MIGRANTS' PERSPECTIVES, MIGRANTS IN PERSPECTIVE

MIGRANTS' PERSPECTIVES, MIGRANTS IN PERSPECTIVE
World Cinema

Edited by Nicole B. Wallenbrock
and Frank Jacob

EDINBURGH
University Press

Edinburgh University Press is one of the leading university presses in the UK.
We publish academic books and journals in our selected subject areas across the
humanities and social sciences, combining cutting-edge scholarship with high editorial
and production values to produce academic works of lasting importance. For more
information visit our website: edinburghuniversitypress.com

© editorial matter and organisation Nicole B. Wallenbrock and Frank Jacob, 2021, 2023
© the chapters their several authors, 2021, 2023

Edinburgh University Press Ltd
The Tun—Holyrood Road
12(2f) Jackson's Entry
Edinburgh EH8 8PJ

First published in hardback by Edinburgh University Press 2021

Typeset in 10/12.5 pt Sabon
by IDSUK (DataConnection) Ltd

A CIP record for this book is available from the British Library

ISBN 978 1 4744 5676 0 (hardback)
ISBN 978 1 4744 5677 7 (paperback)
ISBN 978 1 4744 5678 4 (webready PDF)
ISBN 978 1 4744 5679 1 (epub)

The right of the contributors to be identified as the authors of this work has been
asserted in accordance with the Copyright, Designs and Patents Act 1988, and the
Copyright and Related Rights Regulations 2003 (SI No. 2498).

CONTENTS

List of Figures — vii

1. Migrants' Perspectives, Migrants in Perspective: World Cinema, An Introduction — 1
   Nicole B. Wallenbrock and Frank Jacob

PART I   MIGRANTS' PERSPECTIVE

2. Migrants and Refugees in Moving Image Contemporary Art: Ghazel's "Home (Stories)" (2008) and Bouchra Khalili's "The Mapping Journey Project" (2008–11) — 15
   Valerie Behiery

3. Forced Migration and Fantasies of Return in Palestinian Cinema: *When I Saw You* (Annemarie Jacir, 2012) and *Gate of the Sun* (Yousry Nasrallah, 2003) — 46
   Drew Paul

4. Displacement and the Vicissitudes of Pan-Arabism: Between *The Dupes* (Tewfik Saleh, 1972) and *In the Last Days of the City* (Tamer El Said, 2016) — 68
   Mohannad Ghawanmeh

5. Still/Moving: An Analysis of Recent Films about Transnational Migration from Central America to the USA — 88
   William Brown

CONTENTS

6. Japanese Immigrant Identities on the Brazilian Screen: *Gaijin: Os Caminhos da Liberdade* (Tizuka Yamasaki, 1983) and *Corações Sujos* (Vicente Amorim, 2011)   108
   Frank Jacob

PART II   MIGRANTS IN PERSPECTIVE

7. Communitarian versus Humanitarian Forces in the Dardenne Brothers' *La Promesse* (1996) and *Le Silence de Lorna* (2008)   143
   Colleen Hays

8. This is Not Paradise and the Journey Was Not Worth it: Globalization, Financial Crisis, and the Portrayal of the Sub-Saharan Immigrant in Two Spanish Films   161
   Marta F. Suarez

9. Mobility Constrained and Enabled by Gender: The In-transit *Africaine* of *Hope* (Boris Lojkine, 2014)   186
   Nicole B. Wallenbrock

10. Un/documented Migration in "Borderland Schengen"   205
    Jan Kühnemund

11. Circulating Images of Death: Festival Films and the Syrian Refugee Crisis   230
    Michelle Baroody

The Contributors   256
Index   258

FIGURES

2.1	Ghazel, Marco VII reading the newspaper, film still from "Home (Stories)"	24
2.2	Ghazel, Marco VII on a bench, film still from "Home (Stories)"	24
2.3	Ghazel, Marco I and the moon, film still from "Home (Stories)"	27
2.4	Ghazel, Paola I drawing home, film still from "Home (Stories)"	28
2.5	Bouchra Khalili, film still from "Foreign Office"	30
2.6	Bouchra Khalili, "The Mapping Journey Project," installation view	33
2.7	Bouchra Khalili, still from "Mapping Journey #3"	34
2.8	Bouchra Khalili, still from "Mapping Journey #4"	35
3.1	*When I Saw You*	54
3.2	*When I Saw You*	55
3.3	*When I Saw You*	55
3.4	*When I Saw You*	57
3.5	Bab al-Shams	58
3.6	Bab al-Shams	60
3.7	Bab al-Shams	60
3.8	Bab al-Shams	63
6.1	The dead Sasaki on a heap of cotton in *Corações Sujos*	131
7.1	Assita and Igor embrace in *La Promesse*	149
7.2	Assita and Igor at the train station after the confession in *La Promesse*	150
7.3	Claudy taking water from Lorna in *Le Silence de Lorna*	151

FIGURES

7.4	Claudy and Lorna embrace in *Le Silence de Lorna*	152
9.1	Hope in loose, non-gendered clothing, hoping to pass as male when spotted in *Hope*	190
9.2	Hope attempts to evade her femininity on the truck, but is none the less noticed for her difference	194
9.3	The director pictured on the left of the screen under Léonard's X-ACTO knife in *Hope*	197
9.4	Hope at work in the film of the same name	198
9.5	Hope holds the now dead Léonard in the early morning on the boat in *Hope*	200
9.6	Hope looking towards Spain in *Hope*	201
10.1	The rubber boat and its digital shadow in "Havarie" (Philip Scheffner, 2016)	209
10.2	The asylum seeker from Ethiopia imitates the crouched posture he adopted in the small boat in "La Forteresse" (Fernand Melgar, 2008)	216

1. MIGRANTS' PERSPECTIVES, MIGRANTS IN PERSPECTIVE: WORLD CINEMA, AN INTRODUCTION

Nicole B. Wallenbrock and Frank Jacob

World history forgets and erases in-transit and newly immigrated peoples. Thomas Nail quotes Hegel to underline recorded history's relationship to the migrant figure: "we are concerned only with those peoples that have formed states (because) all the value human beings possess, all of their spiritual reality, they have through the State alone."[1] As visual culture addresses, impacts, and alters what survives as historical fact, the wide-ranging films treated in this volume radically counter the popular visions and assumptions that diminish the stateless and disenfranchised in contemporary history. These films insert in-transit individuals and peoples into a dismissive recorded culture, proving their presence and humanity—accordingly, the majority of films analyzed in this volume transgress mainstream popular currents and instead participate in alternative networks, such as internet, festivals, museums, and art-house circuits. Although each of these films argues for the inclusion of forgotten individuals and peoples, each of the chapters' authors reveals negotiations and compromises that intention and subject matter cannot wholly dispel. This volume thus grapples with such paradoxes in moving images and their formative role in the early twenty-first-century imagination of migration. We ask: How does the filmic migrant alter the public's vision and understanding of off-screen refugees? In what ways does cinema give voice to the invisible and or contribute to a vision of the migrant as a victim lacking agency? A study of point of view embodies the spirit of these questions and demands that we investigate with whom the camera and the narrative align the audience and create suture—does the public identify with the migrants or their "hosts"? For this reason we have organized the volume in two parts of five chapters, "Migrants' Perspective" and "Migrants in Perspective," encouraging readers to reflect on the ways in which a cinematic and narrative gesture may invigorate debates concerning diversity and authorship.

In recent years a paradigm shift in thought concerning migration and issues related to this essential phenomenon of humans past and present occurred; a problem considered rather peripheral in many societies of the industrialized West became one of the most important political and social issues in the early twenty-first century.[2] Nation-states felt threatened by waves of immigrants,[3] and the rise of right-wing movements and parties proved to be a direct consequence of the demographic pressure felt by supposedly homogenous societies.[4] The so-called "refugee crisis" of 2015[5] caused a reconsideration of people on the move by filmmakers and, in response, a more intense reception of these issues by varied screen audiences around the globe.[6] As Dimitris Papadopoulos and Vassilis S. Tsianos underline, the orientation of migrants in images contributed greatly to the public's perception:

> [M]igrants are considered as irregular citizens, they are commonly conceived either as criminals or as being forced to move, not as active creators of the realities they find themselves in or of the realities they create when they move. The category of the illegal migrant is not created, primarily, by a legal context, but by the political and theoretical view in which forms of agency are driven by internal necessities; the legal context only follows to consolidate this perspective and standardise the "migrants" into manageable categories.[7]

This "political and theoretical view" and "perspective" weaves narratives into such visual thought patterns; our approach to film matter parses its relation to the in-transit individual and community, and is guided by a camera's placement and a script's and or dialogue's primary voices. Thus the perspective of this volume's title has both a specific and a fluid meaning: we are interested in the ways in which a camera may depict an in-transit individual's viewpoint, and the ways in which plot and dialogue may insist on journeys and/or the outsiders' understanding of a milieu's culture and associated discrimination. In conjunction, films, with their unusually expensive and exclusive avenues of production, often present a gaze at the traveler or newly arrived needy, which may glorify those that offer help, even while exposing the malevolence of the surrounding laws and society. In these instances, films place the migrants in the hosting society's perspective, limiting shots and narratives that might present the outsider's vision and/or pre-arrival story. The chapters of this volume illustrate film's unique ability to project the in-transit people as "active creators of the realities" in which "they find themselves," while the second part's chapters present the observers of the migrants at times empathizing, questioning, judging, and in some cases determining the realities of those arriving, sometimes as an exercise in self-exploration. As the previous citation of Papadopoulos and Tsianos implies, the perspective proffered by images not only influences the viewer, but in turn results in larger legal implications for migrants. Therefore, it is imperative that we consider the ways in which film matter shapes opinion through its literal and figurative perspective of populations in transit and in refuge. For this reason, migrant is the central and defining word for this volume, around which perspective revolves; it is movement that defines the migrant, while the immigrant settles and the emigrants' past connection to a country suggests their precarious value.[8]

As the following chapter summaries reveal, three central elements—the depiction of the migrants' space, identity, and need—bind these chapters concerning people on the move, and in this way, all of the included work by individual scholars overlaps and intersects, in spite of its varying geographic and thematic focus. The films studied seek to redefine migration in the public imaginary by exposing the forgotten space that defines survival for many (the refugee camp, the geographical landmark of hardship—that is, the sea and desert crossing, or the bordered, illegal, in-transit community). Secondly, the ever-present question of identity intersects most powerfully in the already mentioned suture, and in the ways in which a migrant must reframe their own identity[9] due to different cultural values (such as more equal and, at the same time, more diverse gender roles)[10] or racist reactions from members of their host societies. Hannah Arendt (1906–75), discussing her own fate and that of many other Jews who escaped to the United States from repression in Nazi Germany in "We Refugees," highlights the problems of the nomenclature and identity of migrants in their new environment—migration considered here solely as the act of moving per se—in the first sentence: "In the first place, we don't like to be called 'refugees.' We ourselves call each other 'newcomers' or 'immigrants.'"[11] While it is not primary to this volume, Hamid Naficy's term, accented cinema, applies to many of these works in which a director's migrant past shapes a film's style and subject.[12] A third major interest that the films and the chapters contest is the need at the root of the migrants' departure and journey. The roots of migration usually lie in the historical developments within the region in which the migration began. This could be wars, like the Syrian Civil War, which has been ongoing since 2011,[13] or disastrous economic perspectives due to underdevelopment or corruption. People do not just move. Does cinema reveal and or deny migrants the reasons that forced them to move? Films may assume our knowledge, or film may deny the migrants' experience its preface of violence and poverty.[14] The migrant journey's space, the consequences for identity in forced situations, and the motivating reasons for fleeing (commonly survival, prejudice, and war) link these visualizations and narratives, while the concept of perspective helps us identify over-arching cinematic approaches.

Migrants' Perspective

Our investigation of the camera's ability to give voice to the migrant begins with the marginal space of the museum and the moving art image of two prominent artists of Middle Eastern heritage and European support, although we should also note that such situations can contradict each other—Ghazel at one point was expelled from France and brings her own narrative to her œuvre's primary theme of immigration. These two artists dispel easily stereotyped visions of migration in both popular media and the elite space of the festival and museum; their works unravel the image of the migrant victim and champion the framed migrants as agents of their situations. For example, the artists' liminal presence in the "space-off" allows the dominant undocumented immigrants in Europe a freedom of movement and expression. Employing the theories of Judith Butler, Gilles Deleuze, and Gayatri Chakravorty Spivak, Valerie Behiery demonstrates that the non-linear nature of moving image art allows for radical forms that surpass evoking or aligning with immigrants, and instead claims needed space for the unique voices and journeys of refugees.

The voices captured by Ghazel and Khalili indicate war and political oppression in the Middle East as primary instigators of departure. The following two chapters relate to the complicated resonance of past migration within the Arab world and its memory; Drew Paul's chapter, "Forced Migration and Fantasies of Return in Palestinian Cinema," discusses Yousry Nasrallah's *Gate of the Sun* (*Bab al-Shams*, 2003) and Annemarie Jacir's *When I Saw You* (*Lamma Shuftak*, 2012), while Mohannad Ghawanmeh's chapter historically locates pan-Arabism and traces its evolution in relation to migration through *The Dupes* (Tewfik Saleh, 1972) (the first Arabic-language narrative film to depict immigration) and *In the Last Days of the City* (Tamer El Said, 2016), set in Cairo before the Arab Spring. The experience of forced exile in *When I Saw You* shapes the conception of the migrants' home country; this process of creating fantasies about a return to an almost mythical home anchors a Palestinian film perspective. Both Paul and Ghawanmeh situate the identity of a past home, as a psychological, theoretical space of belonging, informed by the imagined community; Ghawanmeh suggests that technology provides the gateway to a new pan-Arabism that "connects Arabs and provides a sense of community, even when physical borders prevail."

The last two chapters of this part center on films concerning migration issues in the Americas. In his chapter, "Still/Moving: An Analysis of Recent Films about Transnational Migration from Central America to the USA," William Brown locates what writer Eduardo Galeano of Uruguay labeled a migration industry[15] in relation to the US–Mexican border, illustrated by *Sin nombre* (*Nameless*, Cary Jôji Fukunaga, 2009) and *La jaula de oro* (*The Golden Dream*, Diego Quemada-Díez, 2013). Brown's discourse situates the in-transit experience of those leaving Central America for the United States, as well as its impetus. Both films employ still photography to tease the tension between stillness and movement that migration psychologically and physically entails. The Brazilian films of this part's last chapter evoke a similar stylistic concern with a historical approach. "Japanese Immigrant Identities on the Brazilian Screen: *Gaijin: Os Caminhos da Liberdade* (*Gaijin: Roads to Freedom*, Tizuka Yamasaki, 1983) and *Corações Sujos* (*Dirty Hearts*, Vicente Amorim, 2011)" details how the two films of the chapter's title expose a still relatively unknown history of the Japanese in contemporary political debates about immigrant identities within Brazil's national discourse. Frank Jacob explores the controversial history of the Japanese who largely replaced the slave labor on Brazil's coffee plantations after it became illegal in 1888—their descendants suffered from the near-fascistic Estado Novo regime of Getúlio Vargas (President from 1934 to 1945, and 1951 to 1954), who banned the speaking and writing of Japanese. Discriminatory actions and control by employers and the government led to a fractured diaspora with many secret societies who terrorized those who believed the ignoble truth, that Japan had lost the Pacific War—the subject of *Dirty Hearts*. Jacob notes how films at last addressing these phases of immigration reflect an evolution in Brazil's growth as a multicultural society. All of the chapters in the "Migrants' Perspective" section present cinema opened by the eyes and voices of people in search of survival and betterment. These chapters demonstrate film's ability to express the in-transit people's agency, whether in the documentaries which allow migrants to speak directly of their experience, or in dramas that narrativize migration with its failures, successes, and costs.

Migrants in Perspective

While the first half of this volume exposes and analyzes film matter that visually depicts an in-transit or recent immigrant struggle, the second half studies films that empathize with migrants through another's observation or interpretation of their turmoil. The films in this part of the book confront and/or expose the tactical elements of filmmaking and reporting on the migrant crises, as well as the theoretical debates that are implicit in such undertakings. These pictures cater to the elite art-house, festival, and museum public, even while artists frame or fictionalize migrants and/or refugees and their course of travel and tribulations.

The Dardenne Brothers' (the only "canonic" European directors treated in this volume) first widespread art-house acclaimed film, *La Promesse* (*The Promise*, 1996), depicts the life of a young mother from Burkina Faso (Assita Ouedraogo) who suffers at the hands of a Belgian father–son realty scheme. However, as Colleen Beth Hays displays in her study, with *Le Silence de Lorna* (*The Silence of Lorna*, 2008), the Dardenne Brothers expanded to address not only the challenges of women migrants, but the sexual exploitation endemic in their migration. Rather than situating the films with Emmanuel Levinas's concept of ethics regarding the Other (which the directors have cited as an influence), Hays instead locates the communitarian versus the humanitarian forces in civil society—as argued by Michel Foucault.[16] Ultimately, Hays finds that the presence in both films of a Belgian national's liminal, even expendable, existence mirrors that of the immigrants and creates a filter through which the Western spectator can empathize with the challenges of recently arrived women living illegally in Europe. Hays's argument aligns with the following chapter, "This Is Not Paradise and the Journey Was Not Worth It: Globalization, Financial Crisis, and the Portrayal of the Sub-Saharan Immigrant in Two Spanish Films," for both chapters uncover the history of recent immigration and the ways in which recent European film participates in an ideological and territorial discourse. Marta F. Suarez highlights the specific situation of the sub-Saharan immigrant in two twenty-first-century Spanish fiction films—*14 kilómetros* (*14 Kilometers*, Gerardo Olivares, 2007) and *Diamantes negros* (*Black Diamonds*, Miguel Alcantud, 2013). Her study of the "stereotypes that this portrayal constructs and the connections of these labels to subjacent ideas of the Moor invasion, colonialism, orientalism, and market value" illustrates the historic and regional attitudes implicit in such understandings of contemporary migration to Spain.

"Mobility Constrained and Enabled by Gender: The In-transit *Africaine* of *Hope* (Boris Lojkine, 2014)" continues with tensions related by both Hays's and Suarez's previous chapters and film corpus; for the film *Hope*, like *The Silence of Lorna* by the Dardenne Brothers (and Hays's chapter), lays bare the many ways that gender affects the immigration process. Additionally, *Hope*, like *14 Kilometers* (studied by Súarez), finds a sub-Saharan African forced into marriage in a group crossing the Sahara, proving that European cinema has begun to reveal this seldom-witnessed or studied story. Wallenbrock finds that the manner in which the camera proves its subjectivity, with the migrants' point of view provided and then prohibited, can be likened to the ambivalence found in the intra-African in-transit community's practices, as well the French director's self-conscious query in casting himself as the African prostitute's john. The anthropologist field work of Inka Stock in Morocco with sub-Saharan African women verifies the actuality of the situations that the film depicts and problematizes through the artistry of fiction. Wallenbrock, Hays, and Suarez focus on European films concerning women immigrants whose circumstances coerce sex work, and whose camera provides measured empathy and distance.

This part's fourth chapter departs from fiction drama to pursue instead the (loosely defined) documentary "Un/documented Migration in 'Borderland

Schengen,'" by Jan Kühnemund, which exposes films which relate the interplay of European migration policies and migration movements. Films such as *Bab Sebta* (*Door of Ceuta*, Pedro Pinho Frederico Lobo 2008), *Come un Uomo sulla Terra* (*Like a Man on Earth*, Andrea Serge and Dagmawi Yimer, 2008), and *A Sud di Lampedusa* (*South of Lampedusa*, Andrea Serge, 2006) aim to capture migrants en route, while "Havarie" (*Shipwrecked*, Philip Scheffner, 2016) slows a 3 minute and 36 second extreme long shot of a boat crossing the Mediterranean to 90 minutes—simulating the feeling of endless time and space experienced by those on board. "La Forteresse" (*The Fortress*, Fernand Melgar, 2012) and *Sur le rivage du monde* (*Standing at the Edge of the World*, Sylvain l'Espérance, 2012) place cameras even further from Europe (Mali in the latter), but nevertheless link to the European Union's system of biopolitical control. Kühnemund here assesses the "visual–political arena" of European border zones, whose "predictable or consistently linked points of departure and arrival" stretch into the psychological, whereby they control individuals' perception of movement and its foreseeable consequences. The largely self-produced, often short films studied by Kühnemund exist as testaments to the filmmakers' "aesthetic political practice," which renders the unnoticed people visible, and exposes a challenge to the activist directors at the center of the projects: documenting the undocumented.

Festivals represent an important and rare venue for such political, independent films which expose the debacles faced by people in transit, and a consideration of this viewership and its influence on the filmmaking surrounding migration concludes our volume. Like Kühnemund, Michelle Baroody probes equally outlying experimental matter in her chapter "Circulating Images of Death: Festival Films and the Syrian Refugee Crisis," but emphasizes the reception by Western audiences in this specialized sphere. The nature of the festival vehicle permits the exposure of experimental films, by a highly educated, curious Western elite, but "reproduce(s) the images that already circulate in the global imaginary and reinforce(s) the fantasy of safety elsewhere." Baroody finds two films, *Silvered Water* (Wiam Simav Bedirxan, Oussama Mohammad, 2014) and *Our Terrible Country* (Ziad Homsi, Mohammad Ali Atassi, 2014), that subvert the common Western film festival rapport with Syria by examining "the very spectator position" they critique. Baroody expertly guides us through the filmmakers' techniques and the ways in which they repeat, question, and deny the film festivals' common portrayal of Syria. Baroody's interrogation of the festival space, and the ways in which Syrian filmmakers capitalize and query viewer expectations of violence, tightens and unravels a migrant perspective in film by incorporating its interior knowledge of the Western gaze.

By ending with a chapter which, in part, explores our own educated elite spectator position, our volume places the migrants' space, need, and previous circumstances in relief against the distanced acts of observation and study. In this manner, one may view film's recent attention to migration as a pedetic force, which invites its public to contribute in small ways to the many steps taken by countless others. Thomas Nail defines the pedetic force in migration as

> a social force of motion, it is defined by its autonomy and self-motion. It is different from the social forces of centripetal, centrifugal, tensional, and elastic power because it has neither center nor surplus. Instead its movement is irregular and unpredictable . . . It is said that migrants have no social order and no history, but this is not the case. It is precisely the irregularity and unpredictability of certain figures of the migrant that are capable of giving birth to a new form of social motion not defined by expulsion.[17]

This volume's chapters and the films that define them sustain powerful individual statements and yet exist as a part of a whole that refuses to erase and ignore people on the move—even when compromised, these films, some by migrants (as well as these chapters), place the turmoil of the unseen at the center of the viewer's and reader's vision and thought. One may find some stylistic and narrative tendencies in moving images of migrants, just as the process of their journeys, the multitude of pathways and techniques, cannot be forecast or simplified into one type, region, genre, or message. Yet all of these filmic artifacts and their study represent a movement in thought that, in spite of irregularities, aligns with the migrants' motion to include and to be included. These chapters shed light on the in-transit peoples' history and, when necessary, film's ignorance of their arduous, mortal paths. *Migrants' Perspectives, Migrants in Perspective* thus commits to the chaotic, pedetic force expelled by the movement of migrants. As there is no surplus of scholastic, cinematographic, or physical steps, we conclude this introduction as a preface to future endeavors, calling readers to further expose the migrants' situation and critique societies' treatment and understanding of people on the move.

Notes

1. Georg Wilhelm Friedrich Hegel, *Introduction to the Philosophy of History*, trans. Leo Raugh (New York: Hackett, 1988), 41–2, cited in Thomas Nail, *The Figure of the Migrant* (Stanford: Stanford University Press, 2015), 4.
2. On the relation between migration and state power see: Frank Jacob, "Editorial," *Global Humanities 3: Migration and State Power* (2016): 7–12.
3. Frank Jacob and Adam Luedtke, eds. *Migration and the Crisis of the Modern Nation State?* (Wilmington, DE: Vernon Press, 2017).
4. Manuela Caiani and Ondřej Císař, eds. *Radical Right: Movement Parties in Europe* (New York: Routledge, 2019); Ayhan Kaya, *Populism and Heritage in Europe: Lost in Diversity and Unity* (New York: Routledge, 2020); Christian Stecker and

Marc Debus, "Refugees Welcome? Zum Einfluss der Flüchtlingsunterbringung auf den Wahlerfolg der AfD bei der Bundestagswahl 2017 in Bayern," *Politische Vierteljahresschrift: German Political Science Quarterly* 60, no. 2 (2019): 299–323.

5. Angelica C. Dankert, *Europe Under Pressure: The Development of the European Union Under the Influence of the Arab Spring, the Refugee Crisis and the Global Threat of Terrorism* (Marburg: Tectum, 2017); Justin Healey, *The Global Refugee Crisis* (Thirroul: Spinney Press, 2016); Patrick Kingsley, *The New Odyssey: The Story of Europe's Refugee Crisis* (London: Faber and Faber, 2017).

6. The genre of migration films was stimulated by these events, although numerous films related to migration were produced in the years before, dealing with questions of marginalization, political and ideological conflicts, stereotypes, or the construction and reconstruction of immigrant communities and related subcultures. Bettina Dennerlein and Elke Frietsch, "Einleitung," in *Identitäten in Bewegung: Migration im Film*, ed. Bettina Dennerlein and Elke Frietsch (Bielefeld: Transcript, 2011), 8.

7. Dimitris Papadopoulos and Vassilis S. Tsianos, "Crisis, Migration and the Death Drive of Capitalism," *Afterall: A Journal of Art, Context and Enquiry*, 31 (2012): 9.

8. Here we follow the terminology and definitions employed by Nail, *The Figure*, 12.

9. Rina Benmayor and Andor Skotnes, "Some Reflections on Migration and Identity," *Migration and Identity: International Yearbook of Oral History and Life Stories* 3 (1994): 1–18.

10. Birgit Hoyer, *Migration und Gender: Bildungschancen durch Diversity-Kompetenz* (Leverkusen/Opladen: Budrich, 2015). On the relation of gender and migration and its representation in the media see: Myria Georgiou, "Introduction," in *Gender, Migration, and the Media*, ed. Myria Georgiou (London: Routledge, 2012), 1–9; Mara Mattoscio and Megan C. MacDonald, "Introduction: Gender, Migration, and the Media," *Feminist Media Studies* 18, no. 6 (2018): 1117–32.

11. Hannah Arendt, "We Refugees," in Hannah Arendt, *The Jewish Writings*, ed. Jerome Kohn and Ron H. Feldman (New York: Schocken Books, 2007), 264.

12. Hamid Naficy, *An Accented Cinema—Exilic and Diasporic Filmmaking* (Princeton: Princeton University Press, 2001).

13. The dispute about the Syrian immigrants in its national and global contexts is discussed in Clarke Rountree and Founi Tilli, "Introduction," in *National Rhetorics in the Syrian Immigration Crisis: Victims, Frauds, and Floods*, ed. Clarke Rountree and Founi Tilli (East Lansing: Michigan State University Press, 2019), ix–xxx.

14. On the role of poverty for international migration trends see: Aderanti Adepoju, Ton van Naerssen, and Annelies Zoomers, eds. *International Migration and National Development in Sub-Saharan Africa: Viewpoints and Initiatives in the Countries of Origin* (Leiden: Brill, 2008); George J. Borjas and Jeff Crisp, eds. *Poverty, International Migration and Asylum* (Basingstoke: Palgrave Macmillan, 2006).

15. Eduardo Galeano, *The Open Veins of Latin America: Five Centuries of the Pillage of a Continent*, trans. Cedric Belfrage (London: Serpent's Tail, 2009).

16. Michel Foucault *The Birth of Biopolitics: Lectures at the Collège de France, 1978–1979*, ed. Michael Senellart, trans. Graham Burchell (London/New York: Palgrave Macmillan, 2008).

17. Nail, *The Figure*, 125–6.

Works Cited

Adepoju, Aderanti, Ton van Naerssen and Annelies Zoomers, eds. *International Migration and National Development in Sub-Saharan Africa: Viewpoints and Initiatives in the Countries of Origin*. Leiden: Brill, 2008.

Arendt, Hannah. "We Refugees." In Hannah Arendt, *The Jewish Writings*, ed. Jerome Kohn and Ron H. Feldman, 264–74. New York: Schocken, 2007.

Benmayor, Rina and Andor Skotnes. "Some Reflections on Migration and Identity." *Migration and Identity: International Yearbook of Oral History and Life Stories* 3 (1994): 1–18.

Borjas, George J. and Jeff Crisp, eds. *Poverty, International Migration and Asylum*. Basingstoke: Palgrave Macmillan, 2006.

Caiani, Manuela and Ondřej Císař, eds. *Radical Right: Movement Parties in Europe*. New York: Routledge, 2019.

Dankert, Angelica C. *Europe under Pressure: The Development of the European Union Under the Influence of the Arab Spring, the Refugee Crisis and the Global Threat of Terrorism*. Marburg: Tectum, 2017.

Dennerlein, Bettina and Elke Frietsch. "Einleitung." In *Identitäten in Bewegung: Migration im Film*, ed. Bettina Dennerlein and Elke Frietsch, 7–17. Bielefeld: Transcript, 2011.

Foucault, Michel. *The Birth of Biopolitics: Lectures at the Collège de France, 1978–1979*, ed. Michael Senellart, trans. Graham Burchell. London/New York: Palgrave Macmillan, 2008.

Galeano, Eduardo. *The Open Veins of Latin America: Five Centuries of the Pillage of a Continent*, trans. Cedric Belfrage. London: Serpent's Tail, 2009.

Georgiou, Myria. "Introduction." In *Gender, Migration, and the Media*, ed. Myria Georgiou, 1–9. London: Routledge, 2012.

Healey, Justin. *The Global Refugee Crisis*. Thirroul: Spinney Press, 2016.

Hegel, Georg Wilhelm Friedrich. *Introduction to the Philosophy of History*, trans. Leo Raugh. New York: Hackett, 1988.

Hoyer, Birgit. *Migration und Gender: Bildungschancen durch Diversity-Kompetenz*. Leverkusen/Opladen: Budrich, 2015.

Jacob, Frank. "Editorial." *Global Humanities 3: Migration and State Power* (2016): 7–12.

Jacob, Frank and Adam Luedtke, eds. *Migration and the Crisis of the Modern Nation State?* Wilmington, DE: Vernon Press, 2017.

Kaya, Ayhan. *Populism and Heritage in Europe: Lost in Diversity and Unity*. New York: Routledge, 2020.

Kingsley, Patrick. *The New Odyssey: The Story of Europe's Refugee Crisis*. London: Faber and Faber, 2017.

Mattoscio, Mara and Megan C. MacDonald. "Introduction: Gender, Migration, and the Media." *Feminist Media Studies* 18, no. 6 (2018): 1117–32.

Naficy, Hamid. *An Accented Cinema—Exilic and Diasporic Filmmaking*. Princeton: Princeton University Press, 2001.

Nail, Thomas. *The Figure of the Migrant*. Stanford: Stanford University Press, 2015.

Papadopoulos, Dimitris and Vassilis S. Tsianos. "Crisis, Migration and the Death Drive of Capitalism." *Afterall: A Journal of Art, Context and Enquiry* 31 (2012): 4–11.

Rountree, Clarke and Founi Tilli. "Introduction." In *National Rhetorics in the Syrian Immigration Crisis: Victims, Frauds, and Floods*, ed. Clarke Rountree and Founi Tilli, ix–xxx. East Lansing: Michigan State University Press, 2019.

Stecker, Christian and Marc Debus. "Refugees Welcome? Zum Einfluss der Flüchtlingsunterbringung auf den Wahlerfolg der AfD bei der Bundestagswahl 2017 in Bayern." *Politische Vierteljahresschrift: German Political Science Quarterly* 60, no. 2 (2019): 299–323.

PART I

MIGRANTS' PERSPECTIVE

2. MIGRANTS AND REFUGEES IN MOVING IMAGE CONTEMPORARY ART: GHAZEL'S "HOME (STORIES)" (2008) AND BOUCHRA KHALILI'S "THE MAPPING JOURNEY PROJECT" (2008–11)

Valerie Behiery

> "Who the hell wants to protect subalternity? Only extremely reactionary, dubious anthropologistic museumizers. No activist wants to keep the subaltern in the space of difference . . . You don't give the subaltern voice. You work for the bloody subaltern, you work against subalternity."
>
> Gayatri Chakravorty Spivak[1]

The contemporary art world has not remained indifferent to the current situation of migrants and refugees. As recent exhibitions worldwide reveal, curators are foregrounding the lives and deaths of the hundreds of thousands of displaced persons entering Europe and Turkey.[2] Major artists such as Ai Weiwei, Mimmo Paladino, Kader Attia or Vik Muniz are addressing the issue. In addition to photography, installation, sculpture, performance, and public murals and street art, artists are employing filmic media to convey the realities of migrants and refugees, and to challenge the often-xenophobic media, public, and political narratives about them.

The two moving image art projects on undocumented migrants and possibly refugees that I examine here, Ghazel's "Home (Stories)" (2008) and Bouchra Khalili's "The Mapping Journey Project" (2008–11) both, however, predate the media's recent construction of the ongoing phenomenon of the globally displaced into a crisis, a characterization that raises critical questions of timing and motive. Because media conglomerates work closely with governments, their construing of situations into crises often aims at garnering public support for national, political and geopolitical discourses and strategies, including military intervention. While "crisis" seems an apt signifier for the staggering number of migrants who continue risking their lives to enter Europe, the term obscures both the root causes of migration, sometimes traceable to Euro-American power and policy, and the little-known existence of detention camps along the increasingly militarized borders of Fortress Europe.[3]

"Crisis" also legitimizes the media's framing of migrants as nameless, hapless hordes or, on the contrary, as threats to national security, both of which effectuate their dehumanization in public consciousness. This further encourages their real victimization and consolidates the asymmetrical relationship of power between "us" and "them," emblematic of collective Euro-American identities. The desubjectification of perceived "others" possesses a long history in Europe and North America, explaining why this chapter, akin to the other chapters in this volume, is chiefly concerned with the problematics of representation. A critical analysis of "Home (Stories)" and "The Mapping Journey Project" reveals the strategies that allot agency to subjects normally silenced, erased, or spoken for in current media and politicoscapes. It also probes the possible effects of the articulation of "other" subjectivities on Euro-American discourses and perceptions. As Said, Yeğenoğlu, Butler, Gayatri Chakravorty Spivak, and many other scholars have convincingly argued, Eurocentric models are predicated on sustaining the alleged superiority of the Western subject by contradistinction with devalued others.[4]

In her still timely seminal essay "Can the Subaltern Speak?" Spivak highlights the difficulties of external attempts to acknowledge the voice cum agency of the subaltern that equally pertain to marginalized and minoritized communities.[5] She cites, for example, the danger of essentialization that paints communities as monolithic, thereby denying their heterogeneity and that of Western intellectuals, again speaking for the subaltern. For Spivak, the Western subject, even in contemporary critical theory, remains the unstated norm and the production of knowledge therefore only abets the global reach of the Western imperium. Spivak's contention is not so much that the subaltern cannot speak, but that the very structures of Western discourses do not allow them to be heard. Difference instituted by Western colonial and economic power indeed negates the minoritized's access to recognized subjecthood and, at the very least, distorts the enunciations of heterogeneous marginalized individuals. And being heard may effectively require appropriating the externally imposed status of difference and the narratives through which it is produced, including a generalized collective identity that, as Spivak observes, risks reinstating its subordinate position.

However, I here posit that minoritarian voices can make themselves intelligible and serve, like Gramsci claimed, as "counter-hegemonic strategies of resistance," an idea that Deleuze and Guattari's concept of "minoritarian-becoming" further elaborates.[6] The radical potential of marginalized voices is only heightened by the fact that nations considered Western liberal democracies are experiencing an "identity crisis" due to many factors—including (im)migration—that make plural and transnational identities the norm. The dominant representation of migrants and refugees as victims supplies the necessary othered non-subjects constitutive of mainstream modern Western self-identity. Such depictions can be read as a defense mechanism that rejects "an alternative vision of Europe ... based on multiple belonging."[7] Žižek decries "the universalization of the notion of the victim that has accompanied the worldwide triumph of liberal democracy." He postulates that because the image of the victim "is presented as existing outside of ideology," it "exerts an immobilizing fascination on the witness, inciting compassion while thwarting the ability to act."[8] The Slovenian scholar also articulates the intimate link between the sign of the victim and that of the individual-as-threat:

> What we encounter here is again the paradox of victimization: the Other to be protected is good in so far as it remains victim ... ; the moment it no longer behaves like a victim, but wants to strike back on its own, it magically turns all of a sudden into a terrorist/fundamentalist/drug-trafficking Other ....[9]

The image of the victim ensures the passivity of the spectator, while that of the terrorist provokes the equally paralyzing sentiment of fear. Either way, the entwined tropes between which the representation of refugees and migrants oscillates both equally deny subjecthood and individuality.

The political dimension of the voice and agency of marginalized subjects explains why I have purposely chosen two artists who consciously devise innovative forms of representation, forms that avoid speaking for "those who do not enjoy the status of the subject."[10] The importance of art that emphasizes the militarization of borders hidden from the general public cannot be exaggerated and deserves study.[11] However, Ghazel and Khalili address the realities of migrants who are not presently detained and who have managed to penetrate Europe. Nevertheless, their subjects are still bound by a discursive prison whose walls are erected by laws and official documents, social attitudes and privilege, and an outdated notion of citizenship. Both artists intentionally obviate the trap of victimization. The "illegal" migrants and refugees featured in "Home (Stories)" and "The Mapping Journey Project" are agents of their own stories and lives—Khalili, in fact, refers to them as "resistants."

This study posits that, in addition to minoritarian voices, art and visual culture also possess agency and the capacity to effect change. Representations not only proceed from cultural discourses, but also shape their future becoming.[12] They produce, reproduce, and rewrite collective constructs of vision, and consequently, perceptions of the other. Visual texts can therefore shape societal attitudes and hence governmental policies on refugees and undocumented migrants. However, they cannot obviously replace more concrete actions that directly address the many practical factors pertaining to the well-being of the globally displaced.[13]

Terminology: Of Film, Video, and Moving Image

Before I proceed to Ghazel's and Khalili's moving image projects, a word must be said about method and terminology. A visual culture studies perspective informs the following analysis of "Home (Stories)" and "The Mapping Journey Project." This approach, which recognizes the visual as a site intertwined with culture, ideology, politics, and the personal, contextualizes a discussion of contemporary art within an edited volume on film. The reference to moving image art constitutes an even more precise linkage across film-based media. Moving image as a category encompassing mainstream and experimental film, video art, television, and digital media is certainly useful for analyzing the projected image across contexts, media, and technologies. The expression "moving image art" originated in a series of phenomena, most particularly the interdisciplinarization of the arts in the 1960s, which witnessed the migration of film from the black box of the cinema to the white cube of the gallery, resulting in the prevalence of multimedia video art installations throughout the art world. However, while moving image as a classificatory apparatus highlights the visual, temporal, narrative, referential, political, and social concerns that filmmakers and visual artists sometimes share, it must not gloss over, as Tanya Leighton notes, the fact that film and contemporary art possess "different modes of practice, histories, institutions, economic structures and critical languages."[14] Jonathan Walley, in a text comparing avant-garde film and moving image contemporary art, discerns other divergences, such as the relationship to space and viewer mobility:

> The white cube–black box dyad organises a number of oppositions between the art and film worlds: the sculptural space of artists' film opposes the theatrical film's two-dimensionality; the gallery's mobile viewer is distinguished from the seated cinema spectator; the gallery space enables freedom of choice and movement among viewers who come and go on their own time, while the theatrical space of film screenings putatively constricts the viewer's temporal and spatial experience.[15]

These distinctions neither invalidate visual culture and moving image perspectives as interpretative tools, nor dissolve the indisputable historical relationship between film and other arts. As British film critic and curator Mark Nash writes, "The cinema is an integral if not generative part of twentieth-century art and the cinematic a key mode of twentieth-century subjectivity."[16] Moreover, film is itself a heterogeneous category; we speak, for example, of expanded, experimental, avant-garde, auteur, Third cinema, and so on. New subcategories have emerged in the last decades in an attempt to characterize the growing number of films that specifically treat the experience of migration, transborder displacement, and exile, along with the hybrid and often deterritorialized identities they produce. Films defined as "accented cinema" (Hamid Naficy), "intercultural cinema" (Laura Marks), "transnational cinema" (Elizabeth Ezra and Terry Recolen), "post-migrant cinema" (Joanne Leal and Klaus Dieter Rossade) or the "cinema of the borders" (Bruce Bennett and Imogen Taylor) offer further points of convergence with moving image art. Such films intentionally displace what is considered the normative gaze (in Europe or North America), and thereby challenge modernity's conceptualizations of national identity, borders, citizenship, and the global order.[17]

Ghazel and Khalili both studied film theory, but have both subscribed to the more intimate media of video or digital film and the more intimate context of the gallery or art museum. While I propose here that Ghazel's and Khalili's works articulate alternative narratives of migrants precisely because of the different aesthetic, structural, and spectatorial possibilities of moving image art as compared to film, it is not to suggest that the particular freedoms that they offer are, as Nash also notes, somehow intrinsically more radical than those of film.[18]

Ghazel's "Home (Stories)"

Ghazel is best known internationally for her "Me" video series (1997–ongoing), in which the Iranian artist, dressed in a black chador, undertakes a series of activities from sunbathing to driving a motorcycle, or from weightlifting to dreaming "of being a Botticelli Venus." The "heroine" who speaks via the text written on the film conveys an obvious energy. Her embodied performance individualizes a figure normally desubjectified in Euro-American media and visual culture: namely, *the* Iranian woman or *the* reified veiled woman, what cooke calls the "Muslimwoman."[19] The very short films, now numbering over 750, can also be interpreted as a critique of sartorial or other gendered laws and practices in Iran, although overstating this dimension at the expense of others blinds one to the rich politics and complexity of the work.[20] The mostly black-and-white home-movie aesthetic, as well as the autobiographical and humorous nature of the videos, partially masks their biting commentary on the power of representation, bicultural vision, and unequal geopolitical relations. Accessible and funny, "Me" decolonizes Western attitudes and perceptions of Iran by clearing a space for marginalized subjectivity to be sensed and heard.[21] The autobiographical narratives that Ghazel enacts in "Me" always constitute reflections on the world and yet the later videos in the series comment more overtly on specific issues; for example

"Electric Chair" (2000) confronts the death penalty, and "Keep the Balance" (2004) references Abu Ghraib and therefore broaches the taboo subject of torture and human depravity in the infamous Iraqi prison.[22] Politics effectively underwrites all of Ghazel's work—whether video, performance, or drawing—which addresses topics as varied as war, fossil fuels, women's and children's rights, ecology, consumerism, homelessness, and transborder migration.

The concept of the *"mal fait"* or "badly made" forms a critical central strategy of Ghazel's general modus operandi. For example, in the "Me" videos, once the artist thinks of and through the concept and the scene that she wants to enact, she films it spontaneously in one take, in real time with a HI-8 camera on a tripod. Ghazel best expresses her approach and how it differs from classical filmmaking:

> For me, for example, the Me videos would lose their meaning or essence if the lighting and image quality were high quality and "clean." It's because it depends on one's conception of beauty. For me, the aesthetics of the *mal fait* is more powerful than that of the well-made and is also more real. For the Me series, I wanted a home movie aesthetic, not something slick and "movie-like." When I film, I don't ever check the image beforehand; for example, in "I Wanna Go Around the World with a Globe," I accidentally cut off the top of my head. When I saw it, I was surprised but found that it worked, that it was interesting because I had censored a part of my face. I like the aesthetics of imperfection.[23]

Ghazel's presentation of the "Me" series on small television screens, each displaying a different scene, portrays a disregard for technology and the "aesthetics of imperfection," characteristic of her work. The outdated, old TVs intensify the home-movie reference, only further cementing the relationship between "Me's" character and the spectator.

The earliest piece treating the *"sans papiers,"* or the undocumented, is rooted in Ghazel's own life experience. Ghazel left Iran in 1986 to study in France, where she remained after graduation. In 1997, the artist received an official letter stating that her residency permit would not be renewed. Ghazel had often experienced discrimination in France by professors and government officials alike; there were a lot of jokes and comments about bombs. This was the first and only time that the artist experienced the reality of being and feeling "illegal." This situation, which finally resolved itself, became art in Ghazel's *"Urgent"* or, in English, "Wanted," poster series, a translation that works well because of the double entendre. Usually carrying a photograph of the artist with various areas blackened out, the posters' texts are want ads seeking a husband for what the French call a *"mariage blanc,"* meaning a marriage officiated in order for the undocumented party to obtain a residency permit. For example, a very succinct 1999 poster reads: "WANTED, Woman (32 yrs. Old), middle eastern, seeks Husband (passport), only EEC nationality, preferably French, e-mail: maraal@minitel.net." In 1992, when Ghazel secured a ten-year residency permit, the roles in the series were reversed. The artist began offering marriage to someone looking to legalize his situation. In her latest "Wanted" poster, Ghazel, who obtained French citizenship in 2009, seeks to give up or sell her French citizenship.[24] The work, which has created some backlash, was instigated, as she explains, by "this ridiculous and horrible debate about stripping citizens of their citizenship in French politics now."[25] The world's present focus on global migration and the attendant debates on security and citizenship have conferred a renewed relevance upon the series, which has been most recently exhibited in "Deportation Regime: Artistic Responses to State Practices and Lived Experience of Forced Removal" (September 9 to December 16, 2016) at the Center for Art on Migration Politics in Copenhagen.[26] Conversely, the brush with the specter of deportation has inspired Ghazel to work with "illegal" migrants and other marginalized communities in France, Italy, Iran, Denmark, and the United States.

"Road Movie" (2010 and 2012) is Ghazel's first project focusing on homeless, undocumented immigrants. In the series of twelve black-and-white filmed performances, Ghazel sparingly enacts the stories of individuals she encountered in Paris, Teheran, or elsewhere, and with whom she spent varying amounts of time. An examination of "Road Movie 1" conveys the conceptual, aesthetic, and technical choices that the artist made in this project and provides a segue into my analysis of "Home (Stories)." "Movie 1" involves an Afghan teenager, referred to simply as "H," whom Ghazel met only a few times in the 10th *arrondissement* of Paris, where she lives. H was scheduled to tell his story publicly, but he desisted at the last minute. His last-minute withdrawal forced Ghazel, who wanted H to tell the story in his own words, to quickly devise a way of presenting the teenager without "speaking for him." The artist opted for visual, auditory, and textual minimalism. The performance is pared down to the extreme: there is only the artist, a whiteboard, a felt marker that the artist uses to write down the migrant's story, and a cloth serving as eraser. Each silent black-and-white scene is enacted by Ghazel's writing of words on the board, followed by their erasure. The whiteboard therefore carries the filmic impulse of the "movie," in which text has replaced both image and sound, akin to a giant flipbook whose pages turn through Ghazel's performance. This subversion of technology, coupled with the neutral, way of introducing H, almost in summary form, by inscribing his age, gender, nationality, and the way he came to Paris via Pakistan, Turkey, and Greece, precludes sensationalism or victimization.[27] There is, for example, no account of or dwelling on any of the trials or challenges that he had faced and was still facing.

Only twice do H's actual (albeit translated) words to Ghazel intervene via her act of writing. Once they describe his trip: "I was comfortable. I don't remember the details. I've forgotten everything." The second time, H explains why he does not want to perform:

> I won't come in front of those people. I don't want to recount fiction. If I tell the truth, people won't believe me. They will say he is crazy because people watch too many fiction films and they will say that my story is also one of these films.

His words reveal the sixteen-year-old's awareness of being misconstrued and his certainty of its inevitability.[28] They paraphrase and support Spivak, in fact, when she says,

> Subaltern insurgency . . . *is* an effort to involve oneself in representation *not* according to the lines laid down by the official institutional structures of representation. Most often it does not catch. That is the moment that I am calling "not speaking," distinguishing it from the general condition of subalternity where all the speech acts exchanged in subalternity are only accessible to oral history, or a discursive formation different from the investigation.[29]

H's insightful words, cited above, effectively form the film's culmination. By choosing to reproduce them over others, Ghazel acknowledges the difficulties involved in the representation or self-representation of a minoritized subject, as she does when, writing the film credits at the end, she replaces the initial "Road Movie, a film by g with h" with "Road Movie, a film by h with g."

Ghazel literally speaks, or rather writes, for H, yet her dispositive somehow avoids doing so intellectually or ideologically.[30] Her reserve in "speech" and movement, her evocation of the strictest minimum of facts and words, and her semi-invisibility—largely, spectators see her only from the back—create a space for H's experience. It is, however, a space that, akin to Khalili's "The Mapping Journey Project" and, to a lesser degree, Ghazel's "Home (Stories)", is situated outside of the frame, in what film theorist De Lauretis calls the "space-off," defined as "the space not visible in the frame but inferable from what the frame makes visible."[31] Spectators get a sense of H precisely because "Road Movie" uses the unarticulated space beyond the image to render marginalized subjectivity intelligible. The film therefore suggests that the "official institutional structures of representation" in a scopic regime inflected by modernity do not overdetermine the meaning(s) of visual absence both within and beyond the frame, allowing it to act as a strategy of (self-)representation. Moreover, the film's nothing-to-see aesthetic, the use of text, and the very slow deployment of narrative constitute distancing mechanisms between screen and viewer. Such techniques obviate H's fear that the spectator will assimilate just another film into his or her imagination, in the etymological sense of "making similar" that obviously negates the other.

In 2005, Ghazel conducted a two-week art workshop with "illegal" immigrants and asylum seekers in Venice that resulted in the performance "HOME," shown as part of the thirty-seventh Theatre Festival of the Venice Biennale, curated by Romeo Castellucci. Ghazel had previously worked in art therapy in several instances—for example, with teenagers with social problems in Teheran or with prisoners in New York City—but this was, as the artist says, "the first time I married my art therapy, social activism and my art!"[32] In the workshop leading up to their performance, the participants—originally from Afghanistan, Albania, Congo, Iran, Ivory Coast, Kosovo, Kurdistan, and Romania—experimented in different media, such as drawing, storytelling, and performance—to reflect on the notion of home. They were free to look to the past, the future, or their more precarious, unhomed present. Each person decided what he or she wanted to express and how to express it, Ghazel's role being to facilitate, comment on, and help elaborate the immigrants' concepts in light of performance night.[33] Exemplifying Beuys's notion of social sculpture, in which art, life, and action align to transform society, the unique project pushes the boundaries of what constitutes theatre. Much more critically, the participants in "HOME" recast social, political, and national discourses in the European context by (re)claiming and performing their status as subjects and social actors.

The single performance of "HOME" was a festival success, but it was not filmed. In 2007, Ghazel filmed a follow-up to trace any changes in the migrants' situations. "Home (Stories)" is a 43-minute video that references all eight original adults, but was actually produced with only six of them. It is not, however, a documentary about either "HOME" or the migrants' lives, as the montage purposefully confuses the narrative structure. Godard famously said, "[a] story should have a beginning, a middle and an end, but not necessarily in that order," but "Home (Stories)," evincing a completely non-linear structure, has none of the three.[34] It is a quick-paced assemblage of very short, mashed-up, seemingly unrelated scenes. Several of the narrative performances from "HOME" are re-enacted. However, some are shown partially twice and most are followed by new outdoor scenes, often of Marco VII, who, donning a Pink Panther mask, rides by on a bicycle, sits down in a graffitied alley to read a newspaper, walks to and from an unseen place holding a toilet roll, or wanders near a police car (Figs 2.1 and 2.2). His role offers glimpses into the "normal" daily life of a *sans-papiers* on the streets. The scenes' humorous quality dissipates the viewer's preconceived notions, prohibiting either demonization or heroization. Marco VII constitutes a Trickster figure, who not only provides comic relief, but also breaks the rules of linearity, and by inference, of positivist

Figure 2.1 Ghazel, Marco VII reading the newspaper, film still from "Home (Stories)," 2007, reproduced with the permission of the artist.

Figure 2.2 Ghazel, Marco VII on a bench, film still from "Home (Stories)," 2007, reproduced with the permission of the artist.

knowledge. The unpatterned sequencing of indoor and outdoor, short and less short, funny and serious, neutral and engaged scenes ensures that the spectator does not simply comfort his or her predetermined knowledge of migrants and refugees. Non-linear narrative is associated in film theory with the evocation of memory, as described by Kravagna in an article on "Home (Stories)," in which he states that "(t)he film's structure already shows that it does not seek to paint a self-contained picture of a particular situation, but is more interested in significant overlappings of memory, projections of the future and interim adjustment to adverse circumstances."[35] Ghazel's strategic use of the fragment also creates a filmic equivalent of the suspended time and state in which the participants presently find themselves. "Home (Stories)" possesses a surreal or Theatre of the Absurd quality that effectively evokes the ontological domains of memory and subjectivity, thereby assisting the mediation of the migrants' agency. The humor and the disjointed structure re-represent migrants and refugees, and remap the social imaginary.

The individuals wear masks in order to hide their identity. The masks also, as Kravagna observes, refer to the "techniques of inconspicuousness and mimicry that are necessary in illegality." The generic Italian names by which the participants are referred to—Paolo I and Marco I, II, III, IV, V, VI, and VII—equally mark and challenge these necessary assimilative survival strategies of undocumented migrants. However, I disagree with Kravagna when he states that the facial covering "shifts the level from that of the persons involved to that of representative example." I would argue that "Home (Stories)" seeks to avoid at all costs turning the participants into representative types, and that the masks, in fact, actually enact the distorted essentializing and desubjectifying lens of social, cultural, and political discourses through which "illegal" immigrants are often seen. The masks therefore situate the participants' faces, and by extension their bodies and selves, in the space-off. One way of portraying what the ideological strictures of power and knowledge make unrepresentable is to acknowledge this unrepresentability within the image or, here, frame. This also parallels the ideas of De Lauretis, who, in a discussion on the unrepresentability of the engendered subject, proposes that the subject of feminism must move between "the representation of gender (in its male-centered frame of reference) and what that representation leaves out, more pointedly makes unrepresentable," or, as she states in different terms, between "the discursive space of the positions made available by hegemonic discourses and the space-off, the elsewhere, of those images."[36] In addition to their practical function of concealing identities, the masks thus simultaneously communicate the migrants' social unintelligibility and situate the participants' subjectivity beyond the distorting hegemonic discourses disavowing them.

The face is often considered the body's locus of individuality, a function that it obviously loses on a "non-subject." Providing a proxy circumvents this emptying of the face and locates the real face of the subject beyond the frame in the interstitial space of mediation between the migrant and the spectator where intersubjectivity—that is, a relationship between equals—becomes possible. The masks are, moreover, heterogeneous; the white bandana covering the lower face, the full facial black veil that also covers the eyes, the Pink Panther mask, or handmade paper masks with drawn or collaged features therefore reflect the participants' individuality. They also oblige spectators to glean for other indices of personality and, effectively, "Home (Stories)" adduces how much a person can be sensed by his or her voice, gestures, and posture. Performativity, central to Ghazel's entire corpus, conveys agency beyond the verbal through embodied presence in which the body becomes both site and signifier for subjectivity, recognizing their enmeshment while at the same time distinguishing between being and representation, thereby further locating agency outside of the image and frame.

"Home (Stories)" does not, however, exclude sequences that provoke an emotional response, like the interspersed re-enactments of the Venice performances in which each participant speaks about a large drawing that he or she has made on stage. For example, in the film's first scene, Marco I, his face and eyes covered with a black cloth, unrolls and tapes his drawing to the white wall. A central yellow crescent moon, surrounded by stars of different shapes and colors, takes up most of the drawing (Fig. 2.3). On the moon, Marco I drew a house, which his words elucidate: "I don't have a house in Kurdistan. I don't have a house in Europe. Where do I go? To the moon?" He then takes the drawing down and leaves. In the next scene, the camera pans over another of his drawings, depicting planes dropping bombs on a red and black city in flames. A later scene shows Marco I with the same drawing on his lap. Pointing to two people sitting and drinking together at a table at the top of the drawing, he explains that one is George W. Bush and the other is Saddam Hussein. These three very short scenes illustrate how Ghazel employs indirect means of the poetic, the elliptic, and the humorous as a means to achieve what Spivak labels "subaltern insurgency." Marco I appears again later in a longer sequence. Filmed in black and white in a quiet spot on what appears to be a beautiful day, he comes alive as he speaks Italian rather than English to describe his pizza-making job in a restaurant, vaunting forty-five kinds of pizza and producing 250 pizzas a day. The account of his daily life contradicts the perception of "illegal" migrants as lazy and unproductive, and, with covert humor, rewrites a global signifier of Italian culture and national identity, or at least its production, as cross-cultural. Further on the film deploys a very rapid series of shots of the restaurant and of Marco I working, followed by Marco VII in his Pink Panther mask walking down a street holding a pizza box, presumably from Marco I's restaurant. The film's disjointed narrative and time serve as a Brechtian device that maintains a distance between actor and spectator. However, here, Brechtian aesthetics do not so much enhance the spectacle's artifice than provide an alternative space for marginalized subjectivity.

Figure 2.3   Ghazel, Marco I and the moon, film still from "Home (Stories)," 2007, reproduced with the permission of the artist.

After Marco I's second drawing scene and the subsequent few seconds of Pink Panther Marco VII bicycling on an empty street and across the frame is Paola I's 2005 "HOME" performance. Wearing a white mask with drawn facial features, she palpably enjoys telling her story: spectators feel her strong sense of presence, despite the self-crafted mask concealing her face. Before fixing her drawing to the wall, Paola I looks at the camera (Fig. 2.4). Afterwards, she lists, in both French and Italian, everything depicted in her meticulously rendered drawing of a living room, made in part using a ruler.[37] Describing her drawing as a future project, she focuses on the books, cassettes, DVDs, television set, radio, speakers, potted flowers, and even a decorative teddy bear adorning the entertainment center. After finishing speaking, she removes the drawing from the wall and, continuing to hold it up to the camera, slowly walks out of the frame. In the next sequence in which Paola I appears, she enters an empty parking lot at dusk and, with her arms and body alone, spatially draws her fantasy three-bedroom apartment. Viewers empathize with Paola I's compelling performance. The normalcy of the topic enables a subject-to-subject relationship with the spectator, while the absurdity of the scene communicates the woman's situation without pity or pathos. The narrative scenes interspersed throughout "Home (Stories)" allow for viewer identification, but one that is purposefully unsoldered by the work's fragmentary structure.

Figure 2.4 Ghazel, Paola I drawing home, film still from "Home (Stories), 2007," reproduced with the permission of the artist.

While "Home (Stories)" circumvents the migrant-as-victim trope, a few participants offer glimpses into more tragic aspects of their lives: for example, Marco III, who simply states, "I have very bad memories of water," and Marco V, who tells viewers matter-of-factly that both his parents were killed, that he was imprisoned for two years, and that war erupted in his country because it was rich in oil, gas, iron, gold, diamonds, cotton, cocoa, manioc, sugar cane, and plutonium. Marco V does not visibly appear in the film because a friend convinced him not "to do politics" in Italy. He none the less uses humor to relay tragedy, telling viewers that if plutonium can make nuclear bombs, it can also produce energy to make French fries or to turn on the light to dance. However, representation and its ideological underpinnings are the most potent politics addressed in "Home (Stories)." Using multiple aesthetics alongside technical and conceptual structural strategies, Ghazel creates spaces in which the individual voices of undocumented migrants are legible.

Bouchra Khalili

Bouchra Khalili grew up in Morocco, studied film and fine art in France, and now lives and works between Berlin and Oslo. She exhibits her work on the art, rather than the cinema or film festival, circuit. Yet her work in single-channel video, video installation, and digital film clearly reflects the artist's knowledge of and passion for film in its visual precision, use of off-screen space, plotted relationships between voice and image, and experimentation with novel forms of narrative. Acting as an arena for the self-representation of marginalized subjects and the recovery of erased histories, Khalili's art consciously seeks new forms of storytelling, indebted to Pasolini's and Deleuze's discussions on the transformative role of "free indirect discourse" in film.[38] The artist describes the latter, in which narrator and character, and object (camera) and subject, merge to produce new cinematic forms as "a platform used by individuals who perform themselves in their own words" and "own languages," thereby constituting "subjectivities that challenge normative discourse."[39] She considers minoritized subjectivities counter-hegemonic, either individually or soldered into new groups of resistance. Khalili says, "if one approaches a cinematic apparatus emphasizing language, words, self-representation and performativity, the question of subjectivities becomes central, opening up to the possibility of new collectives to come into existence."[40] These ideas reveal simultaneously Khalili's foundation in film theory, and possible strategies that capacitate the self-representation of marginalized subjects.

Khalili's work is associated with undocumented migrants, who feature in many of her projects, such as "Straight Stories" (2006–8), "Circle Line" (2007), and "The Mapping Journey Project" (2008–11). However, it is vital to contextualize these within the framework of Khalili's wider thematic, intellectual, and political concerns and interests. For example, her recent project, "Foreign Office" (2015), explores the forgotten history of Algiers as a center of left-wing revolutionary politics, to which Marxists from Africa, Asia, the Middle East, Latin America, and the United States once flocked. The three-tier installation, first shown at Paris's Palais de Tokyo, consists of a silkscreen print, a series of photographs, and a digital film. The first, entitled "Archipelago," is a type of abstract map of the headquarters of the various liberation movements that Algiers once housed. Set against a monochrome blue background, the locations are marked by small white shapes reproducing the architectural plans of the buildings. Khalili considers this translation of local geography into "islands" a poetic rendering of what remains of the international solidarity movement's inscription in the urban space of Algiers. Maps, like the production of history and knowledge more generally, are indissociable from power and what it seeks to claim and make visible, or, on the contrary, erase. "Archipelago" maps the now-repressed revolutionary past of the postcolonial nation during the 1960s, the heyday of internationalism. The print must be classified as critical cartography that challenges dominant representations of the world traced by nationalism, colonialism, and sometimes racism, explaining the current pre-eminence of alternative mapmaking in both contemporary art and indigenous resistance movements.

Like "Archipelago," the ten color photographs unleash a faded history into the present. Presenting the decayed or abandoned state of sites related to

Marxist Algiers, they also record the material effects of historical erasure and cultural amnesia on the city's architecture. Amongst the places documented are the Hôtel Victoria, where Karl Marx (1818–83) stayed for seventy-two days in the late nineteenth century, as did Eldridge Cleaver (1935–98), head of the Black Panther Party, much later; the Hôtel el Safir, which housed the influential late writer and intellectual Kateb Yacine (1929–89) and the 1969 Black Panther delegation; and the former headquarters of the Democratic Front for the Liberation of Palestine (DFLP). In a review of "Foreign Office," Azoulay observes that the "deserted sites echo both the grandeur aesthetic of French colonialism and its decay."[41] That revolutionaries stayed in colonial-period and colonial-style hotels adds yet another twist to internationalist history. Yet, the photographs transcend the political by foregrounding how vision, both its focal points and its gaps, like those of urban geography, is fashioned by—but can also contest—social, cultural, and national narratives.

While departing from her earlier work, the film "Foreign Office" embodies Khalili's signature form of storytelling; historical facts, figures, texts, and time mesh with real life and people in the present (Fig. 2.5). While Khalili's work can certainly be qualified as intellectual, this dimension never overrides the openness to life, and to chance encounters informing and shaping it in important ways. In

Figure 2.5   Bouchra Khalili, film still from "Foreign Office," reproduced with the permission of the artist.

fact "Foreign Office" features two young Algerian students, Ines and Fadi, whom Khalili met during the scouting trip for the project. The work purposefully deconstructs the plotted antitheticality between life and film, fiction and documentary, and story and history, the last two sharing the same word, *histoire*, in French.

Interested in the forgotten role their city played in liberation politics, Ines and Fadi probe, internalize, and communicate this history. The film depends completely upon the two young adults' engagement with the latter, emphasizing the responsibility that they carry and Khalili's collaborative way of working. The process of their discovery structures the twenty-two minute film, best summarized by Azoulay:

> This journey through time is led by a young male character and a young female character functioning as narrators who switch between languages—Algerian Arabic, Kabyle, French and English—while rummaging old photos, reading and quoting texts, and also playing music and protest songs related to Algiers's revolutionary era between 1962 and 1972. They use storytelling while at the same time examining their role as storytellers in order to reflect on the responsibilities and complexities of such historical explorations.[42]

All of the film's elements attest to the historical and political forces that produce subjectivity, as well as redefine storytelling. "Foreign Office" documents the students' encounter with the revolutionary history of Algiers, thereby also transmitting it to viewers; yet the subtle transformation of the protagonists operated by the encounter and accrued knowledge form the film's nodal storyline. The ability to define theory as embodied praxis constitutes the core strength and singularity of Khalili's work.

Heteroglossia constitutes another of Khalili's recurring motifs. Debates on postcolonial identity in "French" North Africa have focused on language, a complex issue because Arabic, as well as French, is experienced by some as a colonial language. The Maghreb's centuries-earlier Arabicization has meant the exclusion or minoritization of the various Amazigh languages like Kabyle. In "Foreign Office," Khalili consciously mixes languages to create "a kind of utopian language" that she considers a resolution to the region's language issues because it "reflects our multiple identities ... as if we had surpassed those rigid identity assignments in favor of a creolization."[43] This echoes the ideas of Édouard Glissant, whom Khalili often references in interviews. The Martinican theorist relates the concept of monolingualism to that of the sameness structuring Europe's self-identity and relationship to others. He proposes global polylingualism as a means to deconstruct "the hubris of European master cultures and the arrogance with which they consider their languages as the voice of humanity."[44] However, "Foreign Office" advocates multilingualism and therefore plural identities not for Europe, but for Algeria and North Africa more generally. Framing polylingualism and polyculturality as a social, political, and philosophical path forward equally parallels Deleuze's much-quoted concepts of "minoritarian-becoming" and "the storytelling of the people to come."

If Khalili usually addresses the issue of geographical migration to propose an alternative, borderless world, "Foreign Office" equally unbinds the frontiers of time. Ines and Fadi mediate between past, present, and future. Khalili states, in fact, that she never felt that she "was working on the past. It's more a feeling of working on a becoming that is written in the present with the past, in order to look to the future."[45] Time in "Foreign Office" is a non-linear yet overlapping continuum. Past and present meet the future through Ines's and Fadi's performativity and reflection on the role that the occulted history can play in their lives. At the end of the film, Ines compares her generation's disenchantment and desire to leave with those who thought that they could change the world. Fadi, on the other hand, concludes that these stories exist "all around us" and must be collected, translated, and shared. "Foreign Office" demonstrates that we are all migrants in the spaces of time, meaning, being, and becoming.

The four films comprising "Straight Stories" (2006–8) also suture subjectivity and place, albeit very differently. As in all of Khalili's work on migrants, sound and image are disjunct: the migrants' voices are heard, but the migrants are never seen. This preserves the individuals' anonymity, but it also constitutes free indirect discourse. Pisters considers the filmic strategy to be created through techniques like "obsessive framing, zooming, or the dissociation of image and sound," adding,

> [o]ne way to make subjective and objective, fiction and reality, past and present more ambiguous is by disconnecting sound and image. A voice tells us something, and at the same time we see something else. In this way the voice digs up layers of the past or adds aspects of the future that cannot be seen directly.[46]

In "Straight Stories," the dissociation opens up spaces for marginalized subjectivity and their mediation.

Viewers know the migrants' names, such as Magdalena, Anya, Ahmed, and Musa, only through the films' title screens. Listening to the migrants recount their peregrinations and situations, they see long tracking shots of the Strait of Gibraltar or Istanbul, as well as the camera panning in slow motion, fragments of cityscapes devoid of human life. If the waters speak of passage and possibility, the desolate ferry terminals, boardwalks, gates, and fences signal the legal, social, linguistic, and economic borders that the migrants face. In their narration, Ahmed flees Afghanistan, Musa dreams of returning to the Sudan, and Iraqi Anya describes being trapped for over a decade as an illegal migrant in Istanbul, while a series of visual fragments unfurls on the screen, metaphorically imparting their varied journeys and displacement.

The visual disembodiment of the individuals interrupts the gaze and its assumptions. Circumventing "the institutional structures of representations" for subjects who these have rendered unrepresentable obliges viewers to focus on the voices and the stories they tell. This underscores the power and agency of voice, but also of representation; that some images are premediated because vision is produced through collective narratives makes it necessary to bypass visual representation altogether. Khalili's "Straight Stories," however, plots film and vision as encompassing both the seen or on-screen and the unseen or off-screen. The project's dispositive demonstrates that when the image enacts the space of reception or, stated differently, the evocation of something rather than the thing itself, it better enables communication and translation. The films' deployment of cityscapes or "borderscapes" therefore creates an interstitial space in which spectator and migrant can meet.

"The Mapping Journey Project" (2008–11) also disjoins sound and image and avoids mimetic representation as a way to acknowledge subjects excluded from the normative, cultural structures of vision and discourse. In each of the eight videos, a participant succinctly narrates, in a neutral, objective tone, the trajectory of his or her migration while the screen displays a single, static close-up of a map (Fig. 2.6). The only moving feature is a hand that, holding a pen,

Figure 2.6 Bouchra Khalili, "The Mapping Journey Project," installation view, New Museum, New York, 2014, image courtesy of the artist and the Galerie Mor Charpentier, Paris.

Figure 2.7 Bouchra Khalili, still from "Mapping Journey #3," 2009, "The Mapping Journey Project," reproduced with the permission of the artist.

traces the migrants' journeys as they speak (Fig. 2.7). Because the moving image project is an installation, the large-scale, colored, printed maps constitute a key visual and conceptual unifying element that suggests a collectivity, without erasing the migrants' individualities. Under each screen is a bench with headphones that enables the viewers to hear the different stories. In this way, space, scale, compelling visuality, and repetition unite to engage spectators in the distinctive possibilities of the "white cube."

Oblivious to national and continental borders, the individual journeys trace alternative maps that reconfigure the world as an open space of multiple passages (Fig. 2.8). Khalili describes the project as counter-geography, foregrounding not only global migration, but also resistance; as mentioned earlier, she calls those involved in the project "resistants." The artist, in fact, considers "Mapping Journey #3" the "key node" that "illuminates the whole project" because it stresses resistance over migration.[47] It does not narrate a long journey from East to West or South to North, but that of a Palestinian who, living in the West Bank, cannot drive the twenty minutes it would normally take by car to see his fiancée in East Jerusalem; instead, he is obliged "to climb hills, hide from armed military patrols, and walk a whole day."[48] For Khalili, "Mapping Journey #3" highlights that if one limits the project "to issues of migration, then the real point is missed:

Figure 2.8 Bouchra Khalili, still from "Mapping Journey #4," 2010, "The Mapping Journey Project," reproduced with the permission of the artist.

it is essentially about gestures of resistance of different kinds, that all attempt to reach something universal since they all challenge unfair and arbitrary power."[49] This wider theme underwriting "The Mapping Journey Project" reveals critical points of contact with Khalili's more explicitly political projects like "Foreign Office" or the film trilogy "Speeches" (2012–13).

The other journeys traced in "The Mapping Journey Project" also involve detours and lengthened routes, but on a much larger geographical scale. For example, in "Mapping Journey #6," an Afghan man, heading for Italy, traverses Pakistan and Iran before walking to Istanbul, after which, due to a lack of official documents, he has to travel through Bulgaria, Hungary, Austria, Germany, Belgium, the UK, and France before reaching Rome! Seeing migrants and refugees exclusively as terror threats, burdens on the economy, or, on the contrary, victims denies them the agency witnessed in the short videos. Moreover, the eight stories document subjects who normally fall outside of public discourse and history writing, underlining Khalili's commitment to subaltern history and the visibility of subjects that exclusion renders invisible.

The travels and tales of the individuals fleeing violence and or economic hardship are heterogeneous. In "Mapping Journey #1," for example, an Algerian fisherman and diver narrates, in Arabic and French, his journey on a small boat to Sardinia and then Naples, where he arrives hungry and penniless. He finally manages to sneak unnoticed on a train to Milan, where he finds a job distributing flyers for thirteen and a half hours a day. Continuing to Paris, where he finds life difficult, he travels to Marseilles, where fellow Algerians urge him to sell illegal cigarettes. The video ends with him saying that he hopes to join the Foreign Legion in France or elsewhere. In "Mapping Journey #4," a Somali woman recounts in Italian her journey from Somalia, through Ethiopia, the Sudan and Libya, to Lampedusa, the primary hub of migration from Africa to Europe. Although she liked the island because of its many services for migrants and refugees, she was caught by officials and transported to an asylum center elsewhere in Italy. Receiving official documents two months later, the woman was then sent to Bari, where she learned Italian, found a job, and still lives and works. She ends her story by saying that she does not like Italy and plans on leaving for the UK or Norway.

The stories follow a template that provides narrative, visual, and auditory unity. The stories are all short, delivered without pathos and structured through movement and place. Their sparsity mirrors the project's visuality because it incites or requires spectators to fill in the gaps and thereby see the world from the migrants' perspectives. For example, when one hears the Algerian fisherman casually mention the danger of being in a tiny boat in international waters among strong waves and huge ships, one construes the terrifying navigation between life and death. Similarly, when the Somali woman speaks of being caught, spectators must consider the narrator's fear when she was detained, alone, (and then) without knowledge of Italian. The stories' minimalism and neutrality magnify the feelings that are expressed in language. While we attribute the fisherman's dissatisfaction to his vulnerable situation (he has no papers nor employment), the reasons for the Somali's unhappiness are less clear. She now speaks Italian, possesses official documents, and is employed. Some might misinterpret her dislike of Italy as the trope of the "ungrateful migrant." Others will ask themselves why she does not like Italy: is it because of racism, because the quality of life is not what she expected of Europe, or because she does not see any opportunity for social mobility? The toning and paring down of speech evinces the fragment's power, a strategy that implicates spectators who identify with, and thus acknowledge, the subjecthood of migrants. The stories testify that if some migrants are victims of circumstance, they cannot be characterized as victims. On the contrary, their steadfastness and capacity to surpass circumstance demonstrate personal strength, leaving spectators questioning if they could or would undertake such journeys themselves. As in "Foreign Office" and "Straight Stories", "The Mapping Journey Project" also involves multilingualism, reflecting Khalili's emphasis on language in the formation of new collectivities and identities.

Like sound, image in "The Mapping Journey Project" is also reduced to the strictest minimum. While many, including Khalili, do not consider the map a neutral document, its repeated image is engaging and seemingly simple. Yet, as throughout Khalili's work, the dispositive has been carefully conceived so that all elements, such as image, embody the work's concept, and serve as its visual enactment. The blown-up maps provide a terrain for the inscription of the migrants' lives and identities. We do not physiologically see the individuals, but their moving hands and pens, displaying a subtle performance of subjectivity, function as synecdoche. Graphically and metaphorically embedding minoritized subjects in the world and the viewer's frame of vision, they also remap the world. The alternative mappings claim the power of human subjecthood, further underscoring Khalili's idealism or utopianism, in which world and being remain unbounded by outmoded systems of categorization no longer aligned with contemporary realities.

All the on-screen elements—hands, maps, and journeys—are fragments acting as a shorthand for larger realities. The effectiveness of the fragment, however, rests not only in synecdoche, but also in the gaps that it produces, which leave room for the spectators' imagination. By referencing the space of mediation or reception, Khalili integrates it into the image, and demonstrates one way that the artist plots the unseen as an integral part of vision. Fragments and gaps require assemblage; that an assemblage can be configured in myriad ways implies that it can create new realities. "The Mapping Journey Project" effectively depends upon spectators entering the spaces in and between the stories, and those between sound and image, as well as those between the on-screen and off-screen references. Ellipsis here addresses a socio-political issue and functions as an artistic strategy that avoids pedantry. In addition, ellipsis, because unfixed and incomplete, articulates an anti-essentialist conception of world, community, and being. Instead, these are shaped by ever-changing connections in an equally fluctuating present. This shifting rather than static worldview reflects Khalili's espousal of Deleuze and Guattari's use of the assemblage motif to conceptualize society. However, "The Mapping Journey Project" embodies rather than just illustrates this motif. Khalili posits art and life as living theory; her work embraces and even depends on the artistic risks this position involves.

The moving hands and pens, standing in for the migrants' agency, also nomadize the concepts of place, home, and world. The stories propose nomadism as a philosophy that reflects not only the reality of migrants and refugees, but also that of "globalized" contemporary lives, identities, and systems. In journeys #1 and #4, the migrants' travels are not over, suggesting displacement as voluntary. This cosmopolitanism underwriting "The Mapping Journey Project" elucidates the work's capacity to inscribe marginalized subjects into the world through a contemporary nomadic worldview structured by heterogeneity, rather than dualistic difference. Khalili's elegant moving image project is, in fact, a reminder that everyone is a migrant in the spaces of time, meaning, and becoming.

Conclusion

This chapter situates Ghazel's "Home (Stories)" and Khalili's "The Mapping Journey Project" within the respective artists' bodies of work, and examines their representation of migrants and refugees who are often denied subjecthood. The two projects exhibit a striking number of similarities. They make use of brevity, non-linear structures and narratives, and other characteristics of film afforded by the gallery context. Both are also inherently political, draw upon the documentary genre, probe the larger issues surrounding migration, and propose alternative humanistic, because heterogeneous and flexible, individual and collective identities. Featuring migrants of both sexes and various nationalities, "Home (Stories)" and "The Mapping Journey Project" employ micropolitics as a strategy to enable and make "audible" the self-representation of marginalized subjects. Ghazel and Khalili are themselves polycultural; therefore their status as simultaneous insiders and outsiders to Euro-American cultures and discourses informs their work. However, I must stress here that one cannot—as both artists would concede—conflate the experience of undocumented migrants with that of bicultural cosmopolitan artists living and working in various European or North American capitals. None the less, Ghazel's and Khalili's experience of living across cultures certainly abets their understanding of migrants and refugees.

Despite such commonalities, "Home (Stories)" and "The Mapping Journey Project" differ in method, structure, and form. Ghazel works intuitively and spontaneously, actually integrating chance into the technical aspects of filming. Khalili, on the other hand, designs her dispositives meticulously and is consciously informed by theory, a process that does not obviously preclude an experiential dimension. The comparison is not intended to uphold stereotypes about artist and personality types. On the contrary, it is drawn to highlight how two divergent approaches concerned with the representation of migrants and conscious of their erasure both resulted in positing voice as a less corruptible signifier of minoritized subjectivity. "Home (Stories)" and "The Mapping Journey Project" stretch both vision and image to include the unseen; they demonstrate how the intangible subjective spaces of mediation offer possible terrains for the emergence of and encounter with marginalized subjects. From the perspective of art theory, the two works reveal the nexus between theory and praxis, as well as art and activism, a confirmation that political art need not display its politics overtly, or shed its preoccupations with aesthetics and visuality. The two moving image projects were produced before the migration and refugee "crisis"; yet, the topic and lives of the globally displaced have never been as critical as they are currently within the context of increasingly staggering numbers and the normalization of anti-migrant discourse. It is to be hoped that "Home (Stories)" and "The Mapping Journey Project," which continue to circulate, will corroborate Deleuze's proposition that films are speech-acts that operate on reality and can enunciate "the storytelling of a people to come."[50]

Notes

1. Leon de Kock, "Interview with Gayatri Chakravorty Spivak: New Nation Writers Conference in South Africa," *Ariel: A Review of International English Literature* 23, no. 3 (1992), 46.
2. Two examples would be: "A World not Ours," curated by Katerina Gregos at Art Space Pythagorion, Samos, Greece (August 5 to October 15, 2016), and "Deportation Regime: Artistic Responses to State Practices and Lived Experience of Forced Removal" at the Center for Art on Migration Politics (CAMP) (September 9 to December 16, 2016), Copenhagen, Denmark, curated by CAMP's directors, Frederikke Hansen and Tone Olaf Nielsen. I must note that an important difference should be made between exhibits dedicated to the undocumented migrants and refugees and those addressing migration writ large, usually dealing with the biculturality or "unhomed geographies" of non-Western artists living and working partially or completely in Euro-America.
3. The UN Refugee Agency cites the likelihood of dying this year at 1 in 88, just in crossing the Mediterranean. See UNHCR Staff, "Mediterranean Death Tolls Soars, 2016 Is Deadliest Year Yet," *unhcr.org*, October 25, 2016, available at <http://www.unhcr.org/news/latest/2016/10/580f3e684/mediterranean-death-toll-soars-2016-deadliest-year> (last accessed June 15, 2017). On the question of data regarding detention camps, see Michael Flinn, "An Introduction to Data Construction on Immigration-Related Detention" (Geneva: Global Detention Project Working Paper, July 2011).
4. See, for example, Edward Said, *Culture and Imperialism* (London: Chatto & Windus, 1993); Meyda Yeğenoğlu, *Colonial Fantasies: Towards a Feminist Reading of Orientalism* (Cambridge: Cambridge University Press, 1998); Judith Butler, *Precarious Life: The Powers of Mourning and Violence* (London: Verso, 2004); and Gayatri Chakravorty Spivak, "The Rani of Sirmur." In *Europe and its Others, Volume 1, Proceedings of the Essex Conference on the Sociology of Literature*, 128–51, ed. F. Baker, M. Iverson, and D. Loxley (Colchester: University of Essex, 1985).
5. The postcolonial critic distinguishes between the subaltern and the marginalized due to the former's lack of access to the structure and language of imperial culture.
6. Celeste Ianniciello and Michaela Quadraro, "Museum Practices and Migrating Modernity: A Perspective from the South," *Stedelijk Studies Journal* 1 (2014), available at <http://www.stedelijkstudies.com/journal/museum-practices-and-migrating-modernity-a-perspective-from-the-south/> (last accessed June 15, 2017).

7. Ianniciello and Quadraro, "Museum Practices."
8. Áine O'Healy, "Border Traffic: Reimagining the Voyage to Italy," in *Transnational Feminism in Film and Media*, ed. Katarzyna Marciniak, Anikó Imre and Áine O'Healy (New York: Palgrave, 2007), 46. She is referring to Slavoj Žižek, *The Metastases of Enjoyment: Six Essays on Women and Causality* (London: Verso, 1998).
9. Slavoj Žižek, *The Fragile Absolute* (London: Verso, 2000), 60. Žižek articulates the idea in a discussion pertaining to Western military intervention in Kosovo, but it is equally applicable to the representation of the minoritized in general.
10. Judith Butler, *Bodies that Matter: On the Discursive Limits of Sex* (New York and London: Routledge, 1993), 3.
11. A good example would be Peruvian artist Daniela Ortiz's video "FDTD" (Forcible Drugging to Deport), which broaches the little-known U.S. Immigration and Customs Enforcement practice of forcibly drugging deportees removed against their will to make them pliant. See <http://www.daniela-ortiz.com/index.php?/projects/fdtd/> (last accessed November 24, 2020).
12. I also posit that personal experience—that is, subjectivity—inflects vision and therefore artmaking over and beyond what Kaja Silverman calls the "cultural screen," but this complex issue rests beyond the parameters of this study. Suffice it to say here that if the subject has the freedom to see beyond culturally constructed vision, this none the less only further testifies to the inseparability of "text" and vision.
13. However, I am not proposing that either minoritarian voices or art act(s) as absolute or fixed panaceas, but as possibly transformative phenomena or events whose potential effects need to be carefully examined and even questioned.
14. Tanya Leighton, "Introduction," in *Art and the Moving Image*, ed. Tanya Leighton (London: Tate Publishing, 2008), 9.
15. Jonathan Walley, "Modes of Film Practice in the Avant-Garde," in *Art and the Moving Image*, ed. Tanya Leighton (London: Tate Publishing, 2008), 190.
16. Mark Nash, "Art and Cinema: Some Critical Reflections," in *Art and the Moving Image*, ed. Tanya Leighton (London: Tate Publishing, 2008), 444.
17. Bayraktar lists these expressions used to denote the new genre, as well as those who coined them. Nilgün Bayraktar, *Mobility and Migration in Film and Moving Image Art* (New York: Routledge, 2016), 8. Katarzyna Marciniak, Anikó Imre, and Áine O'Healy, for their part, cite, in addition to "cinema of the borders," "cinema of migration" and "cinema of displacement," which they see as obviating the "ghettoizing rubrics" of "ethnic cinema," "minority cinema," or "immigrant cinema." Katarzyna Marciniak, Anikó Imre, and Áine O'Healy, "Introduction: Mapping Transnational Feminist Media Studies," in *Transnational Feminism in Film and Media*, ed. Katarzyna Marciniak, Anikó Imre, and Áine O'Healy (New York: Palgrave, 2007), 9. Other terms have been coined in English and other languages to denote this type of cinema. For further information, see Hamid Naficy, *An Accented Cinema: Exilic and Diasporic Filmmaking* (Princeton: Princeton University Press, 2001); Laura U. Marks, *The Skin of the Film: Intercultural Cinema, Embodiment, and the Senses* (Durham, NC: Duke University Press, 2000); Elizabeth Ezra and Terry Rowden, "General Introduction: What is Transnational Cinema?", in *Transnational Cinema: The Film Reader*, ed. Elizabeth Ezra and Terry Rowden, 1–12 (New York

and London; Routledge, 2006); Joanne Leal and Klaus-Dieter Rossade, "Introduction: Cinema and Migration since Unification," *gfl-journal* 1 (2008): 1–5, available at <http://www.gfl-journal.de/1-2008/leal_rossade.pdf> (last accessed July 12, 2017); and Bruce Bennett and Imogen Tyler, "Screening Unlivable Lives: The Cinema of Borders," in *Transnational Feminism in Film and Media*, ed. Katarzyna Marciniak, Anikó Imre, and Áine O'Healy, 21–36 (New York: Palgrave Macmillan, 2007).
18. Nash, "Art and Cinema," 444–9.
19. miriam cooke, "The Muslimwoman," *Contemporary Islam* 1, no. 2 (2007), 139–54.
20. Ghazel has clearly stated that, for her, the veil is a "couleur locale", meaning part of local culture, rather than a religious imposition on women. See Amin Moghadam, "Ghazel: l'artiste mobile, l'art de la mobilité," *Hommes et migrations* 1312 (2015), 91–7. For an analysis of how the "Me" series succeeds in obviating the binarism inherent in the image of the veil by challenging the patriarchy underwriting definitions of normative female appearance and subjecthood across cultures, see Valerie Behiery, "Alternative Narratives of the Veil in Contemporary Art," *Comparative Studies of South Asia, Africa, and the Middle East* 32, no. 1 (2012), 137–42.
21. She can be heard because the humor subverts the relationship between the spectator and the visibly Muslim other, and sees the former laugh with the latter, creating a space of intersubectivity. See Behiery, "Alternative Narratives," 137–42.
22. This work requires further discussion to address, for example, spectators who have experienced or witnessed torture, or even the use of humor, which could be misinterpreted here. The piece, while highlighting the subjecthood of those who have been dehumanized to an unimageable and horrific extent, is ambiguous. From my perspective, its merit rests in bringing visibility to a subject that power holders wanted to keep out of the public eye and that contradicts what postcolonial critics call the myth of Western benevolence.
23. Ghazel, "Interview" (with Valerie Behiery), *Mea Culpa* exhibition catalogue (March 14 to May 14, 2016) (Dubai: Carbon 12 Gallery, 2016), n.p.
24. After Nicolas Sarkozy was elected President in 2007, Ghazel successfully applied for French citizenship in order to vote against him and stem the rise of right-wing politics in France, more generally. She remains none the less ambivalent about possessing French citizenship.
25. Ghazel, "Interview," n.p.
26. They are also part of the permanent collection of the National Museum of the History of Immigration in Paris, available at <http://www.histoire-immigration.fr/> (last accessed, June 15, 2017).
27. There is a storytelling component to "Road Movie 1" that begins with, "Once upon a time, there was a beautiful country called Afghanistan. For many years, there had been problems." We learn a few facts about H: for example, that he left Afghanistan with someone who did not speak his language. Storytelling is, however, more present in other videos of the series, such as "Road Movie 5," about Ali, the Iranian Kurd.
28. Translation is key to the piece in that Ghazel and H spoke together in Farsi, and Ghazel writes/performs in English, French, or Farsi, depending on the context of the performance.

29. Gayatri Chakravorty Spivak, "Subaltern Talk: Interview with Donna Landry and Gerald MacLean," in *The Spivak Reader*, ed. Donna Landry and Gerald MacLean (New York: Routledge), 306.
30. Bussolini argues that the Foucauldian term "*dispositif*" is best translated as "dispositive" rather than "apparatus," as is usually done. See Jeffrey Bussolini, "What is a Dispositive?", *Foucault Studies* 10 (2010), 85–107.
31. Teresa De Lauretis, "The Technology of Gender," in Teresa De Lauretis, *Technologies of Gender: Essays in Theory, Film, and Fiction* (Bloomington: Indiana University Press, 1987), 26.
32. Personal communication with the artist, December 7, 2016.
33. Ghazel did intervene indirectly by showing her own work to the participants, and also directly sometimes, as she explains: "One of the guys had a false leg and he thought he would come in the performance and take it off. And I said 'No, no, no that's just too hard for the viewers.' I asked them: Charlie Chaplin and Victor Hugo, which one is stronger? Everybody agreed it was Charle Chaplin. So I convinced them to use humor." Claus Pirschner, "Umkämpfte Migrationsräume," Radio FM4, November 4, 2010, available at <http://fm4.orf.at/stories/1667606/> (last accessed June 15, 2017).
34. Godard's statement was a retort to an interviewer who was telling him that a film had to have a beginning, middle, and end. It is quoted in Jean-François Chassay, *Robert Coover* (Paris: Belin, 1996), 28.
35. Christian Kravagna, "HOME (Stories)," *Nafas Art Magazine*, December 2008, <http://u-in-u.com/nafas/articles/2008/ghazel/> (last accessed June 15, 2017).
36. De Lauretis, "The Technology of Gender," 26.
37. An attempt at perspective is evident in the table and couch, although the latter, essentially shown in a bird's-eye view, adds visual interest to the picture.
38. For a short exposition of Pasolini's and Deleuze's conceptions of free indirect discourse, see David Heinemann, "The Creative Voice: Free Indirect Speech in the Cinema of Rohmer and Bresson," *The New Soundtrack*, 2, no. 1 (2012), 1–2.
39. Jonatan Habib Engqvist, "A Map of Utopia" (Interview with Bouchra Khalili), in *The Opposite of Voice-Over* exhibition catalogue (April 2 to June 19, 2016). Stockholm: Färgfabriken, 2016), 11.
40. Engqvist, "A Map," 11.
41. Ellie Armon Azoulay, "Bouchra Khalili: Foreign Office, Palais de Tokyo, Feb. 18–May 17, 2015," *Camera Austria International* 130 (2015), 78.
42. Azoulay, "Bouchra," 78.
43. Thomas B. Lax, "The Translation of a Translation: A Conversation Between Bouchra Khalili and Thomas B. Lax," in SAM Art Projects, *Foreign Office* (Paris: SAM Art Projects), 72.
44. Rosi Braidotti, "The Becoming-Minoritarian of Europe," in *Deleuze and the Contemporary World*, ed. Ian Buchanan and Adrian Parr (Edinburgh: Edinburgh University Press, 2006), 84.
45. Lax, "Translation," 72.
46. Patricia Pisters, "Arresting the Flux of Images and Sounds: Free Indirect Discourse and the Dialectics of Political Cinema," in *Deleuze and the Contemporary World*, ed. Ian Buchanan and Adrian Parr (Edinburgh: Edinburgh University Press, 2006), 181.

47. Engqvist, "A Map," 12.
48. Engqvist, "A Map," 13.
49. Engqvist, "A Map," 13.
50. Deleuze describes this new form of storytelling that can bring minoritized subjects into the field of representation in these terms: "Not the myth of a past people, but the storytelling of a people to come. The speech-act must create itself as a foreign language in a dominant language, precisely in order to express an impossibility of living under domination." Gilles Deleuze, *Cinema II: The Time-Image*, trans. Hugh Tomlinson and Robert Galeta (London: Bloomsbury, 2013), 223.

Works Cited

Azoulay, Ellie Armon. "Bouchra Khalili: Foreign Office, Palais de Tokyo, Feb. 18–May 17, 2015." *Camera Austria International* 130 (2015): 78–9.
Bayraktar, Nilgün. *Mobility and Migration in Film and Moving Image Art*. New York: Routledge, 2016.
Behiery, Valerie. "Alternative Narratives of the Veil in Contemporary Art." *Comparative Studies of South Asia, Africa, and the Middle East* 32, no. 1 (2012): 130–46.
Bennett, Bruce and Imogen Tyler. "Screening Unlivable Lives: The Cinema of Borders". In *Transnational Feminism in Film and Media*, ed. Katarzyna Marciniak, Anikó Imre, and Áine O'Healy, 21–36. New York: Palgrave Macmillan, 2007.
Braidotti, Rosi. "The Becoming-Minoritarian of Europe." In *Deleuze and the Contemporary World*, ed. Ian Buchanan and Adrian Parr, 79–94. Edinburgh: Edinburgh University Press, 2006.
Bussolini, Jeffrey. "What is a Dispositive?" *Foucault Studies* 10 (2010): 85–107.
Butler, Judith. *Bodies that Matter: On the Discursive Limits of Sex*. New York and London: Routledge, 1993.
Butler, Judith. *Precarious Life: The Powers of Mourning and Violence*. London: Verso, 2004.
Chassay, Jean-François. *Robert Coover*. Paris: Belin, 1996.
cooke, miriam. "The Muslimwoman." *Contemporary Islam* 1, no. 2 (2007): 139–54.
de Kock, Leon. "Interview with Gayatri Chakravorty Spivak: New Nation Writers Conference in South Africa." *Ariel: A Review of International English Literature* 23, no. 3 (1992): 29–47.
De Lauretis, Teresa. "The Technology of Gender." In Teresa De Lauretis, *Technologies of Gender: Essays in Theory, Film, and Fiction*, 1–30. Bloomington: Indiana University Press, 1987.
Deleuze, Gilles. *Cinema II: The Time-Image*, trans. Hugh Tomlinson and Robert Galeta. London: Bloomsbury, 2013.
Engqvist, Jonatan Habib. "A Map of Utopia" (Interview with Bouchra Khalili). In *The Opposite of Voice-Over* (exhibition catalogue) (April 2 to June 19, 2016), 8–33. Stockhlom: Färgfabriken, 2016.
Ezra, Elizabeth and Terry Rowden. "General Introduction: What is Transnational Cinema?" In *Transnational Cinema: The Film Reader*, ed. Elizabeth Ezra and Terry Rowden, 1–12. New York and London: Routledge, 2006.

Ezra, Elizabeth and Terry Rowden, eds. *Transnational Cinema: The Film Reader*. New York and London: Routledge, 2006.

Flinn, Michael. "An Introduction to Data Construction on Immigration-Related Detention." Geneva: Global Detention Project Working Paper, July 2011.

Ghazel. "Interview" (with Valerie Behiery). *Mea Culpa* exhibition catalogue (March 14 to May 14, 2016). Dubai: Carbon 12 gallery, 2016, n.p.

Heinemann, David. "The Creative Voice: Free Indirect Speech in the Cinema of Rohmer and Bresson." *The New Soundtrack* 2, no. 1 (2012): 39–49.

Ianniciello, Celeste and Michaela Quadraro. "Museum Practices and Migrating Modernity: A Perspective from the South." *Stedelijk Studies Journal*, 1, <http://www.stedelijkstudies.com/journal/museum-practices-and-migrating-modernity-a-perspective-from-the-south/> (last accessed June 15, 2017).

Kravagna, Christian. "HOME (Stories)." *Nafas Art Magazine*, December 2008, <http://u-in-u.com/nafas/articles/2008/ghazel/> (last accessed June 15, 2017).

Lax, Thomas B. "The Translation of a Translation: A Conversation Between Bouchra Khalili and Thomas B. Lax." In *Foreign Office*, ed. SAM Art Projects, 72–5. Paris: SAM Art Projects, 2015.

Leal, Joanne and Klaus-Dieter Rossade. "Introduction: Cinema and Migration Since Unification." *gfl-journal* 1 (2008), 1–5, <http://www.gfl-journal.de/1-2008/leal_rossade.pdf> (last accessed July 20, 2017).

Leighton, Tanya. "Introduction." In *Art and the Moving Image*, ed. Tanya Leighton, 1–42. London: Tate Publishing, 2008.

Marciniak, Katarzyna, Anikó Imre, and Áine O'Healy, eds. *Transnational Feminism in Film and Media*. New York: Palgrave, 2007.

Marciniak, Katarzyna, Anikó Imre, and Áine O'Healy. "Introduction: Mapping Transnational Feminist Media Studies." In *Transnational Feminism in Film and Media*, ed. Katarzyna Marciniak, Anikó Imre, and Áine O'Healy, 1–18. New York: Palgrave, 2007.

Marks, Laura U. *The Skin of the Film: Intercultural Cinema, Embodiment, and the Senses*. Durham, NC: Duke University Press, 2000.

Moghadam, Amin. "Ghazel: l'artiste mobile, l'art de la mobilité." *Hommes et migrations* 1312 (2015): 91–7.

Naficy, Hamid. *An Accented Cinema: Exilic and Diasporic Filmmaking*. Princeton: Princeton University Press, 2001.

Nash, Mark. "Art and Cinema: Some Critical Reflections." In *Art and the Moving Image*, ed. Tanya Leighton, 444–59. London: Tate Publishing, 2008.

O'Healy, Áine. "Border Traffic: Reimagining the Voyage to Italy." In *Transnational Feminism in Film and Media*, ed. Katarzyna Marciniak, Anikó Imre, and Áine O'Healy, 37–52. New York: Palgrave, 2007.

Pirschner, Claus. "Umkämpfte Migrationsräume." *Radio FM4*, November 4, 2010, <http://fm4.orf.at/stories/1667606/> (last accessed June 15, 2017).

Pisters, Patricia. "Arresting the Flux of Images and Sounds: Free Indirect Discourse and the Dialectics of Political Cinema." In *Deleuze and the Contemporary World*, ed. Ian Buchanan and Adrian Parr, 175–93. Edinburgh: Edinburgh University Press, 2006.

Said, Edward. *Culture and Imperialism*. London: Chatto & Windus, 1993.

Spivak, Gayatri Chakravorty. "Subaltern Talk: Interview with Donna Landry and Gerald MacLean." In *The Spivak Reader*, ed. Donna Landry and Gerald MacLean, 287–308. New York: Routledge 287–308.

Spivak, Gayatri Chakravorty. "The Rani of Sirmur." In *Europe and its Others, Volume 1, Proceedings of the Essex Conference on the Sociology of Literature*, ed. F. Baker, M. Iverson, and D. Loxley et al., 128–51. Colchester: University of Essex, 1985.

UNHCR Staff. "Mediterranean Death Tolls Soars, 2016 Is Deadliest Year Yet," *unhcr.org*, October 25, 2016, <http://www.unhcr.org/news/latest/2016/10/580f3e684/mediterranean-death-toll-soars-2016-deadliest-year> (last accessed June 15, 2017).

Walley, Jonathan. "Modes of Film Practice in the Avant-Garde." In *Art and the Moving Image*, ed. Tanya Leighton, 182–99. London: Tate Publishing, 2008.

Yeğenoğlu, Meyda. *Colonial Fantasies: Towards a Feminist Reading of Orientalism*. Cambridge: Cambridge University Press, 1998.

Žižek, Slavoj. *The Fragile Absolute*. London: Verso, 2000.

Žižek, Slavoj. *The Metastases of Enjoyment: Six Essays on Women and Causality*. London: Verso, 1998.

3. FORCED MIGRATION AND FANTASIES OF RETURN IN PALESTINIAN CINEMA: *WHEN I SAW YOU* (ANNEMARIE JACIR, 2012) AND *GATE OF THE SUN* (YOUSRY NASRALLAH, 2003)

Drew Paul

Yousry Nasrallah's film, *Gate of the Sun* (*Bab al-Shams*, 2003), an epic saga of the trials and tribulations of Palestinian refugees who fled to Lebanon, begins in 1994 with the two primary characters—the aging freedom fighter Younis and his protégé Khalil—in the Shatila refugee camp near Beirut, where they have resided since their expulsion from Palestine in 1948. Another refugee, Umm Hassan, has given Khalil the branch of an orange tree that she brought back from a visit to Palestine, and Khalil has hung the branch on his wall as a memento of Palestine, which reflects the common use of the orange as a symbol of Palestinian identity and affiliation with the land. Younis, upon seeing the oranges hanging from the branch on the wall, commands Khalil to eat the fruit. He says it is important to "eat Palestine," to eat the homeland (*al-watan*). This command is surprising, coming from Younis, who we soon learn is a dedicated resistance fighter (*fida'i*) and whom the residents of the camp treat as a hero. It defies common practices of Palestinian cultural memory in which physical remnants (such as the keys to former family homes in Palestine) and imagery of nature, land, and agriculture (such as oranges and olive trees) function as means of maintaining and commemorating a connection with Palestinian terrain that was severed by migration and exile. The orange signifies nostalgia for a lost self-sufficiency and a simpler, agricultural past. Instead of preserving this symbolically laden connection to Palestine, Younis orders Khalil to consume the homeland. By telling Khalil to eat the orange, he claims that home and homeland are not simply places but rather are sensorially embodied. In other words, Palestine is contained not within objects, which are all perishable like fruit, but within people and their experiences. The moment that he tells this to Khalil is particularly potent, as he represents a subsequent generation that will be tasked with carrying on the legacy of Younis, and others of his generation that is dying out. Thus the orange maintains its place as a signifier of Palestine, but Younis shows that Palestine does not exist on its own; rather, it serves as nourishment and sustenance for Palestinians, the idea that home lies not within the presence of the orange but within the experience of eating it.

The eating of the orange functions as the frame for a long chronicle of the forced migration and exile of Palestinian refugees in Lebanon, appearing at the beginning of *Gate of the Sun* and again, in an abbreviated version, at the start of the second part of the film. Like the acclaimed novel by Elias Khoury upon which it is based, the film aims to be an epic retelling of the Palestinian national narrative through the saga of migration, exile, and resistance. Yet it begins by questioning the nostalgic synecdoche of homeland with the symbol of the orange. This moment, and others in which the film critiques the representation, remembrance, and preservation of Palestine, denote the film's interrogation of the meanings of *watan* in exile. It also allows us to consider, as I do in this chapter, how filmic depictions of migration and exile both reflect and shape the meanings of *watan*. Moreover, the film's interrogation of *watan* in a Palestinian context extends to a global discourse concerning the nation and those who flee it under duress. Always pertinent, the concerns raised by this film from 2003 continue to resonate more globally in the present moment of nearly unprecedented mass migrations and the upheavals they engender. Similarly, though both films are set in an earlier era—*When I Saw You* occurs immediately after the Six Day War in 1967, *Gate of the Sun* takes place in the 1990s with flashbacks to the pre-*Nakba* ("Disaster") era and other earlier periods—they engage with concerns that are of great importance to the topic of mass migration brought about by war and economic collapse that is the focus of this volume.

In this chapter, I consider how mass migration shapes conceptions of the *watan* through an analysis of two films that depict the Palestinian experience of exile in Lebanon and Jordan. I locate distinct conceptions of *watan* found in the two films in the diverging depictions of forced migration and exile. The first, *When I Saw You* (*Lamma Shuftak*), a 2012 film directed by Annemarie Jacir, tells the story of a young boy and his mother, who find themselves in a refugee camp in Jordan after the Israeli conquest of the West Bank in 1967. The son, Tarek, soon runs off and joins a multinational group of guerrilla fighters (a "people's army") in the hopes of one day becoming a *fida'i* and returning home to Palestine. While the film depicts the refugee camp and other aspects of the exilic experience, it shows little of the migration, and instead emphasizes the son's commitment to resistance and return to the lost homeland (*watan*), thus framing *watan* in primarily political terms. The second film, *Gate of the Sun*, directed by Egyptian filmmaker Yousry Nasrallah, depicts the long and tragic history of Palestinians from the Galilee region who were forced from their homes in 1948 and who have lived in squalid refugee camps in Lebanon ever since. The story is told primarily through the memories of Younis, who escaped Palestine as a young man but frequently sneaks across the border to a cave called Bab al-Shams (Gate of the Sun), where he meets his wife, who remained behind. These flashbacks occur within a framed narrative—set in a Shatila refugee camp in the 1990s—in which an elderly Younis has fallen into a coma, and his young protégé Khalil seeks to revive Younis by retelling his stories. *Gate of the Sun* is divided into two parts—"The Departure" (*al-Rahil*) and "The Return" (*al-'Awda*)—and is nearly 4 hours in length, which reflects its ambition to depict the Palestinians' trajectory as an epic saga in a manner that has not been done before. The director devotes the first part of the film, *al-Rahil*, almost entirely to Younis's youth in Palestine, followed by the violence, expulsion, and flight from the Galilee to Lebanon, providing an intense depiction of the moment of migration, in contrast to *When I Saw You*. Moreover, while Tarek desires to cross the border and return home throughout the latter film, it remains an aspiration, but Younis repeatedly makes that exact journey in *Gate of the Sun*.

In this chapter I will begin with a brief overview of representations of migration in films on Palestine before turning to a theoretical discussion of *watan*, exile, and migration. Taking these concepts as a starting point, I argue that the films' distinctive exilic representations of landscapes and border spaces produce competing conceptions of *watan* that can be placed in dialogue productively. *When I Saw You*'s focus on the impetus to return and fight induces nostalgia for a lost transnational leftist resistance. Such a celebration of past ideologies produces a territorially dictated, collective, political definition of *watan* (in short, a modern nation-state–based understanding of nationhood and homeland). By contrast, *Gate of the Sun* intersperses a lengthy depiction of the experience of forced migration with heroic acts of resistance. Through this juxtaposition, the film conceptualizes the relationship to *watan* as one that is personal and experiential rather than territorial. By considering filmic representations of both spaces of exile, such as the refugee camp and the Fedayeen base, as well as the landscapes of Palestine that were lost and the experience of crossing between them, we discern the two films' distinct depictions of *watan* and migration. In this analysis, the experience of forced migration is not merely a severing or a deviation from *watan*, but rather redefines and reconstitutes *watan* in a manner that makes room for tragic modes of reshaping conceptions of homeland and the nation. Therefore, I will conclude by considering what the Palestinian case can tell us about how migration and exile could shape notions of nationhood, homeland, and nationalism for Syrians, Afghans, Algerians, and others in the coming years and decades.

Migration and Cinema in Palestine

The experience of forced migration and the condition of exile has been crucial to the development of Palestinian cinema, both as a medium of cultural expression and as an industry, since its inception. In part, this reflects the centrality of migration to the Palestinian national narrative. The *Nakba* ("Disaster") of 1948, in which approximately 700,000 Palestinians fled the areas of Palestine that became the State of Israel, shattered the cultural, political, and economic fabric of Palestinian society in irreparable ways. Nearly 80 percent of the Palestinian population in what is now Israel became refugees, representing around 50 percent of the total Palestinian population at the time, and major urban centers such as Haifa, Jaffa, and Jerusalem were depopulated.[1] Subsequent waves of migration, most notably the *Naksa* ("Setback") that followed Israel's conquest and military occupation of the West Bank and Gaza in 1967, further altered the fabric of Palestinian society. As a result, Palestinian notions of nationhood, *watan*, were unavoidably transformed; the homeland came to signify what was lost and the necessity to resist and return. Given the tragically formative role of expulsion and exile in the transformation of Palestinian daily life, culture, and politics, an exploration of migration and its representation provides essential tools for understanding contested and conflicting conceptions of the Palestinian *watan*.

The experience of forced migration and the consequential condition of exile proved crucial to the formation of Palestinian cinema, as reflected both in its history as an industry and in the content of the films that have been produced. There are some examples of pre-1948 films from Palestine,[2] but the *Nakba* had the effect of silencing filmmaking for a significant period of time. During the period immediately following the *Nakba*, which Gertz and Khleifi term the "silent period," almost no film production took place, as there was no infrastructure or funding to do so.[3] A flourishing began in the late 1960s, after the war of 1967, and this period of Palestinian cinematic production, which lasted until the early 1980s, was explicitly tied to resistance efforts. Palestinian political organizations such as the Palestine Liberation Organization (PLO) and the Democratic Front for the Liberation of Palestine (DFLP) established film units that aimed to "document their struggle."[4] The word document is key here, because these films are almost exclusively documentaries and tend to focus on political battles and events, conditions in refugee camps and under occupation, resistance, and protest actions.[5] They include some second-hand oral testimonies from *Nakba* survivors[6] and encompass some coverage of conditions within the occupied territories and Israel, but the primary focus during this period remains outside of historic Palestine. These films were produced exclusively in exile, first in Jordan and then, following the expulsion of the PLO from Jordan in 1970,[7] in Beirut, and to a lesser extent in Syria.[8] Not only were they produced abroad; they were screened across the Arab world and elsewhere, but never in Palestine itself.[9] Tragically, many were lost in the wake of the Israeli bombardments and invasion of Beirut in 1982.[10]

The production of films in the West Bank, Gaza, and Israel began in earnest again only in the early 1980s and is thus relatively new.[11] For the first time in Palestinian cinematic history, this wave of films has included many fiction films, alongside continued extensive production of documentaries. Although centered in historic Palestine, the cinema that has emerged remains highly transnational in funding and production, with support from Europe, other Arab countries, and occasionally Israel, as well as in audience, due to the difficulty of reaching Palestinian audiences.[12] In fact, the first film funded almost exclusively by Palestinian money was released only in 2013.[13] This wave was not exclusively exilic like the previous era; as Livia Alexander notes, this tilt towards filmmakers from within historical Palestine is not coincidental but rather reflects the fact that many Palestinian directors, producers, and camera operators gained experience and access to equipment from working as part of Israeli and foreign film crews.[14] Yet even as Palestinian cinema returned home, it remained inseparable from the transnational and the exilic in many ways. Hamid Naficy argues that Palestinian cinema is "structurally exilic," meaning that it is made either in internal exile (under occupation) or in external exile in other countries.[15] While the relatively recent Palestinian support of cinema complicates this claim, it is true that Palestinian films do not benefit from the attributes of a typical national cinema. In such a situation, Hamid Dabashi suggests in his introduction to an edited volume on Palestinian cinema, the nation becomes more crucial to the construct of Palestinian cinema because a national cinema in the traditional sense is unattainable; he terms Palestinian cinema a "stateless"[16] national cinema, defined by a form of "traumatic realism" that is the "aesthetic presence of a political absence."[17] By chronicling, attesting to, and recording the nation's destruction, Palestinian cinema proves inseparable from the nation and its related exile.

Despite the centrality of exile to the development of Palestinian cinema, filmmakers rarely depict the migration experience. More typical is a focus on the conditions of Palestinian life that followed the *Nakba* and the various forms that they took, reflecting a neorealist-inspired aesthetic that has influenced many global and Third cinemas.[18] Not only did temporal distance render the experience of migration a distant, if still highly potent, memory, but by the 1980s, many of the prominent directors resided in Israel and/or the Palestinian territories. Quite a few films from this period focus on representing the dire conditions that Palestinians encountered in exile, including *When I Saw You* and many PLO documentaries, as well the 1972 film *The Dupes* (which a separate chapter in this volume addresses more extensively), directed by Tawfiq Saleh and based on Ghassan Kanafani's novella *Men in the Sun* (1962), and *They Do Not Exist* (1974), directed by Mustafa Abu Ali. A number of films, such as those by Elia Suleiman, or *Salt of this Sea* by Annemarie Jacir (2008), center on the experience of return to Palestine from exile. Yet others, such as a number of films by Hany Abu-Assad, Michel Khleifi, and Rashid Masharawi, center on the living conditions of those who remained behind in Israel, the West Bank, and Gaza. With some notable exceptions, such as Suleiman's *The Time that Remains* (2009), relatively few depict the period around 1948. Thus, the "traumatic realism" that Dabashi describes also might encompass a neorealist, or even neo-neorealist tendency to use present conditions to call attention to political failure and injustice. In this way, while scholars have identified certain neorealist characteristics in Nasrallah's œuvre,[19] his use of flashback here stands apart and suggests a distinct departure from more typical depictions of Palestinian exile.

In both literature and film, moreover, many of the most extensive depictions of the *Nakba* and subsequent waves of migration have come from Arab writers and filmmakers from outside of Palestine, including the book *Gate of the Sun* (1998) and *As if She Were Sleeping* (2007), both by Lebanese author Elias Khoury, *Days of Dust* (1969) by Halim Barakat, and *The Woman from Tantoura* (2010) by Egyptian writer Radwa Ashour. Likewise, in cinema, *Gate of the Sun*, as mentioned above, was directed by the Egyptian filmmaker Yousry Nasrallah, and the 1981 film *Return to Haifa*, though based on Palestinian author Ghassan Kanafani's novella, was made by Kassem Hawal, an Iraqi director who also directed a documentary on the 1982 massacre of Palestinians in the Sabra and Shatila camps. This complex transnational landscape indicates the need to conceive of Palestinian cinema more broadly, as I seek to do by including *Gate of the Sun*, perhaps as a "cinema of Palestine," in order to consider the representation (or lack thereof) of Palestinian migration on screen.

Thus we see that migration is crucial to the conditions that have produced the cinema of Palestine, as it served as a formative experience for so many filmmakers, including those such as Suleiman who has lived and worked in the United States and Europe, as well as at home. However, the relative dearth of depictions of the experience of migration (and when these do exist, they often come from non-Palestinian directors) illuminates a crucial element of the relationship between cinema and the nation in Palestine. It emphasizes the extent to which cinematic production and representations of Palestine are multivalent, decentered, dispersed, and diverse in a manner that extends beyond the dichotomy of exilic cinemas (or "accented cinemas," to use Hamid Naficy's term[20]) and local cinemas. In a body of works that is national in orientation while also transnational by necessity, the *watan* and its relationship to migration, separation, and exile unsurprisingly become contested terrain. When Younis tells

Khalil to eat the orange that represents Palestine and the *watan*—a command made significant only by the separation from Palestine that makes the orange precious—it is an act that prompts us to consider the polyvalent meanings of *watan* and the ways in which cinemas of Palestine engage with its relationship to migration and exile.

Watan and Migration

Watan in the Arabic tradition is a concept that allows for a range of notions of nationhood and relationships between nation and exile. Though, in modern times, many Palestinians define *watan* as "homeland" or "nation," and though it is the root from which terms such as nationalism (*wataniyya*) and citizen (*muwatin*) derive, the word's etymology suggests an idea that is more local in scale. *Lisan al-Arab* defines *watan* simply as "house" (*manzil*),[21] indicating that there should be an emphasis on the *home* in homeland. This is particularly crucial in the instance of migration and exile, for longing (*hanin*) for the *watan* is not simply mourning the nation but mourning an experience of home. Ihab Saloul, in his study of visual representations of Palestinian exile, quotes a Palestinian refugee who emphasizes that what was lost was not material but mental, not just stones but a "whole life: the country, the people, and their entire existence."[22] Home is not only a physical place, as the modern concept of *watan* suggests, but rather a constellation of affective experiences. Sarah Ahmed writes of home as a "lived experience of locality" akin to inhabiting a second skin.[23] It is a sensory experience, which brings us back to the orange in the opening of *Gate of the Sun*: by commanding Khalil to eat the orange, to taste it, to experience and consume it, Younis pushes the definition of *watan* beyond its simplistic modern interpretation and opens up what Ahmed calls a permeability between *watan* and exile, in which the two are not necessarily diametrically opposed, but rather where there is space for home within exile and vice versa.

The term *watan* contains an inevitable loss at its core. Yaseen Noorani, looking at *watan* as a premodern literary trope, argues that *watan* signifies a temporal as well as spatial distance associated with a golden age that was "characterized by natural simplicity" that is "almost by definition lost or transfigured and unrecoverable."[24] He further notes that this pre-existing topos provides an "affective structure" that is transformed in, but not completely abandoned by, the modern idea of a national homeland.[25] Thus, even as *watan* represents a form of national belonging in the present, it also gestures towards an unattainability, and in a sense signifies a form of displacement that is inseparable from the concept of *watan* itself. In Palestine, and perhaps elsewhere, *watan* does the rhetorical heavy lifting, signifying both the modern concept of nation and the long-established, more localized notion of home, as well as exile from both. As Saloul notes, literary and visual texts depict both the singular *Nakba*—the political event that was the establishment of the State of Israel and the resulting expulsions and flights—and many localized *nakbas*, the anniversaries of which are often commemorated on the day each particular village fell.[26] *Watan* is both personal and political, both nation and home, and the representation of *watan* and its loss is infused with these tensions. Saloul's work reveals the difficulty of narrating the loss; one refugee cannot describe his mental image of his home village, as such personal visions are inexplicable, "hard to explain."[27] Discourse fails him, for home is not simply a place but also a life.[28] In this context of multiple overlapping meanings of *watan*, of a non-binary understanding of home and exile, and of the fraught nature of narrating the loss of the *watan*, I locate *When I Saw You* and *Gate of the Sun*. The ways in which these two filmmakers represent migration reflects and contributes to the contested symbolic terrain of Palestine as homeland.

Preserving the Nation: *When I Saw You*

Both films use space and setting to frame the experience of migration and exile. *When I Saw You* centers primarily on three locales: the refugee camp, the Fedayeen training camp, and the vistas of Palestine visible from the other side of the border. The manner in which the film portrays each setting serves both to emphasize the necessity of return and political resistance, and to mourn the loss of the dream of resistance as it existed in the period immediately following 1967, which was the peak of the Palestinian resistance movement after it became clear that the Arab states were not going to rescue Palestine. Early in the film the two main characters, Tarek and his mother, Ghayda, find themselves in a refugee camp in Jordan; they fled from the West Bank and have become separated from Tarek's father, so they wait at the refugee camp, hoping to be reunited with him. Built hastily as a temporary measure to house Palestinians fleeing the territories that Israel occupied in 1967, the film depicts the camp as barren and inhospitable. It is located in a desert region, flat and brown with very little vegetation. Panoramic shots of the camp and the roads nearby emphasize this bareness. Cars and trucks barrel past the camera down dirt roads, churning up dust, and portraying a desolate space for an unwelcome people. The part of the film set in the refugee camp intersperses scenes from Tarek and Ghayda's life with brief shots that reveal various aspects of the functioning of the camp. We see the tin shacks and makeshift tents that house refugees, as truckloads of new arrivals pour in, and families eagerly greet each new truck in search of news of lost loved ones (Fig. 3.1). Long shots of the camp and its vistas emphasize its bareness and hostility, and its fundamental unhomeliness.

Figure 3.1 *When I Saw You* (Philistine Films, 2012).

Tarek spends his days wandering among the shacks and playing in the dirt, particularly after being expelled from school for not conforming to the rules and following the school curriculum, despite his intelligence. His mother is employed as a seamstress in a garment factory, one of many women working like automatons in a dark room in the camp. From Tarek's school to Ghayda's job to the transport of people in the back of trucks like livestock, the camp produces a bland conformity to the institutionalized and industrial conditions of the postwar refugee camps, which are void of any specificity of place or culture. Life in the camp, in short, entails a loss of self and individuality, as well as nationality. As the camp rejects Tarek, he repeatedly begs his mother to leave, telling her that she is "strangling" him by keeping him there. He begins to notice furtive resistance activity as young men leave the camp to go fight for Palestine. He finds that his desire to resist is incompatible with camp life. The camp scenes frame life there as a diversion from or perversion of the *watan*; characters reach or realize the *watan* through resistance and return, both of which necessitate leaving the camp.

Soon Tarek decides to flee the static conformity of the camp, so one day he simply walks out. The camera follows him as he walks past the tents and shacks and into the open desert (Fig. 3.2). A few seconds later it cuts to a long shot of him walking towards the camera in a green-ish field with some trees (Fig. 3.3). This area is already noticeably less barren than the camp, and it begins to bear a greater resemblance to the hills and fields of Palestine, as opposed to the desert of Jordan. This progression repeats itself a couple of

Figure 3.2 *When I Saw You* (Philistine Films, 2012).

Figure 3.3 *When I Saw You* (Philistine Films, 2012).

times, until shrubs have given way to trees, and brown has turned to green. He comes across a pomegranate tree and reaches up to pick one, adding a vibrant red fruit to the now greener landscape, when an older woman sees him. She startles him at first, but upon finding out that he is Palestinian, she offers him several pomegranates and wishes him well. Thus while the camp is barren, escape allows Tarek to breathe, provides him with sustenance, and revives him. Eventually, a freedom fighter finds him and takes him to the Fedayeen base, which is located in a lush forest. Here the trees and forest provide cover—as opposed to the open, exposed camp, which is attacked by the Israelis at one point during the film—and sustenance in the form of small game and plants. No longer playing in the dirt, Tarek is active, engaged in the training drills of the Fedayeen. If the idle hopelessness of the camp strangles him, the commitment to the *watan* through resistance nurtures and fortifies him. The return to a blossoming nature that resembles Palestine also establishes political engagement as a means of preserving a connection to the *watan* in its absence.

When they are not training or hunting, the Fedayeen spend the evenings in communal fashion, eating together and, importantly, singing Palestinian folk songs. They gather around a campfire, and the camera moves between close-up shots of the *kufiyah*-clad fighters as they play the oud and other instruments and sing songs of home, of Palestine and its natural beauty.[29] The singing, with its invocation both of a folk music tradition and of the Palestinian connection to the land that have been severed but not lost, implicates the act of resistance as a form of *watan* preservation. The film's depiction of life in the Fedayeen base shows how resistance functions not only as a form of *watan* reclamation through political victory but also as a means of maintaining the *watan* and its memory in the absence of return through the formation of a new community bound by both politics and culture.

Interestingly, this mode of *watan* preservation and commemoration through resistance occurs in the absence of significant direct depiction of pre-exile Palestine in the film, and the experience of expulsion and flight is not shown. The film ends as Tarek and Ghayda run towards the border in order to return, but the camera never reveals them setting foot on Palestinian soil. Palestine as a space is visible, however, at many points in the film. Indeed, the Fedayeen operate very close to the border, and occasionally throughout the film, Palestine is visible on the other side of the Jordan river valley. Jacir has noted that the title of the film, *When I Saw You*, is at least in part a reference to seeing the landscape of Palestine from the other side of the border.[30] Early in the film, while Tarek subsists at the refugee camp, he glimpses a vista of the hills of Palestine in the distance, shrouded in clouds (Fig. 3.4). He cannot look away; it lures him, even as a vague and undetailed landscape. Palestine is thus physically close but remains abstract, without specificity or detail. The absence of detail allows Tarek and the Fedayeen to imagine Palestine in ways abstracted from the physical reality. It allows the formation of an idealized Palestinian political community in the form of the Fedayeen (who, it bears mentioning, are not exclusively Palestinian), and an imagined *watan* that is formed around a progressive political ideology and a conception of Palestine as a site of natural and cultural beauty through landscapes and music. Yet these abstracted landscapes, at once

FORCED MIGRATION AND FANTASIES OF RETURN IN PALESTINIAN CINEMA

Figure 3.4 *When I Saw You* (Philistine Films, 2012).

distant and close, also reveal a certain degree of emptiness. The resistance, the songs, the forest can provide physical, political, and cultural nourishment for the Palestinian *watan* but cannot replace or substitute for that which has been lost. Thus the impulse to return, which eventually drives Tarek and his mother, remains as Palestine tempts and beckons just across the border.

Consuming the Nation: *Gate of the Sun*

If the camp in *When I Saw You* functions as a site that suppresses political action and dedication to the *watan*, the camp in *Gate of the Sun* develops into a space that produces particular forms of political action and resistance. As in *When I Saw You*, the characters of *Gate of the Sun* reside in a refugee camp—Shatila refugee camp in Beirut, Lebanon. Refugee camps in the film, and Shatila in particular, signify loss, displacement, and terror: not only that which occurred in the *Nakba* but also the repeated horrors that have since befallen Palestinians. Shatila, as the site of the massacre of Palestinians by members of the Lebanese Phalange militia in 1982, is one of the most potent reminders that the *Nakba* was not simply an event that occurred in 1948 but rather what Elias Khoury describes as "a continuous tragedy, a catastrophe without borders in space or limits in time."[31] A significant portion of the second half of the film ("the Return") centers on the visit of a European delegation to the camp which, informed by the writings of Jean Genet[32] and others on the massacres, comes to speak to survivors and witness the camp's development after the massacre. This delegation visit emphasizes the extent

57

to which Shatila post massacre is not simply a camp but a site of transnational political spectacle.

The camp as a space and setting physically reflects the ongoing *Nakba*. Yet Shatila and other camps are sometimes imbued with redemptive qualities, as in Khoury's essay, in which he writes: "in the alleys of the miserable refugee camps they renamed the neighborhoods after their destroyed villages. Their silence was their secret way to make from their loss a way of life."[33] The camps are thus at once sites of this ongoing catastrophe and of continued Palestinian devotion to the *watan*, a duality that *Gate of the Sun* further explores. In contrast to the wide shots and barrenness of the camp in *When I Saw You*, the representation of Shatila in *Gate of the Sun* emphasizes the well-established, if cramped, nature of the camp; over decades, new construction has resulted in a maze of alleyways and haphazardly constructed concrete dwellings. The camera moves through the camp's passages, creating a sense of walking through them and emphasizing the winding close quarters in which the refugees live (Fig. 3.5). The camp's inhabited spaces are often stacked on top of one another. The nooks and passageways also occasionally provide cover for dangerous or lawless activities; thugs hide behind a corner and ransack Khalil's apartment after he departs one day, and in one scene the narrow alleys of a camp offer an easy spot to ambush and kill Khalil's lover, Shams. In many ways the camp serves as a trap and a ghetto, from which there is little hope of escape. To an extent, this recalls Hamid Naficy's argument that the invocation of claustrophobia responds to the experience of exile and the erasure that it threatens.[34] However, here the camp's cramped nature does not simply reflect the alienation

Figure 3.5   Bab al-Shams (*Gate of the Sun*, Ognon Pictures, 2004).

of the refugees and the fear of existential erasure. Shatila thrives as a highly charged Palestinian political space, intervening in the Arab–Israeli conflict and in internecine Palestinian politics, as well as Lebanese and regional affairs. The refugee camps were frequent targets in the Lebanese civil war and their presence has long been controversial. They have also, as Khoury hints in the essay quoted above, long been centers of Palestinian resistance. *Gate of the Sun* draws an important connection between the camp as a physical space and as a political entity; the claustrophobic closeness of the camp's structure serves as a paradigm for the proximity of inescapable politics.

At the time of Khalil's vigil for Younis in the hospital, the PLO and Israel were in the process of signing the Oslo Accords, and the camp witnesses a number of demonstrations against these agreements, which many camp residents see as an abandonment of the refugees and the right of return. At one point, Khalil notes that the PLO used to fund the hospital where he works, but now that money has dried up, as it has been redirected towards funding the security and bureaucratic apparatuses of the Palestinians' new quasi-state in the West Bank and Gaza. The film uses the camp's spatial configuration to emphasize the interconnectedness of politics and daily life for the refugees, as can be seen in one protest scene in the second part of the film. In this scene, set in Shatila in 1994, residents demonstrate against the Oslo Accords and demand continued resistance against Israel with the goal of returning to Palestine. The scene begins with a shot of an orange stand, the sound of chants and slogans barely audible in the distance. This is followed by a series of close-up shots in which protesters talk about their views on the Oslo Accords and the Palestinian resistance and leadership. Then the camera switches to a traveling aerial shot that begins at the elevated level of Younis on the balcony. As the camera moves gradually downward, flapping banners with pro-resistance slogans fill the screen and partially obscure the marchers. Then the camera reaches the level of the protestors and depicts them marching forward, toward the camera (Fig. 3.6). This shot is framed by an electricity pole and the edges of the alleyway, before the camera pans back up, past more banners and flags, then shows Khalil watching from an upper floor balcony connected to Younis's hospital room (Fig. 3.7).

The spatial and temporal framing of this scene emphasizes the intimate and perhaps claustrophobic intermingling of political action with everyday life in the camp. The scene begins with the orange stand and ends with Younis's hospital room, two ostensibly non-political spaces that are nevertheless affected by the political action taking place. The orange stand is empty, and the protest distracts Khalil from Younis until he is implored to close the window. Likewise, the camera framing, which emphasizes close shots and a crowd screen, highlights the limited space in which the protest is taking place. It rarely shows more than a small portion of the protest and protest space, which takes place not in a big square but rather in the winding alleys of the camp. Finally, the juxtaposition

Figure 3.6 Bab al-Shams (*Gate of the Sun*, Ognon Pictures, 2004).

Figure 3.7 Bab al-Shams (*Gate of the Sun*, Ognon Pictures, 2004).

of the protest and the hospital space, where a past hero of the resistance lies comatose as demonstrators call for more resistance, reveals both the unresolved nature of the *Nakba* and the role of the camps in transmitting political consciousness from generation to generation. Although such political awakening takes distinct forms as various issues are confronted, the space of the camp and the experience of inhabiting it render political activity inescapable. The camp is a space of migration that also functions as a site of a continual process: the forming, re-forming, and transforming of the Palestinian *watan*.

The camp's role as site of political consciousness is complemented by scenes set in Palestine itself, which fall under two main contexts: flashback scenes of life in the Galilee before the *Nakba*, which shed light on Younis's formative years and his relationship with his wife, Nahila, and depictions of the relationship between Younis and Nahila after 1948, when Younis would sneak across the border to visit her. Both are mediated by Khalil's recollection of Younis's stories, which, along with the contrast with the environment of the camp, give Palestine a dream-like, otherworldly quality. Like Jacir, Nasrallah depicts Palestine as a lush, fertile space where an organic relationship can be found between its inhabitants and the land itself; the very first scene of both halves of the film, each of which features Younis and Khalil consuming the Palestinian oranges, establishes this connection. But the *watan*, as represented by the orange, is not static and inorganic, but rather must grow and nourish or it will rot. Elsewhere in the film, Younis tells Nahila of his conversations with young freedom fighters, and he recounts a time when the youth asked him about the war of 1948, but instead of giving facts or stories, he answered them by drawing "the moon on the ground, and I said, 'The moon is full once a month. All of the other days it changes. It grows, it shrinks. Change, that is the key!'" In *Gate of the Sun*, underlying the representation of Palestine is the idea of national transformation, a *watan* that must reconstitute and redefine itself in the face of nearly constant tragedy and loss.

A significant part of the film's representation of Palestine focuses on the pre-*Nakba* period; it depicts an agriculturally focused society and its homes, customs, and traditions such as weddings[35] through the story of Younis, his family, and his marriage to Nahila. These scenes have a tendency towards the idyllic, but this does not last long, as ominous changes start to become apparent. In one scene, construction is significantly changing the village, and pupils are learning Hebrew. Already under pressure, the film's depiction of the devastating attacks on Palestinian villages, executions, and expulsions that occur in 1948 reveal the irrevocable transformation that this tragedy brings to the land and to its people. One scene, an olive harvest, begins with a bucolic image of villagers gathering olives. They sing folk songs and shake the olives from the tree as others collect the crop in large straw baskets. The falling olives make a soft rattling sound, and we hear the laughter of children running through the shot. Then the happy yells of the children turn into more urgent screams, as a group of Zionist settlers approaches. The camera pans back and forth more quickly, reflecting the villagers' disorientation, and then cuts to a group of Jewish youth marching into the village, singing their own songs and carrying Israeli flags. While there are other, more graphic and deadly, depictions of the losses of the *Nakba* in the film, this short scene stages a loss of innocence. As the children's laughter turns to cries, we see that the arrival of Jewish settlers in this scene signifies a moment after which life can never really be the same as it was before. While *When I Saw You*, by not depicting such moments, allows Palestine as it exists in Tarek's memory to remain as something to which he desires to return, *Gate of the Sun* represents these moments in great and painful detail, thereby foreclosing on the possibility of preserving Palestine as it existed pre-1948. To be clear, it still seeks to reclaim Palestine in some fashion, but the film also acknowledges that the new Palestine will be transformed in very fundamental ways. The film portrays both pre-1948 life and the horrors of the *Nakba* not as a means of preserving or returning to this now lost way of life but to mourn its loss and trace its transformation.

After 1948, depictions of Palestine in the film focus on the notion of resistance as a personal rather than military act. Younis is a member of the Fedayeen but the representation of his struggle largely centers not on his military activities but on his personal journeys into Palestine to visit Nahila, which leads to the birth of Younis's children. In one scene, the authorities arrest Nahila and force her to sit in a dark room, where they demand to know if she is seeing Younis, and if he is the man who impregnated her. She denies any contact with Younis, and claims that the father of her child is unknown. She opens herself up to accusations of acts of prostitution when she tells the interrogator, "Sajjil, Ana sharmuta" ("Write it down, I am a whore"), which echoes Palestinian poet Mahmoud Darwish's famous line of defiance to the Israeli authorities, "Sajjil, Ana 'arabi" ("Write it down, I'm an Arab"). Nahila then recounts this story to the villagers, who sit in a circle as she tells them, "You know who [my children's] father is. Their father is a hero," a cry greeted with ululations and cheers. While personal sacrifice as resistance might often be framed in terms of martyrdom or death on the battlefield, here it is an act of Nahila persevering in and preserving her marriage to Younis, despite the authorities' attempts to slander and attack.

Yet this form of marriage as resistance too begins to falter, as Younis and Nahila age, Younis becomes busy with a growing leadership role in the resistance, and Israel's increasing control over its borders makes crossing more difficult. Eventually, years pass between Younis's visits to the cave at Bab al-Shams, a gap that the film depicts in its second part, in which Younis does not return to the Galilee (100 minutes into this half of the film). In this scene, the last encounter between the couple on screen, Nahila tells Younis, "You're exhausted and so am I." She tells him to let her speak, to listen to her, and that she and their children have spent their lives simply waiting for his knock. "We've become strangers," she says. This scene, set in and around the cave where the couple meet in secret, stages the fading of this particular mode of resistance by showing the contrast between their earlier meetings and this final encounter. Younis and Nahila sit in a clearing at night, surrounded by trees and the ambient noise of a forest, facing each other. The camera alternates between a shot facing Nahila, with Younis's back to the camera, and a reverse shot of Younis's face, with Nahila's back to the camera. At several moments, in the switch between the shot and reverse shot, the scene jumps between this last encounter between the couple, and a much earlier encounter, when they were both brimming with hope and defiance (Fig. 3.8). This temporal shift juxtaposes young and old versions of Nahila.

Figure 3.8 Bab al-Shams (*Gate of the Sun*, Ognon Pictures, 2004).

While young Nahila's resistance to Israeli harassment and her desire to be a hero excite her, the older Nahila has lost her connection with Younis and finds herself and her children isolated and alone, in a state that took their land and forced them to steal from it. This juxtaposition emphasizes the transition of this generation away from resistance and towards a growing interest in memory as it ages. Yet, Younis's answer to Nahila's monologue is to declare his faith in the new generation of youth that he has mentored, the ones like Khalil who are following in his footsteps. Thus, even as the film mourns the loss of a particular mode of resistance as Nahila, and then Younis, pass away, it also reminds us that this generational transition is not the end of resistance but rather the end of a particular phase, and the beginning of a new one, to be carried by the youth of the camps and perhaps by Younis and Nahila's children, who grew up in Israel. As the *Nakba* generation dies out, the notion of the Palestinian *watan* again shifts, to include not only refugees never born in Palestine, but also those who remained behind and who have never been able to call their home Palestine. If the *watan* cannot change and transform with the passage of time, it will die out, and acknowledging the role of displacement and migration in the shaping of the Palestinian *watan* makes space for this transformation.

Conclusion

In this chapter I have shown a number of ways in which the depiction of migration is intimately connected to conceptions of *watan* and their development in the decades since the *Nakba*. While the location of the *watan* in *When I Saw You*—the barren refugee camp, the distant but tempting landscapes of Palestine—produces an emphasis on political consciousness that reclaims the *watan* and escapes the emptiness of refugee life, *Gate of the Sun* positions the experience of migration as a formative moment in a post-1948

Palestinian conception of *watan*. In *Gate of the Sun*, migration is simply not a detour from the *watan* or a separation from it—though these elements do exist—but it is a constitutive element of the *watan* and has irrevocably transformed it. This produces a more extensive depiction of the experience of migration than is found in many other films about Palestine. The temporal difference between the settings of the two films is an important consideration in analyzing diverging depictions of migration and the *watan*. Since *When I Saw You* occurs immediately after 1967, perhaps we can read it as an act of mourning for a brief, lost moment in which leftist liberation movements sought to reclaim the Palestine that was lost step by step, first in 1948 and then again in 1967. *Gate of the Sun*, directed by Nasrallah, who was born after 1948 and came of age during the decline of these movements in the 1960s and 1970s, produces a decidedly more filtered and distant perspective, as it is set in the 1990s at a considerable temporal distance from the *Nakba* it depicts. The recollections seem to become more distant and hazy, as the hope for a fast return has long faded, revealing both the necessity and the difficulty of commemorating the experience of migration not as a deviation but as a permanent (until now, at least) fixture of Palestinian life.

As the world faces a wave of mass migration that is the biggest since the period following World War II, which was roughly contemporaneous with the *Nakba* of 1948, the tropes and modes of representing migration in Palestine on camera show how the screen reflects changing notions of homeland and political action, not just in Palestine but also elsewhere. Particularly in the case of Syria, in which the waves of migration are so extraordinarily large that they will likely have a substantive impact on how Syrian national identity is understood and constructed (or deconstructed), the Syrian *watan*, as it existed before, probably cannot be recovered. By imagining migration as a constitutive and formative element of the Palestinian *watan* in the post-*Nakba* era, *Gate of the Sun* in particular offers a glimpse of how filmic depictions can refigure conceptions of nationhood in an era of unprecedented mass displacement.

NOTES

1. Rashid Khalidi, *Palestinian Identity: The Construction of Modern National Consciousness* (New York: Columbia University Press, 2010), 21.
2. Hamid Dabashi, "Introduction," in *Dreams of a Nation: On Palestinian Cinema*, ed. Hamid Dabashi (New York and London: Verso, 2006), 9.
3. Nurith Gertz and George Khleifi, *Palestinian Cinema: Landscape, Trauma, and Memory* (Bloomington: Indiana University Press, 2008), 11.
4. Gertz and Khleifi, *Palestinian Cinema*, 22.
5. Gertz and Khleifi, *Palestinian Cinema*, 26–7; see also Livia Alexander, "Is there a Palestinian Cinema? The National and Transnational in Palestinian Film Production,"

in *Palestine, Israel, and the Politics of Popular Culture*, ed. Rebecca L. Stein and Ted Swedenberg (Durham, NC: Duke University Press, 2005), 154.
6. Dabashi, "Introduction," 10.
7. In the events of "Black September" of 1970, Jordanian government forces went to war with the PLO and other Palestinian groups operating in the country, forcing them to move their headquarters to Beirut.
8. Emily Jacir, "Palestinian Revolution Cinema Comes to NYC," *The Electronic Intifada*, February 16, 2007, available at <https://electronicintifada.net/content/palestinian-revolution-cinema-comes-nyc/6759> (last accessed June 15, 2017).
9. Annemarie Jacir, "Coming Home: Palestinian Cinema," *The Electronic Intifada*, February 27, 2007, available at <https://electronicintifada.net/content/coming-home-palestinian-cinema/6780> (last accessed June 15, 2017).
10. Emily Jacir, "Palestinian Revolution Cinema Comes to NYC."
11. According to Linda Mokdad, Palestinian cinema, in the sense of a national cinema that produces films either for domestic consumption or for international circulation at film festivals, did not exist really before the 1980s. Moreover, it is not even clear that significant domestic consumption occurs today, as many films from and about Palestine receive little local release or attention. Linda Mokdad, "The Reluctance to Narrate: Elia Suleiman's *Chronicle of a Disappearance* and *Divine Intervention*," in *Storytelling in World Cinemas,* vol. 1, ed. Lina Khatib (New York: Columbia University Press, 2012), 193.
12. Gertz and Khleifi, *Palestinian Cinema*, 34.
13. This film was *Omar*, directed by Hany Abu-Assad, which was funded with 95 percent Palestinian money. Nana Asfour, "Omar: The Palestinian Oscar Nominee Made Amid Panic and Paranoia," *The Guardian*, February 22, 2014, available at <https://www.theguardian.com/film/2014/feb/22/omar-film-palestine-oscar-hany-abu-assad> (last accessed June 15, 2017).
14. Alexander, "Is There a Palestinian Cinema?," 154–5.
15. Hamid Naficy, "Palestinian Exilic Cinema and Film Letters," in *Dreams of a Nation: On Palestinian Cinema*, ed. Hamid Dabashi (London: Verso, 2006), 91.
16. Dabashi, "Introduction," 7.
17. Dabashi, "Introduction," 11.
18. Saverio Giovacchini and Robert Sklar, "Introduction: The Geography and History of Global Neorealism," in *Global Neorealism: The Transnational History of a Film Style*, ed. Saverio Giovacchini and Robert Sklar (Oxford, MI: University Press of Mississippi, 2011), 3–5.
19. Benjamin Geer, for instance, has compared Nasrallah's film *After the Battle* (2012) with the works of Roberto Rossellini. Benjamin Geer, "Yousry Nasrallah: The Pursuit of Autonomy in the Arab and European Film Markets," in *Ten Arab Filmmakers: Political Dissent and Social Critique*, ed. Josef Gugler (Bloomington: Indiana University Press, 2015), 159.
20. Hamid Naficy, *An Accented Cinema: Exilic and Diasporic Filmmaking* (Princeton: Princeton University Press, 2001).
21. Muhammad ibn Mukarram ibn Manzur, *Lisan al-Arab*, vols 17–18 (Cairo: al-Matba'a al-Kubra al-Amiriya, 1882), 342.

22. Ihab Saloul, "'Performative Narrativity': Palestinian Identity and the Performance of Catastrophe," *Cultural Analysis* 7 (2008), 20.
23. Sara Ahmed, *Strange Encounters: Embodied Others in Post-Coloniality* (London: Routledge, 2000), 89.
24. Yaseen Noorani, "Estrangement and Selfhood in the Classical Concept of Waṭan," *Journal of Arabic Literature* 47, nos 1–2 (2016): 19.
25. Noorani, "Estrangement and Selfhood," 18.
26. Saloul, "'Performative Narrativity,'" 19.
27. Saloul, "'Performative Narrativity,'" 19.
28. Saloul, "'Performative Narrativity,'" 19.
29. As Barbara Parmenter, Carol Bardenstein, and others have shown, Palestine's natural beauty is one of the most enduring tropes of writings of exile and return. See Barbara McKean Parmenter, *Giving Voice to Stones: Place and Identity in Palestinian Literature* (Austin: University of Texas Press, 2010), and Carol B. Bardenstein, "Trees, Forests, and the Shaping of Palestinian and Israeli Collective Memory," in *Acts of Memory: Cultural Recall in the Present*, ed. Mleke Bal, Jonathan V. Crewe, and Leo Spiter (Hanover, NH: Dartmouth College: University Press of New England, 1999).
30. Annemarie Jacir, quoted in E. Nina Rothe, "When I Saw You: Could This Palestinian Film Win the Next Foreign Language Oscar?" *The Huffington Post*, October 25, 2012, <http://www.huffingtonpost.com/e-nina-rothe/when-i-saw-you-movie_b_2014916.html> (last accessed June 15, 2017).
31. Elias Khoury, "Rethinking the *Nakba*," *Critical Inquiry* 38, no. 2 (2012): 262.
32. Genet's *Four Hours in Shatila* was one of the first accounts to be published on the massacre and its aftermath
33. Khoury, "Rethinking the *Nakba*," 262.
34. Hamid Naficy, "Making Films with an Accent: Iranian Émigré Cinema," *Framework: The Journal of Cinema and Media* 43, no. 2 (2002): 27.
35. Weddings prove to be a particularly important concern in films on Palestine, such as *Wedding in Galilee* (dir. Michel Khleifi, 1987), *The Syrian Bride* (dir. Eran Riklis, 2004), *The Kite* (dir. Randa Chahal Sabbagh, 2003), and *Rana's Wedding* (dir. Hany Abu-Assad, 2002).

Works Cited

Ahmed, Sara. *Strange Encounters: Embodied Others in Post-Coloniality*. London: Routledge, 2000.

Alexander, Livia. "Is There a Palestinian Cinema?: The National and Transnational in Palestinian Film Production." In *Palestine, Israel, and the Politics of Popular Culture*, ed. Rebecca L. Stein and Ted Swedenburg, 150–72. Durham, NC: Duke University Press, 2005.

Asfour, Nana. "Omar: The Palestinian Oscar Nominee Made Amid Panic and Paranoia." *The Guardian*, February 22, 2014, <https://www.theguardian.com/film/2014/feb/22/omar-film-palestine-oscar-hany-abu-assad> (last accessed June 15, 2017).

Bardenstein, Carol B. "Trees, Forests, and the Shaping of Palestinian and Israeli Collective Memory." In *Acts of Memory: Cultural Recall in the Present*, ed. Mieke

Bal, Jonathan Crewe, and Leo Spitzer, 148–68. Hanover, NH: Dartmouth College: University Press of New England, 1999.
Dabashi, Hamid. "Introduction." In *Dreams of a Nation: On Palestinian Cinema*, ed. Hamid Dabashi, 7–22. New York and London: Verso, 2006.
Geer, Benjamin. "Yousry Nasrallah: The Pursuit of Autonomy in the Arab and European Film Markets." In *Ten Arab Filmmakers: Political Dissent and Social Critique*, ed. Josef Gugler, 143–64. Bloomington: Indiana University Press, 2015.
Gertz, Nurith and George Khleifi. *Palestinian Cinema: Landscape, Trauma, and Memory*. Bloomington: Indiana University Press, 2008.
Giovacchini, Saverio and Robert Sklar. "Introduction: The Geography and History of Global Neorealism." In *Global Neorealism: The Transnational History of a Film Style*, ed. Saverio Giovacchini and Robert Sklar, 3–18. Oxford, MI: University Press of Mississippi, 2011.
Jacir, Annemarie. "Coming Home: Palestinian Cinema." *The Electronic Intifada*, February 27, 2007, <https://electronicintifada.net/content/coming-home-palestinian-cinema/6780> (last accessed June 15, 2017).
Jacir, Emily. "Palestinian Revolution Cinema Comes to NYC." *The Electronic Intifada*, February 16, 2007, <https://electronicintifada.net/content/palestinian-revolution-cinema-comes-nyc/6759> (last accessed June 15, 2017).
Khalidi, Rashid. *Palestinian Identity: The Construction of Modern National Consciousness*. New York: Columbia University Press, 2010.
Khoury, Elias. "Rethinking the *Nakba*." *Critical Inquiry* 38, no. 2 (Winter 2012): 250–66.
Manzur, Muhammad ibn Mukarram ibn. *Lisan al-Arab*, vols 17–18. Cairo: al-Matba'a al-Kubra al-Amiriya, 1882.
Mokdad, Linda. "The Reluctance to Narrate: Elia Suleiman's *Chronicle of a Disappearance* and *Divine Intervention*." In *Storytelling in World Cinemas*, vol. 1, ed. Lina Khatib, 192–204. New York: Columbia University Press, 2012.
Naficy, Hamid. *An Accented Cinema: Exilic and Diasporic Filmmaking*. Princeton: Princeton University Press, 2001.
Naficy, Hamid. "Making Films with an Accent: Iranian Émigré Cinema." *Framework: The Journal of Cinema and Media* 43, no. 2 (2002): 15–41.
Naficy, Hamid. "Palestinian Exilic Cinema and Film Letters." In *Dreams of a Nation: On Palestinian Cinema*, ed. Hamid Dabashi, 90–104. London: Verso, 2006.
Noorani, Yaseen. "Estrangement and Selfhood in the Classical Concept of Waṭan." *Journal of Arabic Literature* 47, nos 1–2 (2016): 16–42.
Parmenter, Barbara McKean. *Giving Voice to Stones: Place and Identity in Palestinian Literature*. Austin: University of Texas Press, 2004.
Rothe, E. Nina. "When I Saw You: Could This Palestinian Film Win the Next Foreign Language Oscar?" *The Huffington Post*, October 25, 2012, <http://www.huffingtonpost.com/e-nina-rothe/when-i-saw-you-movie_b_2014916.html> (last accessed June 15, 2017).
Saloul, Ihab. "'Performative Narrativity': Palestinian Identity and the Performance of Catastrophe." *Cultural Analysis* 7 (2008): 5–39.

4. DISPLACEMENT AND THE VICISSITUDES OF PAN-ARABISM: BETWEEN *THE DUPES* (TEWFIK SALEH, 1972) AND *IN THE LAST DAYS OF THE CITY* (TAMER EL SAID, 2016)

Mohannad Ghawanmeh

With much of the consideration of migration today pertaining to its impact on Europe, this chapter concerns itself instead with movement within an Arabic-speaking region whose nation-states are challenged politically, militarily and economically, thus undermining perceptions of their ability to serve their populations, let alone migrants to their territories. I keep the term *pan-Arabism* to describe a connectivity, concern, and mutual empowerment across the lands populated by Arabic speakers. Moreover, I argue that a rendition of pan-Arabism has emerged in order to meet the possibilities of the twentieth century. This contemporary pan-Arabism engages a condition of "virtual omnipresence," and replaces the now discredited and moribund Arab nationalism, which is grounded in governmentality. To illustrate the transition from Arab nationalism to regional virtual omnipresence, I examine and compare the Arabic-language films *The Dupes* (1972) and *In the Last Days of the City* (2016), while grounding my analysis in relevant historical developments.

Middle East Migration — Realities and Perceptions

Death by drowning is appalling news. Death of Middle Easterners and Africans by drowning, which prevents them from becoming illegal immigrants or refugees in Europe, is also melodramatic news. Experiences of the subjugated, the impoverished, and the war-stricken, striving and risking all to attain a semblance of a dignified life in the lands of the more fortunate, implicates the more fortunate, whether or not they would consider themselves or their governments responsible. Those in the West who have followed the regular yet sensational accounts of the displacement and migration of Middle Easterners would be justified in assuming that the majority of refugees were on their way or already in Europe. However, Europe hosts the fewest number of displaced people among the world's regions, with less than one-sixth of the number in the Middle East and North Africa.[1] Indeed, although an unprecedented 1.3 million people sought refuge in Europe in 2015, the number of refugees to Europe since 1985 totaled ten times that figure, 13 million,[2] whereas those who have traveled to Middle Eastern countries between 2005 and 2015 totaled 18 million.[3] The refugee/migration crisis is acute, but it is more acute in the Middle East than it is in Europe, in terms of the number of refugees and the resources available to relatively poorer Middle Eastern countries. Despite the recent interest in the migration crisis, it is not a new phenomenon. Thus this study's analysis necessitates an historical account.

Middle Eastern migrants have most commonly traveled to other regions of the Middle East, including within their home countries. Moreover, the number of displaced migrants has more than quadrupled in the span of a decade, not counting unregistered migrants.[4] Studies are sure to abound that examine the impact of immigrant communities upon their countries of residence, and specifically how the resettlement, temporary or permanent, of non-nationals shifts cultural production and discourse in their countries of origin, passage, and destination.

Taking into account the factors that contribute to an unprecedented regional instability, of which migration, especially by refugees, is a central and tragic facet, it is useful to consider governmentality, particularly the governmentalities of the nation-states in the region. To wit, systems of nation-statehood are themselves partly to blame for deprivation and insecurity, inviting an assessment of modes of governmentality other than the nation-state. The most commonly discussed alternative to the nation-state of the Middle East, including by those parties fretting over immigration to Europe, is, of course, the *khilafah* (caliphate). However, such an Islamic conception is not applicable to the integral and implicit discourses of this chapter's decidedly secular filmic texts—*The Dupes* and *In the Last Days of the City*. Rather, in carrying out a comparative analysis of the text, production, and perception of these two films, made over four decades apart, the present chapter charts a discursive evolution in the conception of pan-Arabism. Thus, it begins its exploration with the introduction of modern pan-Arabism at the end of the nineteenth century, moving past the apogee of Arab unity, 1958,[5] and leading up to the year that *The Dupes*, the first of the two films discussed, was made. *The Dupes*, as will be demonstrated, is at once a "pan-Arab production par excellence,"[6] and a repudiation of the pan-Arabism inherent in the foreign policy of Egyptian President Gamal Abdel Nasser. It is also a tale of the fatal immigration of Palestinian refugees. *The Dupes* thus marks the end of the first phase of pan-Arabism. The second phase follows immediately thereafter, beginning in 1974 and concluding in 2016, the year that the other film discussed here, *In the Last Days of the City*, was released. This recent film will serve as a case study for what I argue is a new mode of pan-Arabism, a non-governmental interconnectedness as proposed. Such affinity is nourished by Arabic-language satellite and internet TV and video, to which the Arab masses are commonly and regularly exposed, and is grounded in a shared cultural history, language, and geographic proximity. Migration is a central theme of *City*, in both physical and virtual forms. The city in question is Cairo, a fine site to conclude an examination of the metamorphosis in pan-Arabism conceptually, because of its representing the cultural center of the Arab world in modernity. After all, as Fredric Jameson would have it, film serves as an exemplary cultural form for the examination of urban life, a site of the transmutation from modernity in nationalism to postmodernity in transnationalism.[7] Within the conceptual parameters of this chapter, the latter state would be more accurately characterized as suprastatehood in a transregionalism—a pan-Arab regionalism.

Pan-Arabism—Zenith to Defeat

Considering that I instrumentalize the term pan-Arabism, it is important to clarify its meaning and value to a study such as the present one that looks at migration and the cinema. *Pan* denotes not only a totality but also a totality in unity, as inherent to Arabism. Arabism is a condition of being Arab, itself a description of those whose native language is Arabic. As Albert Hourani has evaluated, the notion that those who speak Arabic should constitute a nation is one that emerged toward the end of the nineteenth century,[8] around the time of cinema's appearance, as is worth noting for the purpose of emphasizing that nationhood, like the cinema, was experienced as part of Middle Eastern societies' encounter with modernity.

Nationhood would take on the form of statehood in the aftermath of World War I, following the 1916 Sykes–Picot Agreement. Political organizing that pursued Arab empowerment in defiance of continued occupation and colonization became more oppositional and more ambitious after World War I, and particularly in the 1930s.[9] Such empowerment then took on the guise of state policy, specifically that of the Egyptian state following the Anglo-Egyptian Treaty of 1936, which granted Egypt greater control over its foreign affairs.[10] By now, discourses around Arab unity had grown more secular,[11] so that an ideology of unity, undergirded by the commonality of Arabic as the language of the Quran, foundational text of the region's pervasive religion, itself became a religion of the commons, as has been characterized by Syrian philosopher and politician Michel Aflaq.[12] This ideology would be dubbed Arab nationalism. It would then form the political ideology of the first Arab nationalist party, one that professed its commitment to unity from the outset: this was the Arab Ba'th party, founded in Syria in 1947, and whose first leader was Aflaq.[13]

The year 1936 was an important one for the development of pan-Arabism. Beside the assumption of greater sovereignty by the Egyptian government, it saw the Palestine Revolt against the British mandate and Jewish immigration, upon which neighboring Arab countries exerted an influence. This is acknowledged by the Peel Commission report,[14] known principally for having been the first official government recommendation of partition in Palestine. It is important to make the point here that Jewish immigration, including the movement of those seeking refuge from the Nazi regime, represents the first of the four waves of migration that this chapter will mark.[15] Support for the Palestinian cause and Arab unity formed the platform for the Bludan Conference in Syria the following year,[16] and the bond between the Arabic-speaking people itself was then enshrined in the founding of the Arab League in 1945. The principal point of commonality between the member states of the League, toothless as it has largely been, was the stance on Palestine. Sociologist Saad Eddin Ibrahim qualifies: "The first and permanent and fiercest dossier for the infant Arab League, nay for the Arab umma [nation of people] as a whole, was Palestine."[17] This has certainly been the case since the founding of the Israeli state, and the forced migration of at least 750,000 Palestinians occurred a mere three years after the Arab League's foundation.[18]

Among these Palestinian refugees was one Ghassan Kanafani, whose family, having left the coastal city of Acre, settled in Damascus, Syria. Syria would form a constitutional and governmental union in 1958 with Egypt under Nasser: the United Arab Republic, soon renamed the United Arab States, with Yemen joining too.[19] Despite fervent enthusiasm for Arab nationalism in Syria, especially on the part of the Ba'th Party and its allegiance, Syria in fact suffered under the Union from the predominance of Egyptian systems. Syrian personalities in administrative government posts, as well as Syrian society at large, did not thrive economically, partly because of the prevalence of Egyptian goods. Further, Nasser's authoritarian tactics were deployed by United Arab State government officials in Syria, so that political parties were outlawed, the press assaulted, and civil rights curtailed. The Union was dissolved in 1961.[20] This blow to Arab nationalists' aspirations within and without was not softened by the ascendancy of the ostensibly Arab nationalist Ba'th to single-party rule in Syria, nor by an Iraqi Ba'th Party coming into power next door, nor by Nasser's intensification of Egypt's foreign engagements and causes, as part of a strategy of "investment" in foreign policy. Such a policy of foreign investment in "liberation" causes targeted the Middle East region particularly and would end disastrously with the Arab–Israeli War of 1967.[21] In 1962, a year after the dissolution of the United Arab States (Republic), Ghassan Kanafani published his novella, *Men in the Sun* (*Rijal fi ash-Shams*), which would become his most highly regarded work and, a decade later, would serve as the source text for *The Dupes*, the first of the two films to which this chapter attends.[22] Having witnessed the fissure of Arab state unity, Kanafani, in hardly subtle terms, called for a Palestinian self-reliance that jettisoned the Arab unity project.

The year 1962 also saw the delayed institution of the distribution activities of the Organization for the Consolidation of the Cinema Under the Ministry of Culture and National Orientation. The Organization (in Arabic, al-Mu'assasa), as the entity was commonly referred to, had been established in 1957 and had taken over four of the existing Egyptian studios. The Organization sputtered while Egypt was part of the United Arab States (Republic), and this had an impact on film directors, whose work was hampered by the Organization's ineffectuality, which continued even after distribution was sorted out.[23] As if to dispel grumbles about its dysfunctionality, the Organization released the expensive ultrascope, color, historical drama *Saladin the Victorious* (*al-Nasir Salahuddin*, Youssef Chahine, 1962), which cast the eponymous Kurdish historical figure, once ruler of Egypt, defeater of the Crusaders, and liberator of the Holy Land, as an antecedent to Nasser.[24] On the whole, the nationalized Egyptian cinema industry backed inconsequential and reactionary productions, and obstructed originality by tightening censorship and lengthening red tape,[25] which is why ambitious Egyptian directors such as Chahine lost patience and left Egypt to work elsewhere.[26]

The most prestigious Egyptian directors Chahine and Henri Barakat moved to Beirut, leaving Cairo, capital of the Arab world and center of the Arab film industry. They departed from a city that had been neglected in the 1960s, as had cinema in Egypt, and as was Egypt itself under Nasser's "foreign investment" policy, which was not returning the promised dividends.[27] Tewfik Saleh, director of *The Dupes*, fought relentlessly to have the censor approve content in each of his films, notable as they were for the overtness of their progressive agenda.[28] Committed to using cinema to effect positive social change, by the late 1960s Saleh had already demonstrated a firm commitment to "cinema (as) a political instrument with which to understand and change the world."[29] Unlike some of his celebrated contemporaries, Saleh was no mere realist, diagnosing social ills and taking measures to preserve their authentic depiction. Rather, his films offer respite from the social problem they tackle, if not prescriptively then in terms of orientation. Saleh had read *Men in the Sun* and wanted to turn it into a film. He was to do just that, and the result demonstrated his diagnosis-to-empowerment narrative model at its finest. However, he would not manage to film *Men in the Sun* in Egypt, not before the Organization was denationalized in 1971.[30] Fed up with the obstruction and meddling in Cairo, he pitched the project elsewhere, to the Egyptian government's counterpart in the rupture from a decade earlier, the Syrian government.

Syria's own national film entity was founded the year after denationalization of Egypt's, the same year as *The Dupes* was produced—1972. The newly founded National Film Organization, if judged on its output in its first decade, was interested in stories of class struggle—in adherence to the mode of social realism, typical of socialist regimes—and in stories of the Palestinian struggle, in keeping with the Ba'th Party's professed commitment to the liberation of the Palestinian people.[31] A film based on *Men in the Sun* served both interests. Saleh got to make the picture he wanted, considering how bold *The Dupes* is both formally and topically, and by filming a script he had adapted. Thus, an Egyptian filmmaker, with a Palestinian mother, wrote and directed a Syrian film adapted from a Palestinian novella, shot in Syria and in Iraq, and whose events take place in Syria (presumably), as well as in Iraq and Kuwait.

As mentioned, *The Dupes* is daring topically, because of the number of countries and regimes it names, references, and implicates. Further, it may be the first Arabic-language narrative film to depict immigration, let alone use it as a tool to diagnose relevant problems in government practice and policy, as Raymond Baker would have it.[32] Baker, however, would likely be surprised to hear Saleh denying that any effect of credibility in *The Dupes*, or any of his other films for that matter, is a consequence of *realism*. For Saleh does not believe that realism is possible in a form so manipulated as the cinema. He does, however, consider that a semblance of realism elicits audience empathy for the people on the screen. Within this quasi-realism mode, Saleh trusts the audience to be able to interpret metaphors.[33] *The Dupes* proffers an example: a person stands by the shore of Shatt al-Arab, the point at which the Euphrates and Tigris rivers converge, near Basra in Iraq. Those aware of the condition of the Palestinians would read Shatt al-Arab as a metaphor for the water borders of Israel.[34] I would add that this shot by the water—a shot that follows the opening sequence, which forebodingly depicts skulls in a barren expanse of desert—represents the oasis never reached, or the possibility that it was reached but proved to be a mirage, just like the illusion of Arab unity. The two overtly contrasted opening shots signal the parable that the film seems to shape into. *The Dupes* hardly appeals to realism; economic migration is presented as the stuff of myth.

By the end of the film we have learned that the skulls in the flashback sequence belonged to three Palestinian men, refugees who have arrived at Shatt al-Arab and wish to be smuggled into Kuwait to find gainful work. We learn their backstories, in flashback. The backstory of the eldest of the three Palestinian migrant workers, attempting to reach Kuwait clandestinely, takes a startling turn when the plot is interrupted with a photomontage of modern Arab history, accompanied by scathing, embittered narration. This sequence integrates an image of Abdulaziz bin Saud (1875–1953), founder of Saudi Arabia, among other rulers and institutions depicted, whom the film implicates in the Palestinian *Nakba* of 1948.

In the second half of the film, we learn in flashback the backgrounds of the desperate men, who are soon to be duped. Their wretchedness, we are shocked to discern, is such that they seek and secure the services of a smuggler, in the tank of his water truck. Heat generated from the smoldering desert sun is what kills them, but it is the delay at the customs office that seals their fate. Borders in *The Dupes* are the site of miserable death for people who neither deigned to recognize nor designed the borders, persons who would have encountered no borders had they lived half a century earlier. Kanafani did indeed hold the Gulf States responsible for the weakening of Arab unity, but the death of his novella's men in the sun is primarily a consequence of their decision to escape their existential problem to pursue personal economic empowerment. To Kanafani, the top priority for Palestinians, destitute refugees among them, is to retrieve and restore control over Palestine. Thus, immigration is a life choice unavailable to any Palestinian who would claim to care about the Palestinian cause; the collective imperative supersedes personal actualization.

As mentioned, Tewfik Saleh's films diagnose social problems and then suggest how to address them. What is the problem, then, in Saleh's text, if it is to be distinguished at all from Kanafani's? And what does Saleh propose as its solution? Saleh employs immigration itself as a metaphor for foreign policy: specifically that of the Nasser government, a policy that had depleted the domestic coffers by supporting "liberation causes abroad." Thus, whereas Kanafani had produced his text in response to the dissolution of the United Arab States as a manifestation of the first Arab national union, Saleh's work gestures to the Nasser regime, which not only had made egregious errors in economic planning but had then suffered a humiliating defeat, in collaboration with other Arab governments, in its war against Israel. In order to evoke the social fatalism of ignoring the homeland, Saleh distinguishes his text from Kanafani's unremitting fatalism by inserting flashbacks often enough and for long enough to lend the impression that sequences taking place in the plot's present time are flashforwards.

Secondly, besides the insertion of the photomontage of Middle Eastern history just mentioned, the only modification that Saleh makes to the novel, and far more controversially, is to its ending. Whereas Kanafani's novella ignores the three men's experience inside the empty water tank once they climb into it, just before arriving at the Iraqi–Kuwaiti border, *Men in the Sun* turns to relating the smuggler's delay at customs, so that the smuggled men re-enter the story once they have crossed the border. The novella closes with the smuggler's cry, echoing, "Why did they not bang the tank's walls?" Saleh's *The Dupes* has the smuggled men do exactly that. The scene in question cuts from the customs office to a shot of the truck, which then tracks toward the tank, as discordant banging fills the soundtrack. Kanafani's narrative posits that those who abandon their home desert their people and are thus irredeemable, whereas Saleh refuses to disempower characters he considers victimized.

According to Saleh's revolutionary impulses, *The Dupes*, when screened to the masses, could dissuade them from jettisoning their responsibilities toward their own society for the sake of pursuing elusive opportunity abroad. Saleh described his film's effect as one "to provoke color and violence," as opposed to the catharsis more common to social-problem films, for Saleh considered his works "revolutionary art."[35] He once observed, "All my movies are rotated, in a way or another, on the themes of poverty and backwardness, a class whose destiny is in the hands of another, and how to attempt to get out of this impasse."[36] Expending effort, whether individual or national, abroad diverted energies from the social revolution necessary for a people to progress economically and intellectually. The social "impasse" could be surmounted only by dealing with problems at home, not by escaping them.

Divestment from Arab integration was thick in the air following the war of 1967, and became integral to Egyptian President Anwar Sadat's (1918–81) touted policy of *Infitah*, literally meaning *opening up*. However, Sadat's worldview was not aligned with Saleh's, despite their common disavowal of Nasser's economic and foreign policy. In fact, Saleh opted not to return to Egypt, doubled down on the Ba'th, the "standard bearer" of Arab unity, and moved to live under the Iraqi Ba'th regime soon after completing *The Dupes*. Saleh worked for the Iraqi government, to be more precise, and would make his follow-up to *The Dupes* in Iraq: this was his final film, *The Long Days* (*al-Ayyam al-Tawilah*, 1980), a dramatization of the origins of the Iraqi Ba'th, with the character of Saddam Hussein portrayed by Hussein's son-in-law.[37] Migration may have offered Saleh occupational opportunity that he lacked in his homeland, and it is arguable that, had Saleh remained in Egypt, *The Dupes* would never have seen the light of day; the light was dimmed, however, when a theatrical screening was denied in several Arab countries, including Syria and Egypt, where the film was shown exclusively in cinema clubs, cultural centers, and universities. Marginalized Egyptians were thus denied the opportunity to be jolted into revolution; the film's aim had been thwarted and Saleh's career would never recover.[38]

In the second film that this chapter examines, two secondary but impactful characters, Hassan and Tarek, are Iraqis who might have been born while Tewfik Saleh lived in Iraq and who would have been too young to remember the developments that led to Saddam Hussein's rise to the country's presidency. Nevertheless, Hussein's tenure would deliver misery for these characters, eventually evoked in *In the Last Days of the City*. I will next trace the continued devolution in Arab nationalism in this film, analyzing the depiction of emigration from Iraq, as well as from Lebanon, the home of the third non-Egyptian character.

War and Occupation, Displacement, and the Devolution of Arab Nationalism

Sadat's *Infitah* (open door, economic liberalization) policy, enacted in 1974, made the capitalistic turn that was Sadat's project, inviting private and foreign investment in Egypt.[39] Sadat had special plans for Cairo, wishing to modernize the city and thus attract the foreign capital that his *Infitah* plan entailed.[40] Sadat's credo of generating wealth in Egypt replaced the priority of nation building, placing an emphasis on the individual for the sake of advancing the collective. A measurable and noticeable, perhaps predictable, outcome of *Infitah* was a culture of consumption. Yet, as sociologist Mona Abaza proposes, consumption was a facet of an undergirding culture of individualism, one that enclosed migration for personal betterment, including that to Iraq and Lebanon.[41] In addition to migration as a physical movement, an "internal migration into religion"[42] took place, which would lead to an increased public display of religiosity, marking twenty-first-century Cairo as depicted in *City*.

As Sadat's *Infitah* policy, in its second year of implementation, was just beginning to reshape Cairo, Beirut entered a long, grueling season as ground zero of the Lebanese Civil War (1975–90). Between 600,000 and 900,000 people fled the country to escape the warfare,[43] but not Bassem, the third non-Egyptian character in *City*. The 1970s would close with a severe blow to Arab nationalism: in 1978, Egypt signed a peace pact with Israel at Camp David that resulted in its expulsion from the Arab League the following year. With the 1990 invasion of Kuwait, which precipitated the Gulf War (1990–1), Saddam Hussein, the standard bearer of Arab nationalism, assailed Arab unity militarily. Ultimately, the Gulf War provided proof that life remained in Arab nationalism as a creature named after Arab unity. Arab public opinion was split over whether to support Hussein in his conquest, and then over the US military campaign that followed. However, most of those who supported Hussein did so because he had dared defy Israel's staunch ally, the United States, persuaded by his ostensible assault on pro-American enterprise in the Middle East. Five million people were displaced by the Gulf War, and the sanctions regime implemented thereafter brought ruin upon Iraq's economy, leaving Iraqi institutions a shell of themselves. The addled Saddam regime survived for over a decade before it was supplanted by the Coalition Provisional Authority, the governing body of the American occupation that followed the US War in Iraq in 2003. The military insurgency that followed unleashed unprecedented violence upon the country's citizenry.[44]

In the Last Days of the City and a New Mode of Pan-Arabism

Arab nationalism would seem to have been consigned definitively to history with the execution of Saddam Hussein in 2006, but that does not mean that pan-Arabism had been extinguished into the bargain. Arab nationalism, a manifestation of pan-Arabism, was a political ideology that sought unity between nation-states populated by Arabs, while pan-Arabism need not be bound to the state, nor to governance for that matter. *In the Last Days of the City* illustrates a new mode of pan-Arabism, underscoring the ethos that would emerge in the protests that spread across the Arabic-speaking region and would collectively be called the Arab Spring. Even though film production began in 2009, before the transregional protests ignited in Tunisia and then spread to Egypt, it registers as a requiem for Cairo that in turn became a requiem for the Mubarak regime (1981–2011). *City* mulls the moment before the revolution that toppled Mubarak.

City marks itself as a pan-Arab film because of how its melds multiple Arabic dialects, character integration and truncation, and auxiliary footage. Decisions in terms of reference, dialect, and colloquial language suggest that director and screenwriter Tamer El Said (along with co-screenwriter Rasha Salti) had a new mode of pan-Arabism in mind. In the four scenes depicting the protagonist Khalid and his three friends visiting Cairo—Bassem from Beirut, Hassan from Baghdad, and Tarek, an Iraqi, from Berlin—the four refer to their home cities repeatedly, but not to their countries of citizenship, except when discussing matters governmental, such as travel, residency, or immigration. As far as the film is concerned, the reunited friends (all filmmakers, announcing *City*'s reflexivity) consider home to be the city in which they each attempt to produce their work. Beyond the matter of referring to cities as home, not the nation-states in which these cities are situated, *City* may be the only film in which multiple Arabic dialects are spoken within the same scenes. Typically, even an independent production such as *City* avoids alienating particular regionalities of Arab audiences with unfamiliar dialects and "foreign" Arabic words. The film embodies its era in this regard; a quarter-century since the first Arabic language satellite service, there are now tens of free-to-air channels on which an Arabic speaker in any Middle Eastern country may listen to a variety of Arabic dialects, with a few clicks of the remote.

The second way that *City* marks itself as a pan-Arab work is in how it integrates and then dispenses with characters. Tarek, who had immigrated to Berlin from Baghdad, is not heard from once he returns to his new home in Europe, having concluded his visit to Cairo. Laila, the protagonist Khalid's resilient love and a resident of Cairo, leaves Egypt herself, not to be heard from or discussed thereafter in the film. It is telling that *City* never divulges Laila's destination, nor any details of her departure. Tarek is criticized by his countryman Hassan for not having produced any work since moving to Berlin. Having sought refuge from a precarious life in Baghdad, Tarek appears to have lost the drive to produce, despite living in the First World art Eden that is Berlin. Having left Cairo with Hassan and Bassem, he is heard from only toward the end of the film, and then principally as he seemingly delivers sorry news that cannot be heard by the audience. We learn that the news was of the death of Hassan, the film's other Iraqi character, who had elected to stay in Baghdad and who had continued filmmaking. Tarek has not only ceased cultural service to his city of origin, Baghdad, but he delivers the news of the cessation of the service of others to Khalid. In a way, Tarek's service to *City* is his personification of an artist who, unbeknownst to himself, ceases contributing to his society of origin, or to his adoptive one, by opting to leave the people among whom he is born.

On the other hand, *City* does invite Bassem and Hassan back, through film fragments they have shot—two sequences from each—in which they capture their respective cities of Beirut and Baghdad. This auxiliary footage expands the region represented on screen, lending it a pan-Arab sensibility. These sequences interpolate *City*'s action, with unassuming transitions, direct cuts. Bassem and Hassan make appearances in their clips, consequently reappearing in *City*. Hassan's latter sequence actually concludes the film: an unintended final statement, a testament. Having gathered that Khalid heard grave news from Tarek by phone, we now may surmise that concluding *City* with the most elegiac of the "movies within the movie" must mean that Hassan has died. Yet his death, like that of Cairo and like that of his ailing, bedridden mother in hospital, is not depicted. The film refuses to pursue a clear conclusion.[45]

Hassan's two segments form part of a project that he had told his friends about earlier: a film about the work of legendary calligrapher Mahdi al-Jubouri, including his contribution to film posters. In the latter of the two segments, we see an old man writing calligraphic script, which later appears as the title of *In the Last Days of the City*, inscribed by al-Jubouri himself, as is seen in the closing credits. Thus *City*, in terms of location, is a Cairo, Beirut, and Baghdad film—a pan-Arab requiem to cities ravaged by war and stripped of their producers of culture, who are often exiled or killed.[46]

Like Hassan, Bassem "contributes" two segments to *City*, shot in Beirut after leaving Cairo.[47] In an earlier reunion scene that occurs on the roof of a building overlooking Tahrir Square, Bassem seethes that he cannot bring himself to shoot the falsehood that is Beirut, the hag that has had work done, the whore, as he describes it. As the friends sip on beer, Bassem remarks that the "catastrophe" called Cairo before them presented itself honestly, with a take it-or-leave-it attitude. Yet, Bassem films upon returning to Beirut, inspired partly by his recent reunion with his friends. Whereas Hassan's film is an ode to the Tigris, the river that runs through Baghdad, his home city, Bassem captures the Mediterranean coast outlying his own city of Beirut. Otherwise, Bassem narrates his film, mentioning his fear of alleyways and then using the stationary camera to film himself walking toward and through an alley. Beirut's rainy coast and Bassem's desire to conquer his fear motivate him to film again at long last. He intends his films to inspire his friends to produce for and of their cities, especially Khalid, who has been shooting for ages, a film whose end is nowhere in sight. By implication, Bassem's film inspires

Tamer El Said, for whom the Egyptian character Khalid stands in the film, to "include" Bassem's piece in *City*, the two-hour work, culled from 250 hours of footage,[48] that El Said managed to complete six years after its principal photography (2008–10) had concluded.

Concurrence of media, of information streams, underscores a facet of life in early twenty-first-century Arab cities, as several scenes of *City* illustrate. Tarek's international phone call to Khalid occurs as international news resounds in the café in which Khalid stands. This scene points unmistakably to an earlier one with a similar concomitance of sound transmitted by communication technologies—we hear the news and the voices of telephone callers in both cases. Earlier in the film, Khalid walks into a café, only to see on a TV there news of an explosion in Beirut. Looking concerned, he reaches for his mobile and rings Bassem in Beirut to ask after him.[49] In this way, *City* declares the twenty-first century one of virtual omnipresence, due to the immediacy of and connectivity to other cities, although rural Middle Eastern areas may not have had internet or cell-phone services by 2010.[50] Thus, an artist as cultural practitioner may serve her city while remaining connected to its people and their cultural production from a distant location, inspiring them and being inspired by them, a possibility that previously would have required frequent travel to such locations.

Yet, *City* is a work that recognizes the privilege inherent in its own production. It acknowledges how Khalid's socio-economic background, including the fact of his being born to a cultural practitioner (a radio program writer and host), has enabled him to disassemble and reassemble the city intellectually and emotionally, according to his continued perception of it, as does Tamer El Said in making *City*. The film acknowledges that its characters' ability to travel by air is alone indicative of their socio-economic class[51]—the class of cultural practitioners, such as the four friends who gather in downtown Cairo, where Khalid insists on living, in a rejuvenated district that has boasted cultural activities and attracted intellectuals, artists, and writers since the 1990s.[52]

Reflecting much of downtown Cairo's revitalization, *In the Last Days of the City* flaunts its secular credentials. Though it lays claim to revolution principally through its formal and structural elements—its multiplicity of dialects, its elliptical narrative, and its integration of several films within itself—it is in its defiance of the Islamization of culture that *City* issues its most strident cry. The signs are unmistakable throughout: beer drinking by the comrades; kisses between the unwed Khalid and Laila; stickers with prohibitive Islamic statements, such as "Thou shalt not look at women," on the walls of an elevator shaft; and a developing aside of mannequins in a storefront losing their secular (Western) clothes, then being obstructed from view by newspaper pasted on the store window, and eventually being covered by black *abayas*. *City*'s camera displays group prayers in open public spaces, indoors and out. *City* captures a protest—documentary footage—in favor of Islamic government. Khalid stares blankly at the signs of increasing religiosity in the city, until his patience expires toward the end of the film and he tears the stickers with the Islamic slogans off the wall. Pan-Arabism had long integrated an address of Islam and adopted discourses drawn from it, and *City* and its director propose a pan-Arabism for the twenty-first century that repudiates the diktats of Islam.[53] Ideas and practices in the service of the culture that the new pan-Arabists wish to develop are secular a priori, even if the Arabic language was once endorsed by the emergence of Islam among Arabic-speaking peoples in whose language the Quran was written.

From Arab Nationalism to Virtual Omnipresence— *The Dupes* to *In the Last Days of the City*

Tamer El Said, director of *In the Last Days of the City*, "hates borders,"[54] which is why he would likely appreciate Kay Dickinson's *Arab Cinema Travels* for including, in its index, multiple entries under *migration* but none under *immigration*, which it uses only once. After all, *immigrate*, like *emigrate*, denotes a crossing of borders and connotes permanence—unlike *migrate*. The pan-Arabism advocated for in *City* is one of mutual empowerment among those working to enrich their hometowns—a community of conscientious and earnest practitioners that can bring a positive change. Many would say it happened between when the film was shot and when it was released—those peaceful protests that erupted across the region.

City is also pan-Arab in its production—though multinationally funded, the production companies are Lebanese and Egyptian, just like the film's screenwriters, Rasha Salti and director El Said. The Lebanese and Iraqi roles are performed by actors from the same national background, who speak accordingly in the film. As *City* integrates footage shot in Baghdad and Beirut, the production recalls that of *The Dupes*. The similarities between the two films do not stop there. Both fared well at film festivals, winning awards and garnering notable acclaim. Both have run foul of the authorities. *The Dupes* screened in Syria but was quickly withdrawn. In Egypt, it was not shown in commercial cinemas, and rarely elsewhere.[55] Nor was it screened in Iraq or, of course, Kuwait.[56] *City* was withdrawn from the state-funded Cairo International Film Festival, reportedly because it had screened in too many festivals already.[57] Additionally, both directors suggest that their films are revolutionary, without openly saying so. In a letter penned by Tewfik Saleh to his good friend, Tunisian film critic Taher Cheria, two years after release of *The Dupes*, a dispirited Saleh insisted that those who create revolutionary art "know what they're doing."[58] Saleh knew what he was doing when he assembled *The Dupes* in a fractured narrative form that emulated the modernist structure of its source text, *Men in the Sun*. Otherwise, the film would not pack the emotional punch that it does.

El Said insists, "To me, a revolutionary film is not a film about a revolution. It has a lot more to do with the art form."[59] He appears to suggest here that *City* is revolutionary because of its daring form, a form that blends narrative and documentary, a film that records its own making. This may sound like nothing much new to those familiar with impressionistic and autobiographical narrative films, but in Egypt, the totality of *City*'s structural and formal elements seemed unprecedented. Veteran Egyptian film critic Samir Farid called *City* "a moment of metamorphosis in the Egyptian cinema."[60]

Most significant, however, is the fact that the two films communicate a vision of responsibility toward one's people and one's hometown within a conception of a borderless region populated by Arabs. Yet, whereas *The Dupes* perceives the collective arrangement as a union between Arab nation-states, *In the Last Days of the City* conceptualizes a condition of cultural and occupational empowerment and personal interconnectivity by way of media technologies that link people in cities, people who strive to serve their cities. In this manner, *City* reassures its audience; out of the ashes of despair a virtual omnipresence connects Arabs and provides a sense of community, even when physical borders prevail. If one cannot cross a border by land, sea, or air, then perhaps the next best thing is to cross virtually.

Notes

1. "Figures at a Glance," *The United Nations Refugee Agency*, available at <http://www.unhcr.org/figures-at-a-glance.html> (last accessed January 14, 2017).
2. Phillip Connor, "Number of Refugees to Europe Surges to Record 1.3 Million in 2015," *Pew Research Center*, August 2, 2016, available at <http://www.pewglobal.org/2016/08/02/number-of-refugees-to-europe-surges-to-record-1-3-million-in-2015/> (last accessed November 26, 2020).
3. Phillip Connor, "Middle East's Migrant Population More Than Doubles Since 2005," *Pew Research Center*, October 18, 2016, available at <http://www.pewglobal.org/2016/10/18/conflicts-in-syria-iraq-and-yemen-lead-to-millions-of-displaced-migrants-in-the-middle-east-since-2005/> (last accessed November 26, 2020).
4. Connor, "Middle East's Migrant Population."
5. See Michael C. Hudson, "Arab Integration: An Overview," in *Middle East Dilemma: The Politics and Economics of Arab Integration*, ed. Michael C. Hudson (New York: Columbia University Press, 1999), 9.
6. Viola Shafik, *Arab Cinema: History and Cultural Identity* (New York: American University in Cairo Press: 2007), 155.
7. Fredric Jameson's dialectical analysis in *The Geopolitical Aesthetic: Cinema and Space in the World System* probes reification of the supranational cultures of late capitalism as film, marked most obviously in the Arab world by the global ascendancy of the United States in the wake of the Soviet Union's demise, which

coincided the emergence of satellite television. Jameson, "Remapping Taipei," in *The Geopolitical Aesthetic: Cinema and Space in the World System* (Bloomington and London: Indiana University Press and BFI, 1992).
8. "The History of Arab Nationalism" is a main component of Albert Hourani's *Arabic Thought in the Liberal Age 1798–1939*, 2nd edn (London: Cambridge University Press, 1983), 260–2.
9. Hourani, *Arabic Thought*, 307–8.
10. Hourani, *Arabic Thought*, 359.
11. Hourani, *Arabic Thought*, 306, 307. Secularism figures in my analysis of both operative films, in terms of opposition to Islamic conservatism, especially in *In the Last Days of the City*.
12. Michel Aflaq, *On the Way of Resurrection (Fi sabil al-ba'th)* (Beirut: at-Tali'ah Publishing, 1978), 20–1.
13. Aflaq, *On the Way of Resurrection*, 10.
14. "Report by the Royal Palestine Commission," *The League of Nations*, 1937, available at <http://www.jewishvirtuallibrary.org/text-of-the-peel-commission-report> (last accessed June 15, 2017).
15. The second is that of Palestinians of the *Nakba*, in 1948; the second is that of Lebanese during the Lebanese Civil War (1975–90); and the third is that of Iraqis after the Gulf War of 1990–1 and the US Occupation of Iraq, beginning in 2003.
16. Hourani, *Arabic Thought*, 292–3.
17. Saad Eddin Ibrahim, *The Eclipse of Arab Nationalism (Khusouf al-qawmiyah al-'arabiya)* (Cairo: Qaba' Publishing, 2000), 69.
18. This figure represents the number of refugees that the United Nations Relief and Works Agency (UNRWA) recorded in 1950, though it is likely that not all Palestinian refugees registered. "Palestinian Refugees," *United Nations Relief and Works Agency*, available at <https://www.unrwa.org/palestine-refugees> (last accessed January 22, 2017).
19. See Hudson, "Arab Integration," 9.
20. See Mustapha Kamil al-Sayyid, "The Rise and Fall of the United Arab Republic," in *Middle East Dilemma: The Politics and Economics of Integration*, ed. Michael C. Hudson (New York: Columbia University Press, 1999), 118–23.
21. See Hudson, "Arab Integration," 9, as well as Raymond William Baker, "Egypt in Shadows: Films and the Political Order," *The American Behavioral Scientist* 17, no. 3 (1974): 396. Baker was likely the first to write deliberately about Tewfik Saleh's work in English and has since gone on to become an influential scholar in Middle Eastern Studies.
22. The novel was voted as fifth in a 2010 polling of the Arab Writers Union, which produced a list of the 105 greatest Arabic language novels of all time. See M. Lynx Qualey, "Top 105," *Arab Literature (in English)*, available at <https://arablit.org/for-readers/top-105/> (last accessed January 2, 2017).
23. See Baker, "Egypt in Shadows," 403–7.
24. Joel Gordon refers to Saladin's portrayal as that of a "pan-Arab champion." See "Nasser 56/Cairo 96: Reimaging Egypt's Lost Community," in *Mass Mediations: New Approaches to Popular Culture in the Middle East and Beyond*, ed. Walter Armbrust (Los Angeles: University of California Press, 2000), 166. Renowned Egyptian film

critic and scholar Samir Farid expressed the opinion, in an interview with Chahine, that the film amounted to "an official expression of the commitment to Nasser as the Arab leader of the ummah in the face of the rupture between Egypt and Syria in 1961." Chahine's response was evasive. See Farid, *Hiwarat fi al-Sinema* (Conversations in Cinema) (Damascus: Ministry of Culture Publications—The Public Cinema Organization, 2008), 82.
25. See Baker, "Egypt in Shadows," 401–2.
26. Chahine is arguably the most renowned of all Arab filmmakers, credited with over forty films as director. His films received at least a nomination at the world's four most prestigious film festivals—Cannes, Berlin, Venice, and Toronto.
27. Farha Ghannam, *Remaking the Modern: Space, Relocation and the Politics of Identity in a Global Cairo* (Los Angeles: University of California Press, 2002), 28.
28. Tewfik Saleh himself related a question that a French critic had once asked him: why Saleh repeated what he was saying in his films, as if to demand that the viewers understand. Tewfik Saleh, "Khawatir hawla hajis al-talaqqi fi al-sinema" (Remarks on Reception Aesthetics in Arab Cinema), *Alif: Journal of Comparative Poetics* 15 (1995): 89, available at <http://www.jstor.org/stable/521700?seq=5#page_scan_tab_contents> (last accessed January 4, 2017). See also Baker, "Egypt in Shadows," 401–2.
29. Baker, "Egypt in Shadows," 413.
30. Baker, "Egypt in Shadows," 404.
31. "al-Makdu'oun" (The Dupes), *The General Organization for Cinema--The National Film Organization*, available at <http://www.cinemasy.com/film.php?id=79> (last accessed January 22, 2017).
32. See Baker, "Egypt in Shadows," 413.
33. Saleh, "Khawatir hawla hajis al-talaqqi fi al-sinema," 87–8.
34. Saleh, "Khawatir hawla hajis al-talaqqi fi al-sinema," 87.
35. Saleh writes about *The Dupes* in the third of three letters in French to his friend Taher Cheria, critic of Tunisian cinema. Tewfik Saleh, "Trois lettres," *Alif: Journal of Comparative Poetics* 15 (1995), 240–1.
36. Saleh, "Trois lettres," 235.
37. Adham Youssef, " On the Seven Films of Tawfiq Saleh: Militant with a Camera," *Mada*, September 3, 2014, available at <http://www.madamasr.com/en/2014/09/03/feature/culture/on-the-seven-films-of-tawfiq-saleh-militant-with-a-camera/> (last accessed November 26, 2020).
38. Saleh, "Trois lettres," 240.
39. See Marvin G. Weinbaum, "Egypt's 'Infitah' and the Politics of US Economic Assistance," *Middle Eastern Studies* 21, no. 2 (1985), 210–11.
40. Ghannam, *Remaking the Modern*, 29–30.
41. See Mona Abaza, *Changing Consumer Cultures of Modern Egypt: Cairo's Urban Reshaping* (Boston: Brill, 2006), 95. See also Kara Murphy, "The Lebanese Crisis and Its Impact on Immigrants and Refugees," *Migration Policy Institute*, September 1, 2006, available at <http://www.migrationpolicy.org/article/lebanese-crisis-and-its-impact-immigrants-and-refugees> (last accessed November 26, 2020).
42. Abaza, *Changing Consumer Cultures of Modern Egypt*, 15. Also see Ted Swedenburg, "Sa'ida Sultan/Danna International: Transgender Pop and the Polysemiotics

of Sex, Nation, and Ethnicity on the Israeli-Egyptian Border," in *Mass Mediations: New Approaches to Popular Culture in the Middle East and Beyond*, ed. Walter Armbrust (Los Angeles: University of California Press, 2000), 95–6.
43. Murphy, "The Lebanese Crisis and Its Impact on Immigrants and Refugees."
44. Judith Miller, "The World; Displaced in the Gulf War: 5 Million Refugees," *The New York Times*, June 19, 1991, available at <http://www.migrationpolicy.org/article/lebanese-crisis-and-its-impact-immigrants-and-refugees> (last accessed November 26, 2020). See also Joseph Sassoon, *The Iraqi Refugees: The New Crisis in the Middle East* (New York: I. B. Tauris, 2009), 2–6, 96–8.
45. Samir Farid notes the film's inconclusiveness in a glowing review, "Akhir ayam al-madina: nuqtat tahawul fi al-sinema al-masriya," *al-Masry al-Youm*, February 16, 2016, available at <http://www.almasryalyoum.com/news/details/893979> (last accessed November 26, 2020).
46. According to El Said, part of the film was shot in Berlin, though, having watched the film twice, I see no sign of this. See Sara Elkamel's interview with the director, "Tamer El Said: Moments in Eternal Cities," *Guernica*, June 13, 2016, available at <https://www.guernicamag.com/tamer-el-said-moments-in-eternal-cities/> (last accessed November 26, 2020).
47. I should note that Hassan's two film segments appear as parts of a single work, whereas Bassem's appear as two different works.
48. Jay Weissberg, "Berlin Film Review: 'In the Last Days of the City,'" *Variety*, February 14, 2016, available at <http://variety.com/2016/film/festivals/in-the-last-days-of-the-city-review-berlin-film-festival-1201705591/> (last accessed November 26, 2020).
49. Within this multiplicity of media, some, such as social media, having detached from established and co-opted entities, would facilitate Arab Spring protests a month and a half after the film's photography was completed.
50. Broadband internet service, necessary for streaming video. According to the World Bank, "In the absence of fiber backbone networks aggregating increasing data traffic and thereby reducing average costs, broadband services are unlikely to be commercially viable in anything other than the major urban areas of a country." See Natalija Gelvanovska, Michel Rogy, and Carlo Maria Rossotto, *Broadband Networks in the Middle East and North Africa* (Washington, D.C.: The World Bank, 2014), 8, available at <https://openknowledge.worldbank.org/handle/10986/16680> (last accessed August 19, 2017). As for cell-phone services, only a third of the Middle East and North Africa region's population had subscribed to such services by 2010, although mobile technology services have since penetrated rural areas appreciably, according to the Groupe Speciale Mobile Association. *The Mobile Economy Middle East and North Africa 2016* (London: GSMA, 2016), 2, 44, available at <https://www.gsmaintelligence.com/research/?file=9246bbe14813f73dd85b97a90738c860&download> (last accessed August 14, 2017).
51. For more on this, see Kay Dickinson, *Arab Cinema Travels: Transnational Syria, Palestine, Dubai, and Beyond* (London: Palgrave, 2016), 163–5.
52. See Abaza, *Changing Consumer Cultures of Modern Egypt*, 40, 171.
53. For more on the intersection between Islamic and Arab nationalist doctrine, see Paul Noble, "The Prospects for Arab Cooperation in a Changing Regional and Global

System," in *Middle East Dilemma: The Politics and Economics of Arab Integration*, ed. Michael C. Hudson (New York: Columbia University Press, 1999), 72–82.
54. See Elkamel, "Tamer El Said: Moments in Eternal Cities."
55. See Saleh, "Remarks on Reception Aesthetics in Arab Cinema," 90.
56. See Saleh, "Trois lettres," no. 3, 240.
57. Samir Farid, "'In the Last Days of the City is a Moment of Metamorphosis in the Egyptian Cinema" [Aakhir Ayyam al-Madina nuqtat tahauwul fi as-sinema al-masriya], *al-Masry al-Youm*, February 16, 2016. http://www.almasryalyoum.com/news/details/893979
58. Saleh, "Trois lettres," no. 3, 240.
59. See Elkamel, "Tamer El Said: Moments in Eternal Cities."
60. See Farid, "Akhir ayyam al-madina nuqtat tahauwul fi as-sinema al-masriya."

Works Cited

Abaza, Mona. *Changing Consumer Cultures of Modern Egypt: Cairo's Urban Reshaping*. Boston: Brill, 2006.

Aflaq, Michel. *On the Way of Resurrection (Fi sabil al-ba'th)*. Beirut: at-Tali'ah Publishing, 1978.

"al-Makdu'oun" (The Dupes). *The General Organization for Cinema--The National Film Organization*, <http://www.cinemasy.com/film.php?id=79> (last accessed January 22, 2017).

al-Sayyid, Mustapha Kamil. "The Rise and Fall of the United Arab Republic." In *Middle East Dilemma: The Politics and Economics of Integration*, ed. Michael C. Hudson, 109–27. New York: Columbia University Press, 1999.

Baker, Raymond William. "Egypt in Shadows: Films and the Political Order." *The American Behavioral Scientist* 17, no. 3 (1974): 396.

Connor, Phillip. "Number of Refugees to Europe Surges to Record 1.3 Million in 2015." *Pew Research Center*, August 2, 2016, <http://www.pewglobal.org/2016/08/02/number-of-refugees-to-europe-surges-to-record-1-3-million-in-2015/> (last accessed November 26, 2020).

Connor, Phillip. "Middle East's Migrant Population More Than Doubles Since 2005." *Pew Research Center*, October 18, 2016, <http://www.pewglobal.org/2016/10/18/conflicts-in-syria-iraq-and-yemen-lead-to-millions-of-displaced-migrants-in-the-middle-east-since-2005/> (last accessed November 26, 2020).

Dickinson, Kay. *Arab Cinema Travels: Transnational Syria, Palestine, Dubai, and Beyond*. London: Palgrave, 2016.

Elkamel, Sara. "Tamer El Said: Moments in Eternal Cities." *Guernica*, June 13, 2016, <https://www.guernicamag.com/tamer-el-said-moments-in-eternal-cities/> (last accessed November 26, 2020).

Farid, Samir. *Hiwarat fi al-Sinema* (Conversations in Cinema). Damascus: Ministry of Culture Publications—The Public Cinema Organization, 2008.

Farid, Samir. "Akhir ayyam al-madina nuqtat tahauwul fi as-sinema al-masriya." *al-Masry al-Youm*, February 16, 2016, <http://www.almasryalyoum.com/news/details/893979> (last accessed November 26, 2020).

"Figures at a Glance." *The United Nations Refugee Agency*, <http://www.unhcr.org/figures-at-a-glance.html> (last accessed January 14, 2017).

Gelvanovska, Natalija, Michel Rogy, and Carlo Maria Rossotto. *Broadband Networks in the Middle East and North Africa*. Washington, D.C.: The World Bank, 2014, <https://openknowledge.worldbank.org/handle/10986/16680> (last accessed August 19, 2017).

Ghannam, Farha. *Remaking the Modern: Space, Relocation and the Politics of Identity in a Global Cairo*. Los Angeles: Univeristy of California Press, 2002.

Gordon, Joel. "Nasser 56/Cairo 96: Reimaging Egypt's Lost Community." In *Mass Mediations: New Approaches to Popular Culture in the Middle East and Beyond*, ed. Walter Armbrust. Los Angeles: University of California Press, 2000.

Groupe Speciale Mobile Association. *The Mobile Economy Middle East and North Africa 2016*. London: GSMA, 2016, <https://www.gsmaintelligence.com/research/?file=9246bbe14813f73dd85b97a90738c860&download> (last accessed August 14, 2017).

Hourani, Albert. *Arabic Thought in the Liberal Age 1798–1939*, 2nd edn. London: Cambridge University Press, 1983.

Hudson, Michael C. "Arab Integration: An Overview." In *Middle East Dilemma: The Politics and Economics of Arab Integration*, ed. Michael C. Hudson, 1–32. New York: Columbia University Press, 1999.

Ibrahim, Saad Eddin. *The Eclipse of Arab Nationalism (Khusouf al-qawmiyah al-'arabiya)*. Cairo: Qaba' Publishing, 2000.

Jameson, Fredric. "Remapping Taipei." In *The Geopolitical Aesthetic: Cinema and Space in the World System*. Bloomington and London: Indiana University Press and BFI, 1992.

Miller, Judith. "The World; Displaced in the Gulf War: 5 Million Refugees." *The New York Times*, June 19, 1991, <http://www.nytimes.com/1991/06/16/weekinreview/the-world-displaced-in-the-gulf-war-5-million-refugees.html> (last accessed November 26, 2020).

Murphy, Kara. "The Lebanese Crisis and Its Impact on Immigrants and Refugees." *Migration Policy Institute*, September 1, 2006, <http://www.migrationpolicy.org/article/lebanese-crisis-and-its-impact-immigrants-and-refugees> (last accessed November 26, 2020).

Noble, Paul. "The Prospects for Arab Cooperation in a Changing Regional and Global System." In *Middle East Dilemma: The Politics and Economics of Arab Integration*, ed. Michael C. Hudson, 60–91. New York: Columbia University Press, 1999.

"Palestinian Refugees." *United Nations Relief and Works Agency*, <https://www.unrwa.org/palestine-refugees> (last accessed January 22, 2017).

Qualey, M. Lynx. "Top 105." *Arab Literature (in English)*, <https://arablit.org/for-readers/top-105/> (last accessed January 2, 2017).

"Report by the Royal Palestine Commission," *The League of Nations*, 1937, <http://www.jewishvirtuallibrary.org/text-of-the-peel-commission-report> (last accessed June 15, 2017).

Saleh, Tewfik. "Khawatir hawla hajis al-talaqqi fi al-sinema" (Remarks on Reception Aesthetics in Arab Cinema). *Alif: Journal of Comparative Poetics* 15 (1995): 85–90,

<http://www.jstor.org/stable/521700?seq=5#page_scan_tab_contents> (last accessed January 4, 2017).
Saleh, Tewfik. "Trois lettres" (no. 3). *Alif: Journal of Comparative Poetics*, 15 (1995): 235–41, <http://www.jstor.org/stable/521689?seq=7#page_scan_tab_contents> (last accessed January 9, 2017).
Sassoon, Joseph. *The Iraqi Refugees: The New Crisis in the Middle East*. New York: I. B. Tauris, 2009.
Shafik, Viola. *Arab Cinema: History and Cultural Identity*. New York: American University in Cairo Press, 2007.
Swedenburg, Ted. "Sa'ida Sultan/Danna International: Transgender Pop and the Polysemiotics of Sex, Nation, and Ethnicity on the Israeli–Egyptian Border." In *Mass Mediations: New Approaches to Popular Culture in the Middle East and Beyond*, ed. Walter Armbrust, 88–119. Los Angeles: University of California Press, 2000.
Weinbaum, Marvin G. "Egypt's 'Infitah' and the Politics of US Economic Assistance." *Middle Eastern Studies* 21, no. 2 (1985): 210–11.
Weissberg, Jay. "Berlin Film Review: 'In the Last Days of the City.'" *Variety*, February 14, 2016, <http://variety.com/2016/film/festivals/in-the-last-days-of-the-city-review-berlin-film-festival-1201705591/> (last accessed November 26, 2020).
Youssef, Adham. "On the Seven Films of Tawfiq Saleh: Militant with a Camera." *Mada*, September 3, 2014, <http://www.madamasr.com/en/2014/09/03/feature/culture/on-the-seven-films-of-tawfiq-saleh-militant-with-a-camera/> (last accessed November 26, 2020).

5. STILL/MOVING: AN ANALYSIS OF RECENT FILMS ABOUT TRANSNATIONAL MIGRATION FROM CENTRAL AMERICA TO THE USA

William Brown

In this chapter, I shall analyze the tension between moving and still images in various films from the 2000s and 2010s that deal with transnational migration from Central America and Mexico to the USA. My main focus will be on *Sin nombre* (Cary Jôji Fukunaga, Mexico/USA, 2009) and *La jaula de oro/ The Golden Dream* (Diego Quemada-Díez, Guatemala/Spain/Mexico, 2013), although I shall also make reference to other films, including *Who is Dayani Cristal?* (Marc Silver, UK/Mexico, 2013). Comparing *Sin nombre* and *La jaula de oro* to *Trade* (Marco Kreuzpaintner, Germany/USA, 2007), I shall argue how the former films give a human face to an issue that might otherwise be reduced to statistics or spectacle. I shall then demonstrate how there is a tension between photography and cinematography in *Sin nombre* and *La jaula de oro* that matches the tension between the process of migration and the desire for (economic) stability or "stillness" that provokes it. Finally, in drawing upon the work of Latin American theorists like Enrique Dussel, Eduardo Galeano, Walter Mignolo, and Aníbal Quijano, I shall demonstrate how the tension between stasis and movement allows these films, and *Who is Dayani Cristal?*, to suggest the history of exploitation and imperialism that has led to numerous humans undertaking the deadly migration from the "periphery" of Central America to the "center" of the USA.

In *Sin nombre*, Sayra (Paulina Gaitan), her young uncle, Orlando (Guillermo Villegas), and her estranged father, Horacio (Gerardo Taracena) all travel from Tegucigalpa in Honduras through Mexico to the US border. Sayra, Orlando, and

Horacio are joined in Tapachula, Mexico, by Mara Salvatruche gang members Lil Mago (Tenoch Huera Mejía), Smiley (Kristian Ferrer), and Casper (Edgar Flores), the latter of whom wants to leave the gang, but who can do so only by killing Lil Mago, the leader of the local Mara branch.

Meanwhile, in *La jaula de oro*, Juan (Brandon López), Sara (Karen Martínez), and Samuel (Carlos Chajon) depart from Guatemala, similarly passing through Mexico, where they meet an Indian boy, Chauk (Rodolfo Domínguez), in their bid to make it north. In each film, only one character manages to make it into the USA—as the journeys of all of the migrants are marked by corrupt police, local gangs, and barriers both geographic and logistic between their point of departure and their destination. As mentioned, both films also share a fascination for photography. However, before looking more closely at these movies, let us consider briefly the issue of transnational migration across Central America and towards the USA in order to gain a sense of the size and scale of what we might call the "migration industry."

The Migration Industry

Sin nombre and *La jaula de oro* both demonstrate how many Latin Americans will travel north in order to seek the "golden dream"—which is the mistranslated English title typically given to the latter film (more on this mistranslation later). While "data are not available on the actual number of migrants that illegally attempt to cross the border in any given year," estimates vary between about 350,000, about 450,000 to 650,000, and up to 3 million in terms of the number of humans who illegally enter the USA from Latin America each year, of whom an unknown number will at some stage be smuggled/trafficked during their journey.[1] It is hard to estimate how many humans are *not* successful in their attempt to enter the United States. The United Nations Office on Drugs and Crime (UNODC) suggests that "the probability of being apprehended at the border is about 20% for Mexicans"—meaning roughly that an additional 660,000 Mexicans alone (that is, not including migrants from other countries) attempt but do not manage to cross the border each year.[2] Given that Mexicans account for about 88 percent of migrants apprehended at the US border, there would roughly be another 70,000 people from elsewhere in Latin America that attempt to reach the USA each year.[3] This means that somewhere in the region of 3.7 million people attempt to enter the USA each year from Latin America.

However, the figure of 3.7 million people does not include those who fail to reach the Mexican–American border, since these figures are estimates concerning those who successfully cross and/or who are apprehended at that border. According to Amnesty International, Mexico's Comisión Nacional de Derechos Humanos (CNDH; National Human Rights Commission) reported the kidnapping in Mexico of 11,000 migrants in 2011, with the Instituto

Nacional de Migración (INM, National Institute for Migration) also reporting that the Mexican government detained 88,501 migrants in 2012.[4] If many kidnappings are not reported, it would seem, then, that as many as 100,000 further migrants never even reach the Mexican–US border. This paints an even bleaker picture in terms of the sheer number of people who embark upon a journey from Latin America toward the USA in a bid to enter the latter country illegally. Furthermore, none of these statistics reflect migrants traveling with visas or border crossing cards, whether or not they subsequently overstay.

Finally, as is reflected in both *Sin nombre* and *La jaula de oro*, the number of children making these journeys is also on the rise. Indeed, according to one journalist in the *Los Angeles Times*, "[t]he number of minors age[d] 12 and younger has grown 117% [in 2014] compared with 2013, while the number of girls younger than 18 caught at the US border was up 77% this year through May. That compares with an 8% increase for males."[5] One estimates, then, that this migration industry is worth about US$6.6 billion annually, with money going mainly to people smugglers, or *coyotes*, and their employers.[6]

Astonishing as these estimated figures are, however, they do not necessarily help us in understanding why these perilous journeys take place. In order to provide a preliminary explanation for why there is such large-scale migration across the Americas, I shall draw upon one of the stated inspirations behind *La jaula de oro*: namely, Eduardo Galeano's famous polemic, *The Open Veins of Latin America*.[7]

In that work, Galeano outlines the systematic way in which Latin America has been bled dry of both its natural and its human resources. This "bleeding dry" is not simply a history of colonialism under (predominantly, though not exclusively) Spanish rule and the exportation of raw materials, including gold; it is also a history of imperialism right through to the present day, leading to what is termed "underdevelopment" in Latin America.

Writing in 1971, Galeano adds that "we [Latin Americans] give ourselves the luxury of providing the United States with our best technicians and ablest scientists, who are lured to emigrate by the high salaries and broad research possibilities available in the north."[8] Half a century later, Galeano's point remains relevant. However, in the contemporary era, such migration consists not only of technicians and scientists, but also of skilled and unskilled laborers alike—as both *Sin nombre* and *La jaula de oro* depict. Many humans in search of nothing more than labor therefore risk their lives simply to get into the USA in the hope of employment and salaries that do not exist in their homelands as a result of the history of exploitation that Galeano details. In other words, the migration industry has expanded since Galeano wrote his incendiary polemic as the gap between rich and poor countries, and the gap between the rich and the poor within and across countries, have widened.

MIGRATION, CINEMA, AND EUROCENTRISM

Given the widening of the gap between rich and poor, the increased scale of the migration industry from Central America to the USA, and the dangers risked by those who pay to undertake such journeys, it should not be surprising that the issue has become a common theme in contemporary cinema, spanning both fiction and documentary. Included among recent films that deal with this topic are *Trade*, *Los bastardos* (Amat Escalante, Mexico, 2008), *Norteado/Northless* (Rigoberto Pérezcano, Mexico/Spain, 2009), *The Girl* (David Riker, USA/Mexico, 2012), *Purgatorio: Viaje al corazón de la frontera/Purgatorio: A Journey into the Heart of the Border* (Rodrigo Reyes, Mexico/USA, 2013), *Who is Dayani Cristal?*, *Desierto* (Jonás Cuarón, Mexico/France, 2015), and *Lupe bajo el sol/Lupe Under the Sun* (Rodrigo Reyes, Mexico/USA, 2016). These, together with *Sin nombre* and *La jaula de oro*, help to raise awareness of the issue of trans-American migration, giving to it a human face that potentially is lost in the (re)production of statistics and/or historical and theoretical analyses. However, filmmakers run various risks when creating cinematic representations of illegal migration and the concomitant issue of human trafficking. For not only can films give to these issues a human face, but they can also (unintentionally?) have the opposite effect: namely, that of dehumanizing migration and trafficking, and the reasons behind them—especially if they offer up what we shall term a Eurocentric perspective. To understand how this can happen, let us look briefly at another film that deals with cross-American migration: namely, *Trade*.

In *Trade*, we see Texan cop Ray Sheridan (Kevin Kline) join forces with a young Mexican man, Jorge (Cesar Ramos), in order to find and bring to safety Jorge's kidnapped thirteen-year-old sister, Adriana (Paulina Gaitan again), who is about to be sold into prostitution. Although the film gestures towards the transnational complexities of human trafficking networks (it features humans trafficked from Poland via Mexico to the USA, and then sold via an internet auction hosted in the Maldives and a bank account in South Africa), it simultaneously presents to us a narrative of the (troubled) white American rescuing the Mexican teenager and then returning her and her brother to Mexico City, where they will be a happy family. In other words, the film does not necessarily suggest the psychological complexities of migration, whereby many humans will willingly enter (and/or be sold) into precarious situations for the sake of economic betterment. Instead, *Trade* offers us a heroic narrative featuring the white American male, and as arguably befits a film by a German director with German and American funding, *Trade* thus provides a Eurocentric treatment of the issues at hand. All of the characters dream of and/or have a better life in the USA, while human trafficking is evil and run by pedophiles. With its pacy editing and dramatic score, *Trade* renders migration and trafficking spectacular, rather than indicating the more banal economic imbalances that lead to such practices.

Scholars such as Aníbal Quijano and Walter Mignolo argue comprehensively that Eurocentrism is a pernicious myth that allows Europe and, by extension, North America to retain a central position in the world system, thereby relegating to a peripheral position those countries, including Latin American ones, that have been dominated and bled dry of their natural resources.[9] As Quijano argues: "the Europeans generated a new temporal perspective of history and relocated the colonized population, along with their respective histories and cultures, in the past of a historical trajectory whose culmination was Europe."[10] With regard to this chapter, a film like *Trade* arguably reinforces this Eurocentric perspective through its white American male hero and through its relatively naïve characterization of human trafficking as work done simply by "bad people" into whose lives we are given neither time nor insight, with huge swathes of Latin Americans wanting to enter the USA for a better life because it simply is "better" there.

The idea that the USA is just "better" (and that its heroic Federal agents can save Mexican girls from otherwise evil human traffickers) reaffirms the Eurocentric notion that the USA is the center and that Mexico and other Central American countries are peripheral—with everyone from the periphery wanting to be at the center. Quijano explains that Raúl Prebisch coined the distinction between center and periphery in order to "describe the configuration of global capitalism since the end of World War II."[11] In doing so, Quijano argues, Prebisch

> underscored, with or without being aware of it, the nucleus of the historical model for the control of labor, resources, and products that shaped the central part of the new global model of power, starting with America as a player in the new world economy.[12]

That model for the control of labor is precisely the flow of resources from the periphery to the center, as we have already discussed in relation to human resources and Galeano: Americans can choose who does or does not enter into their workforce and thus who can make money, while non-Americans are forced into illegal migration because there is little to no labor or money in their homeland.

Argentine philosopher Enrique Dussel also adopts the language of center and periphery in order to propose a "philosophy of liberation," arguing that

> liberation is possible only when one has the courage to be atheistic vis-à-vis an empire of the center, thus incurring the risk of suffering from its power, its economic boycotts, its armies, and its agents who are experts at corruption, violence, and assassination.[13]

However, if Dussel pleads for the periphery to liberate itself, then what liberation is possible when those in the so-called periphery reaffirm the self-imposed centrality of the center by migrating relentlessly towards it in the hope of the so-called "golden dream"?

To find films that avoid a Eurocentric perspective, which itself reaffirms the binary distinction between the controlling center and the impoverished periphery, we must turn our attention to films that involve funding and talent from Mexico and other "peripheral," as opposed to "central," countries. *Sin nombre*, which received production funds from Mexico and the USA, and *La jaula de oro*, which received production funds from Mexico, Guatemala, and Spain, might constitute two such examples.[14]

How this is so needs to be delicately elaborated. For one might argue that in charting the migration of peoples from Honduras, Guatemala, and Mexico towards and into the USA, *Sin nombre* and *La jaula de oro* do not signal a Latin American ethos of liberation so much as a reinforcement of the "golden dream" and the reaffirmation of the USA as center—as also signaled by the presence of American and Spanish funding for the films. That is, the films' narratives and their financing suggest resignation to the USA's role as center, and to Honduras, Guatemala, and Mexico's role as peripheral. However, while the films arguably do chart a deepened pessimism with regard to the possibilities of and for liberation since Dussel wrote his words in 1985, they also reflect a different world that eludes Dussel's analysis, and in which one can find a critique of the center/periphery system. We can analyze the nature of this world by examining the place of the media in the contemporary world system, before then looking more closely at their role in *Sin nombre* and *La jaula de oro* themselves.

The Role of the Media

In describing "imperialist culture" and the "culture of the center," Dussel says that

> the culture that dominates in the present order . . . is the refined culture of European and North American elites. This is the culture that all other cultures are measured against . . . And this culture has the collective means of communication in its hands (the United States originates and transmits 80 percent of the material that is used in Latin America by daily newspapers, magazines, radio, movies and television).[15]

Furthermore, Dussel also asserts that "[t]he designs of the ruling system are imposed univocally on everybody by propaganda, the communications media, movies, and television—through all receptive pores."[16] In other words, according to Dussel, the media play a key role in economic and cultural imperialism.

Social and other forms of psychology have not necessarily resolved the debate over the extent to which the media affect human beliefs and behavior. Furthermore, Dussel describes a Latin American mediascape from the 1980s, while the public confronts a different mediascape in the 2000s, when, as Joseph Straubhaar points out in relation to television, "there is still a tendency [in Latin America] toward preferring cultural proximity, that is, preferring cultural products from a culture similar to one's own" and therefore not from a dissimilar culture like that of the USA.[17] As Straubhaar elaborates elsewhere, "cultural trade within cultural–linguistic regions is large and growing," with "Latin American television markets . . . more likely to import [Latin] American production ideas and genres than American programs in prime time, although they still import many US programs to fill up the rest of the 24-hour broadcast day."[18]

Since Straubhaar asserts almost the opposite of Dussel, in that Latin Americans consume mainly Latin American media, then an issue is raised. In an era of perceived cultural and economic imperialism, in which Latin American countries are reduced to playing a "peripheral" role, how is it that Latin American countries produce and consume their own media products? For surely this latter "independence" from North American media undermines the latter's influence on Latin American culture—which in turn might beg this question: if Latin Americans do not know about North American life because they do not see it in their media, then how is it that they come to have the "golden dream" of travelling north to the USA in search of opportunity and, perchance, fortune? The answer clearly must be that while Latin Americans may, as per Straubhaar and contra Dussel, consume Latin American media products, they none the less still receive and consume sounds and images (or what Dussel would call "propaganda") from the north. And as much is borne out in *Sin nombre* and *La jaula de oro*, to which we can presently turn.

Neither film includes many media that the characters consume or discuss, but what we do see and hear—predominantly music, both diegetic and non-diegetic—tends to be Latin and sung in Spanish. None the less, the Mara Salvatruche gang members whom we see in *Sin nombre* have appropriated terms like "homie" from North American hip hop culture—even if hip hop itself originated as and continues in some quarters to be an expression of resistance against hegemonic (white) culture in the USA. There is also a reference in the film made to Salma Hayek, a Mexican film star who nevertheless has featured in many Hollywood productions. In other words, *Sin nombre* demonstrates at least an implicit North American influence on the Latin American characters. However, I wish more pressingly to argue that a North American influence is felt not so much via media products that are referenced within the films as in the role played by the different media machines or apparatuses that appear in the films, especially photography.

Photography

Although the mise en scène of *Sin nombre* and *La jaula de oro* does not include televisions, which are the focus of Straubhaar's studies, photography and photographic apparatuses serve essential roles. *Sin nombre* opens with a shot of an autumnal landscape, filled with auburn leaves and trees. The camera tracks slowly towards the tree, before we cut to a reverse shot of Casper. As brooding music swells on the soundtrack, the image, improbably large on Casper's wall, suggests a dreamscape: this place, specified in Fukunaga's script as being an image of Texas, is where Casper dreams of going.[19] As much seems confirmed when Casper later tells his girlfriend, Martha Marlen (Diana García), that he wants to accompany her to Six Flags, an amusement park between Dallas and Fort Worth, with the amusement park suggesting the desire for a spectacular, leisure-filled existence in the USA.

Casper also possesses a digital camera. This he keeps in secret, since no doubt his fellow Mara Salvatruche gang members would demand that he share it with them—as I shall discuss below. Notably, it is on this camera that Casper keeps videos of Martha Marlen, the latter's existence as an image suggesting that she, too, exists as much as a fantasy as a real person—while the resonance of her name, Martha Marlen, with the gang that Casper flees, the Mara, also hints at how she might represent a fantasy escape from gang life. As much is also suggested when Casper looks at these images after killing Lil Mago, having boarded the train with Sayra, Horacio, and Orlando at Tapachula. This he does as revenge for Lil Mago's murder of Martha Marlen; the gang refuses their relationship, which now can exist only in images and memories. Although he initially intends to leave the train at Tonalá, Casper remains on board and finally has to give up the camera in order to pay Leche (Héctor Jiménez) to take Sayra across the Río Grande and into the USA. In other words, where the images of Texas and Martha Marlen signify freedom for Casper, the latter gives away the camera and his own chances of crossing into the USA in order to buy "freedom" altruistically for Sayra.

Casper is not the only character for whom photographs connote a sense of freedom. Sayra's father, Horacio, is in Tegucigalpa at the start of the film because he has been deported from the USA. Having left Sayra in Honduras years earlier to grow up with her grandmother, Horacio now carries with him and repeatedly looks at a photograph of the new family that he has created in New Jersey. In *Sin nombre*, then, photography is associated with the supposed better life that the USA enables.

There are similar associations between photography and freedom in *La jaula de oro*. While en route through Mexico, we see Juan and Chauk pose for a photo session in iconic costumes borrowed from the western: Juan is dressed as a cowboy, while Chauk is dressed as an Indian. Quemada-Díez would seem to suggest at this moment that the migration of Latin American peoples (here, from Guatemala) to the USA is influenced by the dream of becoming cinematic (the western as "cinema"), while also reminding us of how today's migration is perhaps no different from that of the initial white settlers in North America. Indeed, as the UNODC report reminds us, "[t]he USA is a nation of immigrants, and its receptivity to immigration has long been one of the country's strengths."[20] In also reminding us of this history, *La jaula de oro* suggests how a nation built upon migration (and the genocide of indigenous populations) has gone on to preclude so many migrants from legally crossing its borders—with the illegal migration industry also resulting in numerous deaths, including those of indigenous Americans like Chauk. Furthermore, that it is a photograph for which the two pose is again significant, as we shall see below.

Galeano writes about how Latin America is

> condemned to suffer the technology of the powerful, which attacks and removes natural raw materials, and is incapable of creating its own technology to sustain and defend its own development. The transplantation of the advanced countries' technology not only involves cultural—and, most definitely, economic—subordination. It has also been shown, after four and a half centuries' experience of proliferating modernized oases amid deserts of backwardness and ignorance, to resolve none of the problems of underdevelopment.[21]

Although Galeano was, as mentioned, writing in 1971, this quotation serves our analysis of *Sin nombre* and *La jaula de oro* since the photographic apparatus also reveals aspects of cultural subordination. That is, the photograph represents the desire to advance economically by migrating to the USA—meaning that more human resources leave the "periphery" of Latin America, which in turn reaffirms the centrality of the USA. None the less, the very stillness of the photographic image here becomes important.

For photography involves still images, while life itself is moving and time-based (and thus more akin to cinema). This is not a question of realism (I am not suggesting that since life and cinema are both moving, cinema is more "realistic" than photography). Rather, the very stillness of the photograph points to the impossibility of the migratory dreams that the characters in both films pursue. That is, Casper's photograph of Texas, Horacio's photograph of his New Jersey family, and the photograph of Juan and Chauk in western costumes all represent a desire for movement in the form of migration, and yet paradoxically they are still images—suggesting that this desire for movement/migration is impossible and will not be realized. This tension between stillness and movement can be seen elsewhere in *Sin nombre* and *La jaula de oro*, as we shall see presently through an analysis of transport in the films.[22]

Precarious Transport

Since they address migration, it is not surprising that transport plays a key role in both *Sin nombre* and *La jaula de oro*. Indeed, even if most characters do not reach their destination, their lives are defined none the less by movement—as they head from Honduras, Guatemala, and Mexico towards the USA. We see travel by foot, by bicycle (Casper in the first moments of *Sin nombre*), in cars and vans (in particular Smiley as he tracks down Casper after the death of Lil Mago), by boats and rafts (across from Guatemala to Mexico, and across from Mexico to the USA), and, of course, in, or rather on, trains, specifically the freight trains that are referred to by migrants as *la bestia*.[23]

Trains unify the space and time of a nation since the rail network defines national boundaries and demands universal time. Trains thus also naturalize the concept of the nation—even if the latter is what Benedict Anderson would call an "imagined community," in that what unites a people is no inherent, human quality, but rather technologies and the management of time and space.[24] Furthermore, Wolfgang Schivelbusch memorably suggests that trains induce "panoramic vision"—a kind of vision not unlike that induced by the cinema, in which the movement of the images presented to the traveler and/or viewer is so fast that details blur and are missed.[25] As is well known, one of the first films ever made is the Lumière brothers' *L'Arrivée d'un train en gare de La Ciotat/Arrival of the Train* (France, 1895), reaffirming this link between cinema and the railway, which both offer a rush of images to viewers/passengers. This stands in stark contrast to photography, in which the stillness of the image gives the viewer time to peruse it at length (even if the image is blurred because taken while the camera was moving).

Given the migratory experiences of their protagonists, the still images of *La jaula de oro* and *Sin nombre* take on a further layer of meaning. For while they may suggest the impossibility of leading a "cinematic" life in the USA (the "home" of cinema), the photographs also symbolize a dream of stasis/stability that provides an escape from the nomadism of economic hardship. This nomadism is underlined by the prominence of transport in the films. But the transport, and in particular the train, also carries a further layer of meaning, for the movement that the train enables played a key role in the creation of the USA—unifying its territory, allowing its population to travel, just as the moving images of cinema have allowed the USA to achieve a cultural "centrality" across the globe. In this way, the railway and cinematic movement are key to the establishment of the contemporary world order (America as center), and yet the protagonists of *Sin nombre* and *La jaula de oro* use the railroad as a means to seek stasis/stability in the USA. For this reason, it is meaningful that the characters in both films do not ride in the train so much as on the *bestia*; the panorama is not something to observe through a window, but something with which to interact and to experience, as evidenced by objects thrown at and from the train, from fruit to stones—particularly in *Sin nombre*. The train journey of the films' protagonists is thus defined not by luxury, but by precarity, as characters fall from the train and die in both films.

In effect, the train comes to be a kind of literalization of the precarious, or what Giorgio Agamben might term the "bare" lives led by the films' characters.[26] That is, the protagonists of *Sin nombre* and *La jaula de oro* are disposable human beings who are physically alive, but whose lives barely have any worth from the perspective of capitalist society, since they are excluded, unable to contribute for lack of opportunity, and thus always close to death. Since Casper's photograph of Texas, Horacio's photograph of his New Jersey family and the images of Juan and Chauk in iconic western costumes suggest a desire for liberation, we get a sense here that photography itself connotes liberation from these bare lives through its stillness, which contrasts with the constant movement of life on the *bestia*. Moreover, the stillness of the photograph suggests how the "golden dream" of life in the USA has become naturalized; like a photograph, this ideology is unchanging and constant—in sharp contrast to their lives. The mistranslation of the title of *La jaula de oro* here becomes significant. For, what to Western audiences is referred to as "the golden dream," suggesting that successful migration to the USA would involve the fulfillment of a fantasy, to Spanish-speaking audiences is more literally a "golden cage." That is, dreams of gold (wealth and riches) in the USA are, in fact, a trap that can lead to death. The mistranslation thus has an ideological component: it reaffirms to English-speaking audiences that coming to America is the dream of those who live south of its borders, which in turn reinforces its own sense of centrality. Meanwhile, the film to Spanish-speaking audiences critiques the migrations of Central Americans to the USA as a "cage"; like being trapped in a static photograph, the characters are trapped in a static ideology of (personal) liberation. The migrants in *Sin nombre* and *La jaula de oro* are thus not only victims, but also proponents of the very ideology that Dussel aims to critique in his work—namely, that the USA is indeed the center and Latin America merely the periphery.

If *Trade* tentatively has an optimistic ending, in that Adriana is rescued and reunited with her family in Mexico, *Sin nombre* and *La jaula de oro* are far more bleak. In the former film, Sayra's arrival in the USA is a muted victory at best, as she wanders in a somewhat discombobulated fashion around southern Texas. Meanwhile, in *La jaula de oro* we see Jorge sweeping up off-cuts in a meat factory—the visual association being that he is not quite a human being, but just "meat" for the capitalist system to feed on. The "stillness"/stability that the characters seek thus remains an impossibility and even suggests morbidity, as reflected by the many migrants' deaths in these films, as well as by the likelihood that, without papers, Jorge's job in the meat factory is informal, precarious, and beneath a living wage; that is,

Jorge is not "living" but somehow "dead." The pursuit of life at an American theme park (America as theme park) is not a dream, but a cage—a cage that, like the photograph, equates to death.

Now, there is a history of theorists who equate photography with death, André Bazin and Roland Barthes being prominent among them. For Bazin, photography is, in some senses, a preservation of life after death, while also being more "objective" than, say, painting, and thus in some senses "determining"/fixing the reality that it depicts (rather than leaving it open and mutable).[27] Meanwhile, Barthes argues that photography, at times, also bring the dead back to life—at moments when it offers to us a *punctum* effect: a person who is absent (in Barthes's case, his dead mother) suddenly is as if back again, "puncturing" our reality, as it were.[28] Where both of these authors see photography as somehow transcending death, though, my point here is that photography is death.

We can turn to *Who is Dayani Cristal?* to clarify this point. The film combines a reconstruction by Mexican film star Gael García Bernal of the migration of Dilcy Yohan Sandres Martínez (whose body was discovered with the words Dayani Cristal tattooed across his chest) from Tegucigalpa to the USA, while also documenting the process of identifying the bodies of migrants found in the desert. Photographs are prominent in the film—but these are typically associated with death, particularly images of Yohan's body that circulate for people to identify. Bianca Micheletti, who works at the Honduran Foreign Affairs Office, at one point explains how migrants to the USA are dehumanized when their illegality takes precedence over their humanity, while a friend at Yohan's funeral speaks of how the USA invests billions of dollars in an inanimate wall to keep migrants, out rather than in human beings. Finally, Robin Reineke of the Colibrí Center for Human Rights explains how "someone had a dream [to come to the USA], but ended up a number, a statistic." Or, we might add, they ended up a photograph—with the photograph thus combining and showing the links between the idea of the "golden dream," death, the inanimate, and, in Yohan's case, anonymity/invisibility. It is only the movie itself (movie because involving moving and not still images) that gives Yohan a name, in the process bringing him "back to life" *à la* Bazin—even if this is in the form of Gael García Bernal.

To return to *Sin nombre*, it is not surprising that names and naming also play a key role. The Mara Salvatruche characters whom we see all adopt nicknames above and beyond their "true" identity: Casper's "real" name is Willy, and Smiley's is Benito. But where Benito happily becomes "Smiley," Casper wants really to be Willy. This is not a desire to "return" to a "true identity." That Willy only employs his "real" name when talking to Martha Marlen and to Sayra suggests rather that his identity as Willy is linked to the dream of reaching America, which is sublimated by these women, of whom he takes (moving) pictures and for whom he sacrifices his camera. Willy is, however, impotent (he significantly, though post-coitally, loses an erection early on in the film)—and his identity as Casper makes this clear, for Willy's Mara name is also that of the popular, "friendly" ghost Casper: connected as he is to photography and a desire to reach the USA, he is also, in some senses, already dead.

THE MARA SALVATRUCHE AND COLLECTIVE ACTION

The enforced nomadism of those living in Tapachula is made clear in *Sin nombre* through the sequences set in the liminal zone of La Bombilla, an area around the city's railway tracks where the Mara have taken control. People only pass through the space, as symbolized by a transvestite water seller whose own liminal status between masculinity and femininity reflects the nomadic nature of the area. Only informal economies exist in La Bombilla, much as there are no opportunities for work in Tegucigalpa or Guatemala City; migration—traveling for work—is therefore the only option, even if this migration reaffirms the USA as center.

Tellingly, however, this reaffirmation of the USA's "centrality" brings with it notions of personal possessions and personal liberation, and a neoliberal ethos of self-improvement ahead of any collective endeavor. If *Trade* focuses on the heroic American white male, often framed in close-up and with fast-paced editing, *Sin nombre* and *La jaula de oro* feature significantly more frequent long shots, which in turn involve slower editing since there is more information for the viewer to parse in each shot, in particular those shots that give a sense of place and/or of crowds. This is especially true of the shots of people huddled atop the *bestia*. In other words, both films show multitudes of people, suggesting a world of collectivity instead of individuality.

However, as the numbers of migrants diminish over the course of the films—with each featuring only one protagonist who makes it to the USA—we also get a sense of how the journey north involves the adoption of an individualist mentality, with migration transformed into a competition where there can be only one "winner."

At the outset of *Sin nombre*, Willy/Casper declares, when others try to use it, that his camera is "mine." Believing in personal possessions, it is fitting that Casper is already thinking of leaving the Mara Salvatruche and heading north. It is both tragic and significant, then, that it is in giving up his camera that he allows Sayra to travel across the border: Casper demonstrates selflessness instead of selfishness, but in so doing, he also denies himself the possibility of entering the USA, where the self is sovereign. However, if Casper undertakes this transition from selfishness to selflessness (with his lack of a fixed identity/self also suggested in his multiple names?), it is interesting that he does this in contrast to his gang life in the Mara.

What follows is not intended as a romantic rewriting of the Mara as a progressive group; their criminal connections are well documented, as is the gang's involvement in human trafficking, child prostitution, extortion, murder, and of course drugs. None the less, there are ways in which the Mara can be understood as adopting a collective sense of identity, as opposed to an individualist one, a collective identity that runs counter, and thus is logically in opposition, to the individualist identities that are central to the ideology of the neoliberal north.

Sometimes referred to as MS-13, the Mara Salvatruche originated in Los Angeles in the 1980s, having since become a transnational institution, with cells, generally located in marginal urban areas, extending from the USA down to Central America.[29] The transnational reach of the organization is seen in *Sin nombre* when Casper introduces Salvadoran gang members to Smiley while touring their base in Tapachula. The inclusively transnational, as opposed to exclusively national, identity of the Mara connotes a preliminary collective identity, which is also made clear by their rejection of personal possessions. For example, when Smiley sees a *chimba*—a form of pipe gun— in the gang's den, Casper tells him to put it down, explaining that what is "from the Mara is for the Mara." It is thus against Mara code when Casper calls his camera "mine" and it is for this reason that he wants to keep it a secret. Furthermore, Lil Mago diverts funds for *mareros* in prison—and in Fukunaga's script he also provides medicine for a gang member's mother.[30] Forasmuch as being a violent gang with links to terrorism, then, there are symptoms in the Mara—as depicted in *Sin nombre* at least—that suggest the desire for an alternative (if strikingly masculine) organization of society, a desire for a different society that is perhaps necessarily illegal, even if it originated in Los Angeles, the city where the individualist ethos of the USA is produced most visibly as cinema.

We also locate this desire for a different society and perhaps even a different human in the gang members' tattoos, especially those on their faces. The members of the Mara have literally transformed their physical appearance from "normal" humans to something new, or "other"—while at the same time painting over their faces, which is the part of a person's appearance that typically differentiates them from other people. This simultaneous assertion and denial of otherness remind us of Dussel's paradoxical suggestion that the contemporary world system has seen otherness deprived of its very otherness and incorporated into a system of the same: "[t]he conquests of Latin America . . . are the dominating ideological expansion of 'the same' that assassinated 'the other' and totalizes 'the other' in 'the same.'"[31]

To resist this deprivation of otherness, one must reassert a different kind of otherness, one that Dussel also links to the human face. In contrast to the homogenized appearance of Westerners, who not only look alike but also seek never to change by seeking never to grow up nor to grow old, Dussel argues that

> the withered face of the Bedouin of the desert, the furrowed and darkened skin of the peasant, the poisoned lungs of the miner whose face never sees the sun—these "apparently" ugly faces, almost horrible for the system, are the primary, the future, the popular beauty.[32]

The Mara—with Lil Mago's tattooed and "ugly" face as its figurehead—can thus be read as equally "horrible for the system," but also symbolic of dissatisfaction with, and of the contradictions internal to, that self-same system of globalized/homogenized neoliberal capital. It is not that we ought to or can condone the violent crimes of the Mara, which indeed resorts to violence and alternative economies since its members do not have access to the "regular" economy—as is made clear by the historical spread of the Mara into Central America as a result of the literal deportation/exclusion of gang members from the USA.[33] None the less, we can recognize in those marked/tattooed and "other" faces a desire for "popular" change.

What is more, Dussel argues that imperialism leads to the consideration of faces as masks; one does not see the other as a person, but as an "instrument"—or whatever opportunity they can provide in the services of reinforcing the centrality of the center.[34] The tattooed faces of the Mara in *Sin nombre* bring conscious attention to the mask that replaces their actual faces in the eyes of the imperialist powers, which otherwise make of migrants (and local workers) forced laborers and "tools"—as per Jorge in the meat factory at the end of *La jaula de oro*.[35] In effect, the Mara, having not been recognized as beings, opt consciously to become what Dussel might call "non-beings."[36]

In this idea of "non-being," a state perhaps even more abject than that of "bare life," we understand the importance of the film's title, *Sin nombre* ("nameless"). Even if the Mara choose new names for their members, the title *Sin nombre* posits that identity as malleable, and that in the contemporary world, most Latin Americans are, in the eyes of Westerners, and perhaps themselves, nameless. As per the title of the third film that I have analyzed: who *is* Dayani Cristal?

In the end credits of *La jaula de oro* we see the names of the real migrants who participated in the film's making. This naming of the film's participants subverts the domination and "namelessness" of Latin America and Latin Americans (likewise, we discover at the end of Marc Silver's documentary that Dayani Cristal is the name of Yohan's daughter). What is more, *Sin nombre* and *La jaula de oro* in themselves subvert the domination of Hollywood cinema, giving a "name" to Mexican, or perhaps more subtly, a transnational Mexican cinema. I should like to end this chapter, then, with a brief consideration of the relationship between Hollywood and Mexican film.

The Mexican Invasion of Hollywood

Writing in *The Hollywood Reporter*, reviewer Neil Young is relatively dismissive of *La jaula de oro*, comparing it to *Sin nombre*, the success of which he justifies through Cary Fukunaga's subsequent invitation to work in "Hollywood" (even though Fukunaga was born in Los Angeles), where he made the (relatively un-Hollywood) adaptation of *Jane Eyre* (UK/USA, 2011).[37] By considering the Hollywood career as the "golden dream" of any filmmaker, Young perhaps betrays his own sense of Hollywood as filmmaking center. None the less, Young also accuses *La jaula de oro* of being a film constructed for film festivals (it is another in "the endless flow of similar consciousness-raising tales clogging the world's film-festival circuit").[38] If this accusation stands, then both films—*Sin nombre* as Hollywood calling card and *La jaula de oro* as festival fodder—pander to the center–periphery distinction between Hollywood and other cinemas.

To speak of Mexican cinema more generally, the high-profile migration of the so-called "three amigos" (Alejandro González Iñárritu, Guillermo del Toro, and Alfonso Cuarón) from Mexico to the USA would suggest something similar: a continuation of the migration of highly skilled workers from Latin America to the USA, as identified by Galeano.[39] However, we can also read this migration of filmmaking talent in a different way, for this migration signals the "Mexicanization" of Hollywood, as much as it does the Hollywoodization of Mexican cinema (which is not even to consider the recent international successes of other Mexican directors, such as Carlos Reygadas and Amat Escalante, among others). That is, under globalization, the film industry is, like the world depicted in both films considered here, truly transnational (as it perhaps has been all along, as suggested by Alan Williams).[40]

In this way, transnational Mexican productions like *Sin nombre* and *La jaula de oro* point to a world of collective, as opposed to exclusively national, cinema. It is a world in which cinema can paradoxically give a face to the otherwise (and at times willfully) faceless or unseen members of society. Included among these are the nomadic migrant who dreams of a "cinematic" life in the USA, the home of cinema, but whose dream is, in fact, not a cinematic life of free movement, but a static cage, as illustrated by the role played in *Sin nombre* and *La jaula de oro* by photographs. The stillness of the photograph suggests a desire for economic stability, while also conveying the impossibility of realizing that desire, the pursuit of which often results in failure and death. Not passengers in the train, but riders on the *bestia*, the migrants move because of economic instability, not because of economic independence. They lead precarious, "bare" lives, with death a constant presence. None the less, the movement around the world of films like *Sin nombre* and *La jaula de oro* may change this situation, helping us to realize that humanity is everywhere and not just in the "center" where individualist and heroic cinema is typically produced.[41]

Notes

1. The initial quotation and the figure of 450,000 to 650,000 attempts to cross the border illegally from Mexico to the USA is taken from the United States Government Accountability Office, *Illegal Immigration: Border-Crossing Deaths Have Doubled Since 1995; Border Patrol's Efforts to Prevent Deaths Have Not Been Fully Evaluated* (August 2006), 42, available at <http://www.gao.gov/new.items/d06770.pdf> (last accessed December 1, 2014). The figure of 350,000 is extrapolated from the Pew Hispanic Center, "Modes of Entry for the Unauthorised Migrant Population" (May 22, 2006), available at <https://www.pewresearch.org/hispanic/2006/05/22/modes-of-entry-for-the-unauthorized-migrant-population/> (last accessed December 1, 2014).. The figure of 3 million is taken from the United Nations Office on Drugs and Crime, *The Globalization of Crime: A Transnational Organized Crime Threat Assessment* (Vienna: United Nations, 2010), 66, available at <https://www.unodc.org/documents/data-and-analysis/tocta/TOCTA_Report_2010_low_res.pdf> (last accessed December 1, 2014). It should be worth noting, however, that when I presented an early version of this chapter at the Department of Spanish and Portuguese, University of California, Los Angeles (UCLA), various respondents suggested that the UNODC figures are inaccurate. I simply cite the figures as given.
2. UNODC, *The Globalization of Crime*, 65.
3. UNODC, *The Globalization of Crime*, 62.
4. See Amnesty International, "Irregular Migrants in Mexico: Ten Urgent Measures to Save Lives," *Amnesty International USA* (March 12, 2013), available at <http://www.amnestyusa.org/research/reports/irregular-migrants-in-mexico-ten-urgent-measures-to-save-lives?page=show> (last accessed December 1, 2014).
5. Tracy Wilkinson, "Exploitation Awaits Migrant Children on Mexico's Southern Edge," *Los Angeles Times* (August 2, 2014), available at <https://www.latimes.com/world/mexico-americas/la-fg-mexico-migrants-20140802-story.html> (last accessed December 10, 2020).
6. See UNODC, *The Globalization of Crime*, 59 and 65–6.
7. Director Diego Quemada-Díez made mention of Galeano's book as an inspiration for his film at a question and answer session after a screening of *La jaula de oro* at the 2013 London Film Festival. See also Eduardo Galeano, *The Open Veins of Latin America: Five Centuries of the Pillage of a Continent*, trans. Cedric Belfrage (London: Serpent's Tail, 2009).
8. Galeano, *The Open Veins of Latin America*, 245.
9. See Aníbal Quijano, "Coloniality of Power, Eurocentrism, and Latin America," *Nepantla: Views from South*, 1, no. 3 (2000), 533–80; Walter Mignolo, "The Geopolitics of Knowledge and the Colonial Difference," *South Atlantic Quarterly*, 101, no. 1 (Winter 2002), 57–96.
10. Quijano, "Coloniality of Power," 541.
11. Quijano, "Coloniality of Power," 539.
12. Quijano, "Coloniality of Power," 539.
13. Enrique Dussel, *Philosophy of Liberation*, trans. Aquilina Martinez and Christine Morkovsky (Eugene, OR: Wipf & Stock 1985), 8.

14. Cary Jôji Fukunaga is an American director, as he attests in an interview. See Edward Douglas, "Exclusive: Filmmaker Cary Fukunaga on *Sin nombre*," *ComingSoon.net*, March 16, 2009, available at <http://www.comingsoon.net/movies/features/53546-exclusive-filmmaker-cary-fukunaga-on-sin-nombre> (last accessed November 22, 2014). Meanwhile, Diego Quemada-Díez was born in Spain, started his film career working with Ken Loach on *Land and Freedom* (UK/Spain/Germany/Italy, 1995), and then moved latterly to Mexico. See Paul MacInnes, "*The Golden Dream*: 'I wanted to convey brotherhood beyond races, beyond nationalities,'" *The Guardian*, June 21, 2014, <http://www.theguardian.com/film/2014/jun/21/diego-quemada-diez-the-golden-dream> (last accessed November 22, 2014).
15. Dussel, *Philosophy of Liberation*, 91.
16. Dussel, *Philosophy of Liberation*, 51.
17. Joseph Straubhaar, "Brazil: The Role of the State in World Television," in *Media and Globalisation: Why the State Matters*, ed. Nancy Morris and Silvio Waisbord (Lanham, MD: Rowman and Littlefield, 2001), 135.
18. Joseph D. Straubhaar, *World Television: From Global to Local* (London: SAGE, 2007), 6.
19. Cary Fukunaga, *Sin nombre* (English version of script), 2007, available at <https://www.raindance.org/scripts/Sin%20Nombre.pdf>, 1.
20. UNODC, *The Globalization of Crime*, 60.
21. Galeano, *Open Veins of Latin America*, 244.
22. A clear contention might be that the images that Casper keeps of Martha Marlen on his camera are moving images, not photographs. That Martha Marlen dies, however, suggests equally a kind of impossibility: she moves in images, but not in real life. Indeed, her "cinematic" existence might be seen as demanding her death: movement is not permitted from the periphery to the center.
23. See Wilkinson, "Exploitation Awaits Migrant Children."
24. Benedict Anderson, *Imagined Communities: Reflections on the Origins and Spread of Nationalism* (London: Verso, 1983).
25. Wolfgang Schivelbusch, *The Railway Journey: The Industrialization of Time and Space in the 19th Century* (Berkeley: University of California Press, 1986).
26. Giorgio Agamben, *Homo Sacer: Sovereign Power and Bare Life*, trans. Daniel Heller-Roazen (Stanford: Stanford University Press, 1998).
27. See André Bazin, *What is Cinema? Volume 1*, trans. Hugh Gray (Berkeley: University of California Press, 1967), 9–16.
28. Roland Barthes, *Camera Lucida: Reflections on Photography*, trans. Richard Howard (London: Vintage, 1993).
29. Sonja Wolf, "Mara Salvatrucha: The Most Dangerous Street Gang in the Americas?," *Latin American Politics and Society*, 54, no. 1 (2012): 65–99.
30. Fukunaga, *Sin nombre*, 37.
31. Dussel, *Philosophy of Liberation*, 52.
32. Dussel, *Philosophy of Liberation*, 44.
33. Wolf, "Mara Salvatrucha," 67.
34. Dussel, *Philosophy of Liberation*, 54.
35. Dussel, *Philosophy of Liberation*, 54.

36. Dussel, *Philosophy of Liberation*, 14.
37. Neil Young, "The Golden Cage (La Jaula de Oro): Cannes Review," *The Hollywood Reporter*, May 22, 2013, available at <http://www.hollywoodreporter.com/review/golden-cage-la-jaula-de-527318> (last accessed December 1, 2014).
38. Young, "The Golden Cage."
39. For a study of the "three amigos," see Deborah Shaw, *The Three Amigos: The Transnational Filmmaking of Guillermo Del Toro, Alejandro González Iñárritu, and Alfonso Cuarón* (Manchester: Manchester University Press, 2013).
40. Alan Williams, "Introduction," in *Film and Nationalism*, ed. Alan Williams (New Brunswick, NJ: Rutgers University Press, 2002), 1.
41. This chapter was produced as part of "TRANSIT: Transnationality at Large—The Transnational Dimension of Hispanic Culture in the 20th and 21st Centuries," a major project funded by the European Commission's International Research Staff Exchange Scheme (IRSES)/Marie Curie Actions, and involving the Universidad Nacional de Córdoba, Universität Konstanz, UCLA, the Universidade de São Paulo, the Universidad Nacional Autónoma de México, the University of Roehampton, London, the Université Blaise Pascal Clermont-Ferrand 2, and KU Leuven.

Works Cited

Agamben, Giorgio. *Homo Sacer: Sovereign Power and Bare Life*, trans. Daniel Heller-Roazen. Stanford: Stanford University Press, 1998.

Amnesty International. "Irregular Migrants in Mexico: Ten Urgent Measures to Save Lives." *Amnesty International USA*, March 15, 2013, <http://www.amnestyusa.org/research/reports/irregular-migrants-in-mexico-ten-urgent-measures-to-save-lives?page=show> (last accessed December 1, 2014).

Anderson, Benedict. *Imagined Communities: Reflections on the Origins and Spread of Nationalism*. London: Verso, 1983.

Barthes, Roland. *Camera Lucida: Reflections on Photography*, trans. Richard Howard. London: Vintage, 1993.

Bazin, André. *What is Cinema? Volume 1*, trans. Hugh Gray. Berkeley: University of California Press, 1967.

Douglas, Edward. "Exclusive: Filmmaker Cary Fukunaga on *Sin nombre*." *ComingSoon.net*, March 16, 2009, <http://www.comingsoon.net/movies/features/53546-exclusive-filmmaker-cary-fukunaga-on-sin-nombre> (last accessed November 22, 2014).

Dussel, Enrique. *Philosophy of Liberation*, trans. Aquilina Martinez and Christine Morkovsky. Eugene, OR: Wipf & Stock, 1985.

Fukunaga, Cary. *Sin nombre* (English version of script), 2007, <https://www.raindance.org/scripts/Sin%20Nombre.pdf> (last accessed May 30, 2014).

Galeano, Eduardo. *The Open Veins of Latin America: Five Centuries of the Pillage of a Continent*, trans. Cedric Belfrage. London: Serpent's Tail, 2009.

MacInnes, Paul. "*The Golden Dream*: 'I wanted to convey brotherhood beyond races, beyond nationalities,'" *The Guardian*, June 21, 2014, <http://www.theguardian.com/film/2014/jun/21/diego-quemada-diez-the-golden-dream> (last accessed November 22, 2014).

Mignolo, Walter. "The Geopolitics of Knowledge and the Colonial Difference." *South Atlantic Quarterly* 101, no. 1 (Winter 2002): 57–96.
Pew Hispanic Center. "Modes of Entry for the Unauthorised Migrant Population." May 22, 2006, <https://www.pewresearch.org/hispanic/2006/05/22/modes-of-entry-for-the-unauthorized-migrant-population/> (last accessed December 1, 2014).
Quijano, Ánibal. "Coloniality of Power, Eurocentrism, and Latin America." *Nepantla: Views from South* 1, no. 3 (2000) 533–80.
Schivelbusch, Wolfgang. *The Railway Journey: The Industrialization of Time and Space in the 19th Century*. Berkeley: University of California Press, 1986.
Shaw, Deborah. *The Three Amigos: The Transnational Filmmaking of Guillermo Del Toro, Alejandro González Iñárritu, and Alfonso Cuarón*. Manchester: Manchester University Press, 2013.
Straubhaar, Joseph. "Brazil: The Role of the State in World Television." In *Media and Globalisation: Why the State Matters*, ed. Nancy Morris and Silvio Waisbord, 133–53. Lanham, MD: Rowman and Littlefield, 2001.
Straubhaar, Joseph D. *World Television: From Global to Local*. London: SAGE, 2007.
United Nations Office on Drugs and Crime. *The Globalization of Crime: A Transnational Organized Crime Threat Assessment*. Vienna: United Nations, 2010, <https://www.unodc.org/documents/data-and-analysis/tocta/TOCTA_Report_2010_low_res.pdf> (last accessed December 1, 2014).
United States Government Accountability Office. *Illegal Immigration: Border-Crossing Deaths Have Doubled Since 1995; Border Patrol's Efforts to Prevent Deaths Have Not Been Fully Evaluated*. August 2006, <http://www.gao.gov/new.items/d06770.pdf> (last accessed December 1, 2014).
Wilkinson, Tracy. "Exploitation Awaits Migrant Children on Mexico's Southern Edge." *Los Angeles Times*, August 2, 2014, <https://www.latimes.com/world/mexico-americas/la-fg-mexico-migrants-20140802-story.html> (last accessed December 10, 2014).
Williams, Alan. "Introduction." In *Film and Nationalism*, ed. Alan Williams, 1–22. New Brunswick, NJ: Rutgers University Press, 2002.
Wolf, Sonja. "Mara Salvatrucha: The Most Dangerous Street Gang in the Americas?" *Latin American Politics and Society* 54, no. 1 (2012): 65–99.
Young, Neil. "The Golden Cage (La Jaula de Oro): Cannes Review," *The Hollywood Reporter*, May 22, 2013, <http://www.hollywoodreporter.com/review/golden-cage-la-jaula-de-527318> (last accessed December 1, 2014).

6. JAPANESE IMMIGRANT IDENTITIES ON THE BRAZILIAN SCREEN: *GAIJIN: OS CAMINHOS DA LIBERDADE* (TIZUKA YAMASAKI, 1983) AND *CORAÇÕES SUJOS* (VICENTE AMORIM, 2011)

Frank Jacob

Introduction

Brazil in general, and the state of São Paulo in particular, are probably the most important regions when one considers global areas of Japanese emigration. The immigrants from Japan who wanted to start a new life in the South American country since the late 1880s, however, were confronted not only with a foreign environment, but also with a stronger perception of their own identity as Japanese; this would oftentimes be experienced as a disadvantageous barrier to acculturation within their new sphere of living.[1] Brazil was not the only target of Japanese immigration in the Americas during the twentieth century,[2] but, as American historian Miriam Kingsberg Kadia highlights, "[i]t was in Brazil, home of the largest Japanese diaspora in the Western Hemisphere, that the criteria of national membership were most contested."[3] In Brazil, Japanese immigrants were torn between a nationalist and sometimes mythical homeland—that is, Japan—and a nationalist host state whose rulers were eager to force the Asian immigrants into Brazilian citizenship by extinguishing their Japanese identity. While the Westernization of Japanese emigrants was considered a success for Japan's modernization and the acceptability of its citizens as equal citizens to those of the Western world,[4] the 1930s and 1940s were determined by a Japanese nationalism that claimed superiority and challenged the existent world order, which had been established in the aftermath of World War I.[5] Since 1908, when Japanese immigration to Brazil began, the identity of this particular immigrant community changed from that of plantation workers in the Brazilian coffee industry, who were supposed to replace slaves in the plantation system, to that of landowners who would dominate the cotton industry of the country in later years due to their ties to Japan. From the mid-1920s, Japanese emigration corporations (*imin gaisha*) also prepared the immigration of thousands of Japanese, who, once in Brazil, would continue to live in relatively remote and homogenous communities.[6]

The majority of Brazilians have remained ignorant of the important history of the Japanese in their country. However, in recent decades, films have begun to address different periods of Japanese–Brazilian memory, confronting larger audiences with the forgotten years of Japanese immigration to Brazil. It must be emphasized that many depictions of the Japanese experience in the South American country present memories—a reimagined history, rather than actual history on the cinema screen[7]—but, as Leslie L. Marsh has emphasized, "[i]n this process of interpreting the past we find the possibility for the emergence of new understandings of citizenship."[8] The *Nikkeijin*, as individual members of the Japanese diaspora are referred to, redefine their own history by such a commemoration, and the "historical episodes that literary and filmic works choose to memorialize and, equally important, those they try to erase are reliable indicators of a *Nikkei* public memory, even if it is still fragmented and partial."[9] Nowadays, the role of the Japanese community in Brazil and its role within global migration trends or issues are twofold, as there are *Nikkeijin* in Brazil, but at the same time, more and more young Brazilians of Japanese descent are emigrating to their ancestral homeland, Japan, where they are referred to as *dekasegi*. Some episodes that seem particularly important for commemoration by the Japanese community in Brazil are related to the establishment of Brazil's *Nikkei* community in the early 1900s, as well as to World War II and the early postwar years, which must be understood as "a period of identitarian uncertainty."[10] In a time period in which ultranationalist feelings within the immigrant community were stimulated by the actions of the home country and the host country alike, the ethnic heritage, as it was kept alive in the Japanese immigrant community, would also "function as a defense mechanism or a safe refuge where individuals feel protected from outside dangers"; hence, at the same time, "these communities [would] also become a site of hierarchical control or a prison house where individuals are repressed."[11]

This chapter will take a look at two episodes of Japanese immigration and how they are depicted in Brazilian migration films for a mainstream public. The first one is *Gaijin: Os Caminhos da Liberdade* (Gaijin: Roads to Freedom, 1980),[12] a French-funded production that was written and directed by Tizuka Yamasaki, who, through it, recounts early Japanese immigration and the immigrants' identity as foreigners (*gaijin*). The film was released at the Cannes Film Festival in May 1980 and was the first milestone in the career of Yamasaki, who is considered to be "one of Brazil's most important cinema personalities"[13] and "is certainly the most famous . . . Nikkei filmmaker"[14] in the South American country.[15] *Gaijin* was the female director's first feature film, and it addresses the historical episode of Japanese immigration to Brazil from the perspective of a young Japanese woman. The film proffers information essential to both this chapter's and this volume's discourse because, to quote historian Jeffrey Lesser, it

> is perhaps the only Brazilian film widely remembered as including Nikkei, and it is one of the few Brazilian films widely remembered as including Nikkei, and it is one of the few Brazilian mainstream movies in which an ethnic minority is both the focus and treated sympathetically.[16]

While revealing memories of the *Nikkei*, *Gaijin* argues for "racial harmony and hybridity in a new, more tolerant Brazil,"[17] and was therefore able to gain attention and provoke positive reactions among those who watched it. *Gaijin*, like Yamasaki's other works, also "represent[s] significant departures in style and substance" and is one example of the new cinema of Brazil's 1980s, when female directors were eventually able to make their voices heard and provide new perspectives on the big screens of Brazilian cinema. In contrast to Brazil's Cinema Novo (1954–72), Yamasaki not only showed emotions but also used the leading female role to make political and activist statements alike—this approach modeling and demanding more input and involvement from women.[18] The film as such is consequently not just a simple commemoration of the past but, as Leslie L. Marsh puts it, "is, thus, very much engaged with challenging hegemonic notions of Brazilian cultural identity rooted in the past as much as it is directed at inventing a new sociability for the future."[19] *Gaijin* ultimately not only tells the story of a Japanese woman who emancipates herself during her experiences as an immigrant from Japan in early twentieth-century Brazil, but also shows a change in her self-identification, turning a Japanese immigrant into a self-confident and strong Brazilian citizen. This transition is also linked autobiographically to the personal history of the director, who, as the first Brazilian–Japanese woman director, presented such a perspective in Brazilian cinema with authenticity.[20] The title of the film itself also raises "the question of whether the Japanese or the Brazilians are the foreigners."[21] Considering the film's standing within Brazilian film history today as an essential element in the national film canon, it is ironic that it was hard for Yamasaki to gain the support of the *Nikkei* community for its realization. The director, however, never let up in her attempts to gain financial support for it, as Yamasaki "understood the lack of support as a combination of sexism and generational conflict, but she eventually prodded community leaders to action."[22]

The second film of interest for the present contribution is *Corações Sujos* (Dirty Hearts, 2011). Directed by Vicente Amorim, it tells another story related to the existence of the *Nikkei* community in Brazil: namely, one related to Shindō Renmei (the League of the Subject's Way), a Japanese secret society whose members refused to accept Japan's defeat in 1945 as a reality. The film is based on Fernando Morais's *Corações Sujos: A História da Shindo Renmei* (Dirty Hearts: The History of Shindō Renmei, 2000),[23] a novel that investigates an "intriguing episode"[24] in the history of Japanese immigration to Brazil. Mostly active in the state of São Paulo, the members of Shindō Renmei committed terrorist acts against those Japanese in Brazil who believed the "lies" that Japan had lost the war. The organization's

> assassins, popularly known as *tokkotai* (a synonym for *kamikaze*), killed with firearms or *katanas* (traditional Japanese swords) at least 23 Japanese Brazilians and wounded 147 others who believed the news about Japan's defeat. The terrorists ... considered their victims *corações sujos* (dirty hearts).[25]

The film therefore provides a different insight into the history of Japanese immigration and the related Japanese identity in its Brazilian diaspora.

Both films refer to the past and yet also reflect on issues that are relevant for the discussion of immigrant identities and the latter's development within host countries. Both in addition highlight the problems that Japanese immigrants encountered in Brazil at different times in the century-long history of the *Nikkei* community in this particular country. After a short survey of this history, which not all readers might be familiar with, the present chapter will then discuss the two films in more detail to show how the history of Japanese immigrants was displayed for a wider Brazilian audience. It will show that popular media, like films focusing on migration, play an essential part, especially in the twenty-first century, in making the role of the Japanese migrant community in Brazil better understood, because films, including the two presented here, provide an insight into the long and painful history of Japanese in Brazil and therefore help to make the ostracized foreigner more visible, especially in a conciliatory way for a minority and its surrounding society.

Early Japanese Immigration to and the Diaspora in Brazil: A Short Historical Survey

It was on June 18, 1908 that a steamer from Japan, the *Kasato Maru*, arrived at the port of Santos and brought to Brazil the first 781 immigrants, who had signed up to work at the coffee plantations in the Brazilian state of São Paulo.[26] That Japanese immigrants were arriving on the shores of the Americas was nothing spectacular, considering that, by 1900, immigration from Japan to the United States, and to Hawai'i in particular, was quite common.[27] Initially, there was little interest in Brazil as a geographical target for immigration from the

East Asian country, although a "Treaty of Amity, Commerce and Navigation" between the two states had been signed on February 20, 1896.[28] Brazil, however, became more important from a migrant's perspective when US restrictions limited the possibilities for Japanese to settle in the United States, particularly Hawai'i, in 1907/8. Due to this new situation and

> Japan then [being] in the throes of an agrarian crisis and undergoing significant demographic pressure, to which mass emigration might serve as a reliable antidote, Japanese emigration companies began desperately searching for other countries that were prepared to receive new groups.[29]

Japanese immigration to Brazil was therefore a consequence of global change with regard to existing migrant routes across the Pacific. However, immigration to Brazil soon intensified; the country offered solid possibilities for the new arrivals after the initial hardships had been surpassed.

Japanese immigration to Brazil is usually divided into three main periods: firstly, 1908–25; secondly, 1926–41, followed by a total halt during the Pacific War and the immediate postwar period; and thirdly, the period since 1953. Since Peru and the US had closed their borders to Japanese immigrants in 1923/4, more and more immigrants arrived in Brazil, which counted 141,732 arrivals between 1924 and 1935—between 1908 and 1923 there had been only 32,366 immigrants.[30] While many people arrived in Brazil over a longer time period, most of the Japanese continued to keep to themselves and, as Takashi Maeyama has remarked, "do not appear to be culturally an associational people."[31] The newly arrived settlers, often farmers, would establish many almost "over-inflated voluntary associations"[32] in their new environment, which also stimulated a continuing separation of the Japanese immigrant community from Japan, whose members were reluctant to integrate into the Brazilian state as members of the Brazilian nation. While the 700,000 women and men that represented the South American country's *Nikkei* community were concentrated in the two neighboring states of São Paulo and Paraná in southeast Brazil, their geographical concentration, as well as the work the Japanese immigrants were involved with, stimulated their reservations about, and consequent prevention of, cultural acclimatization for many members of the Japanese immigrant community. Most of them would begin their work at coffee plantations, but they quickly moved on from being contract laborers to becoming private landowners. Japanese urbanization in Brazil was, however, rather slow, with only 8 percent of the community being urbanized in the 1930s.[33]

Jeffrey Lesser highlights "three critical issues" when considering and trying to understand the role of national identities in the Brazilian context:

The first is that studying those of immigrant descent helps us to understand broad questions of race and ethnicity in Brazil. . . . The second is that individuals represent themselves and are labeled as immigrants in situational ways. Finally . . . in Brazil the category of "immigrant" is often ancestral or inherited, one that can remain even among those born in the country.[34]

In addition to these assumptions about national identities in Brazil, it is important to understand that the immigration-related narrative largely differs from the one in the US. In the latter context, immigrants supposedly profit from the American nation and become better individuals, while in the South American narrative of Brazil's national identity, the immigrants are an important factor in strengthening Brazil through their personal efforts. The nation in Brazil, maybe with the exception of the 1930s and 1940s, is consequently the product of immigration, and not the precondition for the immigrant's transformation into a citizen.[35] To explain this in Benedict Anderson's (1936–2015) terms, the nation is imagined by a community, but this imagined place is redefined by the immigrants' existence, who stimulate the imagination of a better nation, a post-arrival and multiethnic, as well as multicultural, state.[36]

What opened the way for such redefinitions was the abolishment of slavery in Brazil in 1888 as it turned a settler colony of the Caribbean type into an agrarian plantation system that needed to attract labor to remain productive. This stimulated immigration from abroad, mainly from Spain or Italy from the late nineteenth century, and later also from Japan, as Japanese workers were considered less troublesome by the plantation owners than those from southern Europe, whose minds had already been poisoned with anarcho-syndicalist ideas.[37] The immigrants from Japan were consequently handy for Brazilian landowners, especially since

> [t]heir demands for improved working conditions pushed the capitalist elite toward employing Japanese workers, whom they believed were tidy, orderly, and obedient. It becomes clear that the coffee plantation owner desires cheap, easily exploited labor, and he intends to take full advantage of the Japanese laborers.[38]

In contrast to other destinations for Japanese immigration, like Hawai'i, the United States, or Peru, the Brazilian government allowed immigration only by families. The plantation owners had already realized that individuals would hardly ever stay on the coffee plantations, and therefore requested the family structure from the beginning. On the immigrants' side, however, this precondition led to the creation of pragmatic family ties, and adoption was used as an instrument to create the necessary family bonds before one had left Japan. These so-called "constructed families" (*kōsei kazoku*) or "families with companions" (*tsure kazoku*), which were particularly common in the first immigration period (1908–23), can unfortunately not be discussed in more detail here, but are definitely of interest with regard to Brazil's *Nikkei* community and its history. In Brazil itself, the Japanese immigrants formed a particularly strong and often homogenous community among themselves, while all other ethnicities—Brazilian whites, mulattoes, blacks, or other European immigrants—were considered foreigners (*gaijin*): that is, having an identity that could in addition be used for the Japanese themselves and which therefore was problematic for the immigrants, as is shown in the film *Gaijin*, which will be discussed in detail later. Nevertheless, the dichotomy between Japanese immigrants as an in-group and all others as an out-group was considerably potent during the first two decades of the twentieth century and became more divisive during World War II.[39]

Brazilian Immigrants of the First Hour and their Commemoration in Gaijin: Os Caminhos da Liberdade (1980)

Gaijin is a relatively well-perceived Brazilian film that received multiple awards, including Best Picture at the Gramado Film Festival. Due to its success, it was also nominated as the Brazilian contribution to the Berlin Film Festival and received first prize at the International Festival of Latin American Cinema in Havana in 1980.[40] This was important, as the film not only depicted the beginnings of the Japanese immigrant community in Brazil, but also represented an increasing female perspective in Brazilian cinema, and Tizuka Yamasaki was consequently perceived as one of the main representatives of these trends.[41] With "its representation of exploited workers, recuperation of history, and treatment of gender, the film contributes to a renewing discourse on citizenship in Brazil,"[42] especially since the director linked the two aspects of Japanese immigration to Brazil in her film. Due to the fact that she chose to present the topics as a drama instead of a documentary, she was also able to renew the discourse about Brazilian history from a migrant's perspective, that of a Japanese woman in particular.[43] Regardless of the film's later success, Yamasaki faced multiple difficulties with regard to its production. It was her first feature film project with a relatively high budget of US$300,000, but she had to start to seek and raise funding for it four years before actual production could begin.[44]

Yamasaki,[45] who was born in Atibaia (São Paulo) in 1949 and had Japanese immigrant grandparents as well as Japanese–Brazilian parents who worked as vegetable farmers, represented a new phase for Brazil's perception of its Japanese past and offered a vision at the same time. She was not the only woman to attempt this, as many female directors in the late 1970s and early 1980s, such as Suzana Amaral, Norma Bengell, or Tereza Trautman, offered "interpretations of the past that brought excluded political 'others' into view and produced new cultural knowledge on which a democratic Brazilian society could be built."[46] They used melodrama to transport a political message to the audiences: namely, one that offered an alternative for the future Brazilian society. Yamasaki in particular used a female role in *Gaijin* to demand reflections in modern Brazil about identities, not only ethnic ones but also gender identities that were also disputed within the national women's movement. Yamasaki had studied under and worked with famous directors of Brazil's Cinema Novo, like Nelson Pereira dos Santos (1928–2018) and Glauber Rocha (1939–81); however, she became independent early on with regard to the topics and perspectives she wanted to offer to cinema audiences.[47] The production company for the film was Embrafilme, which provided important support for up-and-coming new filmmakers like Yamasaki. Embrafilme soon grew into a nationally well-known distributor and production company, whose low-interest loan program, started in 1970, allowed many filmmakers to realize projects outside the mainstream. Although this program existed, only a few women actually benefited from it during the first years, like Lenita Perroy, who received some funding from Embrafilme for her *A Noiva da Noite* (The Night Bride, 1974). With local support from university programs and smaller prizes, women had to work their way up to secure bigger budgets for their projects. Some even established their own production companies to make their films possible and, as mentioned before, Yamasaki also had to seek financing over a longer time period to eventually commence filming *Gaijin*.[48]

While the further career of Yamasaki is related to other well-known Brazilian film productions, it was her early works in the 1980s—namely, *Gaijin: Os Caminhos da Liberdade* (Gaijin: Paths to Freedom, 1980), *Parahyba, Mulher Macho* (Parahyba, Manly Woman, 1983), and *Patriamada* (Sing, the Beloved Country, 1984)—that laid the foundations of her fame as a director. These early works "harmonize on a common goal to provide feminist interventions in the reconstruction of Brazilian politics and national identity,"[49] but the first film is probably the best remembered, as it addresses multiple problems of Brazil's past and present. Prior to *Gaijin*, the history of the Japanese immigrant community had not been included in films about Brazilian history. Yamasaki combined her political, feminist agenda with family memories and fictional elements, and thereby created a very appealing feature film. The multiple levels of the plot probably made it so successful, as it dealt with more than a historical story or a generational experience, in that it offered something different audiences could relate to or identify with.[50]

Regardless of the fictional plot, Yamasaki wanted to create an authentic impression and hired Japanese actresses and actors to play the leading roles. The director believed "that they would be more apt to convey the experience of cultural shock and sense of disorientation that the first Japanese immigrants experienced in the early twentieth century."[51] She also persuaded some hundred members of the Japanese community of Atibaia to participate in the film, which was shot on location there. The Japanese–Brazilian director hoped that the production would be successful in spite of anti-Japanese bias, and that it would address the discrimination and ostracization that so many Japanese immigrants had experienced in the South American country. She also wanted to emphasize that the future of Brazil would be based on the acceptance and cooperation of the different ethnic and immigrant groups. As Leslie L. Marsh worded it, "Yamasaki's film created an important dialogue between cultural and ethnic groups in the early 1980s and helped to explain the presence of Japanese people and products in São Paulo."[52]

Gaijin[53] gives an intimate insight into the story of Japanese immigrants who came to Brazil in 1908 to work on a coffee plantation, but it is told from the perspective of a young Japanese woman, "thus bringing to the fore female subjectivity and the contribution of Issei women pioneers to the immigration process."[54] At the beginning, the film shows São Paulo in 1980 with shots of the "oriental district" of the city, displaying, among other things, a banner greeting Japanese customers with "Irasshai" (Welcome). The voice of the woman who is to become the main character starts to reflect on the past and sets the current multicultural image of the Brazilian city in contrast with a time when Japanese immigrants had just started to arrive and were far from being an accepted part of society.[55] Titoe (Tsukamoto Kyoko) is a young Japanese woman who has been forced to marry to create one of the artificial families and the family structure that was necessary to gain access to Brazil in the first place; in the dialogue she states, "My brother wanted to go to Brazil. He had to have a family to be eligible. I decided to go too. I had to marry." She thereby represents a repressed individual, not only as an immigrant in a foreign environment but also as a woman who has been forced to marry and thereby to live in a social environment that considered women to be servile supporters of the family. She is consequently not an independent member of the community, whose wishes and dreams need to be considered with regard to any decision. Her name does not appear very early in the film but instead is revealed rather late on, when her husband addresses her after her first hard day at work on the coffee plantation.[56] Titoe's displacement from Japan commences her journey to Brazil, where she transforms from a young girl suppressed by a forced marriage into a self-confident Brazilian woman of Japanese descent.

After the introduction of 1980s São Paulo as a dichotomic space to the city of the early 1900s shown in the film and Titoe's rural Japanese place of origin, a small village in Japan is shown, where a notice informs the people there and the film's audience about the wider context; Brazil is looking for families that want to emigrate to work on its plantations. Titoe thereby becomes a victim of male wishes, joining those Japanese who wait at the harbor for the ship to a supposedly more promising world.[57] Among these people are Yamada (Kawarazaki Jirō), Titoe's new husband, as well as his brother, Kobayashi (Kaneko Ken'ichi). It becomes obvious that Titoe is leaving Japan involuntarily as the voiceover offers this retrospective assessment by the main character. In the film, she is always having flashbacks that show typical images of Japan, like women performing traditional dances in kimonos. Her self as a woman is also destroyed, in a way, by Yamada, who does not accept her freedom as an individual; eventually, especially with regard to her sexuality, he forces Titoe also to accept her identity as a Japanese wife—that is, offering total, including sexual, submission to the husband—when he rapes her. In the film, a mirror visually expresses his invasion of her private space and of her sexuality. Supposedly one of her few personal possessions, the mirror usually shows a close shot of her own face, yet when Yamada rapes her, it is his face that is shown in a close shot in the mirror. Titoe loses not only her Japanese home but also her body, which is violated by her husband, whom she had to follow to foreign shores. The marriage itself must consequently be considered a part of Titoe's dehumanization, as she is treated like a commodity. When she is raped, she eventually stops trying to halt the attack and accepts her fate, at least for the moment, because her identity as a free individual has been completely broken.

When the Japanese immigrants, dressed in Western clothes, insecure and unable to communicate in Portuguese, reach the Santa Rosa coffee plantation near São Paulo, they meet Italian immigrants like Enrico (Gianfrancesco Guarnieri), who makes jokes about the new arrivals by referring to stereotypes about Asian people, especially their eyes. The contrast between the different immigrant groups in Brazil is also emphasized in different situations that the film will describe.[58] The Japanese newcomers also meet Tonho (Antônio Fagundes), the bookkeeper at the plantation, who is nice to the immigrants. The Japanese are brought to their new homes, old buildings that have previously been used for slaves. There seem to be immediate problems, such as the Brazilian diet at the plantation that consists of beans, dried meat, and manioc flour. The Japanese request rice instead, but eventually they adjust to the new culinary demands of their environment. They also become used to the work on the plantation after receiving instructions on how to handle the coffee plants. From their arrival onwards, as Leslie L. Marsh correctly emphasizes, the film's "narrative establishes a clear dichotomy between the innocent (good) immigrant workers and the greedy, violent (evil) plantation owners and staff."[59] The Japanese immigrants are supposed to replace the lost slaves, as a conversation between the plantation owner and a banker, which has been shown before, also underlines. Regardless of the Japanese immigrants' hard work, their dreams of a fast and reasonable income to better their situation disappear when Tonho is eventually forced to deduct money for unjust reasons from the workers' earnings, while the violent plantation overseer, Chico Santos (Alvaro Freire), prevents any resistance to this practice.[60]

The immigrants might be different with regard to their ethnic and cultural background, but exploitation by the plantation owners unites them,[61] and at a little festivity on the plantation Enrico points out the multicultural sphere that the coffee plantation has created. While music is played, migrants of African, Italian, and Japanese descent celebrate, drink, and dance. Titoe, during the dance, leans against a house, flanked by Yamada on one side and Tonho on the other. This image also reflects her position as an immigrant between her Japanese heritage on the one hand and her potential to become part of the Brazilian nation on the other. At this point in the story, however, she still dreams of Japan. Another Japanese immigrant has already crossed the line between the different cultures by engaging with a young Italian woman. This scene was particularly criticized by the Japanese–Brazilian community when the film was shown in 1980, as it was argued that such relations were not historically accurate but rather a product of Yamasaki's political pro-multicultural agenda.

Regardless of the shared experiences of exploitation, the Japanese immigrant workers continue to observe the demands of the immigration company not to resist or engage in strike activities, although life on the plantations is harder than expected and does not provide any possibility for a reasonable income or better prospects in the near future. They are increasingly treated like slaves, forced to work under the control of armed men.[62] The Italian and Spanish immigrants, represented by Enrico in the movie, in contrast engage in more radical attempts to change their current position, influenced by anarcho-syndicalist ideas that they have brought to the "New World" with them. Enrico initially asks for a small bonus from the plantation owner, as the cost of living is quite high. He also tries to win the Japanese plantation workers over to the idea of a strike, as only a united labor force will be able to succeed in the struggle against the owners and men like Chico Santos. The latter eventually uses violence to suppress Enrico's activities and enters his house with some of his men at night to beat up the labor activist. Later in the film, the Italian radical is banished from Brazil for activities that stimulate civil disobedience among the plantation workers. Yamada, on the other hand, is shown as having a reluctant and probably too servile and traditional Japanese mind, as he refuses to criticize the plantation owners and remains submissive and quite immigrant-like—that is, remaining in his role as a foreigner, instead of claiming his rights in the new national context—just as the women and men from Japan were perceived by the authorities and plantation owners alike.[63]

In contrast to this stereotype, Titoe's role in the film's narrative develops, and like the film, "aims for new political and gendered consciousness."[64] The young woman, who initially appears to be shy and controlled by the surrounding males in her environment, eventually turns into more of a free Brazilian individual than the other Japanese immigrants. Being an object of sexual desire in the first part, not only for Yamada but also for Tonho, who seems to seek to be close to her in some situations, she turns into a self-determined subject, free to follow her own ambitions. She gives birth to her daughter, a new community member and a Japanese–Brazilian, and when her husband dies from a disease, she takes over the leadership of the group of Japanese on the plantation. Tonho, who is unable to provide money for medication when Chico Santos refuses to call a doctor, is at the same time beginning to question his own complicity in the exploitative system. With Yamada dead after two years of hard work that led nowhere, and as the Japanese immigrants are unable to secure any substantial savings, Titoe urges them to leave the plantation and seek better prospects in the city. When they are pursued by Chico and his men, Tonho finds the Japanese on their way out, and as she tells him that she would rather die than return to the plantation, the bookkeeper hugs Titoe, kisses her head, and then urges her and the other Japanese to go while he sets a fire on the plantation to distract the other men in pursuit. Tonho thereby confirms Titoe's changed identity and follows her lead with regard to such a change for his own personal identity as a free person. The insecure Japanese immigrant woman has ultimately turned into her strong Brazilian self, and at the end of the film represents "a strong female character through whom the filmmaker proposes an alternative, feminized history of Brazil."[65]

At the close of the film this strong Japanese woman, now settled in Brazil because her daughter is totally unaware of any Japanese past and fully integrated in the new host country, walks through the city of São Paulo, where she now works in a factory, and meets Tonho again, now fully engaged in labor activism.[66] The romance between these two characters is never openly addressed in the film, but the last scene offers the audience a chance to imagine how they might share a future together. As mentioned before, such interethnic romances were criticized as ahistorical by the Japanese community in 1980,[67] but Yamasaki uses them to provide an image of a strategic "break out of the self-imposed isolation of the Japanese community (which the director herself desired in her own life) while motivating affective bonds with members of the larger Brazilian populace."[68] The final outlook therefore "underscores that love can overcome adversity"[69] and, in addition, is able to "offer signs of the protagonist's progressive Brazilianization"[70] as Titoe "enters the mainstream by 'mixing' with Tonho and thus becoming 'Brazilian.'"[71] Many who saw the movie in 1980 realized that there actually was a Japanese–Brazilian community and, for the first time, were confronted with the past suffering of the first Japanese immigrants who had arrived in the country from 1908 on. At the same time, *Gaijin* points to the different identities that coexisted within the Brazilian nation, proposing a shared future that accepts and embraces the country's ethnic and cultural diversity.

The second film about the Japanese migrant community that will be taken into closer consideration here is probably less conciliatory, as it takes a look at what is the most tragic period for the Japanese community in Brazil, but it also highlights how the issue of migration remains vivid within Brazilian film in the twenty-first century.

The Second World War and the Experience of Japanese Immigrants in Brazil

When the Japanese immigrants faced problems in their new environment, they usually channeled their protests through the emigration agencies that had recruited them in the first place. The main contact in Brazil for the Japanese was consequently not the host country's government or its representatives, but organizations that acted on behalf of Japan's interests in terms of expansion. Nevertheless, the working conditions and the exploitation that existed on the coffee plantations also forced individuals and whole families to escape, as depicted in *Gaijin*, to seek a better future in the cities or as private landowners and farmers afterwards. The work on the plantations carried out by the Japanese immigrants, on the other hand, also strengthened the community along ethnic lines, especially since the new arrivals from Japan were kept in a Japanese environment on the plantations, although in some cases exchanges with other plantation workers also took place.[72] From its beginning, however, the history of Japanese immigration to Brazil was probably more diasporic than that of the southern European immigrants, who did not have to overcome a strong language-related or cultural barrier.

When Kōyama Rokurō (1886–1976) arrived in Brazil in 1908 as one of the passengers on the *Kasato Maru*, he was able to serve as one of four interpreters for the Japanese immigrants because he spoke some Spanish. His later career, due to his language skills, would also be different from those of the other new arrivals. In 1921 he founded the Japanese newspaper *Seishū Shinpō* (*Semanario de São Paulo*), which would include advertisements for Japanese shops or services in the city, such as Japanese pharmacies or shoe shops.[73] Such publications, as well as books, were supposed to highlight a particular "whiteness" or elitist status of the Japanese immigrant community.[74] The readers of this paper were the Japanese who had entered the country since 1908, and the immigrants stimulated an increasing trade balance between Brazil and Japan; to name just one example, they helped to transform the position of rice within Brazil's export statistics, turning it from an import into one of the country's top export goods.[75] The state of São Paulo was the main area of settlement for the Japanese immigrants, and a total of 186,769 of them had come to live there by 1940. More than 50 percent of them reached the South American country after 1930, in a period when Japan had adopted a more aggressive foreign policy, which is why the new settlers were also pivotal in expanding Japan's zone of influence in the Americas.[76] Once the Japanese had left the coffee plantations and the *colonato* labor system[77] that dominated there, they fast gained access to private land ownership. This rapid transition from plantation worker to landowner was possible because the Japanese immigrants had kept their connection to their home country and used the emigration agencies to establish links to a Japanese clientele, who would buy directly from the Japanese farming communities in Brazil.[78]

These communities were eventually able to better face the economic changes that hit the South American country in the late 1920s, when the Great Depression spread from the United States. Furthermore, the establishment of the regime of Getúlio Vargas (1882–1954), who governed the country between 1930 and 1945, and again between 1951 and 1954, eroded the hegemonic position of the coffee industry in Brazil. These changes also further strengthened the position of the Japanese, who "had turned to the intensive polyculture of fruit and vegetables, and also to cotton."[79] Cultivation and trade of the latter crop in particular were increased by the Japanese presence in Brazil since 1916, and more and more immigrants from Japan would become involved in the cotton business there. Although it would take until 1933 for the first cotton shipment to leave Port Santos, the value of cotton exports would increase tremendously during the later 1930s.[80] World War I had had an enormous impact on Japan; in particular, the rivalry between the United States and Japan, as well as that between Britain and Japan, in its aftermath led the government in Tokyo to look for new possibilities with regard to international trade partners. Due to developments since 1918, especially those relating to the immigration limits for Japanese settlers in other regions of the Americas and the new necessities for Japanese trade within the global order, the importance of Brazil and its *Nikkei* community increased for the East Asian country as well. Toake Endoh highlights these points when she remarks that

> [w]ith utilitarian interest in transnational profit maximization, pre-World War II Japan considered its emigration policy towards Latin America as an integral part of its colonization enterprise, in which Nikkei capital and labor were deployed onto foreign lands for agricultural development.[81]

The Brazilian government also shared this interest and sent a trade mission to Japan in 1936. The Federal Congressman Joaquim P. S. Filho, the "former Secretary of Labor, Commerce, and Industries, and a renowned patron of Japanese immigration to Brazil," led the mission and also acted "in the capacity of a minister plenipotentiary including renowned businessmen in mining, coffee, and cotton."[82] While no concrete agreement was reached, both parties nevertheless agreed that cotton would fuel the trade relationship of both countries in the years to come. Regardless of this shared interest in trade, the Brazilian environment, especially from the immigrants' perspective, would transform into a more anti-Japanese one once Getúlio Vargas established the Estado Novo after his second coup d'état in 1937.[83] This would also further strengthen Japanese immigrant nationalism as a reaction to Brazilian discrimination, because the former "showed its most public face after Brazil ended its flirtation with fascism and joined the Allies in 1942."[84]

With Vargas's second coup by, the situation of Japanese immigrants in Brazil changed abruptly. Within a month, new legal decrees had been signed to suppress not only foreign language schools but also publications in non-Brazilian languages. Such new legal conditions were, as Mônica Raisa Schpun highlights,

> especially harmful to the Japanese community, which had only been established in the country for a short time and whose members had yet to master the local language and culture, instead retaining extremely close ties to the Japanese institutions that continued to aid them in various ways.[85]

Around 600 Japanese language schools were no longer allowed to operate, and in 1940, strict language censorship by the Vargas government intensified the feeling of foreignness among the immigrants within the Japanese community of Brazil. Foreign-language newspapers were ordered in 1941 to publish at least 50 percent of their content in Portuguese before they were banned entirely later that same year. The readers of the 50,000 copies of the four main Japanese newspapers in the state of São Paulo were therefore left without an official public space they could share as Japanese immigrants in Brazil, and their public space of exchange totally vanished.[86] Lacking their own public space, Japanese publications only circulated clandestinely, and language schools continued to teach children in hidden meetings, a specific experience that *Corações Sujos* also depicts. Financial support for the schools from abroad had already been cut off by Law No. 383 in 1938, which prohibited the latter from receiving funding from abroad, meaning from Japan in particular.[87]

The situation became even worse once the Pacific War began, with Japan's attack on Pearl Harbor in December 1941. The prohibition on the import of Japanese books and other publications did not immediately stop the "consumption" of such goods, especially since used books and magazines were sold by bookstore owners. For Japanese immigrants, the prohibition did not lead to increased assimilation, but rather a further division from the majority of Brazilian society. While Vargas had hoped to bind the immigrants to Brazil by such measures, which would supposedly separate them from their home countries and "Brazilianize" them, there was an antagonistic reaction from the Japanese community.[88] This was probably also the case as Japanese immigrants were often confronted with racist reactions from the Brazilian authorities, who considered the former as a menace to the nation; "the Japanese were seen not only as 'unassimilable,' but also as 'undecipherable,' 'treacherous,' 'disloyal,' and 'fifth-columnists.'"[89] When the war in the Pacific began, the Japanese eventually lost all connections to their country of origin and thereby were weakened not only with regard to their identity but also financially, as support from Japanese companies, friends, or relatives could no longer reach the immigrant community in Brazil. Its members could no longer publicly express their own culture of origin, as the police would notice anything evoking Japan or Japanese that was not considered to be in the Brazilian national interest.

As a consequence of the suppression of the Japanese immigrant community during the war years, ultranationalist secret societies were founded, taking over the distribution of information within the community and acting as a control organ to secure the community's links to Japanese culture. One of the best-known examples of such societies is Shindō Renmei, whose members aimed to preserve the identity of Japanese immigrants by strengthening links among them and by encouraging emperor worship as a cultural practice to achieve it.[90] The founding of societies like Shindō Renmei was stimulated by Japan's defeat in the war, as it divided the Japanese immigrant community into two groups: namely, those who believed in a Japanese victory (*kachigumi*) and those who were willing to accept Japan's defeat (*makegumi*).[91] The latter tried to achieve acceptance for Japanese within Brazil's society and hoped for better assimilation of their fellow immigrants, but it seemed hard, even impossible, to persuade the *kachigumi* to accept the harsh realities. The *makegumi* members had accepted that they were now living in Brazil and that their future was connected with the Brazilian nation.[92] However, they had to combat the rumors and lies spread by Shindō Renmei, whose members fought to ensure that nobody would, at least publicly, believe any Portuguese news about the Japanese surrender and the end of the war. Different societies were established, such as Aikoku Seinendan (the Patriotic Youth Association), Aidō Jissen Renmei (the League for the Promotion of the Way of Love), and Zaihaku Zaigō Gunjin-kai (the Association of Reservists in Brazil), and these societies "did not try to be voluntary, but were compulsory for their members and in the application of their norms."[93] With this goal in mind, the secret societies resorted to violence to punish those with *tenchū* (divine punishment) who were willing to accept Brazilian realities rather than believe in Japanese utopias. Between 1946 and 1947, many assassins related to the secret societies attacked, wounded, and even killed members of the Japanese community, demonstrating the deep divide of the Japanese community in Brazil.[94]

It is worth mentioning here that these secret societies in a way resumed Japanese traditions, as ultranationalist right-wing societies like the Gen'yōsha (Dark Ocean Society) or the Kokuryūkai (Amur Society, often mistranslated as the Black Dragon Society) had tried to force Japan into a more aggressive foreign policy since the 1880s.[95] It is perhaps ironic that such societies founded in Brazil had been identified as a serious problem in Japan by the Supreme Commander of the Allied Powers, whose occupational government had consequently prohibited their existence. A "Paper on [the] Dissolution of Certain Political Parties Associations and Societies in Japan," provided by the Far Eastern Commission's Committee No. 4 (Strengthening of Democratic Tendencies), dated April 16, 1946, and shared by the American authorities with the British Embassy in Washington, highlighted the role of these secret societies in Japan:

> The Genyosha [sic], the parent of this type of society, in its origin consisted chiefly of disgruntled ex-samurai who, seeing the futility of armed revolt to gain their goal of Japanese expansion in Asia, organized pressure groups by which they could exercise a decisive influence upon key members of the government, particularly in the Ministries of War and Foreign Affairs.[96]

The paper wrongly assumed that "[b]oth societies [Gen'yōsha and Kokuryūkai, F. J.] continued their activities throughout the Pacific war; although considerably attenuated they have remained as a baleful influence behind the scenes,"[97] but obviously in Brazil new secret societies were established as a consequence of the war.[98]

The ultranationalist societies thereby reflected the experiences of the immigrants, particularly racial and cultural discrimination, and especially since 1937.[99] Although much smaller than the German community in Brazil, the Japanese were the main target of governmental suppression because their Asian heritage might have identified them as foreigners much more easily than their German immigrant counterparts. Radicalization within the Japanese community was therefore stimulated both from the outside, by the Pacific War and Japan's defeat, and from within, by the Vargas government's anti-Japanese decrees. When Shindō Renmei was founded, supposedly in 1944,[100] the following aims of the society were declared: "(1) diffusion and improvement of the Japanese spirit; (2) preservation of Shintoism; (3) preservation of the Japanese language among the settlers and their descendants; and (4) acceptance of the New Order which Japan was establishing in Asia."[101] They found support among the estimated 100,000 Japanese immigrants who had not been assimilated in Brazil before, and therefore became isolated by the harsh decrees of the Brazilian government.[102] Shindō Renmei was founded by Kikawa Junji, whom Ignacio López-Calvo has described as "a former army officer who, among other Japanese, brought to the Americas a fervor for aggressive nationalism, patriotism, pride, and a Prussian-like militarism that the Meiji government exhibited from 1868 through 1912."[103]

The British Embassy in Rio de Janeiro reported to the Foreign Office in London

> that considerable excitement and alarm have been caused in Brazil lately by the unrest amongst the Japanese colony in the provinces of São Paulo and Paraná which is due to the activities of certain unscrupulous elements (mostly embodied in secret societies such as the Shindo Remmei [sic] or "Divine Association," and the "Black Dragon") which have sought, with considerable success, to convince their countrymen that Japan, despite all statements to the contrary, has won the war.[104]

Foreign newspapers, which also meant Brazilian ones, that reported on Japan's defeat were considered to be propaganda by the Japanese community in the South American country. On the other hand, the members of the *makegumi*,

> those more realistic Japanese who have made attempts to convince their countrymen of the truth are dubbed 'Pessimists' and branded as traitors and defeatists; not only this, they have been threatened with death, and in two cases have paid for their temerity by their lives.[105]

At the same time, the report argues with regard to the radicals of the *kachigumi* that

> [i]t is not to be supposed that the ringleaders of the secret societies necessarily believe themselves in the tales which their credulous hearers swallow so readily. Their motive may be partly a stubborn pride translating itself into a refusal to admit defeat.[106]

As mentioned before, members of the *makegumi* were attacked by Shindō Renmei, and the report by the British Embassy also provides two descriptions of murders committed by the society in March 1946, which will be quoted here in some detail:

> Ikuta Mizobe, the managing director of the Cooperative Agricola at Bastos in the province of São Paulo. This unfortunate worthy, who was shot dead in his own backyard by a gunman concealed behind a bush . . . had already received a notification that his life was forfeit, apparently because a) he had distributed copies of a Brazilian newspaper giving the facts about Japan, and b) he had been collecting materials for a report to the authorities on the activities of the secret societies. . . . The second murder was perpetrated in a far more brazen fashion in the city of São Paulo itself. . . . [D]uring the past month [March 1946, F. J.], groups of fanatics belonging to the 'Black

> Dragon" had been gradually assembling in the town for the purpose of carrying out "executions" of persons "sentenced to death" for disloyalty to their Emperor and country.... [On April 1,] five of these zealots made tracks for the house of Tshuzabo Nomura, a well-known "cooperative" who lives in the suburbs of São Paulo and, obtaining entry by a ruse, killed the defenseless man as he lay in bed. At the second time a group of five attacked the residence of Shigemitsu Furuya, who twenty years ago was Japanese Ambassador at Buenos Aires, but, in spite of a lively fusillade, lasting twenty minutes, their intended victim was unharmed.[107]

The government reacted with the arrests of 400 men, and according to the report,

> amongst these are Colonel Yungi Kikawa, who has been described as the chief man behind the movement, Tsuguo Kishimoto, a naturalized Brazilian, who has been taking advantage of the situation to extort money from his compatriots, and Kamechiti Shioti, a doctor of medicine and man of fortune.[108]

According to Japanese contacts of the British Embassy, the propaganda put out by these societies had been quite successful the previous month, and countless members of the Japanese community were expecting a visit from Emperor Hirohito (1901–89), who would declare Japan's victory in the war. Such a "phenomenon was observable in Brazil only," because the Japanese immigrant community had been cut off from news about the war and Japan's defeat, and "[i]n a country like America, where the Japanese population have newspapers in their own language, the secret societies' clandestine propaganda could have been met effectively."[109] Attempts to counter the secret societies' propaganda were not successful, and it was suggested by the Swedish ambassador in Brazil that the government in Stockholm

> should urge the Tokyo authorities to address a message to the Japanese colony here, explaining the true position of things and exhorting them to accept the inevitable and to stop persecuting their compatriots and disturbing the law and order of the country whose guests they are.[110]

Shindō Renmei had consequently directed international attention to the Japanese community in Brazil, and the fact that around 150,000 of its members, "literate people living in Brazil,"[111] believed in Japan's victory at the end of the Pacific War raised a lot of questions and often gave rise to disbelief. However, the non-existent public space for Japanese immigrants in the Estado Novo, even more so during the war years, had created a hidden space of exchange that had been dominated by secret societies like Shindō Renmei. The latter had launched "a counterattack on the way national identity was defined"[112] and requested that their immigrant community in Brazil remain as Japanese as possible by worshipping both Japan's emperor and nation. The immigrants should consequently not self-identify as Brazilian of Japanese origin, but remain actively Japanese abroad, representing the expansive efforts of their East Asian home country. Sociologically, the society could be successful to this extent, as a majority of the Japanese immigrants to Brazil had continued to live in secluded and geographically segregated farming communities that had been separated from the rest of the country, and their connections with Japan had been interrupted since 1941 as well.[113]

When the Brazilian Army and the Departamento de Ordem Política e Social (Department of Political and Social Order) arrested the leading members, in addition to the young men who had been responsible for the attacks and assassinations—the so-called *tokkotai*—there were questions about how to deal with them, especially since Shindō Renmei's leaders claimed that the organization had more than 100,000 members. In 1946 and 1947, more than twenty people had been killed by the *tokkotai* and more than 140 members of the Japanese community in Brazil had been wounded. After the arrests, around 400 leaders of the secret organization were in Brazilian custody, but they would also refuse to accept the truth according to papers that the Japanese government had presented to prove the end of the war and Japan's defeat.[114] The members of the *makegumi*, whose lives could now continue without death threats, established the Nihon Sensai Dōhō Kyūen Kai, or Comite de Socorro as Vitimas de Guerra do Japdo (Committee for the Relief of the War Victims in Japan), and collected money that was sent to Japan to help the common people in the aftermath of the war.[115] The Federal Intervenor in the state of São Paulo, José Carlos de Macedo Soares (1883–1968), had no easy task in determining the future of the former Shindō Renmei members, who were considered to be a part of Brazil's future in spite of their previous terrorist acts. As Jeffrey Lesser put it, Soares "could have dismissed the Shindo Renmei as a bunch of kooks, but he did nothing of the sort. Instead he prohibited newspapers from publishing news of Japan's defeat and ordered the term 'unconditional surrender' taken out of all official communications."[116] Instead of shaming the Japanese community in Brazil, the politician chose to use a Japanese strategy to deal with a damaging past; he simply ignored it and offered this particular immigrant community a way to look positively towards their own future as a part of the Brazilian nation. When films and texts address this episode in the history of the Japanese immigrant community, it still seems to evoke reactions like shame or a wish to forget for Japanese and Brazilians alike. Ignacio López-Calvo emphasizes with regard to this aspect that "Nikkei authors and filmmakers admit that, in their ancestors' past, not only dignity, pride and glory can be found, but also shameful episodes and humiliating wounds."[117]

Although immigrants had started to arrive again from different parts of Japan after World War II,[118] ethnic expressions of Japaneseness in Brazil changed over the decades, especially since the community altered its own shape as the "initial community dissolve[d] and first-generation immigrants fade[d] in influence and number,"[119] meaning that the Japanese immigrant population also diversified after the end of World War II. The initial warnings against assimilation were eventually overcome by the *Nikkei*, although many obviously continued to "believe that their cultural heritage ... is the reason for their limited success in a hostile environment."[120] Those who argue that their Japaneseness hinders them from advancing socially in Brazil still believe in Japan as a valid alternative, especially since the home country of their ancestors "continues to provide the tangible rewards of employment and scholarships for full-blooded Japanese competent in the language."[121] Some members of the *Nikkei* community in Brazil consequently still consider Japan to be a more financially secure space to work in, and since the 1980s, the direction of migration, traditionally from Japan to Brazil, has been reversed and more *Nikkei* are actually returning to Japan.[122] The economic crisis of the 1980s and 1990s transformed the South American country from a place of immigration to one of emigration, with many descendants of Japanese immigrants of the first half of the twentieth century leaving for Japan again. They became *dekasegi*, who considered their East Asian country of origin as the best option for their future, and lawmakers in Tokyo further stimulated this trend with a law that gave Brazilians the possibility of working in Japan.[123]

The history of Japanese immigration to Brazil and the stories related to this particular immigrant community consequently provide multiple angles and perspectives for Brazilian filmmakers to address the past, and since the 1980s, different films have tried to evoke broader discussions about it. Two of these will now be taken into closer consideration to show what attempts were made to stimulate the discourse, and how the community and its problems were presented to a broader audience in the South American country.

Brazilian Nationalism and Japanese Responses: Shindō Renmei and its Depiction in *Corações Sujos* (2011)

The film *Corações Sujos*, directed by Vicente Amorim, addresses the division of the Japanese community in Brazil as a consequence of World War II and the defeat of Japan. As described above, the partition of the Japanese immigrants into *kachigumi* and *makegumi* during the 1940s intensified a conflict between Brazilian nationalism that attempted to forcefully Brazilianize the Japanese in the country, and Japanese nationalism that tried to resist exactly that while preserving and honoring the Japanese heritage. The film is based on Fernando Morais's *Corações Sujos: A História da Shindo Renmei* (2000), a text that Ignacio López-Calvo has called "a hybrid of historical essay, novel, testimonial, and biography."[124] The author, who has no links to any kind of Japanese ethnic heritage, none the less argues that the Japanese immigrant community in Brazil was treated as a scapegoat for many things during the Estado Novo, and that antagonism between Brazilian nationalism and Japanese immigrants was also stimulated by repressions of the latter by the police, to name just one example that is also addressed in the film. Many Japanese were, according to rumors, considered to be spies, gathering information and acting as some kind of fifth column to prepare an invasion by the Imperial Japanese Army. Amorim also avoids adopting a one-sided perspective when he describes the history of Shindō Renmei by evoking the reasons why so many Japanese immigrants were obviously attracted by such an ultranationalist organization.

Corações Sujos, like *Gaijin*, is also told from the perspective of a female character: namely, Miyuki Takahashi (Tokiwa Takako), a Japanese teacher who witnesses the ways in which the extreme ideas of Shindō Renmei corrupt her husband, photographer Takahashi (Ihara Tsuyoshi). In this way of telling the story, Amorim, as López-Calvo highlights, "does not focus on Yellow Peril stereotypes . . . but on the causes of the protagonist's radicalization and, by extension, of his social group's sudden turn to fanaticism."[125] The historical mix of repression by the government and anxieties within the *Nikkei* community—that is, the twofold perspective on the process of radicalization of the Japanese immigrant community during the 1940s—is provided in a moving and melodramatic narrative. The film's beginning provides the historical frame for its setting with some information about the situation in Brazil since 1937 and especially in the 1940s: that is, how Japanese immigrants had not been allowed since the beginning of the Pacific War to read or publish their own newspapers, and how Japanese-language education had been prohibited. In addition, the first shots of the film show cotton, a cash crop, as mentioned above, highly related to the previous success of the *Nikkei* community in Brazil.

Takahashi resembles one of the frequently encountered Japanese individuals of these years, who addresses his customers only in Japanese, and needs the help of a young girl, Akemi Sasaki (Celine Fukumoto), to translate for him. During a break, she asks the photographer why he does not speak Portuguese. His answer is simple: "Because I am Japanese." Akemi is puzzled: "My father is also Japanese, but he speaks Brazilian, too." This scene already highlights one aspect that was so important for the success of Shindō Renmei: namely, the lack of language skills of many Japanese immigrants, who therefore cannot read Brazilian newspapers. The other aspect—the conflict between the respective nationalisms of the Brazilian state and the Japanese immigrants—is addressed in one of the following scenes. Watanabe (Okuda Eiji), a former

Japanese officer probably representing the historical leader of Shindō Renmei, has invited other Japanese to his house for a celebration, where they also put up a Japanese flag. The police officer, Cabo Garcia (André Frateschi), and his men interrupt the event and humiliate the Japanese, especially by cutting down the Japanese flag and using it as a cleaning rag. Garcia emphasizes to the Japanese: "This is Brazil! Here is Brazil!" He thereby highlights the Brazilian nationalism that offended many Japanese, who feared the loss of their cultural identity and tended to believe that Shindō Renmei would secure it.

Akemi's father, Sasaki (Shun Sugata), represents the *makegumi*, and as he and Aoki (Issamu Yazaki) listen to Brazilian radio, since they understand Portuguese, they learn from the news bulletin that Japan has actually lost the war. When Watanabe assembles his men to seek revenge for the earlier humiliation, Takahashi joins them and they march to the police station to request the death of Corporal Garcia. Earlier, his wife had bound a Japanese war flag around his hips under his clothes, in a ritual similar to the one that young *kamikaze* pilots performed. The attempt at revenge fails, however, and the Japanese are taken into custody. Aoki, who translates for the police, is accused of being a traitor (*hikokumin*), and Takahashi tells him that those who believe that Japan has lost will no longer be Japanese. With the help of a Brazilian lawyer of African descent—leading to some racist remarks by the police—the Japanese are, nevertheless, allowed to leave.

Watanabe then assembles his followers and declares that "[t]he enemy is among us." With a *"Tennō heika banzai"* (Long live His Majesty the Emperor) that is shouted out three times, the Japanese underline their loyalty to their spiritual leader, whose aim is to preserve their true Japaneseness spirit, their *yamato-damashii*.[126] The Brazilian authorities, in the meantime, intensify their efforts to suppress secret Japanese-language schools, and when Takahashi *sensei*'s course is interrupted, only Akemi is able to speak in Portuguese with the police officer in charge. The conflict thereby intensifies and Watanabe orders Takahashi to kill Aoki, who has already been harassed with signs on his wall claiming that he is a traitor. In reference to the film's title, Takahashi names the reason why he has to kill Aoki: "Your heart has become dirty." Once he has killed the *makegumi* member, his wife finds Takahashi kneeling on the floor in front of the dead body with the sword in his hands. She becomes his accomplice when she cleans the floor.

Her loving husband increasingly transforms into a fanatic, reading the messages of Shindō Renmei out loud during supper at home as well. Sasaki tries to counter such false information, asking the cotton factory workers to believe him and the Brazilian authorities who explain that the war is over and Japan has been defeated. Sasaki also tries to highlight the fact that the immigrants are no longer Japanese and that Brazil has become their new home, to which they are supposed to adapt. Watanabe departs, and most of the men with him, leaving Sasaki with few friends, but the truth, which he later reveals to his wife, seems to be obvious: "I am also finished." His wife, Naomi (Yo Kimiko), argues that she could never be well if her husband was killed and that she would have to go back to Japan then. Sasaki's house is also secretly marked with the signs for *kokuzoku* (traitor to the fatherland), and his wife receives a death note from Watanabe himself. Those who supported Sasaki's claim are systematically killed before Takahashi is sent to Sasaki to kill him as well. As they fight, the men fall into a consignment of cotton and the stabbed Sasaki eventually dies on a heap of it, his blood leaving a red mark in its center, resembling the Japanese flag (Fig. 6.1).

After the murder, Takahashi hides in the countryside in a cotton hut, and Miyuki seems to be haunted by the certainty that her husband has become a murderer. She kills all the chickens in their backyard because she can no longer stand their noise, which resembles the voices that are making steady accusations.

Eventually, Takahashi finds out the truth about the end of the war and realizes that Watanabe has only been using him when he is requested to forge some photographs. His doubts increase, which is why Watanabe decides that the photographer must also be killed. The latter, however, survives the assassination attempt and walks to Watanabe's house, where he kills the leader of the local secret organization. He then goes to the police, where he emphasizes that his Japaneseness has been changed, as he now accepts Brazilian law and deserves to live a dishonorable life, knowing that he has killed two men, two friends, whose only fault was believing the truth.[127]

Figure 6.1 The dead Sasaki on a heap of cotton in *Corações Sujos* (Downtown Filmes, 2011).

Years later, the photographer is now the owner of a little shop and Akemi enters it, not knowing who the man is. However, when she sees a photo of herself on the wall, she recognizes Takahashi. She leaves the store immediately and Takahashi is surprised to be confronted with his own past, the girl whose father he has killed. However, Akemi leaves and is not interested in talking for long, although she seems to have forgiven him.[128] The last scene shows Miyuki, who says: "Due to the war I have lost the man I love." Amorim thereby reflects upon the division of the whole Japanese immigrant community during the war. Miyuki has lost her husband to the fanatical ideas of Shindō Renmei, and like many Japanese, she has lost friends and family to the secret society's influence. The film consequently provides an intimate perspective on the overall historical events of 1946/7. At the same time, it carefully tries to explain why so many Japanese were under the influence of secret organizations that argued that Japan had won the war. It was a response to Brazilian nationalism and the forced homogenization attempts since 1937, the non-existence of a Japanese public space, and their anxieties about their own identities as foreign immigrants in a hostile environment that stimulated the radical fanaticism of ordinary men during and immediately after the Pacific War. *Corações Sujos* consequently presents the identity conflicts of ordinary Japanese women and men who were separated not only from the Brazilian majority but also from their land of origin. They deal with this situation in different ways, but the experience as such definitely transforms their own identities, just as the immigration experience transformed Titoe's identity some decades before.

Conclusion

Brazil's history is highly determined by immigration from Africa, southern Europe, and Japan. The relevant migrants' perspectives consequently offer insight not only into their migration-related stories but also into the transformation of Brazil, especially during the twentieth century. Very often, Japanese immigrants in Brazil were confronted with problems created in relation to their specific identity and their emancipation from an immigrant community to one that was an essential part of the Brazilian nation.

Both films discussed in the present contribution deal with questions of assimilation that would turn Japanese immigrants into Brazilian citizens.[129] *Gaijin* was a first successful attempt to bring the question of Japanese identities in Brazil to wider recognition, and the film turned out to be so popular that a sequel, *Gaijin 2: Ama-me Como Sou* (Gaijin 2: Love Me As I Am, 2005), was shot to continue the story of Titoe and her daughter, Shinobu (Nobu McCarthy), in Brazil. The sequel not only shows how the Japanese immigrants increasingly became part of the intercultural and multiethnic community of Brazil, it also directs the audience's focus to the fate of the *dekasegi*, who leave Brazil for

Japan due to the economic crisis of the 1990s. Between 1990 and 2005, more than 250,000 of them left the South American country, making their reversed migration flow more than visible.[130] *Corações Sujos* also highlights how some aspects of the history of the Japanese immigrant community in Brazil are still sufficiently important to be shared with wider audiences and discussed within and outside of the *Nikkei* community there.

Both films that I have explored highlight the role the Japanese have played within Brazilian history, which is a history of migration. The present chapter has also highlighted how the issue of Japanese immigration and adaptation to, or absorption into, Brazilian society has been discussed by cinema directors. There are plenty of other aspects that could also be discussed, such as interethnic relationships, or the identity of Japanese–Brazilians of the second or third generation, as well as the self-perception of their ancestors in later decades. These issues, however, are beyond the scope of the present work. Nevertheless, several perspectives on migration, and therefore on the migrants themselves, including the migrants' own views, remain important topics for Brazilian film in the twenty-first century.

Notes

1. Pierre Chaunu, "Un Petit Aspect du grand problème unitaire: La Minorité japonaise au Brésil," *Annales: Histoire, Sciences Sociales* 3, no. 4, *L'Amérique du Sud devant l'histoire* (1948): 472.
2. On the Japanese diaspora in the Americas see, among others Eiichiro Azuma, *Between Two Empires: Race, History, and Transnationalism in Japanese America* (New York: Oxford University Press, 2005); Yuji Ichioka, *The Issei: The World of the First Generation Japanese Immigrants, 1885–1924* (New York: Free Press, 1988); Stewart Lone, *The Japanese Community in Brazil, 1908–1940: Between Samurai and Carnival* (New York: Palgrave, 2001); Daniel Masterson, *The Japanese in Latin America* (Urbana: University of Illinois Press, 2004).
3. Miriam Kingsberg, "Becoming Brazilian to Be Japanese: Emigrant Assimilation, Cultural Anthropology, and National Identity," *Comparative Studies in Society and History* 56, no. 1 (2014): 70.
4. Kingsberg, "Becoming Brazilian to Be Japanese," 72.
5. On the role and impact of World War I in Japan see Frank Jacob, "Japan und der Erste Weltkrieg: Außenpolitische Chancen, wirtschaftlicher Boom und gesellschaftlicher Diskurs an der globalen Peripherie des Krieges," in *Erster Weltkrieg. Globaler Konflikt—lokale Folgen. Neue Perspektiven*, ed. Stefan Karner and Philipp Lesiak (Innsbruck: Studienverlag, 2014), 389–402; Frank Jacob, "Der Erste Weltkrieg als ökonomisch–soziale Zäsur der japanischen Moderne," in *Tōkyō in den zwanziger Jahren. Experimentierfeld einer anderen Moderne?*, ed. Stephan Köhn, Chantal Weber, and Volker Elis (Wiesbaden: Harrassowitz, 2017), 17–32; Frank Jacob, "Japan and the Great War: Imperialist Ambitions Abroad, Social Change and Protest at Home," in *Zeiten des Aufruhrs (1916–1921): Globale Proteste, Streiks*

und Revolutionen gegen den Ersten Weltkrieg und seine Auswirkungen, ed. Marcel Bois and Frank Jacob (Berlin: Metropol, forthcoming).
6. Kingsberg, "Becoming Brazilian," 72.
7. On this aspect see in more detail Pierre Nora, ed. *Les Lieux de mémoire*, 3 vols (Paris: Gallimard, 1984–92).
8. Leslie L. Marsh, *Brazilian Women's Filmmaking: From Dictatorship to Democracy* (Urbana: Illinois University Press, 2012), 89.
9. Ignacio López-Calvo, *Japanese Brazilian Saudades: Diasporic Identities and Cultural Production* (Boulder: University of Colorado Press, 2019), 46.
10. López-Calvo, *Japanese Brazilian Saudades*, 47.
11. López-Calvo, *Japanese Brazilian Saudades*, 109.
12. The film is also sometimes referred to by the title *Gaijin, a Brazilian Odyssey*.
13. Jeffrey Lesser, "A Reflection on Foreignness and the Construction of Brazilian National Identities," *Luso-Brazilian Review* 50, no. 2 (2013): 61.
14. Jeffrey Lesser, *A Discontented Diaspora: Japanese Brazilians and the Meanings of Ethnic Militancy, 1960–1980* (Durham, NC, and London: Duke University Press, 2007), 63.
15. Scott Nygren, *Time Frames: Japanese Cinema and the Unfolding of History* (Minneapolis: University of Minnesota Press, 2007), 221.
16. Lesser, *A Discontented Diaspora*, 63.
17. López-Calvo, *Japanese Brazilian Saudades*, 54.
18. Marsh, *Brazilian Women's Filmmaking*, 96.
19. Marsh, *Brazilian Women's Filmmaking*, 100.
20. Nygren, *Time Frames*, 224–5.
21. Lesser, *A Discontented Diaspora*, 64.
22. Lesser, *A Discontented Diaspora*, 64.
23. Fernando Morais, *Corações Sujos: A História da Shindo Renmei* (São Paulo: Companhia das Letras, 2000).
24. Walnice Nogueira Galvão, "As musas sob assédio: indústria cultural e globalização," *Iberoamericana, Nueva época* 4, no. 14 (2004): 102.
25. Ignacio López-Calvo and Kathleen López, "Cultural Celebration, Historical Memory, and Claim to Place in Júlio Miyazawa's Yawara! A Travessia Nihondin-Brasil and Uma Rosa para Yumi," in *Imagining Asia in the Americas*, ed. Zelideth María Rivas and Debbie Lee-Distefano (New Brunswick, NJ: Rutgers University Press, 2016), 170.
26. Mônica Raisa Schpun, "Japanese Brazilians (1908–2013): Transnationalism amid Violence, Social Mobility, and Crisis," in *A Century of Transnationalism: Immigrants and their Homeland Connections*, ed. Nancy L. Green and Roger Waldinger (Urbana: University of Illinois Press, 2016), 84.
27. John M. Liu, "Race, Ethnicity and the Sugar Plantation System: Asian Labor in Hawaii, 1850–1900," in *Labor Immigration Under Capitalism: Asian Workers in the United States before WWII*, ed. Lucie Cheng and Edna Bonacich (Los Angeles: University of California Press, 1984), 186–201.
28. "Treaty of Amity, Commerce and Navigation between the Federal Republic of Brazil and the Empire of Japan," February 20, 1896, National Archives of Japan [Japanese Center for Asian Historical Records (JACAR)], A03020323999.

29. Schpun, "Japanese Brazilians (1908–2013)," 86.
30. Schpun, "Japanese Brazilians (1908–2013)," 86–7.
31. Takashi Maeyama, "Ethnicity, Secret Societies, and Associations: The Japanese in Brazil," *Comparative Studies in Society and History* 21, no. 4 (1979): 589.
32. Maeyama, "Ethnicity, Secret Societies, and Associations," 590.
33. López-Calvo, *Japanese Brazilian Saudades*, 590.
34. Lesser, "A Reflection on Foreignness," 54–55.
35. Lesser, "A Reflection on Foreignness," 56.
36. Benedict Anderson, *Imagined Communities: Reflections on the Origin and Spread of Nationalism* (London: Verso, 1983).
37. On transatlantic radicalism, especially in Brazil, see Carlo Romani and Bruno Corrêa de Sá e Benevides, "The Italian Anarchists' Network in São Paulo at the Beginning of the 20th Century," in *Transatlantic Radicalism*, ed. Frank Jacob and Mario Keßler (Liverpool: Liverpool University Press, forthcoming.
38. Marsh, *Brazilian Women's Filmmaking*, 101.
39. Maeyama, "Ethnicity," 591–2. See also Takashi Maeyama, "Ancestor, Emperor, and Immigrant: Religion and Group Identification of the Japanese in Rural Brazil," *Journal of Inter-American Studies and World Affairs* 14, no. 2 (1972): 151–82.
40. Marsh, *Brazilian Women's Filmmaking*, 97.
41. Rosana Cássia Kamita, "Relações de gênero no cinema," *Estudos Feministas* 25, no. 3 (2017): 1401.
42. Marsh, *Brazilian Women's Filmmaking*, 97.
43. Nygren, *Time Frames*, 224.
44. Lesser, *A Discontented Diaspora*, 64; Marsh, *Brazilian Women's Filmmaking*, 97.
45. Her first name, Tizuka, is a Brazilianization of the Japanese first name, Chizuko.
46. Marsh, *Brazilian Women's Filmmaking*, 90.
47. Melissa A. Fitch, *Side Dishes: Latina American Women, Sex, and Cultural Production* (New Brunswick, NJ: Rutgers University Press, 2009), 119; Marsh, *Brazilian Women's Filmmaking*, 94–6.
48. Marsh, *Brazilian Women's Filmmaking*, 18–22.
49. Marsh, *Brazilian Women's Filmmaking*, 89.
50. Lesser, *A Discontented Diaspora*, 65; López-Calvo, *Japanese Brazilian Saudades*, 126; Marsh, *Brazilian Women's Filmmaking*, 99.
51. Marsh, *Brazilian Women's Filmmaking*, 99.
52. Marsh, *Brazilian Women's Filmmaking*, 100.
53. For a detailed discussion of the film see Lesser, *A Discontented Diaspora*, 64–73; López-Calvo, *Japanese Brazilian Saudades*, 126–30.
54. López-Calvo, *Japanese Brazilian Saudades*, 126.
55. Marsh, *Brazilian Women's Filmmaking*, 97–8; Nygren, *Time Frames*, 225.
56. Nygren, *Time Frames*, 225–6.
57. Marsh, *Brazilian Women's Filmmaking*, 98.
58. Marsh, *Brazilian Women's Filmmaking*, 101; Memória Sindical, "Gaijin—Caminhos da Liberdade," available at <https://memoriasindical.com.br/cultura-e-reflexao/gaijin-caminhos-da-liberdade-2/> (last accessed April 20, 2020).
59. Marsh, *Brazilian Women's Filmmaking*, 102.

60. López-Calvo, *Japanese Brazilian Saudades*, 128.
61. Marsh, *Brazilian Women's Filmmaking*, 104.
62. López-Calvo, *Japanese Brazilian Saudades*, 128.
63. Lesser, *A Discontented Diaspora*, 65.
64. Marsh, *Brazilian Women's Filmmaking*, 105.
65. López-Calvo, *Japanese Brazilian Saudades*, 129. Also see Nygren, *Time Frames*, 226.
66. On this scene see López-Calvo, *Japanese Brazilian Saudades*, 125–6; Marsh, *Brazilian Women's Filmmaking*, 106–7.
67. It can be assumed that they existed historically as well, although there were probably not many cases.
68. Marsh, *Brazilian Women's Filmmaking*, 105.
69. Marsh, *Brazilian Women's Filmmaking*, 107.
70. López-Calvo, *Japanese Brazilian Saudades*, 130.
71. Lesser, *A Discontented Diaspora*, 65.
72. Maeyama, "Ethnicity," 592.
73. *Semanario de São Paulo*, September 7, 1923: 2.
74. Jeffrey Lesser, "From Japanese to Nikkei and Back: Integration Strategies of Japanese Immigrants and their Descendants in Brazil," in *Displacements and Diasporas: Asians in the Americas*, ed. Wanni W. Anderson and Robert G. Lee (New Brunswick, NJ: Rutgers University Press, 2005), 115.
75. Lesser, "From Japanese to Nikkei and Back," 114–15.
76. Emilio Willems, "The Japanese in Brazil," *Far Eastern Survey* 18, no. 1 (1949): 6.
77. Under this system every family was assigned a certain number of coffee plants and could use the soil in between for additional farming of vegetables. This was also a reason for the Brazilian government to request immigration by Japanese families.
78. Schpun, "Japanese Brazilians (1908–2013)," 89–90.
79. Schpun, "Japanese Brazilians (1908–2013)," 91.
80. Toake Endoh, *Exporting Japan: Politics of Emigration to Latin America* (Urbana: University of Illinois Press, 2009), 172.
81. Endoh, *Exporting Japan*, 175.
82. Endoh, *Exporting Japan*, 171.
83. Maeyama, "Ethnicity," 597. On the *Estado Novo*, see Nelson J. Garcia, *Estado Novo: Ideologia e propaganda política* (São Paulo: Loyola, 1982).
84. Lesser, "From Japanese to Nikkei," 116.
85. Schpun, "Japanese Brazilians (1908–2013)," 92.
86. Anna Maria Theis-Berglmair, "Öffentlichkeit und öffentliche Meinung," in *Handbuch der Public Relations*, ed. Romy Fröhlich, Peter Szyszka, and Günter Bentele, 3rd edn (Wiesbaden: Springer VS, 2015), 399–410.
87. Schpun, "Japanese Brazilians (1908–2013)," 93.
88. Schpun, "Japanese Brazilians (1908–2013)," 94.
89. Schpun, "Japanese Brazilians (1908–2013)," 96.
90. Handa Tomō, *Imin no Seikatsu no Rekishi* (Sao Paulo: Centro de Estudos Nipo-Brasileiros, 1970), 673.
91. Maeyama, "Ethnicity," 601; Schpun, "Japanese Brazilians (1908–2013)," 97.
92. Maeyama, "Ethnicity," 602.

93. Maeyama, "Ethnicity," 601.
94. Maeyama, "Ethnicity," 601; Schpun, "Japanese Brazilians (1908–2013)," 97.
95. Frank Jacob, *Japanism, Pan-Asianism and Terrorism: A Short History of the Amur Society (The Black Dragons) 1901–1945* (Bethesda, CA: Academica Press, 2014).
96. Nelson T. Johnson, Confidential Report C4-004, April 16, 1946, National Archives UK, Foreign Office, Foreign Office files for Japan, 1946–1952, FO 371-54138, No. F-6420/95/23.
97. Johnson, Confidential Report C4-004.
98. Of course, when we consider the term "secret societies" here, we must consider them to have been secret with regard to their organizational structures, members, and assassination attempts when they were active, while some activities did not remain secret and can be studied today.
99. López-Calvo, *Japanese Brazilian Saudades*, 143–4.
100. López-Calvo, *Japanese Brazilian Saudades*, 148 names 1942 as the founding year.
101. Willems, "The Japanese in Brazil," 8.
102. Willems, "The Japanese in Brazil," 8.
103. López-Calvo, *Japanese Brazilian Saudades*, 148.
104. British Embassy Rio de Janeiro, Report No. 126, to Ernest Bevin, M.P., His Majesty's Principal Secretary of State for Foreign Affairs, April 16, 1946, National Archives UK, Foreign Office, Foreign Office files for Japan, 1946–1952, FO 371-54138, No. F-6447/95/23, 1.
105. British Embassy Rio de Janeiro, Report No. 126, 1.
106. British Embassy Rio de Janeiro, Report No. 126, 1.
107. British Embassy Rio de Janeiro, Report No. 126, 2.
108. British Embassy Rio de Janeiro, Report No. 126, 2.
109. British Embassy Rio de Janeiro, Report No. 126, 3.
110. British Embassy Rio de Janeiro, Report No. 126, 4.
111. Lesser, "From Japanese to Nikkei," 116.
112. Lesser, "From Japanese to Nikkei," 116.
113. Emilio Willems and Hiroshi Saito, "Shindo Renmei: Um problema de aculturação," *Sociologia* 9 (1947): 133–52.
114. Lesser, "From Japanese to Nikkei," 117; López-Calvo, *Japanese Brazilian Saudades*, 146.
115. Maeyama, "Ethnicity," 602.
116. Lesser, "From Japanese to Nikkei," 118.
117. López-Calvo, *Japanese Brazilian Saudades*, 147.
118. Teiichi Suzuki, *The Japanese Immigrant in Brazil: Narrative Part* (Tokyo: University of Tokyo Press, 1969), 172. Japanese immigration to Brazil took off again after 1952, when Japan had signed the peace treaty with forty-eight enemy countries. Schpun, "Japanese Brazilians (1908–2013)," 98.
119. Christopher A. Reichl, "Stages in the Historical Process of Ethnicity: The Japanese in Brazil, 1908–1988," *Ethnohistory* 42, no. 1 (1995): 32.
120. Reichl, "Stages in the Historical Process of Ethnicity," 36.
121. Reichl, "Stages in the Historical Process of Ethnicity," 36–7.
122. Schpun, "Japanese Brazilians (1908–2013)," 100–2.

123. Schpun, "Japanese Brazilians (1908–2013)," 100.
124. López-Calvo, *Japanese Brazilian Saudades*, 155.
125. López-Calvo, *Japanese Brazilian Saudades*, 150.
126. Michael Carr, "Yamato-Damashii 'Japanese Spirit' Definitions," *International Journal of Lexicography* 7, no. 4 (1994): 279–306; Saitō Shōji, "*Yamatodamashii" no bunkashi* (Tokyo: Kōdansha, 1972).
127. López-Calvo, *Japanese Brazilian Saudades*, 154.
128. López-Calvo, *Japanese Brazilian Saudades*, 153.
129. On the role of assimilation with regard to in- and out-groups, see Kingsberg, "Becoming Brazilian," 67.
130. Lesser, "From Japanese to Nikkei," 118.

Works Cited

Anderson, Benedict. *Imagined Communities: Reflections on the Origin and Spread of Nationalism*. London: Verso, 1983.

Azuma, Eiichiro. *Between Two Empires: Race, History, and Transnationalism in Japanese America*. New York: Oxford University Press, 2005.

Carr, Michael. "Yamato-Damashii 'Japanese Spirit' Definitions." *International Journal of Lexicography* 7, no. 4 (1994): 279–306.

Chaunu, Pierre. "Un Petit Aspect du grand problème unitaire: la minorité japonaise au Brésil." *Annales: Histoire, Sciences Sociales* 3, no. 4, *L'Amérique du Sud devant l'histoire* (1948): 472–4.

Endoh, Toake. *Exporting Japan: Politics of Emigration to Latin America*. Urbana: University of Illinois Press, 2009.

Fitch, Melissa A. *Side Dishes: Latina American Women, Sex, and Cultural Production*. New Brunswick, NJ: Rutgers University Press, 2009.

Garcia, Nelson J. *Estado Novo: Ideologia e propaganda política*. São Paulo: Loyola, 1982.

Handa Tomō. *Imin no Seikatsu no Rekishi*. Sao Paulo: Centro de Estudos Nipo-Brasileiros, 1970.

Ichioka, Yuji. *The Issei: The World of the First Generation Japanese Immigrants, 1885–1924*. New York: Free Press, 1988.

Jacob, Frank. "Japan und der Erste Weltkrieg: Außenpolitische Chancen, wirtschaftlicher Boom und gesellschaftlicher Diskurs an der globalen Peripherie des Krieges." In *Erster Weltkrieg: Globaler Konflikt—lokale Folgen. Neue Perspektiven*, ed. Stefan Karner and Philipp Lesiak, 389–402. Innsbruck: Studienverlag, 2014.

Jacob, Frank. *Japanism, Pan-Asianism and Terrorism: A Short History of the Amur Society (The Black Dragons) 1901–1945*. Bethesda, CA: Academica Press, 2014.

Jacob, Frank. "Der Erste Weltkrieg als ökonomisch–soziale Zäsur der japanischen Moderne." In *Tōkyō in den zwanziger Jahren: Experimentierfeld einer anderen Moderne?*, ed. Stephan Köhn, Chantal Weber, and Volker Elis, 17–32. Wiesbaden: Harrassowitz, 2017.

Jacob, Frank. "Japan and the Great War: Imperialist Ambitions Abroad, Social Change and Protest at Home." In *Zeiten des Aufruhrs (1916–1921): Globale Proteste, Streiks und Revolutionen gegen den Ersten Weltkrieg und seine Auswirkungen*, ed. Marcel Bois and Frank Jacob (Berlin: Metropol, forthcoming).

Kamita, Rosana Cássia. "Relações de gênero no cinema." *Estudos Feministas* 25, no. 3 (2017): 1393–1404.

Kingsberg, Miriam. "Becoming Brazilian to Be Japanese: Emigrant Assimilation, Cultural Anthropology, and National Identity." *Comparative Studies in Society and History* 56, no. 1 (2014): 67–97.

Lesser, Jeffrey. "From Japanese to Nikkei and Back: Integration Strategies of Japanese Immigrants and their Descendants in Brazil." In *Displacements and Diasporas: Asians in the Americas*, ed. Wanni W. Anderson and Robert G. Lee, 112–21. New Brunswick, NJ: Rutgers University Press, 2005.

Lesser, Jeffrey. *A Discontented Diaspora: Japanese Brazilians and the Meanings of Ethnic Militancy, 1960–1980*. Durham, NC, and London: Duke University Press, 2007.

Lesser, Jeffrey. "A Reflection on Foreignness and the Construction of Brazilian National Identities." *Luso-Brazilian Review* 50, no. 2 (2013): 53–63.

Liu, John M. "Race, Ethnicity and the Sugar Plantation System: Asian Labor in Hawaii, 1850–1900." In *Labor Immigration Under Capitalism: Asian Workers in the United States Before WWII*, ed. Lucie Cheng and Edna Bonacich, 186–201. Los Angeles: University of California Press, 1984.

Lone, Stewart. *The Japanese Community in Brazil, 1908–1940: Between Samurai and Carnival*. New York: Palgrave, 2001.

López-Calvo, Ignacio. *Japanese Brazilian Saudades: Diasporic Identities and Cultural Production*. Boulder: University of Colorado Press, 2019.

López-Calvo, Ignacio and Kathleen López. "Cultural Celebration, Historical Memory, and Claim to Place in Júlio Miyazawa's Yawara! A Travessia Nihondin-Brasil and Uma Rosa para Yumi." In *Imagining Asia in the Americas*, ed. Zelideth María Rivas and Debbie Lee-Distefano, 158–83. New Brunswick, NJ: Rutgers University Press, 2016.

Maeyama, Takashi. "Ancestor, Emperor, and Immigrant: Religion and Group Identification of the Japanese in Rural Brazil." *Journal of Inter-American Studies and World Affairs* 14, no. 2 (1972): 151–82.

Maeyama, Takashi. "Ethnicity, Secret Societies, and Associations: The Japanese in Brazil." *Comparative Studies in Society and History* 21, no. 4 (1979): 589–610.

Marsh, Leslie L. *Brazilian Women's Filmmaking: From Dictatorship to Democracy*. Urbana: Illinois University Press, 2012.

Masterson, Daniel. *The Japanese in Latin America*. Urbana: University of Illinois Press, 2004.

Memória Sindical, "Gaijin—Caminhos da Liberdade," <https://memoriasindical.com.br/cultura-e-reflexao/gaijin-caminhos-da-liberdade-2/> (last accessed April 20, 2020).

Morais, Fernando. *Corações Sujos: A História da Shindo Renmei*. São Paulo: Companhia das Letras, 2000.

National Archives UK, Foreign Office, Foreign Office files for Japan, 1946–1952, FO 371-54138, Code 23 File 95.

Nogueira Galvão, Walnice. "As musas sob assédio: indústria cultural e globalização." *Iberoamericana, Nueva época* 4, no. 14 (2004): 95–106.

Nora, Pierre, ed. *Les Lieux de mémoire*, 3 vols. Paris: Gallimard, 1984–92.

Nygren, Scott. *Time Frames: Japanese Cinema and the Unfolding of History*. Minneapolis: University of Minnesota Press, 2007.
Reichl, Christopher A. "Stages in the Historical Process of Ethnicity: The Japanese in Brazil, 1908–1988." *Ethnohistory* 42, no. 1 (1995): 31–62.
Romani, Carlo and Bruno Corrêa de Sá e Benevides. "The Italian Anarchists' Network in São Paulo at the Beginning of the 20th Century." In *Transatlantic Radicalism*, ed. Frank Jacob and Mario Keßler. Liverpool: Liverpool University Press, forthcoming.
Saitō Shōji. "*Yamatodamashii*" *no bunkashi*. Tokyo: Kōdansha, 1972.
Schpun, Mônica Raisa. "Japanese Brazilians (1908–2013): Transnationalism amid Violence, Social Mobility, and Crisis." In *A Century of Transnationalism: Immigrants and their Homeland Connections*, ed. Nancy L. Green and Roger Waldinger, 84–105. Urbana: University of Illinois Press, 2016.
Suzuki, Teiichi. *The Japanese Immigrant in Brazil: Narrative Part*. Tokyo: University of Tokyo Press, 1969.
Theis-Berglmair, Anna Maria. "Öffentlichkeit und öffentliche Meinung." In *Handbuch der Public Relations*, ed. Romy Fröhlich, Peter Szyszka, and Günter Bentele, 3rd edn, 399–410. Wiesbaden: Springer VS, 2015.
Tomō, Handa. *Imin no Seikatsu no Rekishi*. Sao Paulo: Centro de Estudos Nipo-Brasileiros, 1970.
"Treaty of Amity, Commerce and Navigation between the Federal Republic of Brazil and the Empire of Japan," February 20, 1896, National Archives of Japan [Japanese Center for Asian Historical Records (JACAR)], A03020323999.
Willems, Emilio, "The Japanese in Brazil." *Far Eastern Survey* 18, no. 1 (1949): 6–8.
Willems, Emilio and Hiroshi Saito. "Shindo Renmei: Um problema de aculturação." *Sociologia* 9 (1947): 133–52.

PART II

MIGRANTS IN PERSPECTIVE

7. COMMUNITARIAN VERSUS HUMANITARIAN FORCES IN THE DARDENNE BROTHERS' *LA PROMESSE* (1996) AND *LE SILENCE DE LORNA* (2008)

Colleen Hays

> The majority is unaware of the minority, it's a social law. The majority lives in the belief of being the all. How would it be otherwise because all of the institutions and all of the customs are its mirror? Rare and precious are individuals from the majority that find the mirror.
>
> La majorité ignore la minorité, c'est une loi sociétale. La majorité vit dans l'évidence d'être le tout. Comment pourrait-il en être autrement puisque toutes les institutions et toutes les coutumes sont son miroir? Rares et précieux sont les individus de la majorité qui trouvent le miroir."[1]

Belgian directors Luc and Jean-Pierre Dardenne, also known as the Dardenne brothers, write and direct internationally known films that have twice won the Palme d'Or, the highest honor at Cannes, as well as numerous awards from other international film festivals. They are famous for their documentary style and realistic depiction of the blue-collar workers after the collapse of the coal industry in 1960s Wallonia (the Francophone area of Belgium). However, some of their films consider the plight of the most marginal members of Belgian society: immigrants. Although the Dardenne brothers released another film in 2019 that also investigates the immigrant experience, *Le Jeune Ahmed*, and also wrote and directed *La Fille inconnue* (2016), about a doctor seeking to retrace the death of an African prostitute, this chapter focuses on *La Promesse* (The Promise, 1996) and *Le Silence de Lorna* (Lorna's Silence, 2008), two films that investigate the plight of female immigrants and the Belgian response to their predicament, with developed, immigrant women characters. Although there are many differences between the female immigrants in each of the two films, they share fear, exploitation, and a lack of agency in their lives in Belgium. In *La Promesse*, Assita (Assita Ouedraogo) has just arrived with her baby from Burkina Faso to live in squalid conditions with her illegal-immigrant husband, Hamidou (Rasmané Ouédraogo). After he has an accident and she is widowed, she becomes dependent upon Igor (Jérémie Rénier), a Belgian adolescent whose abusive father, Roger (Olivier Gourmet), has forced him to work in the illegal-immigrant trade. In *Le Silence de Lorna*, the titular character (Arta Dobroshi) is an Albanian immigrant who has recently obtained Belgian citizenship by virtue of her marriage of convenience to Claudy, a Belgian drug addict, played by Jérémie Rénier (the staple actor of the Dardenne brothers, who had played Igor in *La Promesse* as a young teen), arranged by Lorna's john, Fabio (Fabrizio Rongione). Assita represents Otherness to an occidental European viewer, wearing vibrant African fabrics and carrying her baby around her waist in a *kitenge*. And while the Eastern European Lorna of *Le Silence de Lorna* appears assimilated to Belgian culture, she also lives on the edge of society.

Previous research on these films concentrates on their neorealistic focus, along with the themes of capitalism and development of the protagonists' sense of morality; scholars (such as Sarah Cooper and Philip Mosely) chiefly explore the films' relation to Emmanuel Levinas's concept of ethics regarding the Other. Thus, though several have written on the economic and moral considerations in *La Promesse* and *Le Silence de Lorna*, none has compared and contrasted the films in the same study; nor have they demonstrated the films' perspective on the female immigrant,[2] an absence in Dardenne scholarship that this chapter addresses. As an introduction, I will first examine the Dardenne brothers' general representation of immigrants in their œuvre before considering their specific portrayal of the female immigrant in *La Promesse* and *Le Silence de Lorna*. Next, I will explore the role of empathy provoked in the spectator by these films; while the Dardenne brothers explain that their permanent challenge is to avoid pathos,[3] this sentiment does not preclude their creating compassion and insight in the spectator. This chapter argues that the representation in both films of a male Belgian national's liminal, even expendable, existence mirrors that of the female immigrant, creating a filter through which Western spectators can experience empathy and understanding for those who do not fit their own profile. This contrasts with the trajectory of a film such as Philippe Lioret's *Welcome* (2009), which, while telling the story of an Iraqi who immigrates to France, emphasizes instead the French protagonist's evolution from a citizen who is indifferent to the immigrants' plight to one who awakens and actively tries to help them. In *La Promesse* and *Le Silence de Lorna*, the viewer associates the Belgian nationals' desperation and estrangement from mainstream Belgian society with those of the immigrants, thereby providing a conduit through which the Westerner can better relate to the latter's misery. Consequently, the film effects change not through pity and objectification but via identification with the principal male Belgian protagonists. In this way, the spectator's bond with the male Europeans leads to a revelation of the immigrants' situation, yet still through the prism of Otherness. In conclusion, I consider Michel Foucault's discussion of the communitarian versus the humanitarian forces in society, or the belief that the human need to self-identify as a member of a tribe supersedes a call to empathy for the Other, for these films in fact, elicit empathy for the outsider through exploiting such a tribal association.

Representation of the Immigrant

The Dardenne brothers portray the immigrants' lives in both films as exceedingly bleak and demoralizing due to their exploitation by Belgian nationals. While the principal immigrant roles are female, the representations of male immigrants in both films reinforce the general plight of this minority grouping within Belgian society. In *La Promesse*, Roger, with son Igor at his side, uses the male immigrants' desperate circumstances for his own profit. The immigrants have thus no option but to overpay for unclean, cold apartments with dilapidated furniture, reeking of sewage. Roger offers to help them by lowering their rent in exchange for construction work on his house, although they will still be responsible for buying heating oil and other necessities. Under this arrangement, the immigrants are expendable because there are always more arriving. When Roger's boss in the trade of illegals tells him that the police need to round some up to give the appearance of enforcing the law, Roger designates a group of four sacrificial Eastern European males. Roger's response to Hamidou's accident on the job reveals his opinion of an illegal immigrant's worth: not only does he remove the tourniquet that his son put on Hamidou's leg to stop the bleeding, but he refuses to take him to the hospital. In contrast, *Le Silence de Lorna* studies Lorna and her boyfriend, Sokol, both Albanian and both involved with Fabio, a Belgian taxi driver, who expands his criminal trade to involve Eastern Europeans and Russians seeking Belgian citizenship. Sokol lives above subsistence level, but has made dangerous compromises to do so; he works in German nuclear reactors, receiving 1,000 Euros for each minute he spends inside. In summary, the male immigrants in both films take great chances to come to Western Europe to live out their dreams, even risking deportation and death, while being exploited by Belgian nationals.

Although both female immigrant characters come from areas of the world where Islam is the predominant religion, the films lack Muslim signifiers, allowing the Western audience to relate more easily to the immigrants' situation. Assita in *La Promesse* comes from Burkina Faso and Lorna is Albanian (although her country of origin is unclear), rather than being from areas that provide the highest percentage of non-European Union immigrants to Belgium: Morocco, Turkey, or the Republic of Congo.[4] While Burkina Faso, formerly a French colony (Upper Volta), had a high rate of migration in 1996, movement was not intercontinental and Burkinabés chiefly moved to the Ivory Coast.[5] Assita purchases a sheep for sacrifice—an act that recalls Islam—but her religious activity focuses on animism, a minority pagan religion in Burkina Faso. She performs such actions as cutting open a chicken to read its entrails and visiting a shaman who practices divination to determine if her husband is dead. Western viewers might observe these acts as primitive and superstitious, but they do not associate them with Islam in the same way that they would characters praying on rugs or visiting a mosque. Lorna, conversely, never invokes any religion and the dialogue does not reveal if she is an ethnic Albanian from Albania, Kosovo, the Republic of Macedonia, or another Balkan state. Thus, the two female immigrants, and the films themselves, effectively avoid identification with Islam and protect the European viewer from possible alienation on the basis of anti-Muslim sentiments. The fact that these characters speak mostly French intensifies their relationship with European spectators, and an even larger art film public that follows French-language features.

Both characters are strong and resolute in their plans for survival, and also display nurturing, maternal qualities. For example, in *La Promesse*, after Hamidou's disappearance, even though she is an illegal immigrant, Assita begins a determined quest to find her husband and insists on going to the police department to give them his description. In *Le Silence de Lorna*, when Lorna begins to sympathize with heroin addict Claudy, she sternly refuses his requests to leave the apartment (even taking the key away from him so that he cannot go out and find drugs) and intuits his lies. However, later in the film she lets him help her—she has no other options—and she nurtures him in return, even preparing him a meal in true maternal fashion. With regard to Lorna, the audience does not know why or when she came to Belgium—the mass exodus from the Balkans took place in the 1990s— and she does not appear to be a refugee. Instead, Lorna seems driven by a dream of financial success in Europe, and of owning a snack bar with her boyfriend in Belgium. To accomplish the first step of becoming a Belgian citizen, Lorna arranges with Fabio that she will marry a Belgian drug addict, Igor, who also agrees to an arrangement to supply him with drugs. The plot revolves around provoking an overdose in Igor, which will then allow Fabio to profit by charging other men 10,000 Euros to marry Lorna (now a new Belgian widow) to gain European citizenship—in particular, a rich Russian, whom we meet in the second half of the film. Near the beginning of the movie, as the audience learns of her part in the scheme, the Western European viewer might experience echoes of the stereotypes attributed to Albanians: involvement in prostitution, clandestine immigration, and drug and arms trafficking.[6] Lorna eschews a personal relationship with Claudy—she is single-mindedly progressing toward her goal of citizenship. This coldness distances the viewer, however, just as some of Igor's actions do before he promises to care for Assita. However, when Lorna witnesses Claudy's desperation, she waivers and does what she can to save him (short of telling him that his life is in danger).

Both female characters' strength and determination are mediated by their caring acts: Assita loves her child and eventually accepts Igor, and Lorna looks after Claudy. This contrasts strongly with their partners' behavior: Hamidou gambles away his money and cannot pay the rent or for heat for his family, and Sokol abandons Lorna once he sees that she is condemned by Fabio. Thus, the Dardenne brothers created female immigrant characters who, though forceful and resolute, are also approachable and loving, thereby ultimately creating a safe audience space to view them.

The Westerner as the Other

In the roles of the adolescent Igor and drug addict Claudy, Jérémie Rénier depicts male Belgian nationals living on the periphery of society. Igor has left middle school and is doing an apprenticeship with a mechanic, which he abandons because his father Roger demands his labor. We meet him at the mechanic's service station, where Igor politely fixes an older woman's car, then steals her money and lies to her about it. This leaves the audience with a cynical attitude toward the young, seemingly charming teen. His stealing is emblematic of other instances when he habitually collects an exorbitant amount of money from illegal immigrants at his father's bidding. When the film begins, Roger's relationship with Igor is not clear: Roger treats Igor as a subordinate co-worker/pal and attempts to eliminate the father–son bond, later telling Igor to call him "Roger" and not Dad. He seduces him by giving him a matching tattoo and a matching ring, as though Igor is joining his gang.[7] Igor works tirelessly with the immigrants, doing the same work they do; however, his motivation is to serve as his father's lieutenant. Igor is therefore comfortable being Roger's right-hand man and has a place in the latter's domain, but lacks a substantial link to broader Belgian society as his life is defined by his role in Roger's world. He is at Roger's beck and call: besides giving up the apprenticeship, he is called away from his friends whenever he is needed, Roger allowing him no other link to the outside world. The audience, witnessing how Igor is a child enmeshed in a problematic relationship with his father, realizes that he is not just a delinquent who willingly dupes people but rather an abused child, and better understands Igor's actions.

When Assita arrives with her baby to live with Hamidou, Igor is immediately curious and feels drawn to her. We share in his voyeurism as he peeks though an opening in the wall to see her caring for her baby soon after her arrival, an intimate family moment. Even though Igor knows it would not please his father, he gives Hamidou free heating oil for his family, which foreshadows his break from Roger's world. One day, when government inspectors arrive at Roger's house searching for immigrant laborers, Hamidou rushes to hide and falls from the house, seriously injuring himself; Igor goes to help him. Hamidou extracts a promise from Igor to protect his family if he himself cannot. From this moment, the break between father and son becomes inevitable. When Roger discovers that Igor has given some of his own money to Assita, he beats him, stopping only when his girlfriend shouts that he might kill Igor. In this scene, the camera is focused on Roger's back, his largeness looming over the much smaller Igor. Igor recoils into the fetal position, emphasizing his helplessness, and shields his face so that we see only his fearfulness, provoking audience sympathy. Roger's girlfriend pulls him off Igor, saying that Roger could have killed him. Although Roger later tries to repair the relationship, this event informs Igor and the viewer that Roger could indeed end Igor's life if he disobeyed again. Igor is thereafter further isolated because he can no longer trust Roger and he has no other strong relationships. He is truly in a liminal space.

Assita's isolation mirrors Igor's. She has come to Belgium to be with her irresponsible husband, who has gambled away the money that he owes Roger for her journey and more. Roger says he will deduct from Hamidou's earnings to pay for Assita's journey, further compromising the well-being of Assita and her baby. Assita, like Igor, is industrious and she tries to manage. When Hamidou goes missing, she is isolated. Her family ties in Belgium are non-existent, and she cannot find a place in Belgian society as a recently arrived, illegal immigrant of color with a baby. Her outsider status is underlined in a scene where she waits for Igor below a bridge over the highway. Two men standing on the bridge above urinate on her and her baby, then ride their motorcycles down to her level, crushing her bag and beheading her religious statuette. Roger's earlier attack on Igor is echoed when Nabil (Hachemi Haddad), Roger's paid henchman, bursts into Assita's apartment to feign a sexual assault so that Roger can come to her aid and gain her trust. Again, in this violent scene we see the attacker from behind, enhanced by a back shot, with mostly a side view of the victim's contorted face. This assault prepares the viewer for Roger's final solution: selling Assita into prostitution, a destiny for many female African immigrants.[8]

Thus the viewer, whether consciously or subconsciously, makes a connection between Igor—exploited and beaten by his father with no other close alliance—and Assita, the only black female immigrant in Roger's slum house, who is neglected by her husband, left widowed without recourse, and is in danger from Roger. This connection becomes more concrete after Assita and Igor argue and she shouts at him to leave. Igor then rushes to embrace Assita. During this 15-second embrace, the camera focuses on Igor's desperate face, his head resting on Assita's shoulder as he tries to avoid crying; we see only the arm of her dress, her face out of frame because of her greater height, thus underlining her adulthood (Fig. 7.1).

Assita tells him to let go, but he is clings on and she stops pushing him away. When he does break from her, we see in a shot–reverse shot that she is staring at him in bewilderment while he looks up at her and tries to dry his tears. I would disagree with Lauren Berlant's description of the scene: "They bicker and scream, but ultimately he forces her to shut up and submit to giving him what he wants: a hug."[9] Assita does not submit—she makes a conscious decision to hug Igor, and the viewer can only hypothesize the reason. However, the embrace asks the audience to associate the young white Belgian male with the Burkinabé mother: Igor has made a physical connection with the Other, and the embrace literally bonds them. The contact is significant because, up to this point, Igor has only acted on his promise to Hamidou to take care of Assita, and has not attempted any personal recompense. However, the embrace testifies to his vulnerability and desire for connection: Assita's skin color and status in Belgium are not relevant to Igor's needs. As the film ends with Assita and Igor leaving

Figure 7.1 Assita and Igor embrace in *La Promesse* (Les Films du fleuve, 1996).

Figure 7.2   Assita and Igor at the train station after the confession in *La Promesse* (Les Films du fleuve, 1996).

the train station together after he tells her husband is dead, the viewer does not question the bonding of the Western European to the Burkinabé (Fig. 7.2); Igor's evolution from an exploiter of immigrants to someone who accepts and is responsible for Assita prepares the audience to also accept Assita as belonging in Western society.

In *Lorna's Silence*, the drug addict Claudy is much like the male immigrants in *La Promesse*: dispensable. An emaciated Rénier[10] portrays a Belgian national whose drug addiction isolates him from society, his only visitor being his drug dealer. Claudy is portrayed as an invalid, further alienated by unemployment and without apparent family ties. He is not demonized but rather infantilized, creating some audience sympathy for his relative innocence in the arranged marriage scheme. On the other hand, we are distanced, as he appears to be "just a junkie," as other characters refer to him. From almost the beginning of the film he says that he wants to get clean, which essentially keeps him prisoner in his and Lorna's apartment because the drug dealer is lurking outside the door. His lack of freedom resembles that of an illegal immigrant, whom the outside world threatens with discovery—both are essentially prisoners.

In the first shot of the film, we see Lorna opposite a bank teller, who is counting the money that she is depositing in an account, saving for an apartment that she and her boyfriend, Sokol, plan to buy. She will soon have more to deposit after Claudy's overdose, as he will never receive his share of the money agreed for the sham marriage. As Luc Dardenne states, Lorna could not be transformed "into a poor emigrant, victim of the evil Belgians, since she participates in the plot."[11] If that were the case, the West European audience would pity her, and she would have no agency. Lorna determines their living arrangements in the sterile apartment—all white walls with no decoration—which echoes their relationship. She orders Claudy around, telling him to shut the curtains or to remove his "bed," a piece of foam hidden under her own proper bed, at night. She finds his music and his attempts to construct a relationship annoying, and even his very presence in the small, bleak apartment bothers her. He is often in a physically subaltern position, unable to stand straight, weakened from drug abuse and then withdrawal pains. However, as Claudy makes a genuine decision to get clean, he slowly draws the previously detached Lorna into his life.

As Lorna grudgingly helps Claudy to become sober, her resolve to objectify him weakens, though only gradually. In one scene that takes place during Claudy's withdrawal, as he writhes on the floor with cramps and begs for water, she serves him water in a bowl on the floor; he laps it up, underlining his subhuman status (Fig. 7.3). But with each service he demands of her—buying him medicine, helping him to the hospital, staying with him as he waits to be admitted, bringing his CD player to the hospital—she becomes more attached to the prospect of his successful detoxification. Her change of heart is illustrated when she goes into his hospital room and briefly watches him sleep, something she never would have done in their apartment. As she watches him struggle, she is no longer in agreement that he must die; Fabio, however, has informed her that if he does not die from a self-inflicted overdose, one would be forced on him. As Fabio states, Claudy deserves no better: he is just a junkie whose death does not count, a sentiment that Lorna's boyfriend, Sokol, repeats. Fabio believes a divorce from Claudy would make the police too suspicious, but nevertheless, Lorna searches for a way to avoid murder and decides on a quickie divorce, based on claims of domestic violence, even though it will be risky for her.

In order save Claudy's life, Lorna proceeds with her plan to divorce him and urges him to hit her in the hospital room. When he retorts, "I may be a junkie, but I've never hit a woman," she smacks her head against a metal window and succeeds in obtaining a divorce. This causes Claudy to despair, as his one

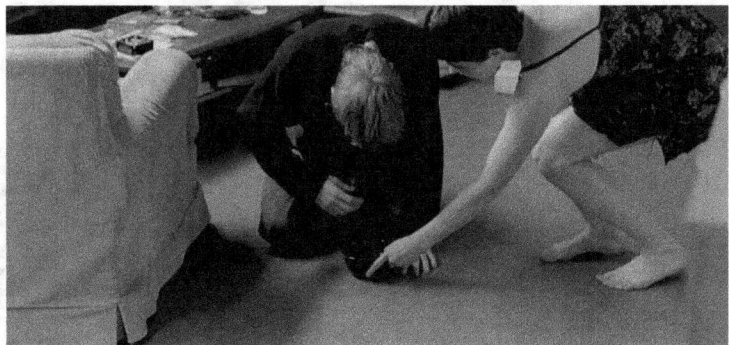

Figure 7.3 Claudy taking water from Lorna in *Le Silence de Lorna* (Les Films du fleuve, 2008).

human connection is deserting him. There follows an echo of an earlier scene, in which Claudy begged Lorna to lock him in to save him from his dealer, even clinging to her leg so that she could not easily walk away, and throwing his apartment keys out of the window to ensure that he cannot leave. In this later scene, their roles are reversed: as Lorna announces their impending divorce, she struggles with a desperate Claudy to keep the keys so that he cannot go to his dealer. They wrestle and she manages to lock the door; this time, it is she who throws the keys out of the window. Claudy collapses on the floor of the entryway and weeps. Lorna quickly disrobes and runs to him. Altering a trope used in the film in which Lorna never raises Claudy from his subaltern position, whether he is on the floor writhing in pain, clinging to her leg, or otherwise in a submissive position, she pulls him up to her level. She removes his shirt and he removes his pants. In a scene that recalls the one in *La Promesse* in which Assita and Igor cling to each other, Lorna and Claudy first look each other in the eyes for several seconds before they clutch one other, an embrace lasting 34 seconds, and establishing a connection and an equality (Fig. 7.4).

In a medium side shot—the audience sees only the door handle and not Claudy's face—we see the side of Lorna's face and both of their backs, with their arms in movement as they caress each other. This is a long, passionate embrace, which leads to a love-making scene at the door, the line of sight being from the entryway, with the door handle and means of escape now meaningfully obscured. The plain-white, arched entry frames them and focuses the audience's attention on the human connection. It is a redemptive embrace, allowing the audience to alter their perception of Claudy and of Lorna. He is

Figure 7.4   Claudy and Lorna embrace in *Le Silence de Lorna* (Les Films du fleuve, 2008).

no longer an infantile, grasping junkie, but a man capable of offering himself to another as an equal. The spectator's sympathy at this point grows into hope for him, for his future existence, and we ultimately become invested in his staying alive. We can recognize Claudy as ourselves—a person with dreams and potential; he later even talks of getting a job. Simultaneously, our view of Lorna evolves. She is no longer the cold, opportunistic immigrant who profits from a European's planned death to open a café. She has evolved into a person who regrets her part in a murder plot and tries to save a life. At potentially great cost, she breaks from a criminal scheme that exploits a Belgian national, finally recognizing Claudy's and her own humanity. Their bodily connection not only unites them, but it induces viewers to associate the newly caring immigrant Lorna with the newly redeemed Claudy. Effectively, the film encourages the audience to identify Lorna with Claudy and to identify with both in sympathy.

Claudy's murder occurs regardless. Subsequently, Lorna attributes a missed menstrual period to a pregnancy by him. In *Au dos de nos Images II*, Luc Dardenne states that this "phantom child is not only one of guilt (she ought to have told Claudy what was being plotted against him) but also of love."[12] Jean-Luc says they are surprised "by the number of readers [of the screenplay] who want her to expect Claudy's child, as though they want her to be able to buy herself back."[13] He further mentions one reader who believed that Lorna was pregnant, in spite of the narrative. Due to Lorna's passionate belief that the child inside her is alive and because of her attempts to save the fantasized child, the audience feels compassion for her. While the imaginary child represents Lorna's attempt to atone for her sin of silence, he/she also legitimizes and normalizes Lorna as the mother of a mixed child with automatic Belgian citizenship. She is no longer the Other, transformed through her relationship with Claudy.

Referring to Dardenne brothers' pre-2007 films (encompassing *La Promesse*), Sarah Cooper writes: "The Dardenne brothers' cinema is not one of empathy through conventional identificatory routes, but is one of proximity."[14] She explains that the camera position in Dardenne brothers' films does not exactly replicate the point of view of the characters; it is rather in a position of proximity, and therefore "guards against identification on the part of the spectator," but leaves us with a closeness to them and registers "both the other characters' and our own distance from those filmed."[15] Martin O'Shaughnessy states that the Dardenne brothers' cinema demands an ethical spectatorship that "lies in a detached proximity to the main protagonists."[16] He further asserts: "In the same way that the protagonists are forced to recognize their being-with-others, we are forced to be with the characters."[17] I disagree and would say, rather, that the main characters' detached proximity does not endure during the course of these two films and neither does the spectators' distance. In fact, as both mixed couples with differing citizenship and needs—Assita and Igor, and Lorna and Claudy—are increasingly in close proximity, they become increasingly united. Concurrently, the spectators' point of view becomes one of acceptance and empathy, as we recognize and acknowledge our commonalities with the immigrants and subconsciously minimize their foreignness.

COMMUNITARIANISM VERSUS HUMANITARIANISM IN CIVIL SOCIETY

If the ideas concerning civil society as described by Michel Foucault are applied to these two films, a sharper portrait of Belgium's relationship with immigrants emerges. In a lecture on April 4, 1979, at the Collège de France, Foucault explains that civil society is not an immediate reality, but rather forms a part of modern governmental technology.[18] He explains that civil society is, instead,

> much like sexuality and madness, what I call transactional realities (réalités de transaction). That is to say, those transactional and transitional figures that we call civil society, madness, and so on, which although they have not always existed are nonetheless real, are born precisely from the interplay of the relationship of power and everything which constantly eludes them, at the interface, so to speak, of governors and governed.[19]

We thus find a definition of civil society as intrinsically connected to governing powers, unlike the more common concept of civil society as existing outside of the realm of government agencies.[20] Foucault's comments on the second and fourth essential characteristics of civil society, which he takes from Adam Ferguson, apply most obviously to *La Promesse* and *Le Silence de Lorna*, which depict immigrants as immobilized by a web of capitalist and state structures.[21]

Regarding the second characteristic, Foucault explains that civil society "assures the spontaneous synthesis of individuals."[22] By this, he means that there is no forced relationship, no agreement to subjection, and although the value of individuals depends upon their value to the group, that value is not to be attributed solely to the group but also ascribed to each individual. People come together because of interests—and Foucault says these are not economic interests, although this unity of interests performs via the same mechanism as the mechanism of economic interests: that is, the shared interests of the individual and the whole.[23] To begin his discussion, Foucault cites Ferguson's four civil society bonds: "instinct, sentiment, sympathy, and the feelings of benevolence people feel for one another or of loathing for others, disgust for the troubles of some and pleasure in the hardships of others."[24] Foucault states that these bonds bring people together in "units," and then lead individuals to support the views of the group. "Civil society is not humanitarian but communitarian," he says,[25] stating that one can see it on all levels: familial, village, corporate, and even national. Furthermore, the economic bond, which brings economic subjects together, can lodge itself in the medium of civil society because of shared interests.[26] However, when this does happen, the bonds of benevolence and so on, and the economic egotism inherent in the economic bond dissociate. Fundamentally, the economic bond, once inserted into civil society, threatens its spontaneous bonds.

If we look at the main characters in *La Promesse* and *Le Silence de Lorna* from the perspective of Foucault's civil society, we note that all four were financially dependent upon others at the beginning of the films and shared an economic bond: Igor was a servant to his father, who assured his economic security; Assita was tied to her husband's financial situation, tenuous as it was; Claudy, who could not work and had a relationship only with his dealer, was financially supported by a criminal arrangement; and Lorna joined with criminals in a murderous, money-making scheme. They all had important economic considerations and felt an impetus to continue these economic bonds; however, each, at some point, abandoned these economic ties for human and humanitarian bonds, breaking free of their one-time communitarian unit that no longer served their wishes. They chose to remake their bonds based on criteria other than economic concerns. Igor and Assita begin to support one another after their traumas involving Roger. Claudy turns the corner and chooses to live by virtue of having a relationship with Lorna, deserting his drug dealer; and Lorna gives up her financial interests, as well as taking risks with her life, to honor her bond with Claudy. The characters evolve in such a way that economic interests are not central to their choices; instead, they choose to bond with people who are outside their community, forging new communities.

If we then look at these films from a broader spectrum—one of audience reception—it can be said that viewers are also encouraged to make new choices. Many Western Europeans are part of a broad group with many common interests; sociologists Mitchell Dean, and Kaspar Villadsen term this "community or civil society" (34),[27] one in which Foucault would say that the individuals are linked by feelings of benevolence for one another, and possibly loathing for others.[28] One may assume that the majority of the Western European audiences for *La Promesse* and *Le Silence de Lorna* would identify more universally with blond, native French speakers Igor and Claudy, and less with immigrants Assita and Lorna. Although Igor and Claudy are clearly antipathetic early in the films—Igor's robbery of the old woman and Claudy's drug dependence repel us—they are not performing as members of the idealized Western European unit. Igor exploits people and Claudy is a junkie; both are members of the demi-monde. However, as they morph into personages who decide to change their lives—followed up by the concerted efforts they make—Western European viewers can allow Igor and Claudy into their unit; they are deserving of the community's benevolence in a communitarian, tribal-like response. When Claudy and Igor then receive Assita and Lorna fully into their lives—symbolized by the couples' strong embraces—the viewer can then identify with the Belgian males' acceptance of the Other. This holds true, even as we watch them go outside of Western choices for companionship. Thus, in relation to the viewers' growing acceptance, Assita and Lorna become more complex and less unidimensional. No longer stereotypical immigrants that we mistrust or ignore, they have become individual women whose dilemmas touch us. Their ability to provoke a humanitarian response in the viewer derives from Igor's and Claudy's reception, which, in fact, can enlarge viewers' communitarian perimeters.

Let us now turn to Foucault's explanation of the fourth characteristic of civil society—that it could be called "the motor of history." Foucault believed that economic bonds, based on economic egotisms within civil society, always threaten to tear it down. As economic bonds are constantly challenged and reformed to be more advantageous to the individual, they cause the "dissociation of the spontaneous equilibrium of civil society."[29] He further states that the principle of dissociative association is also a principle of historical transformation.[30] This process is what Foucault calls the motor of history in civil society: "It is egoistic interest, and consequently the economic game, which introduces the dimension through which history is permanently present in civil society, the process through which civil society is inevitable and necessarily involved in history."[31]

To return to the films, I would suggest that the dissolution of the main characters' initial bonds in *La Promesse* and *Le Silence de Lorna* is a sort of dissociative association. Their interests are no longer served by remaining in those units: instead of economic egotism being the driving force for their departure, self-preservation and a need to be needed are at play. Igor's responsibility for Assita and Claudy's love for Lorna lead the audience not only to accept the immigrant characters but also to understand the relationship between characters without judgment. If we adapt Foucault's idea pertaining to economic structure—that dissociative association drives the motor of history—this concept can also be applied to cultural structure. *La Promesse* and *Le Silence de Lorna* cause us to think differently about the immigrants in the films and to broaden our understanding of the challenges faced by such immigrants. As Constance De Gourcy states: "the cinema [is] a faithful witness of the stakes of its time [and] shows the way in which a society builds its relation to the otherness through the appearance of the foreigner."[32] Through our acceptance of Assita and Lorna, our communitarian bonds are challenged, if not completely broken, and we experience some level of dissociative association.;Via Igor and Claudy, the male Western characters, we experience a sort of historical transformation, even if on a small scale, reflecting the unique power of film to communicate complex dynamics and impact social change.

Notes

1. Luc Dardenne, *Au dos de nos images II (2005–14)* (Paris: Éditions du Seuil, 2015), 33.
2. Titles that treat the films through Levinas's lens include Philip Mosely, *The Cinema of the Dardenne Brothers: Responsible Realism* (New York: University of Columbia Press, 2013); Joseph Mai, "*Silence* and Levinas's Ethical Alternative: Form and Viewer in the Dardenne Brothers," *New Review of Film and Television Studies* 9, no. 4 (October 2011): 435–53; Michèle Bissière, "De *La Promesse* (1996) à *l'Enfant* (2005): le cinéma éthique des frères Dardenne," *Dialogues et Cultures* 56 (2010): 108–16; and Sarah Cooper, "Mortal Ethics: Reading Levinas with the Dardenne Brothers," *Film Philosophy* 11, no. 2 (August 2007): 68–87.
3. Qtd in Bissière, "De *La Promesse* (1996) à *l'Enfant* (2005)," 109.
4. Marco Martiniello and Andrea Rea, "Belgium's Immigration Policy Brings Renewal and Challenges," *Migration Information Source*, Migration Policy Institute (October 1, 2003), available at <https://www.migrationpolicy.org/article/belgiums-immigration-policy-brings-renewal-and-challenges> (last accessed December 16, 2017).
5. Bonayi Dabore, Hamidou Kone, and Siaka Lougue, *Recensement général de la population et de l'habitation de 2006 (RGPH-2006): anaylse des résultats définitifs. Thème 8: Migrations*, Ministère de l'économie, Comité National du Recensement, Bureau Centre du recensement, Burkina Faso (October 2009), available at <http://www.insd.bf/n/contenu/enquetes_recensements/rgph-bf/themes_en_demographie/Theme8-Migrations.pdf> (last accessed December 16, 2017).
6. Stéphane Bouchet, "La Mafia albanaise gangrène l'Europe," *Le Parisien*, May 28, 2000, available at <http://www.leparisien.fr/faits-divers/la-mafia-albanaise-gangrene-l-europe-28-05-2000-2001403117.php> (last accessed December 1, 2020).
7. While I find Roger abusive, I do not agree with Laura E. Ruberto that Roger's actions border on pedophilia. She states: "A shower scene in which Roger helps Igor wash mud off his legs and feet—shot with a hand-held camera and lots of close-ups of unclothed flesh, has a soft porn effect." Laura E. Ruberto, "Neo-realism and Contemporary European Immigration," in *Italian Neo-Realism and Global Cinema*, ed. Laura E. Ruberto and Kristi M. Wilson (Detroit: Wayne State University Press, 2007), 254. In fact, Roger is helping Igor remove his wet socks so that he can wash Hamidou's blood off Igor's feet, blood that implicates them both.
8. As of 2008–9, 60 percent of female sex workers in Belgium were migrants and 26 percent of these were from Africa. TAMPEP 8, WP4 Mapping (January 24, 2010), available at <https://webgate.ec.europa.eu/chafea_pdb/assets/files/pdb/2006344/2006344_d4_deliverable_t8_annex_10_d_national_reports_mapping.pdf> (last accessed December 16, 2020).
9. Lauren Berlant, "Nearly Utopian, Nearly Normal: Post-Fordist Affect in *La Promesse* and *Rosetta*," *Public Culture* 19, no. 2 (2007): 276.
10. Although he is a drug addict, he is not pursued as a criminal because there was a tolerance for individual heroin use and an emphasis on treatment in Belgium. "The ambitious 'Drug and Drug Action Program' (3 February 1995) reflects a global and transversal policy of reducing risks to health and specific crime (Duprez et al., 2005; Kaminski, 1996; Kaminski, Mary, 1999). In line with the government's drug plan,

it intends to become independent of global security plans. The drug field, translated into a 'program of action', will stimulate the birth of ten specific measures." Two of these specific measures are "la mise en place de maisons d'accueil socio-sanitaires pour consommateurs de drogues marginalisés" (the establishment of socio-medical shelters for marginalized drug users) and "l'organisation optimale et l'augmentation de l'offre de soins aux consommateurs de drogues" (optimal organization and increase of the supply of care to drug users). Caroline Jeanmart, "Entre cadre légal et pratiques de consommations: l'usage de drogues illicites en Belgique francophone," *Déviance et société* 32, no. 3 (2008): 288.
11. Dardenne, *Au dos de nos images II*, 70.
12. Dardenne, *Au dos de nos images II*, 39.
13. Dardenne, *Au dos de nos images II*, 86.
14. Cooper, "Mortal Ethics," 84.
15. Cooper, "Mortal Ethics," 85.
16. Martin O'Shaughnessy, "Ethics in the Ruin of Politics: The Dardenne Brothers," in *Five Directors: Auteurism from Assayas to Ozon*, ed. Kate Ince, 80 (Manchester: Manchester University Press, 2011).
17. O'Shaughnessy, "Ethics in the Ruin of Politics," 80.
18. Michel Foucault, *Birth of Biopolitics, Lectures at the Collège de France 1978–1979*, ed. Michael Senellart, trans. Graham Burchell, 297 (London and New York: Palgrave MacMillan, 2008).
19. Foucault, *Birth of Biopolitics*, 297.
20. According to the United Nations, civil society is "the 'third sector' of society, along with government and business. It comprises civil society organizations and non-governmental organizations" (available at <http://www.un.org/en/sections/resources-different-audiences/civil-society/> (last accessed December 1, 2020)). Although this is not the only definition of "civil society," it is a common one. Civil society is generally seen to be a force outside the areas of government and business.
21. Adam Ferguson was a Scottish philosopher and historian of the Scottish Enlightenment. Foucault uses his *An Essay on the History of Civil Society* (1767) in his lecture of August 4, 1979. The four essential characteristics of civil society that Foucault borrows from Ferguson are: firstly, civil society is a historical–natural constant; secondly, civil society assures the spontaneous synthesis of individuals; thirdly, civil society is a permanent matrix of political power; and fourthly, civil society constitutes the motor of history.
22. Foucault, *Birth of Biopolitics*, 300.
23. Foucault, *Birth of Biopolitics*, 301.
24. Foucault, *Birth of Biopolitics*, 301.
25. Foucault, *Birth of Biopolitics*, 302.
26. Foucault, *Birth of Biopolitics*, 302.
27. Mitchell Dean and Kaspar Villadsen, *State Phobia and Civil Society: The Political Legacy of Michel Foucault* (Redwood City, CA: Stanford University Press, 2016), 34.
28. Foucault, *Birth of Biopolitics*, 301.
29. Foucault, *Birth of Biopolitics*, 306.
30. Foucault, *Birth of Biopolitics*, 306.

31. Foucault, *Birth of Biopolitics*, 307.
32. Constance De Gourcy, "Le Cinéma a besoin de l'individu, les migrants ont besoin du cinéma pour redevenir des individus. Entretien avec Andrea Segre," *Revue européenne des migrations internationals*, 32, nos 3 and 4 (2016): 2, available at <https://journals.openedition.org/remi/8209> (last accessed November 30, 2020).

WORKS CITED

Berlant, Lauren. "Nearly Utopian, Nearly Normal: Post-Fordist Affect in *La Promesse* and *Rosetta*." *Public Culture* 19, no. 2 (2007): 273–90.

Bissière, Michèle. "De *La Promesse* (1996) à *l'Enfant* (2005): le cinéma éthique des frères Dardenne." *Dialogues et Cultures* 56 (2010): 108–16.

Dabore, Bonayi, Hamidou Kone, and Siaka Lougue. *Recensement général de la population et de l'habitation de 2006 (RGPH-2006): anaylse des résultats définitifs. Thème 8: Migrations*, Ministère de l'économie, Comité National du Recensement, Bureau Centre du recensement, Burkina Faso (October 2009), <http://www.insd.bf/n/contenu/enquetes_recensements/rgph-bf/themes_en_demographie/Theme8-Migrations.pdf> (last accessed December 16, 2017).

Dean, Mitchell and Kaspar Villadsen. *State Phobia and Civil Society: The Political Legacy of Michel Foucault*. Redwood City, CA: Stanford University Press, 2016).

Bouchet, Stéphane. "La Mafia albanaise gangrène l'Europe." *Le Parisien*, May 28, 2000, <http://www.leparisien.fr/faits-divers/la-mafia-albanaise-gangrene-l-europe-28-05-2000-2001403117.php> (last accessed December 1, 2020).

Cooper, Sarah. "Mortal Ethics: Reading Levinas with the Dardenne Brothers." *Film-Philosophy* 11, no. 2 (August 2007): 66–87.

Dardenne, Luc. *Au dos de nos images (1995–2005)*. Paris: Éditions du Seuil, 1996.

Dardenne, Luc. *Au dos de nos images II (2005–14)*. Paris: Éditions du Seuil, 2015.

De Gourcy, Constance. "Le Cinéma a besoin de l'individu, les migrants ont besoin du cinéma pour redevenir des individus. Entretien avec Andrea Segre." *Revue européenne des migrations internationales* 32, nos 3 and 4 (2016): 2, <https://journals.openedition.org/remi/8209> (last accessed November 30, 2020).

Foucault, Michel. *The Birth of Biopolitics: Lectures at the Collège of France, 1978–1979*, ed. Michael Senellart, trans. Graham Burchell. London and New York: Palgrave MacMillan, 2008.

Jeanmart, Caroline. "Entre cadre légal et pratiques de consommations: l'usage de drogues illicites en Belgique francophone." *Déviance et société* 32, no. 3 (2008): 285–302.

Mai, Joseph. "*Silence* and Levinas's Ethical Alternative: Form and Viewer in the Dardenne Brothers." *New Review of Film and Television Studies* 9, no. 4 (October 2011): 435–53.

Martiniello, Marco and Andrea Rea. "Belgium's Immigration Policy Brings Renewal and Challenges." *Migration Information Source*, Migration Policy Institute (January 6, 2017), <https://www.migrationpolicy.org/article/belgiums-immigration-policy-brings-renewal-and-challenges> (last accessed 17 December 2020).

Mosely, Philip. *The Cinema of the Dardenne Brothers: Responsible Realism*. New York: University of Columbia Press, 2013.

O'Shaughnessy, Martin. "Ethics in the Ruin of Politics: The Dardenne Brothers." In *Five Directors: Auteurism from Assayas to Ozon*, ed. Kate Ince, 59–83. Manchester: Manchester University Press, 2011.

Ruberto, Laura E. "Neo-realism and Contemporary European Immigration." In *Italian Neo-Realism and Global Cinema*, ed. Laura E. Ruberto and Kristi M. Wilson, 242–58. Detroit: Wayne State University Press, 2007.

TAMPEP 8, WP4 Mapping (January 24, 2010), <https://webgate.ec.europa.eu/chafea_pdb/assets/files/pdb/2006344/2006344_d4_deliverable_t8_annex_10_d_national_reports_mapping.pdf> (last accessed December 16, 2020).

United Nations. *Civil Society*, <http://www.un.org/en/sections/resources-different-audiences/civil-society/> (last accessed December 1, 2020).

8. THIS IS NOT PARADISE AND THE JOURNEY WAS NOT WORTH IT: GLOBALIZATION, FINANCIAL CRISIS, AND THE PORTRAYAL OF THE SUB-SAHARAN IMMIGRANT IN TWO SPANISH FILMS

Marta F. Suarez

This chapter explores the portrayal of sub-Saharan characters in two films, *14 kilómetros/14 Kilometers* (Gerardo Olivares, 2007) and *Diamantes negros/ Black Diamonds* (Miguel Alcantud, 2013). The first is representative of "journeys of hope" and was released before the financial crisis (2008–12), while the second looks at exploitative practices in a land of opportunity that has become less so. These two films illustrate shifts in the fictional narratives of Spanish immigration cinema. While *14 kilómetros* moves into African territory to explore the causes of migration, *Diamantes negros* examines illegal recruiting practices in Spain and the vulnerability of the immigrant in a neoliberal Europe. In the case of *14 kilómetros* and against a backdrop of strengthening border controls, the film emphasizes the dangers of the journey and the interrelations between the border measures and the immigrants' precarity.[1] In the case of *Diamantes negros* and following other narratives of the time, Spain is constructed no longer as a place of opportunity, but as one of disappointment that incites further mobility.

EU Membership and Migration Flows

After entering the European Union (EU) in 1986, Spain experienced an economic boost that contributed as a crucial pull factor in the growth of immigration. Belén Agrela[2] points out that, although the increase in immigration started to be perceived as a global phenomenon at the end of the 1990s, Spain's status as a receiving country supposed a complete transformation, turning it from a country of emigration to one of immigration in just under twenty years of joining the EU.[3] With the incorporation of Spain into the EU, the number of immigrants settling in the Iberian country increased to unprecedented recorded levels, from under 2 percent of the total population in 1999 to around 12 percent ten years later.[4] The rising numbers of immigrants heightened anxieties over this new *other* but also acted as symbols of the success of the Transition,[5] European membership, and the thriving economy. The last two decades of the twentieth century saw Spain racing to meet all the requirements to join the Schengen area and adopting the euro during the first stages of the process. Spanish film joined these efforts in what Núria Triana Toribio and Ignacio Echevarría name a "culture of the transition," a collective desire to support the processes of democratization and Europeanization of Spain.[6] In this context, the Spanish film academy and film organizations validated, through awards and funding, themes and narratives that would appeal to European taste.[7]

As part of the conditions for its new membership, Spain was required to strengthen its external borders[8] and guard "Fortress Europe."[9] From this moment on, immigration control and border reinforcement became key points in the government's political agenda. In this new role of guardian of the European borders, Spain sees itself as the protector of Europe and Europeanness, which involves not only controlling its borders but also, to some extent, regulating its practices to conform with the imagined West.[10] In the context of heightened anxieties over the porosity of the border, the Spanish news media often reported on immigration with pieces about undocumented immigrants and illegal entry, paying particular attention to the border between Spain and Africa. With alarmist headlines about the number of immigrants arriving on the Spanish coasts or jumping the fence in the enclave of Melilla on the African continent,[11] the media problematized African immigration by using terms like "wave," "massive arrival," "avalanche," or "tide."[12] Yet, it is important to note that African immigrants were not the most numerous group at the time and, in fact, the figures for sub-Saharan immigration are among the lowest in this period. In 2012, at around the time that the films analyzed here were made, the Observatorio Permanente de la Inmigración (OPI)[13] reported under 7 percent of non-European immigration in Spain, with over 53 percent from Latin America and 36 percent from Africa. While the numbers are high, of this 36 percent, over 70 percent were from Morocco, with Senegal as the only sub-Saharan country reaching the level of 5 percent. Despite the much higher numbers of Moroccans in Spain, narratives around their personal migratory experiences have been much fewer than those addressing sub-Saharan immigration. Notable exceptions are the films *Retorno a Hansala/Return to Hansala* (Chus Gutiérrez, 2008), *Un novio para Yasmina/A Fiancée for*

Yasmina (Irene Cardona, 2008), *El rayo/Hassan's Way* (Fran Araújo and Ernesto de Nova, 2013), *Slimane* (José Ángel Alayón and Mauro Herce, 2013), and *A escondidas/Hidden Away* (Mikel Rueda, 2014).

The differences in the portrayals of the North African and the sub-Saharan African are varied. On the one hand, North African immigration suffers from identification with the historical medieval Moor, a pejorative word that designated the Berber and North African nomadic groups that arrived and settled in the south of Spain from 711 until 1492. Events related to this period are usually contained in cultural and historical texts with narratives of the "Moorish invasion," and the subsequent battles to reconquer the occupied land. As Daniela Flesler points out, the contemporary North African immigrant is often conflated with notions derived from this historical past.[14] While this chapter does not occupy itself with images of the North African, the fear of invasion permeates media accounts of undocumented African immigrants arriving on small fishing boats (*pateras*[15]) on the Spanish coasts. Leslie B. Rout affirms, in this regard, that sub-Saharans have historically been less present in the collective memory than North Africans.[16] In this sense, the portrayal of the sub-Saharan increases the distance and constructs a less familiar *other*. By doing so, the pull factors of immigration to Spain are rooted less in postcolonial ties and more in global desirability. Additionally, the connections between Spain and Africa are minimized. In emphasizing belonging to Europe and increasing the distance from Africa through a focus on the less familiar African immigrant, Spain detaches itself from the old European saying that "Africa begins at the Pyrenees."[17] Drawing on work by Edward Said,[18] this ambivalence towards Africa has been described by Ignacio Tofiño-Quesada as a paradox at the heart of Spanish orientalism, indicating that it is "the narrative of a country that Orientalizes and indeed colonizes the Other ... but which is described as Oriental itself."[19] This position is shared by Susan Martin-Márquez, who concludes that the fact that Spain is a nation "at once Orientalised and Orientalising" brings a profound sense of disorientation to its national identity.[20] This level of complexity was acknowledged by Said himself in the very first pages of the 2002 Spanish edition of *Orientalism*,[21] where he concedes that Spain could be considered an exception in the general European context described in his book.

During democracy and up to the second decade of the 2000s, narratives exploring Spanish colonialism usually depicted Latin America. In a way, the shared history with the African territories had been sunk into the collective historical memory gap surrounding the Francoist regime and sustained by the Pacto del Olvido (Pact of Forgetting).[22] Many scholars noted in this period the lack of cultural engagement with the postcolonial situation of the former African colonies.[23] In this context, the sub-Saharan becomes the representation of the new unfamiliar and racialized immigrant. On film, echoing some of the narratives in the news media, the sub-Saharan immigrant has often been linked to violence and potential death also, in images that not only emphasize the hardship of the journey, but also turn the spotlight on Spanish society. For example, early immigration cinema up to the immigration crisis usually confines violence within identifiable threats linked to individuals. *Bwana* (Imanol Uribe, 1996) presents a family of Spaniards observing and interacting with the sub-Saharan protagonist, only to leave him behind when a group of neo-Nazis arrive on the scene, presumably abandoning him to his death. *Taxi* (Carlos Saura, 1996) engages with targeted violence towards marginalized groups, while *Poniente/West* (Chus Gutiérrez, 2002) fictionalizes a real-life attack on immigrants in the town of El Ejido two years earlier. Beyond Spain, *14 Kilómetros* and *Querida Bamako/Dear Bamako* (Omer Oke and Txarly Llorente, 2007) address the dangers of crossing the border and the risk to life it involves, themes also present in *Retorno a Hansala* and *Ilegal/Illegal* (Ignacio Villar, 2003), and portrayed through immigrant drownings near the coast. There is something problematic in the scenes of suffering that permeate both news media and film. In the case of sub-Saharan immigrants, their experience is continuously connected to violence, the threat of death, sexual assault, and poverty. While these are elements that are indeed linked to much of the African migration experience, the constant portrayal of the African immigrant in these terms constructs an image of helplessness that reinforces the role of Spain as savior, or, at least, its potential to become one. The limitations derived from using these tropes in films that aim for social criticism is briefly addressed by Montserrat Iglesias Santos (2013),[24] Jorge Pérez (2015), and Lidia Peralta (2016). For example, Santos indicates that, although many films include humanitarian commitment and social criticism, there is a trend for what she calls *buenismo* or *buenrollismo* (a "goody-goody" attitude), which overemphasizes passivity and victimization. In a similar argument, Pérez[25] names this kind of cinema "NGO-films" in order to encapsulate the "good intentions" of the filmmakers, but also to call attention to their limitations and, fundamentally, their failures in terms of ethical accountability for neoliberal practices, "the root causes of migratory displacement," and the "historical matrix of the Mediterranean." Finally, Peralta[26] addresses it as "ambivalent cinema of social criticism" for its potential to raise awareness about the lives of undocumented immigrants while struggling to escape the stereotypes. Another issue that arises from the emphasis on suffering, vulnerability, and precarity is that when the film aims to promote sympathy, this is done through the witnessing of hardship instead of through identification. By doing so, the film indirectly supports a meritocracy of suffering, where the place of the sub-Saharan in the national space is earned through resilience and pain. This chapter does not question that suffering is indeed part of the sub-Saharan migratory experience; nor does it suggests that film should move away from highlighting these tragic conditions. What it does note, however, is that the repetition of the same images across the Spanish national space constructs reductive understandings of sub-Saharan Africa that negate the region's big industrialized cities, local economies, universities, and, in general, any image that challenges the binaries constructed around Eurocentrism. It is not until the revision of historical memory aligns, first, with the financial crisis and, later, with the Syrian and Saharawi conflicts that Spanish cinema sets out to rediscover Africa and the causes of displacement, this time highlighting positions of similarity and understanding instead of difference.

Also discussing the apparent silence of Spain regarding its African colonial past, Debra Faszer-McMahon and Victoria L. Ketz[27] approach Ricci's work[28] on the invisibility of Guinean literature in Spain and the Iberian country's disregard for African postcolonial texts. However, they continue, the lack of interest in its own postcolonial sub-Saharan production at this time contradicts, in a sense, the high visibility of the sub-Saharan migrant in films,[29] leading the authors to question the reasons for over-representing narratives of sub-Saharan male migrants in contexts of cultural conflict and segregation. Another explanation for the over-representation of these narratives relates to Spain's desire to emphasize its Europeanness, contrasting itself with a less familiar *other*. Antumi Toasije (2009) explains on this matter that Africa has been constructed as the "unknown other," not because there has been no contact between sub-Saharan countries and Spain, but as a result of erasing memory and facts within this relationship. For Toasije, black migrants have been depersonalized "in all public discourses. Spanish authorities have used new forged geographic epithets such as 'Sub-Saharans', accompanied by expressions such as avalanche (avalancha), flux (flujo), and so on."

Spanish Immigration Cinema

Spanish immigration cinema was firmly established in the 1990s.[30] *Las cartas de Alou/Alou's Letters* (Montxo Armendáriz, 1990) is considered to be the film that inaugurated the genre, having one of the first non-European protagonists in Spanish cinema. The film was very successful on the critics' circuit, as its two Goya awards[31] attest. Alou, an undocumented immigrant, moves around Spain from menial job to menial job until he is detained and repatriated, only to travel back to Spain again. The film encourages audiences to sympathize with Alou through the portrayal of his daily life and the friendships he makes. Nevertheless, it also calls for tolerance and acceptance of the *other* by noting the racism and prejudice of some of the Spaniards in the film. Uribe's *Bwana* portrays the few hours that follow the irregular entry of Ombasi, an African immigrant who was in a capsized boat. Also successful with the critics, *Bwana* was the winner of the Golden Seashell at the San Sebastián Festival (1996) and was chosen as the Spanish entry for the 69th Academy Awards. The film highlights the racism of Spain through the actions of the nuclear family. Connecting this story to common images in the media of undocumented crossing and death, the narrative emphasizes the ignorant and racist attitudes of the other characters: the Nazi group that beat up the protagonist, and the family who watches him, caught between fascinated and fearful. *Taxi*, also nominated for the Golden Seashell at the San Sebastián Film Festival (1996) but losing to *Bwana*, delves into similar themes to portray a seemingly ordinary Spanish family who use their taxi company to exert violence on those they consider undesirable. This initial period thus sees filmmakers approach African immigration with a spotlight on the host, the prejudice embedded in society, and the violence experienced by the immigrant. These underlining themes continue in the first years of the 2000s with films such as *Salvajes/Savages* (Carlos Molinero, 2001), *Poniente*, and *El traje/The Suit* (Alberto Rodríguez, 2002).

It is also around this time that fiction narratives about the journey from Africa to Spain emerge. The elections of 1996 put the Popular Party in power for the first time. Following the implementation of the Schengen agreement in 1995, Spain initiated the process of strengthening surveillance and border controls. One of the first measures was the development and implementation of the SIVE (External Surveillance Integrated System), which was ready by 2001 around the Canary Islands and parts of Andalusia. In the years that followed, the system was expanded to other areas of the border and the African enclave of Ceuta. This hardening of the borders diverted immigration routes and encouraged reliance on illegal networks of human smugglers. The journey to Spain became more dangerous.

With the SIVE expanding and rumors growing of a regularization process ("Normalización"), the arrivals increased in number and frequency. This regularization took place in 2005, with the media often reporting on long queues of immigrants wanting to submit their forms and, therefore, also drawing attention to the number of undocumented immigrants in the country. Instead of the process reducing the number of undocumented immigrants, regularization in fact attracted more immigrants, who hoped for a new regularization process. In 2006, Spain saw a summer of unprecedented arrivals in the Canary Islands by sea, with a total of over 30,000 immigrants in over 500 boats that year.[32] Known as "the crisis of the *cayucos*," these events increased anxieties over the arrivals. In the news media, reports on the "illegal" condition of these immigrants and the trespassing over the border stressed concerns over that border's porosity and, thus, the need to strengthen it. For María Martínez Lirola,[33] the press approaches the African immigrant in terms of either threat or victim, emphasizing his or her difference from the Spaniard but also erasing the difference between African immigrants, particularly those from sub-Saharan countries. When their representation is examined through a victimizing lens, the sub-Saharan is usually depicted in the news media as requiring protection and assistance, which is generally provided by the Spaniard,[34] such as in scenes of rescue, medical assistance on the beach, groups of migrants covered with blankets handed out by the Spanish authorities, or people receiving food. By repeating these scenes of rescue, the stories direct the point of view towards Spaniards, who appear as the bearers of aid, and muddle cultural and ethnical differences among the immigrants.[35] This narrative of Spanish rescue often coexists with the notion of "invasion," evoked via the continuous reporting of *pateras* arriving quietly at night.

It is against this background that Spanish immigration cinema expands its focus from the 1990s interactions between Spain and the new immigrant, and looks over its shores at the hardships of the journey and the realities of the immigrants' homeland. Even though these films connect African immigration with illegal entry, low-skilled labor, and border crossing, they do so to inspire sympathy in the audience by individualizing the immigrants' experience. Although fiction film has not been as prolific at exploring the journey as documentary film, the films *Ilegal, 14 kilómetros, Querida Bamako* (and, to some extent, *Retorno a Hansala*) are representative of this trend. Focusing on interpersonal relationships between Spaniards and immigrants, other films highlighted the entrapments of a system that criminalizes undocumented immigrants and forces them to find ways to regularize their status, such as *Princesas/Princesses* (Fernando León de Aranoa, 2005), *Agua con sal/Water with Salt* (Pedro Pérez Rosdo, 2005), and *Un novio para Yasmina*.

Studies around immigration cinema in Spain also proliferated with the start of the millennium. Isabel Santaolalla's work of 2005[36] is a landmark study in notions of otherness and immigration in Spanish cinema, and continues to be referenced to this day. In the same year, journalist Eduardo Moyano published a monograph on migration and cinema, with an emphasis on the notions of memory, mobility, and racism.[37] Moyano's volume aims to establish connections between the Spanish migrant past and contemporary immigration in Spain, also paying attention to mobility within the Spanish borders and portrayals of the internal *other*. A further volume by Chema Castiello explores three thematic narratives in immigration cinema: journey, rejection, and *convivencia* (coexistence).[38] These three groups intersect with Yosefa Loshitzky's categories,[39] although a closer inspection highlights the absence of second- and third-generation diasporic filmmaking in Spain at the time. What these three foundational works highlight is the filmmakers' conscious desire to force audiences to reflect on the immigrant's condition and to expose racism in Spain. For example, Castiello (2005) indicates that the Spanish directors of immigration cinema in this period share the intentions of "testimony," "social reflection," and "demand for changes" by showing "reality" and denouncing it.

However, for that same reason, many scholars have found limitations in the films included in the period of study covered by these foundational works (1990–2005), indicating that many of them are centered around Spain's reaction to the *other* or the consequences of a hardening border, and not so much around the *other*'s experiences.[40] That is, that they are more about Spain than about the immigrant. The only notable exception in their period of study is *Cartas de Alou*, where the African immigrant is the central subject, something that would become more common only in the late 2000s.[41] Santaolalla[42] refers to it as "exceptional" and a "fetishist text of the Spanish anti-racist discourse," while M. Van Liew rates it for its "tone of great humanity and attitudinal diversity."[43] In contrast, Guido Rings indicates that it is "an excellent example" of the values of the Council of Europe's film fund, as it is a film that "strengthen[s] human rights, racial tolerance and multicultural acceptance."[44] However, many of these scholars also call attention to the othering of Alou through an exoticization of his body.[45] Being the first film to address African immigration directly, along with the problems arising from problematic integrations, *Cartas de Alou* set the model for many of the films that followed.

14 KILÓMETROS

This film was written and directed by Gerardo Olivares, a filmmaker with extensive experience in documentary filmmaking and state television. Winner of the best film at the Seminci Valladolid Festival, it is a favorite of festival circuits, school curricula, and exhibitions. The title refers to the distance between Africa and Spain at its narrowest point in Gibraltar, contrasting the short distance with a narrative that presents a long and painful journey. The film follows the journey to Spain of Violeta, a young woman from Mali, and brothers Buba and Mukela, from Niger. The characters meet at a mid-point near the Sahara and continue the journey together. However, Mukela dies in the desert and Violeta separates from Buba at a checkpoint, reappearing only in the last ten minutes of the film, when she joins him to cross the Strait in a *patera*. In the final scenes and after reaching Spain, a nearby patrol is alerted to their arrival and attends the area, searching for the newcomers. Buba and Violeta hide in the nearby forest, where they are discovered by a member of the Guardia Civil.[46] However, and against what would be expected, the Guardia Civil leaves the scene quietly, and this allows the protagonists to run back to the beach. Aligning with Loshitzky's category of journeys of hope,[47] the film uses documentary-style techniques and on-screen maps to guide the audience through this journey.

Although inspired by real accounts of immigration, the film is limited when illustrating the reasons for the journey and the difficulty of the decision to leave, something that *Querida Bamako*,[48] however, does very well. In *14 kilómetros*, Buba and Mukela ponder going to Europe and daydream of Buba finding a job as a soccer player. Discussing the wealth and abundance of Europe, they refer to the continent as a land of opportunity, where money can be found under rocks. The brothers are portrayed as free of financial worries but dreaming of wealth. They have no dependants and seem to co-share an apartment, where Buba has his own room, decorated with soccer memorabilia. Working as a mechanic, Buba's only complaint is that his boss profits from his labor without doing anything himself. By presenting the characters in this light, the film paints Europe as a land of opportunity and wealth, a reading that is reinforced by the intertitle at the end of the film, which, in terms of "them" and "us," anchors Spanish immigrants to the realization of dreams.[49] Buba and Mukela's longing for Europe is presented to the audience as a desire to become wealthy and famous, combined with a distorted idea of the opportunities available. While these are similar objectives to those of the protagonists of *Diamantes negros*, in *14 kilómetros* the decision to emigrate is presented on screen as an impetuous one made by the protagonists, whereas in *Diamantes* the youngsters are lulled into a false sense of security with fake promises. As a consequence, the motivations in *14 kilómetros* connote impulsivity and a thoughtless assessment of the journey, where the pull factor of Europe surpasses any risk. Mukela indicates that he wants to "live like the whiteys in soap operas," while Buba follows him but is only half convinced that he will fulfil his hopes of becoming a soccer player. Buba and Mukela's motivations are thus grounded on their desire to participate in Bauman's liquid modernity, the society of consumers.[50]

In Violeta's case, her portrayal takes on a gendered dimension. She is running away from a forced marriage to a much older man, who abused her when she was a child. In her narrative, the motivation to migrate aligns with her desire to be freed from this arrangement, and to do so safely. It is a story of liberation that has the woman's body at its center and where Europe appears as the space where the risk cannot follow. Indeed, Violeta considers migrating only to Europe, and not to a different town or country, indicating that, in order not to be found and killed, she needs to go as far as possible, where "far" does not seem to indicate geographical distance but a cultural one. The context does not suggest that any pursuit could take place, as the man is portrayed as weakened by age and having no influence. Thus, the African woman is constructed against the Western woman, aligning with Talpade Mohanty's notion of "third world woman," and with feminist discourses that position "Western women as secular, liberated, and in control of their own lives."[51] Not only is Europe the place where this liberation can be secured, but during the journey Violeta's body is continually assaulted by the men in her life, including Buba, and she is driven to prostitution to survive. The narrative minimizes this assault by not exploring remorse, reparations, or even acknowledgment when, at the end, Buba tells Violeta to join him in the *patera*. In their first conversation since the assault, Buba refers to it as "a misunderstanding," and although Violeta initially closes the door to him, she immediately runs after him into the street, where they embrace tightly. The opportunity to go to the promised land leads Violeta to forgive Buba, Europe being once more the place where gendered abuse is supposedly left behind.

The film neglects to consider the emotional impact of displacement, uprooting, and migration; none of the characters longs for their homelands or the people left behind. With reasons anchored in the pursuit of wealth and self-determination over the body, the goals of the journey align with Europe's self-identification with capital and freedom. Since the characters start their journeys in Niger and Mali, it is a missed opportunity not to contextualize the socio-political circumstances of these countries, both affected at the time by political instability and armed conflict. Indeed, although many of the fiction narratives of immigration cinema of this period reassert the figure of the immigrant as economic migrant, Wim Naudé (2008)[52] determines that the reasons for migrating in sub-Saharan countries are more complex and include a combination of financial hardship, armed conflict, and environmental factors. In *14 kilómetros* the motivations of the three characters are condensed into the acquisition of wealth and escape from a forced marriage, but the way that these reasons are illustrated on screen offers a simplistic view that circumvents looking at the wider picture in these countries. Consequently, the film directs the sympathy of the audience towards the individuals and their plights on the journey, but avoids raising any concerns over the state of the Global South, the impact of neoliberalism and foreign debt, or the political issues that derive from ineffective decolonization. Instead, it questions the choice to leave Africa and implies that it is precisely emigration that is perpetuating poverty, and not poverty that perpetuates emigration. By doing so, the film roots the characters to Zygmunt Bauman's producer society and, therefore, a heavy modernity characteristic of the industrializing and developing world.[53]

This connotation is encapsulated in a dialogue that takes place around a campfire. Shortly after being rescued by the Tuaregs from the desert and now restored to health, Buba questions their determination to remain in Africa when so many people emigrate to Europe. The Tuaregs reply that it would be inconceivable to them because the land is rich if one knows how to harvest it. Grabbing a handful of soil (and connecting to Laura U. Marks's "haptic visuality"[54]), the Tuareg explains that, with knowledge and effort, even the dry land of the desert is workable. Moreover, ignoring foreign debt and neocolonialism, one of the Tuaregs claims that Africa's poverty is a consequence of emigration, and that if the same effort were invested in opening businesses in Africa instead of reaching Europe, they could all lift the economy and help to create jobs. The answer trivializes the migrant experience and the postcolonial history of many of these countries. Thus, the film adopts a Eurocentric point of view that presents Europe as a promised land and, at the same time, makes the home country responsible for its own poverty. By doing so, the film emphasizes the appeal of Europe as a pull factor but distracts from creating an understanding of the variety of push factors motivating the journey.

The film showcases for a Spanish audience the hardship of the desert and the empty borderlands, lingering at the same time on the beauty of the African landscapes. In the scenes introducing the main characters, the camera explores the busy market and fishing shores, before showing Buba working as a mechanic, and later Violeta, listening in her bedroom to the dowry exchange. These spaces, the home and the auto repair, function as the only true anthropological places that the characters inhabit in the film. From there on, the characters will enter a journey through non-places, "the archetype of the traveller."[55] In the film and outside the small towns, Africa is constructed as a mosaic of non-places, a space of heavy modernity where a society of consumers is not possible.[56] The African landscape outside the characters' hometowns, such as the desert and the empty lands around the border, is hostile and dangerous. The only settlement that they encounter is the Tuareg camp, by its nature nomadic and therefore mobile. The Tuaregs' suggestion that Africa remains in poverty because the youth are leaving for Europe implies that their desire to become part of the society of consumers is what is keeping Africa a society of producers. Similarly, Europe as a place of consumption is evoked not only through dialogue but also through props that connote the symbolic capital[57] of their reference. For example, Violeta starts her journey with a shopping bag on which is written "Paris," whereas Buba takes with him the match ball that his brother bought for him. However, the characters lose all their initial possessions in the course of the journey, and arrive on a beach in an isolated area, far from tourist or urban centers. The film therefore ends with the question of whether the undocumented Violeta and Buba would be able to enter the land of opportunities not just physically, but organically, and participate in the liquid modernity of the host country.

In this sense, it allows a reading of hope and integration, with its open ending after the successful journey.[58] Yet, another reading suggests that the characters remain in a non-place, and thus the possibility of integration into the socio-anthropological space of Spain is negated. A similar view is held by Pérez, who sees this ending as utopian and unrealistic.[59] Since the beach in immigration cinema is often a symbolic seascape of death,[60] the characters' return there might not be a symbolic fresh start but, rather, a reminder of the liminality of the immigrant condition, the difficulties of integration, and the hardships still to come. For Pérez, the border official stands for the model Spanish citizen and, as long as these citizens "treat the arriving migrants with the same mercy as this fictional officer, the casualties of migratory movements to Europe might vanish, and we would all live in a happy-go-lucky multicultural world." The scene manifests the erasure of the border control or, at least, a caring response. In the aftermath of the tragedy in Ceuta and the "express deportation" agreements (2005),[61] the film provides a border official who, quite literally, "gets out of their way" and leaves the immigrants to continue their journey on Spanish soil.

What these authors do not note is that this is not the only act of kindness the protagonists have experienced at the border. On the other side and on their way to the *patera*, Buba begs one of the smugglers to let Violeta join the group, even though she does not have enough money. After some protests and a dubitative short pause, he instructs them to get into the truck. Thus, the kindness at the border refers to both the smugglers and the border control officers, the two having the power to prevent or allow the crossing. By ending with scenes built on binary themes (departure/arrival, night/day, smuggler/border officer), the film metaphorically offers two sides of the same coin and expresses an interrelation. In this case, the hardening of border controls intensifies the precarious conditions under which the immigrant attempts this journey. Thus, the acts of kindness by individuals with (in)formal control of the border offer a conclusion of hope. However, by doing so, the film emphasizes actions at the micro level of individual encounters, yet fails to recognize the issues at a macro social level, such as systemic racism and institutional violence. Whereas immigration films of this period might also include abuses of power,[62] these appear as fundamentally linked to individual actions. This would change after around 2010, with more of an emphasis on the limitations and inefficacy of the authorities to protect the immigrant, the bureaucracies that harm them, collective corruption in systems of power, or organized networks seeking to exploit or profit from the immigrant.[63]

Thus, *14 kilómetros* anchors itself on the aims of immigration cinema to bring understanding and sympathy to a Spanish audience that was influenced by the portrayals by the news media. The film is categorized by Pérez as "NGO-film," or one that is "conceived with a genuine motivation to foster an ethics of solidarity and, thereby, to generate social awareness about the issues at stake when dealing with immigration."[64] However, as Pérez also argues, these films, as non-governmental organizations often do, "fail to account for the whole picture of the historical matrix of the Mediterranean."[65] The film is, in this sense, reductive, and constructs Africa through a Spanish gaze for a Spanish audience accustomed to these stereotypes. By doing so, it uses common clichés to lead spectators to focus on the adversities of the journey instead of the characters' particular backgrounds. For this reason, the treatment of the immigrant experience is oversimplified and might reinforce some of the stereotypes in the news media that construct the sub-Saharan immigrant as in need of protection. The sympathy comes, then, from the witnessing of hardship and not through character identification, which, in a sense, is the same compassion shown by the border patrol officer at the end of the film. The *other* remains the *other*, but a suffering *other* evidences the worth of Spain and calls for protection.

Just as Spanish immigration cinema was exploring the implications of stricter border surveillance and immigration control, the financial crisis (2008–12) hit. With the rise in unemployment, both Spaniards and immigrants were leaving the country to look for opportunities elsewhere. Films around this period explore expulsions from the Spanish landscape or into the underground economies, in a country transformed from a land of opportunity into a land of disappointment, where financial struggle affects both Spaniards and immigrants. *El rayo* approaches the return journey to Morocco as a consequence of the crisis, whereas, in *Amador* (Fernando León de Aranoa, 2010), financial struggles lead the Spanish daughter and Latin American carer to pretend that Amador is still alive, so they can both continue to be paid. Coinciding with global concerns over transnational organized crime, many of these films also note the role of networks seeking to profit from the immigrant: for example, the sweatshops and illegal street trading in *Biutiful* (Alejandro González Iñárritu, 2010), human trafficking in *Evelyn* (Isabel De Ocampo, 2012), fake businesses charging for non-existing contracts in *La venta del paraíso/The Sale of Paradise* (Emilio Ruiz Barrachina, 2012), or the dishonest soccer scouts in *Diamantes negros*. We will now turn to the last of these films.

Diamantes negros

Diamantes negros/Black Diamonds (2013), by Miguel Alcantud, was co-produced by Spain and Portugal. Like *14 kilómetros*, it featured mainly on the film festival circuits, winning the audience award at the Festival de Málaga 2013 but barely making 24,000 euros at the box office. The film engages with irregular practices in the recruitment of under-age African soccer players for European leagues. The recruits are made to sign an exploitative and binding contract with soccer scouts, under the impression that this will guarantee them trials with the big clubs in the European leagues, as well as state-of-the-art training facilities. Instead, the youngsters are given fake papers, left alone in an apartment, and sent for trials with lower-league teams. The scouts produce forged identity cards and student visas while hoping for one of the youngsters to become a promising star by the age of eighteen, when it becomes legal, under soccer regulations, to transfer these players. The sub-Saharan immigrants in this film have not started the journey out of desperation. Instead, they are lured into leaving by an organized network exploiting the appeal of Europe. For the protagonists, Amadou and Moussa, Spain is just a step in the journey, as they long to settle in France instead. As with many other fiction films engaging with the immigrant experience after the crisis, Spain is not presented in the background of the story as a land of opportunities that closes the door to the immigrant, but instead as a land where these opportunities are none the less scarce,[66] motivating further journeys.

Amadou and Moussa, two young teenagers from Mali, are among the best players in the local youth soccer team. They are approached by Spanish scouts, who promise to take them to Europe to play soccer, in exchange for an administrative fee. Once the young men arrive in Spain, the scouts are unable to find them a team, and it becomes evident that the contacts the scouts claimed to have were a fabrication. When Amadou goes with a different scout to Portugal to play a trial for one of the big teams, one of their initial contacts, Pablo, evicts Moussa into the street out of spite. At this stage, the audience is led to believe that the plot will continue with Amadou's narrative of success and Moussa's narrative of failure. Yet, Amadou undergoes a similar fate when, after suffering a leg injury, he is abandoned at a railroad station without any papers. The youngsters have to resort to crime to survive, with Moussa ending up in a youth penitentiary center for drug dealing, and Amadou buying his return tickets with money gained from thieving. In the end, Moussa is released by Pablo, who has found him a place on a team in Estonia helping a rising star, whereas Amadou returns to his hometown and is rejected by both family and friends.

The young footballers are thus denied space not only in the consumer society but also in the producer society. Holding the promise of cultural capital in the form of soccer talent, they are discarded throughout the narrative once it does not materialize. Indeed, the dialogue suggests that this talent is not enough, as they lack the technical skills of European-trained sports players. Moussa becomes instead a product to be consumed, when a promising soccer player requests players from Mali to keep him company and make him feel more at home. The film calls attention to the inefficacy and dehumanization implicit in systems related to authority and immigration control, going beyond the individual to explore institutionalized behaviors. For example, the lack of controls around student visas encourages the activities of the scouts, the legal use of contracts exclusively in Spanish impedes the understanding of the conditions agreed, Moussa's experiences in the penitentiary highlight humiliation and dehumanization, the attendants at the police station whom Amadou approaches ignore his pleas to help him return home because he has no proof of origin, and Moussa is quickly released to Pablo without much investigation. Whereas *14 kilómetros* ended the journey in Spain, as if it were the last stop on the migratory journey, *Diamantes negros* emphasizes the obstacles to integration after the young men's arrival, delineating the narratives around the notions of expulsion[67] and waste[68] in the consumer society and liquid modernity.

The main characters in this film are presented as substantially different, in both background and personality. This approach reinforces the message that this could happen to any youngster, also stressing the impact of these recruitment practices on poorer households. The film opens with cross-cutting scenes of Amadou and Moussa playing soccer, highlighting their different economic status within their local town. Amadou is introduced in a field next to a dumping ground, where he plays against some younger children. In shallow focus, the camera focuses on the piles of waste at the back and the cows that wander around the edges. Moussa, however, is introduced in soccer gear, playing on a field surrounded by greenery, which the audience will recognize later as the fields around his house. Throughout the scenes that follow, Moussa and Amadou are constructed as coming from different economic backgrounds in Mali. For example, Moussa attends school and is supported financially by his father. His family's wealth is evident in the big family house, where he lives with his parents and siblings, and his father's two other wives. In contrast, Amadou works for the local store and is the only breadwinner in his household, supporting a sick mother and two siblings. His situation of financial struggle is further conveyed through mise en scène: Amadou wears the same clothes every day, whereas Moussa has a range of outfits, including a variety of sportswear. Furthermore, whilst Amadou has to share the little food he gets among the family, Moussa's family is able to organize a big barbeque event at short notice to greet the scouts. By positioning these characters in such different family and financial backgrounds, the narrative emphasizes the pull of Europe and the symbolic capital of soccer. Whilst Moussa longs for the fame of some African players in the European leagues, Amadou wants to earn enough money to provide his mother with hospital treatment and improve the family's well-being. Europe, thus, functions as a place of wealth, fame, and recognition, to which Spain is a door. In this context, the film connects different European countries through soccer, creating a network of leagues and scouts that participate in the dubious practice of recruiting youngsters under false pretenses. The locations in Spain, Portugal, and Estonia work alongside other references to big European teams to create an idea of Europe as a unit. No longer a model example of financial improvement and political stability, Spain anchors itself in the European and the Global, reconfiguring notions of national identity.

In the end, Moussa accepts his role as companion if it means not returning to Mali, whereas Amadou learns of the sacrifice the family made to pay for his journey and is rejected by his friends and family. Contrasting with *14 kilómetros*, this film emphasizes issues of value and human capital in a globalized world. Amadou's family sell his younger sibling to a local trader in exchange for money to pay Amadou's fees, whereas Moussa's family collects the sum from the community. After a knee injury, Amadou loses all the human capital that the scouts want to exploit, whereas a humbler Moussa acquires renewed human capital once he accepts his place in the new team, developing another player's human capital. The friends become, in this way, representative of the categories of recycled lives and wasted lives that Bauman links to current processes of globalization and the immigrant other.[69]

The journey in itself is short and is undertaken by plane, moving away from the notions of invasion and threat that the *pateras* evoked. Throughout the first scenes, Amadou and Moussa appear fascinated by the lights in the plane, the escalators at the station, and the hot water faucet in the apartment. However, this vision of Europe soon takes a turn, and the friends end up homeless on the street. The non-places in the film highlight their mobile status and the impossibility of settlement, yet these are places to which the scouts take them, such as the station in Lisbon where Amadou is left undocumented and without money, or from which they can be released, such as the penitentiary center in Madrid. These interactions highlight the scouts' power to integrate or discard the immigrant, emphasizing the way in which neoliberal practices decide the latter's fate.

Diamantes negros continues to depict stories of hardship and pain. However, these take place after arrival in the Spanish space. Far from being the land of opportunity of previous films, Spain does not retain its allure once Moussa and Amadou arrive there. The characters' undocumented status and lack of opportunities drive them to poverty and criminality. In this context, the film approaches notions of human value derived from their talent to play soccer and the irregular recruiting practices that put African youngsters in positions of vulnerability. The recruiting process, however, draws attention to criminal or illegal practices in Spain that ultimately exploit the immigrant. By doing so, it starts to interrogate the role of Europe in encouraging migration to supply its needs, at the same time that it implicitly criticizes the inefficacy of the systems and procedures that are supposed to protect the immigrant from these practices. Moving the gaze from the individuals to the system, *Diamantes negros* illustrates a shift towards narratives around globalization, neoliberalism, and Europe's responsibility to curtail exploitative recruiting practices.

Conclusion and Afterthoughts

Whereas *14 kilómetros* continues the European trend of journeys of hope and underlines the allure of Europe, in *Diamantes negros* this allure is manipulated by Spanish networks to ensure their business transactions. As Spain reached the second decade of the millennium, a series of events aligned that shaped more recent cinema. The Law of Historical Memory (ley de Memoria Histórica, 2007[70]) brought to the forefront debates around collective memory, while corruption cases involving top politicians and the Crown[71] motivated a revision of the Transition and the agents involved. On the one hand, interrogation of the past gave rise to explorations of the colonial role of Spain in Africa in fiction films such as *Palmeras en la nieve/Palm Trees in the Snow* (Fernando González Molina, 2015) or *Neckan* (Gonzalo Tapia, 2015). On the other hand, narratives around corruption and globalization further encouraged themes of global crime, corrupt authorities, and neoliberalism, such as in *Alacrán enamorado/Scorpion in Love* (Santiago Zannou, 2013) or *El niño/The Kid* (Daniel Monzón, 2014).

As Spain left the financial crisis behind and started to rebuild its economy, the refugee crisis began to heighten anxieties in Europe that threatened the very core ideals of the Schengen area. Following a revival in the collective memory of the traumas of the war, Spain oscillated between adopting humanitarianism through the role of the rescuer and increasing controls under European pressure. A series of fiction films emerged in more mainstream cinema, exploring global inequality and the tragedies forcing displacement. What changes from previous depictions of the causes behind emigration is that, in many of these more contemporary films, the Spaniard travels to Africa beyond the more familiar Morocco, emphasizing the need to see beyond the national space to truly understand human tragedy. Many of these films promote early audience identification through more familiar Spanish actors, bringing to the mainstream aims of sympathy and understanding that previously had been somewhat relegated to Spanish immigration cinema. These films address global inequality, postcolonialism, corruption, criminal networks, and the role of the West in challenging these issues. Although some of these problems had been explored previously in films such as *También la lluvia/Even the Rain* (Icíar Bollaín, 2010) they were rooted in a Latin American context, of which Spain retains a vivid collective memory, or in documentary films such as *Hijos de las nubes/Sons of the Clouds* (Álvaro Longoria, 2012), with a more limited reach. *El cuaderno de Sara/Sarah's Notebook* (Norberto López Amado, 2018) and *El viaje de Marta/ Marta's Trip* (Neus Ballús, 2019) take the viewer to Congo and Senegal, while the acclaimed *Adú* (Salvador Calvo, 2020) travels across the African continent in an ensemble narrative.

Thus, the more contemporary Spanish films connect Spain with the global – not just Europe – and engage with issues of humanitarianism, conviviality, and the West's responsibility to address some of the issues affecting the continent. There is much to explore regarding the way that Spain presents itself as part of the Global North, the embracing of narratives of the savior, or even the impact that global streaming and distribution have had on reconfiguring ideas of Spanishness. While it is not possible to attend to these elements in this chapter, it is important to note that narratives around the African migrant in the early stages of Spanish immigration cinema approached immigration within a reduced scope linked to poverty, irregular status, and integration into Spain. With tragedies of drowned immigrants inundating the media and border controls increasing every year, Spanish film moved the camera to the African continent to explore the individual circumstances that lead to migration. The crisis brought narratives around the more vulnerable condition of the immigrant and the rise of criminal networks profiting from desperation. Alongside these, debates over the historical memory inspired a wave of screen narratives revisiting events of the last century, which promoted a revision of history related to the former Spanish African colonies of Equatorial Guinea, the Spanish Sahara, and the Spanish Protectorate of Morocco. Having crossed the border into sub-Saharan Africa with a box-office hit (*Palmeras en la nieve*), mainstream cinema has continued to show an interest in exploring other African territories through the eyes of Spanish characters. These changes in mainstream cinema have also been supported by the interrogation not only of historical events, but also of the hegemonic institutions involved, with some filmmakers in the new millennium inciting change and exploring themes and modes of production traditionally not favored by the Spanish Film Academy.[72]

Notes

1. Judith Butler, *Precarious Life: The Powers of Mourning and Violence* (London: Verso, 2006).
2. Belén Agrela, "Spain as a Recent Country of Immigration: How Immigration Became a Symbolic, Political, and Cultural Problem in the 'New Spain,'" Working paper no. 57 (La Jolla: University of California–San Diego, 2002). Belén Agrela and Gunther Dietz, "Nongovernmental Versus Governmental Actors? Multilevel Governance and Immigrant Integration Policy in Spain," in *Local Citizenship in Recent Countries of Immigration*, ed. Takeyuki Tsuda (New York: Lexington Books, 2006), 205–34.
3. This trend was only temporarily reversed during the financial crisis, when a high number of both Spaniards and immigrants left Spain for other countries.
4. Ana María López Sala and Ruth Ferrero Turrión, "Economic Crisis and Migration Policies in Spain: The Big Dilemma." Annual conference, Centre on Migration, Policy and Society, University of Oxford, 2009.
5. The "Transition" is the term by which the passage from Franco's dictatorship (1939–75) to the democratic general elections of 1982 is known. Until recently, this period was seen as a successful model that united the nation, quickly reinstated a democracy, and initiated the steps that would lead to membership of NATO (1992) and the EU (1986).
6. Núria Triana-Toribio, *Spanish Film Cultures: The Making and Unmaking of Spanish Cinema* (London: Bloomsbury, 2016). I. Echevarría, "La CT: un cambio de paradigma," in *CT o la cultura de la transición: Crítica a 35 años de cultura española*, ed. G. Martínez (Barcelona: Mondadori, 2012), 25–36.
7. Pierre Bourdieu, *Distinction: A Social Critique of the Judgement of Taste* (Cambridge, MA: Harvard University Press, 1984).
8. Daniela Flesler, *The Return of the Moor: Spanish Responses to Contemporary Moroccan Immigration*, Purdue Studies in Romance Literatures, vol. 43 (West Lafayette, IN: Purdue University Press, 2008).
9. Belén Agrela Romero, "Políticas de inmigración y prácticas sociales con mujeres inmigrantes: discursos, representaciones y significaciones," in *Delitos y fronteras: mujeres extranjeras en prisión*, ed. María Teresa Martín Palomo, María Jesús Miranda López and Cristina Vega Solís (Madrid: Editorial Complutense, 2005), 139–82.
10. Flesler, *The Return of the Moor*.
11. Maria Martinez Lirola, "Multimodal Representation of Sub-Saharan Immigrants as Illegal: Deconstructing Their Portrayal as Victims, Heroes and Threats in a Sample from the Spanish Press," *Bulletin of Hispanic Studies* 93, no. 4 (2016): 343–61. María Martínez Lirola, "Discursive Legitimation of Criminalization and Victimization of Sub-Saharan Immigrants in Spanish El País and ABC Newspapers," *Representing the Other in European Media Discourses* (Amsterdam/Philadelphia: John Benjamins, 2017), 135–54.
12. María Carmen Albert Guardiola, Eva Espinar Ruiz, and María Isabel Hernandez Sanchez, "Immigrants as Threats. Migratory Processes in Spanish Television," *Convergencia – Revista de Ciencias Sociales* 17, no. 53 (2010): 49–68. Juan José

Igartua, Carlos Muñiz, and Lifen Cheng, "La inmigración en la prensa española: aportaciones empíricas y metodológicas desde la teoría del encuadre noticioso," *Migraciones: Publicación del Instituto Universitario de Estudios sobre Migraciones* 17 (2005): 143–81.
13. The OPI is one of the Spanish institutions that study and report on immigration in Spain. The data can be accessed through their website at <http://extranjeros.inclusion.gob.es/es/Estadisticas/> (last accessed December 10, 2020).
14. Flesler, *The Return of the Moor*.
15. A *patera* is a type of small open boat with a shallow draft, commonly used to transport undocumented migrants from Morocco to Spain.
16. Leslie B. Rout, *The African Experience in Spanish America: 1502 to the Present Day*. Cambridge Latin American Studies, vol. 23 (Cambridge: Cambridge University Press Archive, 1976).
17. A remark often attributed to Alexandre Dumas.
18. Edward Said, *Orientalism* (New York: Vintage Books, 1978).
19. Ignacio Tofiño-Quesada, "Spanish Orientalism: Uses of the Past in Spain's Colonization in Africa," *Comparative Studies of South Asia, Africa and the Middle East* 23 nos 1 and 2 (2003): 4.
20. Susan Martin-Márquez, *Disorientations: Spanish Colonialism in Africa and the Performance of Identity* (New Haven, CT: Yale University Press, 2008), 8–9.
21. Edward Said, *Orientalismo* (Madrid: Debate, 2002; Spanish edition only), 1.
22. The "Pacto de Olvido" is an agreement reached by the political parties during Spain's Transition, which involved not discussing the Francoist past. The pact aimed to ensure that democracy was established and that old wounds were not reopened. A desire to leave behind the backwardness that the Francoist era had come to represent, and a Europeanization derived from the preparations to join the EU, encouraged the population to tacitly observe this agreement. It was not until the new millennium that discussions over the historical memory and revisions of the past started to take place in wider political and social discourses.
23. Isabel Santaolalla, "Ethnic and Racial Configurations in Contemporary Spanish Culture," in *Constructing Identity in Contemporary Spain: Theoretical Debates and Cultural Practice*, ed. Jo Labanyi (Oxford: Oxford University Press, 2003). Alberto Elena, "Back to Africa? Colonial History and Postcolonial Dynamics in Recent Spanish Cinema," in *(Re)viewing Creative, Critical and Commercial Practices in Contemporary Spanish Cinema*, ed. Duncan Wheeler and Fernando Canet (New York: Intellect, 2014), 65–78. Antumi Toasije, "The Africanity of Spain: Identity and Problematization," *Journal of Black Studies* 39, no. 3 (2009): 348–55.
24. M. Iglesias Santos, *Imágenes del otro: identidad e inmigración en la literatura y el cine* (Madrid: Biblioteca Nueva, 2013).
25. J. Pérez, "Reframing Accountability in Spanish Immigration Cinema: Mediterranean Modernity and the Shortcomings of 'NGO-Films.'" *Journal of Mediterranean Studies* 24, no. 2 (2015): 219–220.
26. L. Peralta García, *Los nuevos héroes del siglo XXI: las migraciones subsaharianas vistas por el cine en España y África* (Barcelona: Editorial UOC, 2016), 46–7.

27. Debra Faszer-McMahon and Victoria L. Ketz, eds, *African Immigrants in Contemporary Spanish Texts: Crossing the Strait* (Farnham: Ashgate, 2015), 16.
28. C. H. Ricci, "African Voices in Contemporary Spain," Hispanic Issues 37 (2010): 225.
29. Faszer-McMahon and Ketz, African Immigrants, 17.
30. Isabel Santaolalla, *Los "otros": etnicidad y "raza" en el cine español contemporáneo*, Humanidades, vol. 50 (Madrid: Prensas Universitarias de Zaragoza, 2005). Chema Castiello, *"Los parias de la tierra:" emigrantes en el cine español* (Madrid: Talasa, 2005). Eduardo Moyano, *La memoria escondida: cine y emigración* (Madrid: Tabla Rasa Libros y Ediciones, 2005).
31. The Goya awards are the most prestigious film awards in Spain
32. José Maria Rodriguez, "Spain's Handling of the Cayuco Boat Crisis," *EurActiv* (June 14, 2017), available at <https://www.euractiv.com/section/justice-home-affairs/news/spains-handling-of-the-cayuco-boat-crisis/> (last accessed December 10, 2020).
33. María Martínez Lirola, "Approaching the Representation of Sub-Saharan Immigrants in a Sample from the Spanish Press," *Critical Discourse Studies* 11, no. 4 (2014): 482–99.
34. Athanasia Batziou, *Picturing Immigration: Photojournalistic Representation of Immigrants in Greek and Spanish Press* (Bristol: Intellect, 2011), 51.
35. Antolín Granados Martínez, "Es virtual la realidad de la inmigración?: la construcción mediática de la inmigración extranjera en España," in La inmigración en España: contextos y alternativas, vol. II, ed. Francisco Javier García Castaño and Carolina Muriel López (Granada: Laboratorio de Estudios Interculturales, 2002), 437–48.
36. Santaolalla, *Los "otros."*
37. Moyano, *La memoria escondida.*
38. Castiello, *"Los parias de la tierra."*
39. Yosefa Loshitzky, *Screening Strangers: Migration and Diaspora in Contemporary European Cinema* (Bloomington: Indiana University Press, 2010).
40. Flesler, *The Return of the Moor*; Santaolalla, *Los "otros"*; I. Gordillo Álvarez, "El diálogo intercultural en el cine español contemporáneo: entre el estereotipo y el etnocentrismo." *Revista Internacional de Comunicación Audiovisual, Publicidad y Literatura* 1, no. 4 (2007): 207–22; A. Davies, *Spanish Spaces: Landscape, Space and Place in Contemporary Spanish Culture* (Liverpool: Liverpool University Press, 2012); Peralta García, *Los nuevos héroes del siglo XXI*; M. van Liew, "Immigration Films," in *Contemporary Spanish Cinema and Genre* (Manchester: Manchester University Press, 2019).
41. Davies, *Spanish Spaces*, 145.
42. Santaolalla, *Los "otros."*
43. van Liew, "Immigration Films", 260.
44. CoE (Council of Europe) Mandate, 1992 (ratified 2017), available at <https://www.coe.int/en/web/conventions/full-list/-/conventions/treaty/220> (last accessed December 10, 2020); qtd in Guido Rings, *The Other in Contemporary Migrant Cinema: Imagining a New Europe?* (Abingdon: Routledge, 2016), 2.
45. Santaolalla, "Ethnic and racial configurations in contemporary Spanish culture." Santaolalla, *Los "otros."* I. Santaolalla, "Body Matters: Immigrants in Recent Spanish,

Italian and Greek Cinemas," in *European Cinema in Motion*, ed. D. Berghahn and C. Sternberg (London: Palgrave Macmillan, 2010), 152–74. I. Ballesteros, "Xenofobia y racismo en España: la inmigración africana en *Las cartas de Alou* (1990) de Montxo Armendáriz y *Bwana* (1996) de Imanol Uribe." In I. Ballesteros, *Cine (ins)urgente: Textos fílmicos y contextos culturales en la España postfranquista* (Madrid: Editorial Fundamentos, 2001), 205–32. I. Ballesteros, "Screening African Immigration to Spain: Las Cartas de Alou and Bwana," *Chasqui* 34 (2005): 48–61. I. Davies, "Raza y etnicidad: desafíos de la inmigración en el cine español," *Letras Hispanas* 3, no. 1 (2006): 98–112. D. Q. Burkhart, "The Disposable Immigrant: The Aesthetics of Waste in Las Cartas De Alou," *Journal of Spanish Cultural Studies* 11, no. 2 (2010): 153–65. Rings, *The Other in Contemporary Migrant Cinema*.
46. The Guardia Civil is a police force of military origin, in charge of security and order outside urban centres, such as on highways or the border.
47. Loshitzky, *Screening Strangers*.
48. The film was directed by Omer Oké and Txarli Llorente. Its choral narrative mixes fiction and testimonies, calling attention to the hardship of the border, the difficulties of integration due to having an undocumented status, and the inefficacy of the systems in place to promote integration. Before this film, Oké was the Director of Immigration of the Basque government, where he developed a regional immigration policy. As a representative of both an accented cinema and political messaging, the film is innovative in its treatment of sub-Saharan immigration in the context of Spanish immigration cinema.
49. Just before the credits roll, the words of writer Rosa Montero appear on screen: "They will continue to come and they will continue to die, because history has demonstrated that there is no wall capable of containing the dreams."
50. Zygmunt Bauman, *Liquid Modernity* (London: John Wiley & Sons, 2013).
51. Chandra Talpade Mohanty, "Under Western Eyes: Feminist Scholarship and Colonial Discourses," in *Media and Cultural Studies: Keyworks*, 2nd edn, ed. Meenakshi Gigi Durham and Douglas M. Kellner (London: Wiley: 2012), 361.
52. Wim Naudé, *Conflict, Disasters and No Jobs: Reasons for International Migration from Sub-Saharan Africa*, WIDER Research Paper, no. 2008/85 (Helsinki The United Nations University World Institute for Development Economics Research (UNU-WIDER), 2008).
53. Bauman, *Liquid Modernity*.
54. Laura U. Marks, *The Skin of the Film: Intercultural Cinema. Embodiment, and the Senses* (Durham, NC: Duke University Press, 2000).
55. Marc Augé, *Non-places: Introduction to an Anthropology of Supermodernity* (London: Verso, 1995), 86.
56. Zygmunt Bauman, *Work, Consumerism and the New Poor* (London: McGraw-Hill Education (UK), 2004).
57. Bourdieu, *Distinction*.
58. I. Ballesteros, *Immigration Cinema in the New Europe* (Bristol: Intellect, 2015). B. Zecchi, "Veinte años de inmigración en el imaginario fílmico español," in *Imágenes del otro: identidad e inmigración en la literatura y el cine*, ed. Montserrat Iglesias Santos (Madrid: Biblioteca Nueva, 2010), 157–84.

59. Pérez, "Reframing Accountability in Spanish Immigration Cinema," 225.
60. Fiona Noble, "Beyond the Sea: Seascapes and Migration in Contemporary Spanish Cinema," *Bulletin of Hispanic Studies* 95, no. 6 (2018): 637–57. Davies, *Spanish Spaces*.
61. After weeks of being harassed by the Moroccan police in a nearby immigrant camp, a group of people waiting to cross the fence separating Morocco from Ceuta decided to attempt to jump it collectively one night. Over 700 people attempted to cross. At some point in the chaos, the Spanish border guard started shooting and in the urgency many got tangled up in the razor wire. The exact number of deaths and injuries is unknown, although reports suggest that many were injured and at least fifteen died. Many of those arrested were subjected to what is called "devoluciones en caliente" (express deportations), being left in the desert without their injuries being attended to or their data being processed. The event led to outcry among many groups working with immigrants, yet the media reported it only briefly. It would take almost a decade to remove the razor wire and investigate the circumstances.
62. See, for example, *Princesas/Princesses* (2005).
63. See, for example, *Biutiful* (2010), *Evelyn* (2012), or *A escondidas* (2014).
64. Pérez, "Reframing Accountability in Spanish Immigration Cinema," 217.
65. Pérez, "Reframing Accountability in Spanish Immigration Cinema," 215.
66. See, for example, *La venta del paraíso/The Sale of Paradise* (2012), *El rayo* (2013), or *Diamantes negros* (2013).
67. Saskia Sassen, *Expulsions: Brutality and Complexity in the Global Economy* (Cambridge, MA: Harvard University Press, 2014).
68. Zygmunt Bauman, *Wasted Lives: Modernity and its Outcasts* (Cambridge: Polity Press, 2004).
69. Bauman, *Work, Consumerism and the New Poor*. Bauman, *Wasted Lives*.
70. The law was proposed by the socialist government in 2004 and implemented in 2007. It aimed to close the gap in Spain's non-existent transitional justice by, among other actions, removing the remaining symbols of the Francoist regime (such as street names and statues); lending government support to locating and identifying victims in mass graves; and granting automatic Spanish nationality to direct descendants of the exiled. The law incited debates that had long been dormant.
71. Some of the most notorious corruption cases in Spain in recent times have implicated top politicians of the Popular Party, including the President of the Valencian Community, Francisco Camps; the Valencian mayor, Rita Barberá; former Treasurer, Luis Bárcenas; former Minister of the Economy, Rodrigo Rato; or the King's brother-in-law, Iñaki Urgandarín.
72. Triana Toribio, *Spanish Film Cultures*, 16.

Works Cited

Agrela Romero, Belén. "Políticas de inmigración y prácticas sociales con mujeres inmigrantes: discursos, representaciones y significaciones." In *Delitos y fronteras: mujeres extranjeras en prisión*, ed. María Teresa Martín Palomo, María Jesús Miranda López and Cristina Vega Solís, 139–82. Madrid: Editorial Complutense, 2005.

Agrela, Belén. "Spain as a Recent Country of Immigration: How Immigration Became a Symbolic, Political, and Cultural Problem in the 'New Spain.'" Working paper no. 57, La Jolla: University of California–San Diego, 2002.

Agrela, Belen, and Gunther Dietz. "Nongovernmental Versus Governmental Actors? Multilevel Governance and Immigrant Integration Policy in Spain." In *Local Citizenship in Recent Countries of Immigration*, ed. Takeyuki Tsuda, 205–34. New York: Lexington Books, 2006.

Albert Guardiola, María Carmen, Eva Espinar Ruiz, and María Isabel Hernandez Sanchez. "Immigrants as Threats. Migratory Processes in Spanish Television." *Convergencia – Revista de Ciencias Sociales* 17, no. 53 (2010): 49–68.

Alcantud, Miguel, director. *Diamantes negros*. 2013.

Augé, Marc. *Non-places: Introduction to an Anthropology of Supermodernity*. London: Verso, 1995.

Ballesteros, I. "Xenofobia y racismo en España: la inmigración africana en *Las cartas de Alou* (1990) de Montxo Armendáriz y *Bwana* (1996) de Imanol Uribe." In I. Ballesteros, *Cine (ins)urgente: Textos fílmicos y contextos culturales en la España postfranquista*, 205–32. Madrid: Editorial Fundamentos, 2001.

Ballesteros, I. "Screening African Immigration to Spain: Las Cartas de Alou and Bwana." *Chasqui* 34 (2005): 48–61.

Ballesteros, I. *Immigration Cinema in the New Europe*. Bristol: Intellect, 2015.

Batziou, Athanasia. *Picturing Immigration: Photojournalistic Representation of Immigrants in Greek and Spanish Press*. Bristol: Intellect, 2011.

Bauman, Zygmunt. *Liquid Modernity*. London: John Wiley & Sons, 2013.

Bauman, Zygmunt. *Wasted Lives: Modernity and its Outcasts*. Cambridge: Polity Press, 2004.

Bauman, Zygmunt. *Work, Consumerism and the New Poor*. London: McGraw-Hill Education (UK), 2004.

Bourdieu, Pierre. *Distinction: A Social Critique of the Judgement of Taste*. Cambridge, MA: Harvard University Press, 1984.

Burkhart, D. Q. "The Disposable Immigrant: The Aesthetics of Waste in Las Cartas De Alou." *Journal of Spanish Cultural Studies* 11, no. 2 (2010): 153–65.

Butler, Judith. *Precarious Life: The Powers of Mourning and Violence*. London: Verso, 2006.

Castiello, Chema. *"Los parias de la tierra:" emigrantes en el cine español*. Madrid: Talasa, 2005.

CoE (Council of Europe) Mandate, 1992 (ratified 2017), <https://www.coe.int/en/web/conventions/full-list/-/conventions/treaty/220> (last accessed December 10, 2020).

Davies, A. *Spanish Spaces: Landscape, Space and Place in Contemporary Spanish Culture*. Liverpool: Liverpool University Press, 2012.

Davies, I. "Raza y etnicidad: desafíos de la inmigración en el cine español." *Letras Hispanas* 3, no. 1 (2006): 98–112.

Echevarría, I. "La CT: un cambio de paradigma." In *CT o la cultura de la transición: crítica a 35 años de cultura española*, ed. G. Martínez, 25–36. Barcelona: Mondadori, 2012.

Elena, Alberto. "Back to Africa? Colonial History and Postcolonial Dynamics in Recent Spanish Cinema." In *(Re)viewing Creative, Critical and Commercial Practices in*

Contemporary Spanish Cinema, ed. Duncan Wheeler and Fernando Canet, 65–78. New York: Intellect, 2014.

Faszer-McMahon, Debra and Victoria L. Ketz, eds. *African Immigrants in Contemporary Spanish Texts: Crossing the Strait*. Farnham: Ashgate, 2015.

Flesler, Daniela. *The Return of the Moor: Spanish Responses to Contemporary Moroccan Immigration*. Purdue Studies in Romance Literatures, vol. 43. West Lafayette, IN: Purdue University Press, 2008.

Gordillo Álvarez, I. "El diálogo intercultural en el cine español contemporáneo: entre el estereotipo y el etnocentrismo." *Revista Internacional de Comunicación Audiovisual, Publicidad y Literatura* 1, no. 4 (2007): 207–22.

Granados Martínez, Antolín. "Es virtual la realidad de la inmigración?: la construcción mediática de la inmigración extranjera en España." In *La inmigración en España: contextos y alternativas*, vol. II, ed. Francisco Javier García Castaño and Carolina Muriel López, 437–48. Granada: Laboratorio de Estudios Interculturales, 2002.

Igartua, Juan José, Carlos Muñiz, and Lifen Cheng. "La inmigración en la prensa española: aportaciones empíricas y metodológicas desde la teoría del encuadre noticioso." *Migraciones: Publicación del Instituto Universitario de Estudios sobre Migraciones* 17 (2005): 143–81.

Iglesias Santos, M. *Imágenes del otro: identidad e inmigración en la literatura y el cine*. Madrid: Biblioteca Nueva, 2013.

López Sala, Ana María and Ruth Ferrero Turrión. "Economic Crisis and Migration Policies in Spain: The Big Dilemma." Annual conference, Centre on Migration, Policy and Society, University of Oxford, 2009.

Loshitzky, Yosefa. *Screening Strangers: Migration and Diaspora in Contemporary European Cinema*. Bloomington: Indiana University Press, 2010.

Marks, Laura U. *The Skin of the Film: Intercultural Cinema, Embodiment, and the Senses*. Durham, NC: Duke University Press, 2000.

Martínez Lirola, María. "Approaching the Representation of Sub-Saharan Immigrants in a Sample from the Spanish Press." *Critical Discourse Studies* 11, no. 4 (2014): 482–99.

Martínez Lirola, María. "Multimodal Representation of Sub-Saharan Immigrants as Illegal: Deconstructing Their Portrayal as Victims, Heroes and Threats in a Sample from the Spanish Press." *Bulletin of Hispanic Studies* 93, no. 4 (2016): 343–61.

Martínez Lirola, María. "Discursive Legitimation of Criminalization and Victimization of Sub-Saharan Immigrants in Spanish El País and ABC Newspapers." In *Representing the Other in European Media Discourses*, ed. Jan Chovanec and Katarzyna Mokek-Kozakowska, 135–54. Amsterdam and Philadelphia: John Benjamins, 2017.

Martin-Márquez, Susan. *Disorientations: Spanish Colonialism in Africa and the Performance of Identity*. New Haven, CT: Yale University Press, 2008.

Mohanty, Chandra Talpade. "Under Western Eyes: Feminist Scholarship and Colonial Discourses." In *Media and Cultural Studies: Keyworks*, 2nd edn, ed. Meenakshi Gigi Durham and Douglas M. Kellner. London: Wiley: 2012.

Moyano, Eduardo. *La memoria escondida: cine y emigración*. Madrid: Tabla Rasa Libros y Ediciones, 2005.

Naudé, Wim. *Conflict, Disasters and No Jobs: Reasons for International Migration from Sub-Saharan Africa*. WIDER Research Paper, no. 2008/85. Helsinki: The

United Nations University World Institute for Development Economics Research (UNU-WIDER), 2008.
Noble, Fiona. "Beyond the Sea: Seascapes and Migration in Contemporary Spanish Cinema." *Bulletin of Hispanic Studies* 95, no. 6 (2018): 637–57.
Olivares, Gerardo, director. *14 kilómetros*. 2007.
Peralta García, L. *Los nuevos héroes del siglo XXI: las migraciones subsaharianas vistas por el cine en España y África*. Barcelona: Editorial UOC, 2016.
Pérez, J. "Reframing Accountability in Spanish Immigration Cinema: Mediterranean Modernity and the Shortcomings of 'NGO-Films.'" *Journal of Mediterranean Studies* 24, no. 2 (2015): 215–29.
Ricci, C. H. "African Voices in Contemporary Spain". *Hispanic Issues* 37 (2010): 203–32.
Rings, G. *The Other in Contemporary Migrant Cinema: Imagining a New Europe?* Abingdon: Routledge, 2016.
Rodriguez, José Maria. "Spain's Handling of the Cayuco Boat Crisis." *EurActiv* (June 14, 2017), <https://www.euractiv.com/section/justice-home-affairs/news/spains-handling-of-the-cayuco-boat-crisis/> (last accessed December 10, 2020).
Rout, Leslie B. *The African Experience in Spanish America: 1502 to the Present Day*. Cambridge Latin American Studies, vol. 23. Cambridge: Cambridge University Press Archive, 1976.
Said, Edward. *Orientalism*. New York: Vintage Books, 1978.
Said, Edward. *Orientalismo*. Madrid: Debate, 2002.
Santaolalla, Isabel. "Ethnic and Racial Configurations in Contemporary Spanish Culture." In *Constructing Identity in Contemporary Spain: Theoretical Debates and Cultural Practice*, ed. Jo Labanyi. Oxford: Oxford University Press, 2003.
Santaolalla, Isabel. *Los "otros": etnicidad y "raza" en el cine español contemporáneo*, Humanidades, vol. 50. Madrid: Prensas Universitarias de Zaragoza, 2005.
Santaolalla, Isabel. "Body Matters: Immigrants in Recent Spanish, Italian and Greek Cinemas." In *European Cinema in Motion*, ed. D. Berghahn and C. Sternberg, 152–74. London: Palgrave Macmillan, 2010.
Sassen, Saskia. *Expulsions: Brutality and Complexity in the Global Economy*. Cambridge, MA: Harvard University Press, 2014.
Toasije, Antumi. "The Africanity of Spain: Identity and Problematization." *Journal of Black Studies* 39, no. 3 (2009): 348–55.
Tofiño-Quesada, Ignacio. "Spanish Orientalism: Uses of the Past in Spain's Colonization in Africa." *Comparative Studies of South Asia, Africa and the Middle East* 23, nos 1 and 2 (2003): 141–8.
Triana-Toribio, Núria. *Spanish Film Cultures: The Making and Unmaking of Spanish Cinema*. London: Bloomsbury, 2016.
van Liew, M. "Immigration Films". In *Contemporary Spanish Cinema and Genre*, ed. Jay Beck and Vicente Rodríguez Ortega. Manchester: Manchester University Press, 2019.
Zecchi, B. "Veinte años de inmigración en el imaginario fílmico español." In *Imágenes del otro: identidad e inmigración en la literatura y el cine*, ed. Montserrat Iglesias Santos, 157–84. Madrid: Biblioteca Nueva, 2010.

9. MOBILITY CONSTRAINED AND ENABLED BY GENDER: THE IN-TRANSIT *AFRICAINE* OF *HOPE* (BORIS LOJKINE, 2014)

Nicole B. Wallenbrock

Introduction

The film *Hope*, in which a Nigerian woman and a Cameroonian man meet crossing the Sahara, relays often ignored findings in migration studies to the fiction screen. Although many reports and visual sources portray dangerous and deadly boat journeys, *Hope* reveals the crossing of the Sahara Desert, an arduous path that precedes boat travel for many. While the press seldom mediatizes "in-transit" sub-Saharan African communities of North Africa, such groupings are central to *Hope*. In these clusters, Africans may live for months or even years before individuals risk their lives in an attempt to reach Europe (though others may decide to return home). The path of the Africans traveling in *Hope* follows this unreported trajectory; when crossing the Sahara, they exercise ongoing mobility which permits strategized movement with the impeding goal of an undocumented crossing. Yet, later halted in Morocco, the characters suffer from involuntary immobility, which forces them to remain in a country on their route and impedes their movement towards their desired destination (Europe). An exception in the realm of fiction film, *Hope* shifts sub-Saharan migrants from the media-mandated boat crossing—which still occurs in the film's climactic final ten minutes—and exposes a forgotten, lengthy, but also dangerous leg of the journey. *Hope* contradicts previous depictions of immigration, for as anthropologist Inka Stockton notes: "Transit represents a challenge to dichotomist representations of mobility and immobility."[1]

In addition, the inclusion of a female who begins the migration process alone singularizes *Hope*. The spectator witnesses many situations of sexual violence and discrimination against the character Hope (played by Endurance Newton) during her migration journey. Yet her survival and participation in an economy depend upon the very female status that suffers through such violence and oppression (marriage, prostitution, pregnancy). The plight of the female character unearths the vicissitudes of mobility for women in transit; Hope's status as a woman both constrains and enables her mobility, suggesting the complications of gender and the dimensions of their influence on the migration process. Camera work in *Hope* further complicates a reading of gender in migration; our view of the migrants is at times omniscient, but at others assumes a male character's perspective. In summary, *Hope*'s unique cinematic situation complicates the African migration debate, centered on continental politics and human rights, with the ever-present but frequently overlooked questions of how gender functions in North Africa's often ignored in-transit communities.

In the following chapter, I will first review some details of contemporary inter-African and African migration to Europe. This information will aid our close reading of four sequences that present a situation of danger and survival for African women in transit. Inka Stock's article, written and researched roughly a year before *Hope* was filmed (2012), provides an ethnographic account of the fiction film's veracity. The first two sequences selected for our study cinematically highlight Hope's gender as the primary factor in abuse and survival; these scenes provide a vehicle for a debate on the applicability and the limits of Giorgio Agamben's term *homo sacer*.[2] The third scene we will examine questions the European spectacle that surrounds the debate on gender and in-transit migration. In this sequence, the director's self-conscious gesture exposes gender, in-transit migration, and the legacy of French colonialism as bound by the cinematic apparatus. The chapter concludes by studying the film's ending when Hope perceives Europe, and the camera at last grants her a point of view. This lesser-known film uniquely imparts important details of African migration in the early twenty-first century, as well as the negotiations undergone when a European lens presents such phenomena.

In Transit

A note on the vocabulary surrounding immigration should commence this study: in particular, several consistently used terms, *irregular* and *illegal*. Although *Hope* concerns the debacles of irregular migration (meaning, broadly, "crossing borders without proper authority or violating conditions for entering another country"[3]), the legality of their status remains in flux—the majority of migrants who enter one country illegally, often in the course of their journey, enter another legally. Additionally, after entering a country without permission, one may seek residence, whereby a legal migration process may ensue. Such inconsistencies render the term *illegal migration* inadequate, while *irregular* and *in-transit* more completely describe the everchanging status of those traveling in pursuit of a life in another geographic region.

While travel through the Sahara Desert does not bar one's intended boat travel when reaching the coast, the desert scenes that commence *Hope* nevertheless trouble a visual trope of the African migrant at the coast and or on the water—many other fiction films from Francophone networks, such as *Welcome* (Philippe Lioret, 2009) and *Le Havre* (Aki Kaurismaki, 2011), set in France, *Harragas* (Merzak Allouache, 2009) in Algeria, and *La Pirogue* (Moussa Touré, 2012) in Senegal, maintain the Mediterranean boat image as necessary to expose the problem. However, Mary McAuliffe and Adrian Kitimbo explain that, in fact, Africans more frequently migrate to neighboring countries and remain on the continent. They conclude that "[t]he number of African migrants is not negligible and has increased since the 1990s. However, intra-regional migration continues to outpace extra-regional migration."[4] In precolonial times, the Sahara and Sahel region represented "intensive population mobility" due to "a (caravan) trade, conquest, pilgrimage, and religious education."[5] While colonialism's borders largely destroyed the natural migration that existed between North and West Africa (one thinks specifically of the Berlin conference of 1884/5, in which European leaders drew borders and claimed different regions), Saharan migration remains an age-old phenomenon. We should also note that despite the frequent mediatization of such feats and their failures, the majority of Africans in transit do not attempt to reach Europe, and if attempting to cross the Mediterranean Sea, frequently travel by plane. In fact, of the difficult-to-calculate statistics in which 1,015,078 reached Europe in 2015,[6] only a percentage traveled by boat (221,454 reached Spain, Greece, and Italy by boat in 2015, 10,495 in 2018, 1.8 million between 2014 and 2018).[7] Nevertheless, the main characters in *Hope*, Justin and Hope, remain bound by the dream of Europe and a Mediterranean Sea crossing, which is an ambition for many. *Hope* does invoke a Western media obsession with the African desperate to reach Europe, and even pictures boat travel in its climactic conclusion. Yet, the film also portrays the ignored and denied intra-African migration as an aspect of an in-transit lifestyle that precedes an intercontinental journey. While some studies allege that women make up 20–30 percent of the sub-Saharan Africans migrants in Morocco,[8] at present there is no objective source concerning the gender of sub-Saharan migrants that seek Europe and or that are en route in Morocco; women are often reluctant to participate in interviews, and male migrants provide most of the information. In addition, if illegal in-transit and immigrant persons may not wish to risk their lives or homes by speaking to researchers, sex workers will be still more unlikely to describe their past or present situation. Françoise Guillemaut writes,

> [t]he occultation of the place of migrants in prostitution and that of prostitution in the work on the history of migration reveals to us how much the situations lived by foreign women, as well as their testimony (especially if they are outside the norms of marriage or family reunification and do not present themselves as victims), are poorly documented because they face a combination of forms of oppression and suppression of their testimony and experience. This occultation is not just due to chance.[9]

For this reason, the media frequently provide an image of the typical transit immigrant as a young, single man, and absents the women who are less visible, especially those that hide in the shadows of sex work, which, if threatened, may risk their mobility, economic solvency, and ultimately survival. Inka Stock writes, "[w]hen they are mentioned women migrants are often described as being under male control during their migratory project . . . women's mobility appears to be forced and not of their own volition."[10] The complexity of a situation that may be in part forced, in part decided by women, does not often receive press attention or a narrative platform, as such stories refuse a simplistic gender binary formulation.

Sequence 1: Gender in the Sahara

As the noun "hope" describes the yearning and belief that inspire many Africans to undertake a life-risking journey, it may not initially be apparent that the film title also modifies a female character. (In fact, Inka Stock finds that many African women en route name their children after optimistic concepts such as Hope, to empower their journey.) Describing both a woman and a concept, Hope propagates a gendered symbolism that then dominates the film's powerful conclusion. Yet, our introduction to the character iterates no such symbolism and, in fact, obliterates such facile coding. Opening in the bright desert to the slight sounds of a person stirring formula into water, the film first relates the physical hardship of geography, and its toll on the crouched figures. In this visual realm of human survival and masculinity, director Boris Lojkine situates the actress Endurance Newton, whom we meet not as a woman, but as a presumed male in a medium-long shot, wearing loose clothing (Fig. 9.1). However, when two men discuss the stranger, and one suggests that the outsider is a woman, a survival technique unravels. One man then approaches and speaks roughly to the traveler, accused of being in drag, before the man grabs and scrutinizes her face, which bares the marks of Yoruba scarification. To verify his claims, the man violently opens her jacket to see and touch her chest.

Figure 9.1 Hope (on the left) in loose, non-gendered clothing, hoping to pass as male when spotted in *Hope* (Zadig Films, 2014).

In this way, the opening scene introduces immigration as bound to a specific brutal geography and a dogmatic gender hierarchy which receives little media coverage. In fact, in consideration of Francophone films concerning immigration, the majority take place on the coast or at sea, thus erasing the agony of the foot migration through the Sahara, which precedes the boat attempts for many. Senegalese productions depict a different trajectory, as some Senegalese also depart by boat from their nation's coast (*La Pirogue*; *Atlantiques*, Mati Diop, 2019). I should also add here that Jacques Audiard's César-winning *Dheepan*, filmed in the year *Hope* was released, 2014, unconventionally followed a Sri Lankan immigrant unit from the boat to a life outside Paris and generally represents an evolution in Francophone immigrant depictions. Still, five years after *Hope*'s premiere, there has been no other fiction feature to depict such in-transit life in the Sahara, and the brutality that individuals endure for the chance to sail to Europe. Furthermore, in the majority of fiction films concerning migration, sexuality and gender themselves present the heteronormativity of the male characters. While *Harragas* depicts one Algerian woman on board for Europe, she follows a boyfriend, and the plot and dialogue rely on the sexual tension caused by her presence in a masculine realm. *Atlantiques* never attempts to depict the boat voyage, but the film starkly pronounces gender division; the young men who work in construction plan their sea crossing when they are not paid—when they drown, the young women they leave behind are inhabited by their ghosts. Thus while *Atlantiques* transgresses genre expectations in a film about the "lost generation" (as Mati Diop said in a Q and A after a screening of *Atlantiques* at the New York Film Festival), it maintains the media's gender binary bias concerning immigration, and denies the *migrante*'s voice or volition.

Five years before *Atlantique*s, the CNC (Centre National du Cinéma et de l'Image Animée, the French government film board) and its distributor, Pyramide, exclusively targeted with *Hope* a French audience that was ill prepared for this gender unveiling and its geographic locus. The first few minutes of the film do not invoke the freedom of a pre-gendered person, as described by Monique Witteg.[11] Instead, the non-gender represents a form of containment dictated by survival circumstances; or, if viewing the character Hope as more obviously in drag, before being outed as a woman who will then be perceived as such, we find the desert induces gender fluidity. Helen Nabasuta Mugambi's words concerning the relevance and particularity of gender in African studies resonate today: "Gender . . . as a socially constructed mark of identity, is particularly vulnerable to transformation when socio-economic forces are intensified by internal migrations, militarization, and cultural globalization."[12] Although we do not meet Hope or learn of her identity before her migration journey, we witness several steps of transformation; she has rejected femininity for protection before being forced to assume a woman's role by men. The scene reveals that the basic needs of food and safety, threatened by the migration journey, mutate gender for the lone woman, and these same survival needs, under patriarchal threat, then force her to identify as a woman. As subsequent scenes reveal, marriage and prostitution, only possible in this context as a woman, are common survival mechanisms for those in transit. Thus, the moment that men discover Hope's sex, her life depends on the expression of gender norms and sexual labor, reinforced cinematically by lack of a viewpoint.

The theories of Giorgio Agamben, expounded in *Sovereign Power and Bare Life* (1998)[13] and *The State of Exception* (2003),[14] generally apply to clandestine immigration and its filmic portrayal (I previously have written on the subject in an article entitled the *Homo Sacer on the Norman Coast* in regard to *Le Havre* and *Welcome*).[15] Agamben's term bare life equally applies to the immigrants' situation in *Hope*, for the population exists illegally as a "hidden norm" incorporated by the larger political structure. The empty Algerian desert, scattered with immigrants, relates to a zone both in and outside of the government's sovereign power, that remains little controlled, in part because of the extreme temperature and the desert's vast expanse. *Hope* impresses the fear involved in migration and the need to stay within your nationality's clan in opening intertitles that read in the second person, "beware of police and bandits." To this extent, *homo sacer*, a term from ancient Roman law that described prisoners, applies, for a *homo sacer* lacked a citizen's rights, but was also considered unworthy of execution. The sub-Saharan Africans en route and in hiding in North Africa similarly suffer such a bind, lacking citizenship where they dwell, and yet denied the right to move by law. The immigration the Africans seek consequently counters international dictates, which force them into a survival mode—they travel largely by foot through the desert, before hiding near the coast in continual efforts to raise money to board a boat.

However, while Agamben's vocabulary applies generally to twenty-first-century displaced peoples, and the various films that expose such matters, further questions ensue. In fact, Agamben's theory fails to confront the status of race, and of sexuality, and thus never locates the doubling or tripling of discrimination within the *homo sacer* underworlds. Ewa Płonowska Ziarek concurs, saying that "Agamben's analysis of this aporia from antiquity to modernity misses . . . the negative differentiation of bare life along racial, ethnic, and gender lines."[16] More precisely, as it pertains to this chapter, Agamben neglects gender within the state of exception, and the bias against the gender minority of sub-Saharan immigrants, women. By demonstrating divisive and violent gender rhetoric within the African communities, *Hope* exposes a fracturing of desperation fueled by statelessness. In fact, in an interview with me, Boris Lojkine vaguely expressed this criticism from immigrant activists: his film *Hope* related the strife between sub-Saharan men and women while in transit, and thus countered a more holistic call to European action. Yet, such a filmic revelation of violent behavior against a female character does not insinuate her point of view. In fact, a preference for a male perspective (though not an overtly sexualized gaze) proffers more space to Hope before the male characters (and the camera) consider her female. Now defined as she in this first sequence, and soon revealed as the titular Hope, the sole woman immigrant participates in what Luce Irigaray once described as a phallogocentric economy,[17] that cinema in part emulates by viewing her from a male character's perspective in shots that increasingly tighten. This European vision of women traded as objects amongst men remains pertinent with respect to the camera's vision, but yet dissolves with our plot and setting. For while Hope's livelihood as a migrant in the Sahara is initially threatened by being traded by men, it soon elicits a survival mode that the men lack. Françoise Guillemaut's research with African women in Lyon reveals that "their desire to migrate takes precedence over the possible repugnance of sex work, and that in any case, they do not want to be repatriated."[18] Such research suggests that an element of volition combines in these forced circumstances, and that although African women prostitutes may be considered victims, often their situation demonstrates strategizing for immigrating and the associated economizing of their own finances.

The complexity of understanding the agency involved in the sex work practiced by women in transit projects into the camera's splintered relationship to a female perspective in *Hope*. In fact, Boris Lojkine explained that he had originally written the script as uniquely fixated on the Cameroonian man's journey. However, after he added a romantic storyline, Lojkine realized that the most interesting element of the film lay in the lone female's battles. Additionally, Lojkine explained to me, he and the casting director chose Endurance Newton because she superficially evoked androgyny. He explained that the actress could be "belle mais pas sexy" (beautiful but not sexy), and could thus relate the truth of women hiding gender signifiers while immigrating. However, the near-drag also heightens the suspense at the beginning of the film. In this way, we witness a parsing of the bare-life community by gender difference, which the European camera then upholds and teases, inculcating spectators in the hetero-male gaze of gender emphasis and distinction. Furthermore, the later forced marriage of Hope to Léonard (Justin Wang), which then provides Léonard with a new source of income—his wife's sex work—continues to narratively obfuscate subject and object, victim and agent. Eventually, Hope falls in love with her husband (and he with her), and the money that she earns in the most horrible of abusive circumstances, when she is essentially kidnapped to live and work in a brothel, ultimately buys her and Léonard a place on a boat.

The Off-screen Rape

In the scene directly after the first desert sequence the camera continues its suture with Léonard, aligning the audience with the camera's perspective, which is also that of its male protagonist. Here we recognize the characters previously seen trekking through the desert, now seated aboard an open-back truck. The public begins to identify Léonard as a protagonist; shots of his head turning, coupled with shots of his field of vision, convey his awareness of the woman amongst them. This technique bolsters the spectator's identification with Léonard and reciprocates his fascination. Through his point of view, we see Hope's continued attempt to evade any trace of femininity's difference: namely, through covering herself, in a hat and hood. In the silence dictated by hiding, men use the occasion of close bodies to touch her—Hope swipes and pushes their hands away and then reaffirms her grip on her clothing. Intercut shots of Léonard glancing to the side connote his enchantment, while denying Hope's vision of the experience. In this way, the film repeats a scenario in which men watch Hope before touching her. Hope's eyes remain half-shut, and even when directly across from the camera, her eyes and actions never return Léonard's interest.

A cut reveals an ellipsis, although the camera remains in the same position in the truck. It is night, and now the sounds of Algerian soldiers speaking in French and Arabic permeate the previous silence. The soldiers' comments and bustle relate the traveling Africans' precarity under the state's sovereign power through what appears to be mundane and routine for the soldiers. Camera movement follows a soldier's flashlight to roam around the truck, stopping briefly to read each face's unique features for a second before continuing. This shot and the flashlight then glimpse the back of a man's jacket, which reads France in thick bold letters. Directly afterwards, the light finally locates Hope's blank expression, a face aiming to be read as plain and neuter, if not masculine. Yet, the soldiers' procedure, which typifies the state of exception, enforces Hope's gendered exclusion, distinction, and identity. Hope's isolation as a hetero-male visual interest, through the eyes of Léonard and now the soldiers, and further modified by the signifier France, posits a self-conscious query into the suture, as this French production by a French director typifies a male perspective that, in this instance, victimizes Hope (Fig. 9.2).

When the soldiers exit with Hope, the following shots and sound design suggest her rape and its horrific nature without depicting it. We hear the cries of a woman while a montage sequence captures the pained faces of the African men in the truck, each for a brief few seconds before passing to another's grimace, a technique which imparts the solidarity of the group and their collective helplessness. As they hope to survive under the all-powerful sovereignty, intervention cannot be attempted. While we as spectators do not fear our own mortality in these moments, we do experience the same division between the sounds of pain and the absence of vision, not unlike the in-transit men in the truck. In fact, the spectators' inability to halt the oppressive rule on screen analogizes the public's inability to change global immigration policy, and a shared powerlessness pervades. Of course, without words, without movement, the men's subtle expressions serve as blank projections for the audience, who

Figure 9.2 Hope attempts to evade her femininity on the truck, but is none the less noticed for her difference (Zadig Films, 2014).

may also perceive the men's steady stares and silence as a lack of courage. If the camera remains with the outsiders, who listen but do not intervene, the sound design's steady female screams force one to simultaneously visualize and sympathize with the terror. *Hope* here fully evokes a doubling of the state of exception for the woman; the state permits the soldiers' interpretation of the law which follows their most malign desires, and those who represent bare life do not (and arguably cannot) protect the attacked. Instead, they must protect their own superior status within such otherness, proving her inferiority and victimization.

These instances, early in the film, establish the surrounding men's violent demand of sex with women, who are a scarcity in the depicted migration landscape. Hope is here the object of exchange, at the center of a violent economy. While drag-dress permitted her mobility at the film's beginning, the camera's and the characters' revelation of her sex now determine, while never curtailing, her ability to move. In this way, as the research of Inka Stock also demonstrates, gender both constrains and enables movement.

A French Self-critique

In the third sequence under discussion, the director's self-casting comments on the entire production—the word "France," written on a jacket in the shot that directly precedes Hope's rape by the Algerian soldiers, already teased out this critique. However, to fully locate Lojkine's self-criticism, one should first situate *Hope* in the French tradition of ethnographic film. In interviews, Lojkine, who had previously directed two documentaries on Vietnam, confesses that his goal with *Hope* "was to make a film that was equal parts fiction and documentary," and freely acknowledges the influence of Jean Rouch (1917–2004). In fact, like *Hope*, the œuvre of Rouch, who began in ethnographic film (*Les Maîtres fous*, 1955) and pioneered *cinéma-vérité* (*Chronique d'un été*, Jean Rouch and Edgar Morin, 1961), blurs categorical distinctions. By drawing on the active participation of his African subjects, in both writing and editing, Rouch pioneered a field that Paul Stoller terms ethno-fiction. In a self-reflective article, "On the Vicissitudes of the Self: The Possessed Dancer, the Magician, the Sorcerer, the Filmmaker, and the Ethnographer," Rouch describes his own understanding of the film production process as the creation of "a shared anthropology."[19] Rouch argues that by empowering his African subjects, he disables the inherent voyeurism of ethnographic film.[20] While the African communities did not directly contribute to the storyline or the post-production in *Hope*, a comparison can be made, as the non-actor cast improvised all of their dialogue.[21] Although the majority of the action takes place outdoors and is shot in natural lighting, for scenes set in huts Lojkine relied on the communities' suggestions to ensure authenticity.

In this way, elements of the real signify the fiction within, enhancing the ethnographic quality of the film. Thus, the Western director observes and records the cultures of foreign peoples for a French public (the film was uniquely funded by CNC and TV5 Monde, and did not premiere in Africa, like his second production filmed in Africa, *Camille*, which was produced by Canal+ and CNC). Ethnography, the branch of anthropology that studies a group of non-Western peoples, and ethnographic film, cinema that portends an objective view of such people under study, has, from its inception, battled with the directors' positionality; directors may distort factual reporting with fiction (Robert Flaherty's *Nanook of the North*, 1922, ultimately created a false narrative) or pose questions to the subjects, asking the viewer to reflect on the directors' role (*Chronique d'un été*). It follows that the same tension between filmmaker and subject, present in all ethnographic film, lies in *Hope*, as it evokes a French view of African immigration. Thus, the inability of the Western intellectual, as explicated by Gayatri Chakravorty Spivak, to comprehend and theorize the impoverished person's experience in the Global South, applies to both *Hope*'s director and its discerning viewer.[22] The viewer may ask if *Hope*, in its fictional, authored presentation by a French man for a European audience, speaks for Africans seeking boat immigration. Furthermore, does their contribution to the director's realism proffer a shared vision of their misery? Additionally, does the camera's framing of the doubly marginalized woman exploit her subjectification?

Lojkine spent in total three months in Morocco living in the sub-Saharan African ghettos that are featured in the film and with the non-actor cast, in order to frame the actuality of migration and immigrants for European visual consumption, with the altruistic aim of revealing such hardship to a Northern public. Although Lojkine pursued an insider status by spending time with Africans in Morocco, his inability to speak the African languages and dialects, and his authority over the production and the budget, enhanced the neocolonial dynamic of his camera as it shot Africans. It is precisely his self-casting in a brief sequence that critiques the financial dynamic, and simultaneously mines the actors' anger for heightened dramatic tension. In the scene, Lojkine appears as a French client partaking of Hope's services in a hotel, when Léonard, Hope's husband, who at this point in their journey dually serves as her pimp and protector, enters to steal the client's wallet with the threat of an X-ACTO knife (Fig. 9.3).

While we never see Lojkine in bed with Hope, his Frenchness (he utters "c'est qui?" when Léonard knocks), the hotel setting, and his perceived nudity—only a blanket covers his chest—indicate not only his fragility but a consumer privilege. An occidental financial status enables the camera's exoticizing function for the European public. However, the scene's nuance derives from the acting, which, diegetically and non-diegetically, teases colonial gender imperatives and their cinematic recasting. Lojkine divulged that the actor playing Léonard, Justin Lang, "felt negative, bottled-up feelings towards me.

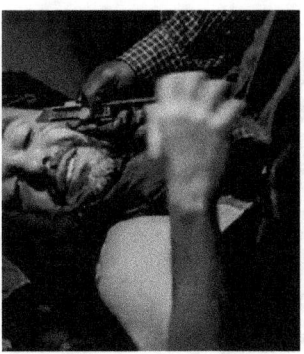

Figure 9.3 The director pictured on the left of the screen under Léonard's X-ACTO knife in *Hope* (Zadig Films, 2014).

In this scene, he took total pleasure in attacking the tourist character, and the effect was to 'unblock' him." The blocking empowers Léonard's rage as, standing above the director, he holds the X-ACTO knife to his neck while threatening him. In our conversation, Lojkine added that he had been giving orders to the actors for a few months, which also led to Justin's more persuasive depiction of anger towards the European. In both cases, the director's self-casting as a European buying sex from an African man's wife encouraged his African actor's antagonism; for in the scene, it is not only a European actor symbolizing domination and empire, but the precise French man whose perspective and wallet granted a chance, but also dependence.

However, the prostitute as an object of desire and exchange remains exterior to this powerful scene of theft and mortal threat. We see Léonard's point of view entering the hotel and knocking on the door, before he attacks the john, but we only glimpse Hope standing in a bra (Fig. 9.4). This quick glance suggests the nude state in which she works, while reinforcing Léonard as the camera's dominant point of view and the exchange of a woman as phallocentric, an economy intensified by the turmoil of poverty and travel. Léonard does not (and again in the context, cannot, without risking his life) defend Hope when she is raped by the Algerian soldiers, and he categorically views his wife as a financial instrument for, even after he falls in love with her, he pimps her and later, due to pressure, trades her to other Africans. Still, her prostitution to a European provokes Léonard's anger more than any other act, as it evokes the racial tension entwined with the Global North's historical domination of Africa, a sensation that resonates both on and off screen. In this way, Lojkine, the French director of a film about African immigration, admits, encourages, and protests his presence and gaze on Africans in transit. The French wallet and its transfer complicate the ambivalence of the male and female perspective, and

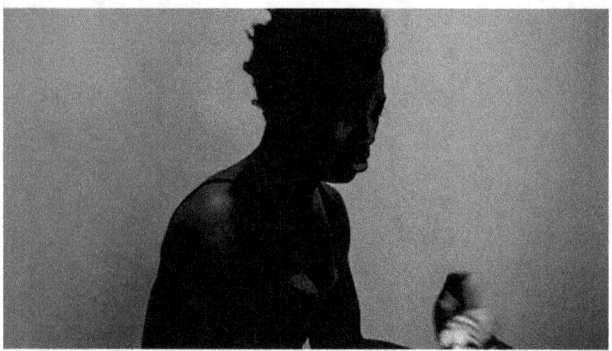

Figure 9.4 Hope at work in the film of the same name (Zadig Films, 2014).

insert the French film into the debate around an in-transit African woman's layered mobility. Lojkine's *Hope* reveals the global tragedy of the Africans in transit and the women in transit, whose mobility depends on their gender, which is also a constraining force. However, this particular scene, which depicts a financial exchange violently bound to the French john/director, also examines the nature of ethno-fiction and the financial order which permits such cinema. The African woman, who remains the nexus of the exchange while being almost ignored by the camera, exists in ambivalence and shadow as her gender both endures violence and provides an income. After running, she walks hand in hand with Léonard, as she loves the man who has forced her into marriage, and who relies on her prostitution for an income and for theft scenarios. Although her future at times seems determined by men, her gendered body also provides a means of survival, and ultimately the female body secures the boat journey. If the screen and a male-dominant point of view deny Hope's power when she is being observed and traded, the film's documentary aura fails to eradicate the truth of the fluctuating mobility of African women in transit. Ultimately, the resilience of these women, and their emblem, dominates the film's publicity and conclusion.

Hope's Point of View

Therefore, Boris Lojkine's *Hope* not only reveals the *homo sacers* of sub-Saharan African migration but indicates the complicated web of power within in-transit African communities, and the ways in which gender both permits and prohibits movement. European access to other cultures cannot be disentangled from a patriarchal, neocolonial vision, and the self-reflection imbues Lojkine's portrait of Africa with the very tools of its realization—the European wallet. Lojkine aimed to produce a melodrama, and when he realized that the most elusive character generated the audience's empathy and fascination, he then allotted Hope the title and brandished her as a symbol of the film and of in-transit African struggles. In fact, Lojkine says that the female character's increasing importance to the narrative was a decision made, in his words, "en dépit de moi-même" (in spite of myself).

The camera work equally reveals Hope's increasing value as she transitions from a subject at which men look, into an object of exchange. At last, her own point of view dominates the spectator's vision and the camera aligns in a suture with the film's female character. It is only in the closing minutes, after the death of the true male protagonist, Léonard, that the camera at last grants Hope a field of vision. At this point in the film, Hope is visibly pregnant, and though the father cannot be determined because she has had many partners as a prostitute, she believes that Léonard is the biological father. In a tragic ending which demonstrates the ways in which gender can, in fact, enhance mobility, the pregnant Hope, who has paid the proper fee for the boat journey, leaves the Moroccan brothel where she has been separated from Léonard, but where she has been minimally paid. Hope's pregnancy depicts a norm of many African women's migration journey: Stock cites studies by Mghari (2008),[23] Keygnaert et al. (2009),[24] Médecins sans Frontières (2010),[25] and Kastner (2010)[26] that find many in-transit Africans become pregnant.[27] To illustrate the danger and currency of African women who do leave by boat, as I edit this chapter on October 7, 2019, thirteen African women, some of whom were pregnant, were found dead on a shipwrecked boat near Lampedusa. While the subject was not addressed in the film *Hope*, one should note interviews and studies that find that some, in fact, attempt boat journeys while pregnant, hoping that being with child will prevent them from being repatriated, and that the future child's European citizenship will allow for family unification.[28] This background informs Lojkine's drama and script, but the dialogue only expresses the parents' hopes that their child will lead an easier life in Europe—this accessible dialogue relating to all parents' wishes for their offspring. Many work for years to finance a clandestine boat journey across the Mediterranean: Françoise Guillemaut finds that the passage cost nearly 50,000 euros in 2007. Hope is at last able to pay the fee and may perhaps be given priority because of her pregnancy, and one imagines that her character's chances of staying in Europe would be high.[29]

However, a climactic night sequence ruins the possibility of the African parents escaping together to Europe, for Léonard, who plans to join Hope who is boarding a boat, is suddenly stabbed before the boat's departure. Several low-lit shots portray a difficult night journey on the boat, and after an ellipsis we see the travelers in the stark gray light of morning. Here, at last, the film illustrates Hope's vision: she looks down at her hands, the palms covered in Léonard's blood. In this first shot to adopt a female point of view, we have a reflection of self, the woman looking at her body and viewing the tactile, visual suggestion of its responsibility for Léonard's death. Finally, with Léonard dead, we see the migration journey through an in-transit woman's perspective, and a traumatic self-examination is the camera's first instinct. After she screams from shock, we catch her vision of the blue sea, nestled between the shifting outlines of obscured passengers, who cry out in joy at seeing Spain from the boat. Hope struggles to enjoy her vision of Europe and what it symbolizes. Instead, she seeks to grant the vision to her dead lover, and yells "Regarde!", before taking her hands to his lifeless head and moving it to face the sea (Fig. 9.5).

The camera then remains fixed in a medium close-up on her for 20 seconds as she holds the now dead Léonard, a shot that reconfigures her as an emotional subject, and draws heavily on Christian imagery, a likeness of Mary holding Jesus. Thus, the woman immigrant's perspective—teased, denied, and then granted—primarily reveals the mortality of her male counterparts, and the futility and shifting optimism of blue, still surrounded by men. In this way, *Hope*'s plot suggests the confused state of African women in transit, whose fluctuating mobility derives from the degradation, discrimination, reproductive capacity, and resilience of their gender. The film visually presents the chaos surrounding the perception of African women in transit, as we view Hope, the only developed female character, as secondary until her perspective dominates at last. With regret, and reticence, she glimpses a European future.

On a closing note, a symbolic wallet joined the wallet prop from the scene in which the director played the role of a prostitute's john—for this relationship

Figure 9.5 Hope holds the now dead Léonard in the early morning on the boat in *Hope* (Zadig Films, 2014).

Figure 9.6   Hope looking towards Spain in *Hope* (Zadig Films, 2014).

continued after the performances and festival premieres, illustrating that the film too represented mobility for the Africans in the production. Both leads had European ambitions: Justin Lang, the actor playing Léonard, had already once reached Europe by boat but was forced to return, and Endurance Newton, who plays Hope, had desired a European future but could not find a way to leave. Therefore, the film represented new contact with Europe and its possibilities. In addition to their salaries for the film (which Lojkine did not disclose), the director offered to finance a business in Africa for each of them. While Endurance Newton leads a calm life and has a home and children, the director said that Justin Lang continues to see him as a white man, whom he further defines as "a money faucet in this African's eyes." His businesses fail and he continues to call Lojkine for financial help. Lojkine bemoaned the situation with a rhetorical question that contradicted his film's best intentions, "Dois-je payer toujours pour cette coupabilité coloniale?" (Must I pay forever for this colonial guilt?). This colonial guilt and neocolonial compromise encapsulate *Hope*, whose titular character finally and briefly escapes the screen's frame. However, even as the other passengers exalt at seeing Spain, all that the audience witnesses of the imagined *Africaine*'s vision is shifting blue water (Fig. 9.6).

Notes

1. Inka Stock, "Gender and the Dynamics of Mobility: Reflections on African Migrant Mothers and 'Transit Migration' in Morocco," *Ethnic and Racial Studies* 35, no. 9 (2012): 1578.
2. Giorgo Agamben, *Homo sacer: Souveräne Macht und bloßes Leben* (Frankfurt am Main: Suhrkamp, 2002).
3. Bill Jordan and Franck Düvell, *Irregular Migration: The Dilemmas of Transnational Mobility* (Cambridge: Edward Elgar, 2002), 15.

4. Marie McAuliffe and Adrian Titimbo, "African Migration: What the Numbers Really Tell Us," *World Economic Forum*, June 7, 2018, <https://www.weforum.org/agenda/2018/06/heres-the-truth-about-african-migration/> (last accessed December 3, 2019).
5. Hein de Haas, *Irregular Migration from West Africa to the Maghreb and the European Union: An Overview of Recent Trends* (Geneva: International Organization for Migration, 2008), 15.
6. "Migration to Europe in Charts," *BBC News*, September 11, 2018, available at <https://www.bbc.com/news/world-europe-44660699> (last accessed September 22, 2019).
7. United Nations High Commissioner for Refugees as featured in Patrick Kingsley, "Migration to Europe is Down Sharply. So Is It Still a 'Crisis'?," *New York Times*, June 27, 2018, available at <https://www.nytimes.com/interactive/2018/06/27/world/europe/europe-migrant-crisis-change.html> (last accessed September 22, 2019). While this chapter focuses on a film produced in 2013/14, the above article describes how African migrancy to Europe has largely diminished, due in part to the Italian government's plan to work with small Libyan militias that have prevented the smuggling business, and European deportation agreements with Sudan, Niger, and most notably Turkey. While I cannot describe these consequences in any detail, a slave trade in Libya has been documented.
8. Stock, "Gender and the Dynamics of Mobility," 1578.
9. "L'occultation de la place des migrant-e-s dans la prostitution et celle de la prostitution dans les travaux sur l'histoire des migrations nous révèlent combien les situations vécues par les femmes étrangères, de même que leur parole (spécialement si elles sont en dehors des normes du mariage ou du regroupement familial et ne se présentent pas comme des victimes) sont peu documentées, parce qu'elles se heurtent à une conjonction de formes d'oppression et de suppression de leur parole et de leur expérience. Cette occultation n'est pas seulement due au hasard." Françoise Guillemaut, "Femmes africaines, migration et travail du sexe," *Sociétés* 99 (2008): 96.
10. Stock, "Gender and the Dynamics of Mobility," 1579.
11. Monique Witteg, *The Straight Mind and Other Essays* (Boston: Beacon Press, 1992), describes the baby as free, and only imprisoned by gender regulations once biological signs are found.
12. Helen Nabasuta Mugambi, "The 'Post-Gender' Question in African Studies," in *Africa After Gender?*, ed. Catherine Cole, Takyiwaa Manuh, and Stephen Miescher (Bloomington: Indiana University Press, 2012), 289.
13. Agamben, *Homo sacer*.
14. Giorgo Agamben, *State of Exception* (Chicago: University of Chicago Press, 2005).
15. Nicole Beth Wallenbrock, "Clandestine Boat Immigration in French Film: The Homo Sacer on the Norman Coast: *Welcome* (2009) and *Le Havre* (2011)," *Global Humanities* 3: Migration and State Power (2016): 123–39.
16. Ewa Płonowska Ziarek, "Bare Life on Strike: Notes on the Biopolitics of Race and Gender," *South Atlantic Quarterly* 107, no. 1 (2008): 89–105.
17. Luce Irigaray, *Ce sexe qui n'en est pas un* (Paris: Éditions de Minuit, 1977). In one of her essays, Irigaray describes a phallocentric economy with Marxist vocabulary.

See, for an English translation: "Women on the Market," in Luce Irigaray, *This Sex Which Is Not One*, trans. Catherine Porter and Carolyn Burke (Ithaca, NY: Cornell University Press, 1985), 170–91.
18. "[L]eur envie de migrer prime sur l'éventuelle répugnance au travail du sexe, et que dans tous les cas elles ne veulent pas être rapatriées." Guillemaut, "Femmes africaines," 94.
19. Jean Rouch, "On the Vicissitudes of the Self: The Possessed Dancer, the Magician, the Sorcerer, the Filmmaker, and the Ethnographer," in *Ciné Ethnography* (Minneapolis: University of Minnesota Press, 2003), 87–101.
20. Furthermore, much as Rouch enabled African directors, Lojkine continues to train with African film students and encourages their own productions.
21. Lojkine has, in recent interviews, suggested a similar practice in *Camille*, his newest film, which is set in Central Africa.
22. Gayatri Chakravorty Spivak, "Can the Sub-Altern Speak?," in *Marxism and the Interpretation of Culture*, ed. Cary Nelson and Lawrence Grossberg (Basingstoke: MacMillan, 1988), 271–313.
23. Mohamed Mghari, *La Migration irrégulière au Maroc*, Rabat: Centre d'Études et de Recherches Démographiques (CERED), 2008, available at <https://iussp2009.princeton.edu/papers/92040> (last accessed September 9, 2010).
24. Ines Keygnaert, Seline van den Ameele, Jeroen Keygnaert, Altay Manco, and Marteen Temmerman, "La Route de la souffrance: rapports des résultats de la recherche: la violence sexuelle et transmigrants subsahariens au Maroc: un partenariat participatif pour prévention," University of Ghent, 2009, available at <https://biblio.ugent.be/publication/979677> (last accessed December 10, 2020).
25. Médecins sans Frontières, *Violence sexuelle et migration: la réalité cache des femmes subsahariennes arrêtées au Maroc sur la route de l'Europe* (Rabat: MSF Spain, 2010).
26. K. Kastner, "Moving Relationships: Family Ties of Nigerian Migrants on Their Way to Europe," *African and Black Diaspora: An International Journal* 3, no. 1 (2010): 317–51.
27. Stock, "Gender and the Dynamics of Mobility," 1580.
28. Stock, "Gender and the Dynamics of Mobility," 1588.
29. The fee, if it is not paid in full, puts women into debt and forces them into prostitution, a situation referred to as debt bondage (Guillemaut, "Femmes africaines," 98).

Works Cited

Agamben, Giorgio. *Homo sacer: Souveräne Macht und bloßes Leben*. Frankfurt am Main: Suhrkamp, 2002.

Agamben, Giorgio. *State of Exception*. Chicago: University of Chicago Press, 2005.

de Haas, Hein. *Irregular Migration from West Africa to the Maghreb and the European Union: An Overview of Recent Trends*. Geneva: International Organization for Migration, 2008.

Guillemaut, Françoise. "Femmes africaines, migration et travail du sexe." *Sociétés* 99 (2008): 91–106.

Irigaray, Luce. *Ce sexe qui n'en est pas un*. Paris: Éditions de Minuit, 1977.

Irigaray, Luce. "Women on the Market." In Luce Irigaray, *This Sex Which Is Not One*, trans. by Catherine Porter and Carolyn Burke, 170–91. Ithaca, NY: Cornell University Press, 1985.

Jordan, Bill and Franck Düvell. *Irregular Migration: The Dilemmas of Transnational Mobility*. Cambridge: Edward Elgar, 2002.

Kastner, K. "Moving Relationships: Family Ties of Nigerian Migrants on Their Way to Europe." *African and Black Diaspora: An International Journal* 3, no. 1 (2010): 317–51.

Keygnaert, Ines, Seline van den Ameele, Jeroen Keygnaert, Altay Manco, and Marteen Temmerman, "La Route de la souffrance: rapports des résultats de la recherche: la violence sexuelle et transmigrants subsahariens au Maroc: un partenariat participatif pour prévention," University of Ghent, 2009, <https://biblio.ugent.be/publication/979677> (last accessed December 10, 2020).

Kingsley, Patrick. "Migration to Europe is Down Sharply. So Is It Still a 'Crisis'?" *New York Times*, June 27, 2018, <https://www.nytimes.com/interactive/2018/06/27/world/europe/europe-migrant-crisis-change.html> (last accessed September 22, 2019).

McAuliffe, Marie and Adrian Titimbo, "African Migration: What the Numbers Really Tell Us." *World Economic Forum*, June 7, 2018, <https://www.weforum.org/agenda/2018/06/heres-the-truth-about-african-migration/> (last accessed December 3, 2019).

Médecins sans Frontières. *Violence sexuelle et migration: la réalité cache des femmes subsahariennes arrêtées au Maroc sur la route de l'Europe*. Rabat: MSF Spain, 2010.

Mghari, Mohamed. *La Migration irrégulière au Maroc*. Rabat: Centre d'Études et de Recherches Démographiques (CERED), 2008, <https://iussp2009.princeton.edu/papers/92040> (last accessed September 9, 2010).

"Migration to Europe in Charts." *BBC News*, September 11, 2018, <https://www.bbc.com/news/world-europe-44660699> (last accessed September 22, 2019).

Nabasuta Mugambi, Helen. "The 'Post-Gender' Question in African Studies." In *Africa After Gender?*, ed. Catherine Cole, Takyiwaa Manuh, and Stephen Miescher, 286–301. Bloomington: Indiana University Press, 2012.

Rouch, Jean. "On the Vicissitudes of the Self: The Possessed Dancer, the Magician, the Sorcerer, the Filmmaker, and the Ethnographer." In *Ciné Ethnography* (Minneapolis: University of Minnesota Press, 2003), 87–101.

Spivak, Gayatri Chakravorty. "Can the Sub-Altern Speak?" In *Marxism and the Interpretation of Culture*, ed. Cary Nelson and Lawrence Grossberg, 271–313. Basingstoke: Macmillan, 1988.

Stock, Inka. "Gender and the Dynamics of Mobility: Reflections on African Migrant Mothers and 'Transit Migration' in Morocco." *Ethnic and Racial Studies* 35, no. 9 (2012): 1577–95.

Wallenbrock, Nicole Beth. "Clandestine Boat Immigration in French Film: The Homo Sacer on the Norman Coast: *Welcome* (2009) and *Le Havre* (2011)." *Global Humanities* 3: Migration and State Power (2016): 123–39.

Witteg, Monique. *The Straight Mind and Other Essays*. Boston: Beacon Press, 1992.

Ziarek, Ewa Płonowska. "Bare Life on Strike: Notes on the Biopolitics of Race and Gender." *South Atlantic Quarterly* 107, no. 1 (2008): 89–105.

10. UN/DOCUMENTED MIGRATION IN "BORDERLAND SCHENGEN"

Jan Kühnemund

Introduction

Drawing on two documentary films set in the borderlands established by the interplay of European migration policies—migration control and policy implementation on the one hand and migration movements on the other—this chapter specifically investigates visualizations of undocumented migration.[1] What is currently framed as the *European refugee crisis* is, in this regard, understood as the acute manifestation of a predicament that has been ongoing for at least a decade now and that is, at the same time, inseparably linked with current European paradigms of repulsion and exterritorialization.[2]

This chapter has consequently also to account for the fact that undocumented migration has a history in many regards. On a *political* level, it is entangled with a Europeanization process that contrasts internal freedom of movement with tight external borders, and that settled on a particular culture of border control[3] and governmentality.[4] On a *social* level, immigration has been perceived as a threat to European societies and is entangled with integration discourses that emphasize discipline[5] and assimilation, and that still misinterpret migrants as representing the "Other." On a *spatial* level, it rests upon a dialectical relationship of mobility and immobility, and adheres to the logic of control and surveillance. On a *visual* level, eventually, undocumented migration grounds in specific iconologies, stereotypes, and figures that must be considered crucial elements of image politics, deployed, in return, to justify policy measures, societal exclusion, and spatial structures at the same time.[6]

Anticipating those dimensions and critically approaching the crises of migration from an altogether different angle, the documentary films "Havarie" (Philip Scheffner, 2016) and "La Forteresse" (Fernand Melgar, 2008) scrutinize the assumption of a linearity of migration movements with predictable or consistently linked points of departure and arrival. They investigate the visual–political arena of what I would like to call *Borderland Schengen* by means of cinematic approaches—and they illustrate that those borderlands are by no means limited to the proximity of European demarcation lines. Instead, undocumented migrants are potentially confronted with the European migration regime and its borders literally everywhere: in the European metropolises, as well as in the proximity of the Spanish exclaves Ceuta and Melilla, on the outskirts of Mali's capital Bamako as well as in Al Kufrah prison in the middle of the Libyan desert.

"Havarie" will be used to investigate documentary films' awareness of their mediality and entanglement with image politics. The film successfully overcomes the makers' failed attempt to find an adequate image for the *refugee crisis*. Instead, it establishes a peculiar narrative space in which the film's being film reverberates throughout and reflects an incident at sea in the mirror of its being watched. A sequence from Fernand Melgar's "La Forteresse" will, secondly, be used to illustrate the contradiction between the refugee's subjectivity and its iconology—the narrative and the stereotype. The incident documented in this sequence can also be read as referring to performative modes aiming at offering the refugees a space in which they can reclaim and reappropriate their narrative in the first place.

Both films apply distinct strategies in order to challenge the self-evidence of the predominant iconologies of "illegality" and placeholders of the crisis. In doing so, they also critically reflect their own mediality and entanglements with the migration control apparatus. Emphasizing the fictional capacity of documentary films[7] and deploying performative–affective images of non-actualizable (Deleuze) migration experiences, they scrutinize at the same time a linear representation–meaning nexus and representational aspirations of documentary film in general. Moreover, the films grant their protagonists a specific opacity (Glissant)[8] in order to establish an image space in which they can be accounted for as discursive subjects. The films' understanding of the visuality of undocumented migration is consequently characterized not only by the figures they depict and by the narratives accounted for, but also by the specific perception and visual construction of spaces, routes, and places of migration, which together compose a transnational visual–political topography of undocumented migration that eventually directs the attention to a particular autonomy of migration.[9]

A Refugee Crisis?

The supply of images that illustrate what the media commonly refer to as the *European refugee crisis* seems to be infinite. At the same time, however, most images draw upon and reiterate a limited number of narratives and figures—and rather than an acute crisis, they bear witness to "a perpetual emergency."[10] What many images of specific events, and of political responses to them, share is their self-evidence. Such images include groups of people in unseaworthy boats; military vessels combing through international waters, fulfilling the European Frontex mission; young men clandestinely crossing fences; border patrols lowering the Schengen Area's turnpikes; a child's body washed upon the shore; and military staff and private security companies intending to stop migration from happening by erecting fences that primarily result in diverting migration routes, making them more dangerous. There are also scenes and photos of troublesome-looking European politicians at their summits selling yet another concept, directive, response, or policy; the politicians profess to struggling for humanitarian solutions that eventually turn out to be primarily rhetorical and symbolic. Rather than bearing witness to the solution of a crisis, however, the political responses presented are part of specific image politics at work, of an engineering process that links the images to acts of testimony, authentication, and annotation.[11]

If what we see in those images represents a *refugee crisis* at all, then it is a perpetuating crisis in slow motion—and a *border* crisis. It is apparent that large numbers of people are on the move; we can trust the respective images enough to state that we can see it; and the movement is even comprehensible and hardly surprising—and, above all, nothing really new. The majority of the images illustrate migration and flight as dramas that, however, draw on well-known figures, icons, and metaphors: the victim, the threat, the refugee, the "waves," "floods," and "swarms" of people, illegal acts of border-crossing and of smuggling, the fence, the boat, Lampedusa, the sea. They tell the old tale of "Us" and "Them"—they know their "Other" very well. They leave no questions, no doubt; they homogenize, they victimize, and they emotionalize. But what they have on offer is rarely more than pity or fear, or a complex combination of both. The current predicament is, in other words, extremely visual and the set of icons representing migration, illegality, and the crisis at the same time must be considered extremely stable. The iconic dead body, for example, of the "dark-haired toddler,"[12] Aylan Kurdi, does not fundamentally put this representational regime in question; rather, it fuels the visual and the news industry.

While "illegalized immigration is a highly iconic topic"[13] that is, due to its very character, almost exclusively visible through the media, the "illegal immigrant" may, however, be considered a symbolic resource that can be strategically deployed and rewritten; by means of alternative narratives and/or a hybrid positioning, films potentially thwart hegemonic orders.[14] The borderland, in this regard, may be understood as both a conflict zone and a contact zone. It is consequently another of this chapter's central presumptions that there are other images too, other narratives and figures—sometimes even the same narrative wrapped in other images, the same images wrapping alternative narratives: icons that refuse to be consumed easily, images that have the potential to account for motivations, aspirations, and subject positions. This chapter argues that such images can be found in contemporary documentary films about undocumented migration; moreover, even against the background of the omnipresent *crisis*, documentary film is considered one of the very few places where the increasingly complex and relevant issues of visibility and recognition of undocumented migrants at the European Union's fringes are being raised at all.

By exploring documentary films dedicated to the phenomenon of undocumented migration, this chapter investigates an apparent contradiction. If visibility is, however, understood as a category of knowledge and the document in question as a visual technology, the contradiction turns into an obvious interdependence. Documentary film, in this regard, cannot be primarily concerned with trying its best to be the most adequate reproduction of reality and truth, but must reflect its mediality and its entanglement with mechanisms of knowledge production and image politics—the migration apparatus, in other words. The production of the documentary image in this regard is, above all, a practice—and it may, in an analogy to Benz and Schwenken's statement about migration practices, be considered a stubborn practice itself.[15]

"Havarie"—Shipwrecked in the Middle of Everywhere

My first example is the German film "Havarie" (2016).[16] It is based on a video clip that the German filmmaker Philip Scheffner found on YouTube and blew up to cinematic dimensions; "Refugees"[17] was originally shot by a tourist—the Ulsterman Terry Diamond—on board the cruise ship *Adventure of the Seas* and captures its coincidental encounter with a rubber boat[18] carrying thirteen refugees in distress on the Mediterranean Sea some 38 nautical miles off the Spanish coast.[19] Slightly more than 3 and a half minutes in length, the clip, for most of its duration, focuses on a black patch lying a couple of hundred meters in the distance. Halfway through, the shaking, handheld camera shortly pans right and left alongside the ship and we see other tourists observing the scene. There is no further explanatory comment and, for the longest part of the film, all we hear is indistinct chatter and the hum of the ship's engine. The tourist holding the camera says very little—and without the usual comment, without the usual frame, the scene has a scarily self-evident character, as if it is mere routine. Pointing at the sea, the camera zooms back and forth every so often. Suddenly, two of the men on the rubber boat wave in the direction of the cruise ship—and the camera zooms back in astonishment, as if to bring some distance between the cameraman and its involuntary protagonists, as if the familiar icons have unexpectedly come to life. After this short incident, the camera zooms back in and gets as close as possible.

By capturing the incident at sea, Diamond certainly aimed at documenting a real event—he used the camera on his cell phone as a tool to help him to handle an exceptional experience. What Scheffner does to this footage in "Havarie" changes its character fundamentally. Firstly, he decelerates the film drastically—instead of 25 frames per second, his film presents 1 frame per second; the original length of 3 and a half minutes is stretched to 90 minutes, reportedly exactly the period for which the two boats lay alongside each other. He strips the clip from its context; all the icons and fragments of reality and authenticity are there but edited beyond recognition. Immediacy divided by 25: roughly 5,500 primarily blue images slowly pass our eyes, one by one, every single one recognizable for exactly 1 second. The rubber boat shakes and bounces before our eyes, it blurs, it sidles about in the frame's fringes, seems to move out of sight but always returns to the center of the image. And it often has—what an adequate metaphor for migration movements through the European borderlands—some kind of a digital shadow, on the one hand blurring the boat's concrete form but at the same time anticipating and preceding the boat's movement, which is actually the movement of the camera—the shadows always move first (Fig. 10.1).

Figure 10.1 The rubber boat and its digital shadow in "Havarie" (Philip Scheffner, 2016).

Secondly, Scheffner disconnects images and sound. While, on the visual level, the exposition of the images' mediality seems to make the question of the representative function of the images obsolete, different audible layers open up a parallel narrative space that contributes to giving the whole film an overall fictional texture. On the audio level, different narratives—recorded independently and then edited into some kind of dialogue—take turns and sometimes also overlap[20]: a woman in France and her husband in Algeria, separated by the Mediterranean Sea, talk about their challenging and involuntarily transnational relationship; the bridge of the *Adventure of the Seas* communicates with Cartagena Sea Rescue; the crew of a Ukrainian cargo ship reflect on their experiences; one of the cruise ship's managers and its first officer talk about losing their spatial and temporal sense of orientation on board —and the producer of the original film material, Terry Diamond, talks about his memories of the brutal British rule in Northern Ireland. While, most of the time, we hear a clock ticking to the rhythm of the frames switching—or maybe it is the other way around—what we hear has a cinematic and fictional dimension itself. Often, we hear only indistinct sounds instead of talking: a running water faucet, street noise, a motorbike in the distance, teacups on the kitchen table, birds singing in the park; we see a film without actually seeing its images, our minds turn into a screen and are, at the same time, still confronted with what we actually see—a shipwrecked boat, the blue sea.

The different narratives span a trans-social web across the Mediterranean Sea and beyond, from Algeria to Spain, from France to Algeria, from Ukraine to Spain, from Northern Ireland to Algeria—and back again; it is a web of relationships and affection, but one of conflict, fear, and anger as well, the Mediterranean both connecting and separating the spheres. And the narratives become knotted to the images we see, like in a ball of transnational and trans-social strings, relationships, memories, and ambitions, so that, eventually, sound and image in a way come to coincide again. This is particularly the case when the husband in Algeria seems to stand on the beach with a friend, reflecting upon the several unsuccessful attempts they have made to cross over to Europe. And this is even more the case when, in the middle of the film, the camera slowly pans to the right and to the left. Originally a sequence of hardly 15 seconds, it now takes more than 6 minutes—we are abducted to the "hyper-present and monstrous"[21] world of the cruise liner; in parallel, we hear the radio communication between the rescue units. What we see and what we hear seem to coincide at least partially—but, in fact, all we realize is the harsh contrast between the different life realities.

This coincidence of simultaneity and blurring is omnipresent in "Havarie," and it directs the attention not only to the tension between what is in the image and what is not in the image, but also to the tensions at the level of the image itself. Terry Diamond's statement recalling the moment when he realized that the dark patch in the distance was, in fact, a rubber boat carrying refugees also demonstrates visual disorientation. He talks about having asked himself questions and picturing himself in their place—but then surrenders to the non-actualizability of the experience: "you can never replicate that; you can only assume . . . ."

Scheffner compounds the visual disorientation by decontextualizing the footage. The only localization provided at the beginning of the film reads "37° 28.6′ N, 000° 3.8′ E", the geographical coordinates in the Mediterranean Sea where the incident apparently took place. The awkward accuracy of the geographical localization of the incident creates a strong contrast to the generic quality of the image itself. Those coordinates are, at the same time, so precise and yet so abstract and meaningless that, instead of providing orientation, they locate the incident in the middle of nowhere—or rather in the middle of everywhere. Geographical precision is not Scheffner's cinematographic goal—he needs the viewer to lack orientation in order to contour the Mediterranean as an image space and a political space. He makes the viewer the screen, and, as Nicole Wolf puts it, "that we start creating images in our heads is not an accident, that we experience the intimacy of spaces and relations is not random, but follows admirable aesthetic political choices."[22] And Scheffner not only stretches 200 seconds into 90 minutes, he also strips the moment of recognition from its temporal dimension; stretching the incident to eternity, he wrenches the images away from an assumed authenticity or reality to an, in all regards, illuminated world.

Terry Diamond, coincidentally, works as a security guard in Belfast, staring at CCTV monitors all night long; his reflections about his job sound paradigmatic in the context of the images we see while we hear him talk: "You're always on edge, you're waiting on the unforeseen. And it's sometimes when you least expect it, that's when it can happen," he says. "And sometimes you can be distracted by certain images and they're not an important security image and that's when you miss something else." At many other points, elements on the different levels seem to be duplicated or reiterated in a slightly varied way, which additionally emphasizes the film's mediality. The camera's pan, capturing the crowd at the cruise ship's railings, disturbingly reminds us of our own position as spectators. And most prominently, the film throughout reiterates the aspect of waiting—everybody is waiting for something to happen, longing even: the people on the rubber boat, the spectators on the cruise ship, the people in France and Algeria, those on the Ukrainian cargo ship and we as the viewers.[23] The spectating turns into waiting. In the end, nothing happens at all; none of the narratives comes to an end or a solution.

And while, throughout the film, the radio communication between the cruise ship captain and Cartagena builds up, as if it were striving towards some kind of a climax—while Cartagena Sea Rescue advises the cruise ship to maintain visual contact with the rubber boat but not to take the refugees on board, a rescue operation is initiated—the film eventually stops without providing the relief of a successful rescue operation or its dramatic failure. Yet eventually, it becomes apparent that, actually, it is not only the people on the rubber boat who are shipwrecked but the viewer as a spectator as well, and with him/her the representative function of the images: the images Scheffner evokes neither represent anything tangible nor feed into an economy of emotions. Separating our senses—looking, listening, bodily affect—allows him to put the emphasis on little details. Eventually, this relocation of the crisis is not limited to the spectator's gaze but goes much further because, as Wolf put it, "[w]hen our senses meet again, a turbulence seems to arise, forcefully locating the crisis in our very own bodies."[24] To summarize what actually *happens* in the film is consequently almost impossible because it takes place on an affective, non-actualizable level. Breaching the self-evidence of the situation by means of the multiplication of screens and the confrontation of the viewer with his/her knowledge, Scheffner eventualizes an apparently unremarkable and yet singular incident. And while the film certainly tells the viewer something about Europe's dealings with the refugee crisis, it also makes the mediality and visuality of migration itself its central concern. It confronts the spectator with the activity of viewing itself and with the knowledge, perceptions, expectations, and also self-images linked to the gaze in the image space of migration. At the same time, the film fundamentally blurs the icon of the undocumented migrant, and he/she vanishes into an opaque space.

How the film exposes its mediality may also be understood as the attempt to illuminate the subjectivity of the filmmaker's perspective and refusal of a notion of a master narrative of undocumented migration. In particular, embedding its figures and narratives in a self-reflexive approach to its mediality—being conventionalized and being entangled with the control apparatus—"Havarie" outlines a mode in which the image can avoid being consumed by dominant discourses, in which it even has a resistive core. The film in this regard perceives its mediality as a result of a process of *becoming* medial: that is, as a process of medialization by means of a sometimes stable, sometimes volatile reification of stratified, engineered, and mediated dispositives.[25]

Borderland Schengen

The narrative space that "Havarie" spans must not least be understood as aiming to shift the responsibility for the current predicament away from the undocumented migrants and to the European migration regime. The film finds an innovative way to react to the arsenal of familiar depictions of the *European refugee crisis*. And although those images may be taken at very different geographical locations, at the same time they are all set in a specific migration space, a space that is, on a more general level, primarily framed by a Europeanization process that, in return, is heavily entangled with migration movements.[26] It must be assumed that one of the primary goals of the Schengen Area as a political entity is, in fact, to define and constantly redefine the course, shape, and permeability of European borders and border zones, the shape and relationship of European centers and peripheries, regular and irregular routes, eligible and ineligible movers and travelers.

The process of European integration has, since its early stages, been accompanied by an inside and outside binary that seeks to determine if a person should be permitted to enter the European Union.[27] The underlying culture of border control is linked to specific border practices that deploy different surveillance and visualization mechanisms and tools. In addition, it relies on an exterritorialization of border policies, border facilities, and border spaces in general, and the entanglement of the border with a specific image politics. Europe's borders are made and performed; they are constantly and strategically changing, shape-shifting depending on the respective challenge—they are characterized by this flexible organization of geography and space, physically and socially manifest. Contemporary European border zones consequently reach far beyond actual demarcation lines and thus establish a "heterogeneous and hierarchized space of circulation within graduated zones of sovereignty."[28] At the same time, this border zone is constantly being redefined, restructured, and rehierarchized by the concrete interplay of a highly flexible policy implementation and everyday migration movements. Scheffner aims to reorganize this space—at least symbolically—to put into focus the moments of border construction and border crossing, and their implications for borders as social spaces.

For this chapter I would like to frame this border zone as *Borderland Schengen*—a transnational space emerging from the interplay of the visual, the political, the social, and the spatial. It imparts the remote, hidden spaces of migration management and detention in Europe and the continent's capitals, as well as the countless places and "dangerous and fragmented"[29] routes of migration carving through what is perceived as the continent's fringes and peripheries, the transit countries in Eastern and South-eastern Europe, as well as on the African continent. It establishes a border zone in which various transnational networks, migration projects, border-crossing practices, spatial strategies and strategic knowledge, visualization techniques and technologies, policy-implementation strategies, and clandestine economies overlap and establish a specific geography of undocumented migration. Temporally and spatially fragmented by means of specific political tools—for example, the Dublin Regulations and the concurrent Eurodac database, the border zone is established as a space of permanent—spatial, social, legal—transit, or of hypermobility.[30] This is a space in which mobility and immobility unpredictably take turns, in which a person's legal status can change in the blink of an eye under the condition of potential surveillance, and in which social networks constantly have to be re-established—either due to the legal and political mechanisms structuring the migration spaces or in connection with strategic decisions taken by the person concerned.

Borderland Schengen consequently consists not only of the heavily patrolled border zones in the proximity of Schengen's political borders or its checkpoints and demarcation lines, but also of zones of exception and strategically *exterritorialized* thresholds—sites between states and liminal zones of exception.[31] However, the border is also inscribed in the bodies of the undocumented migrants themselves, by means of their conditioning, their being lost in time and space, and their wounds and scars. In "Havarie," they are invisible yet tangible in the protagonists' narratives of exclusion and separation. The principles of exterritorialization and flexibility stretch the border-crossing situation and the state of liminality for those who are considered ineligible ad infinitum both temporally and spatially—which is most obvious in the virtual dialogue between the separated Algerian–French couple; the physical manifestations of borders are complemented by a specific visuality and image politics of the border, as well as by social conditioning connected to panoptical visibility, social control, and surveillance technologies. The two films used in this chapter also show that, for undocumented migrants, moving through *Borderland Schengen* means to continuously move along the border, to continuously negotiate borders, and to be permanently exposed to dislocating geopolitical powers. As Mountz points out, being detained in *Borderland Schengen* implies not only a legal and jurisdictional ambiguity, with waiting and uncertainty, but also the hardship of understanding where and by whom one has been detained—often discovering that one has lost a specific status or belonging during the journey across borders.[32]

At the same time, however, with regard to the spatial manifestation of *Borderland Schengen*, one has to note that the specific interplay of migration control and migration movements at work condenses not only in the actors and discourses but as well in the places, routes, practices, and routines that continuously structure and restructure it as a transnational social space—the social and narrative, but also geographical, space that "Havarie" enquires into serves as a perfect example of this. The most evident effects are the changes in migration routes over time,[33] which are based on an interplay of migration surveillance and migration movements. If a route becomes less favorable because control measures succeed in establishing an effective blockage, not only do the points of entry to the European Union change but also the whole preceding mobility and smuggling infrastructure that adapts to the new situation. Such a successful blockage in return has to be understood as being constituted by means of a complex constellation of physical border facilities and the exchange of information and experiences within trans-social migration networks—networks which are inseparably linked to the visual emergence of the border itself and narratives of failure. While this kind of reconfiguration of spaces and routes on a macro-level takes some time, on a micro-level it happens frequently—the boat we see in "Havarie" hence represents a specific structural element of the European migration regime rather than a singularity. Simultaneously, migration movements may, in this regard, be understood as "an imperceptible force which renders the 'walls around the world' irreversibly porous."[34] This autonomy of migration is the paradigmatic driving force behind processes such as European integration—at the same time, it is its worst nightmare.[35]

Borderland Schengen hence is by no means drafted exclusively by acts of policy making and implementation, or migration movements; it also encompasses the visual–political space that emerges in documentary filmmakers' enquiries of the multifaceted interplay of migration policy and control, and migration movements; films such as the two used here contribute to the reconfiguration of Borderland Schengen as a topographical layer that is overlapped with the politically, visually, and legally structured spaces of migration control and migration management. In modifying its iconologies, figures, spaces, and routes, its stories, histories, narratives, and motivations by means of performative–affective images and specific appropriation techniques, they help to re-establish it as a counter-topography[36] in which commonalities and differences, visibilities and invisibilities, are reordered strategically—not least in order renegotiate the social, visual, political, and spatial conditions of European borderlands.

"La Forteresse"—The Fortress of What One Knows

My second example comes from Fernand Melgar's "La Forteresse" (2008). The film enquires into the microcosm of a Swiss reception center, primarily by means of observation. Various layers of representation and narration overlap in a triangular way: firstly, the camera captures statements by refugees on film and observes day-to-day life in the center; secondly, the refugees are interrogated by federal authorities; and thirdly, the camera also selectively documents some of those interrogations and contrasts the different perspectives with each other. One scene in "La Forteresse" specifically illustrates the various layers and conventions of narration and representation in *Borderland Schengen*. In this sequence, Melgar takes up the case of a young Somali from different angles: firstly, the viewer observes him telling the story of his flight to a pastor at the center, and, afterwards, the conversation between two federal decision makers discussing the case. In the first part of the sequence, roughly 3 and a half minutes long, one of the center's pastoral counsellors talks with the Somali and empathically follows the story of his provenance and flight.

As if he were confessing, the man gives an account of his story in a plausible, even shockingly illustrative way. He reports coming from Somalia and uncovers the scars he carries from having been shot in the legs several times. He talks about having walked through the Sudanese and Libyan deserts with badly injured legs for several weeks to eventually reach the Mediterranean Sea. There, he reports, he entered a small pirogue, which he had to share with about fifty other refugees. Again and again referring to his bodily experiences, and in order to supply evidence, he not only exposes his scars but also imitates his crouched posture in the small boat (Fig. 10.2). The pastor's empathic amazement triggers the man to continue and to provide more and more detail; he allows him to take possession of his narrative. Calmly, the camera gaze rests upon the Somali's face for most of the conversation—grasping the horrors of the trip in his countenance; the narrative and the man's body become one; the medium close-up camera angle is interrupted only by a few close-ups of the counsellor; there is also an interpreter present, but we see her rarely and always from behind.[37]

The story then culminates in an episode that took place on the group's tenth day at sea. After a little boy had died of thirst, the other refugees cut his body in pieces and ate it. Both the pastor and the translator react with bewilderment, and the camera also stares at the man for a couple of seconds, as if to express speechlessness. He looks away, nervous and ashamed. As if to release the tension, the next shot shows the pastor holding, caressing the Somali's hand, while the pastor asks him what he thinks about Switzerland and all its riches, the cars, the food, especially in contrast to what he has been through. Laughter spells relief.

Figure 10.2 The asylum seeker from Ethiopia imitates the crouched posture he adopted in the small boat in "La Forteresse" (Fernand Melgar, 2008).

What at first appears to be quite naïve, or at least some kind of displacement activity, turns out to complete the Somali's narrative. He expresses gratitude and appreciation for being given food, medication, and shelter and for being treated by the Swiss in a humane way—an assessment that is clearly contradicted in the second part of the sequence. In this scene, the federal decision maker explains to a colleague that the Somali's asylum claim has been rejected because she did not find his story plausible. She presumes that he made up the story because it was too accurate and stereotypical with regard to the details of the journey, and at the same time too imprecise and vague when it came to the man's personal background and motivation. She claims that he was not able to convince her that it was really him who made the journey—as if he was telling another person's story. What struck her most about his story, she states, is that she cannot imagine how he walked through the desert for thirty days with fractured legs. Her colleague is apparently extremely surprised and argues that, on first listen, he found the story remarkable but credible.

Beyond Melgar's giving an account of an event in order to outline the intolerable Swiss and European asylum system, and his—implicit—politically motivated fundamental critique of it, the filmmaker here puts the focus on the sheer contrast between the individual's experience and the decision-making authorities' failure to grasp it. For the film itself, it is irrelevant if, or to what extent, the Somali's narrative can be considered appropriately rendered. The film exposes the conventions and representational orders illustrated by the contrast of the two scenes—and in the fact that while there certainly is a truth behind the narrative, a reason forcing this young man to leave his home country in order to try his luck in Europe, the authorities apparently assume that in their interrogations they are able to differentiate performative and representational aspects of the asylum seekers' narratives, that they are able to tell the truth from the lie.

This moment of fundamental failure is an immanent element of the procedures themselves and it starts with the asylum seeker being forced to actualize his experience in a way that allows him to present a consistent and comprehensible narrative in order to claim asylum in the first place. Melgar emphasizes this dramatic failure by means of a sequence in which the links between the viewer, the experience, and the images are suspended—he is even able to avoid inviting pity to spell out the relief of a partial actualization of the Somali's experience. Representation in this setting necessarily fails on all levels; neither can the affective experience be adequately represented or "be translated into words without doing violence to the totality of awareness,"[38] nor can the viewer directly incorporate it into his/her conceptual world. Furthermore, the interrogator's attempt to locate truth and authenticity outside the Somali's account fails.

The affect, however, steers our attention to the extent to which a refugee's fate depends on such a procedure of interpretation that apparently adheres to representational paradigms and conventions. The Somali's narrative is not accounted for *as it is* but against the backdrop of a set of stereotypical figures, practices, and narratives. The decision maker's appreciation of the interrogation—which, and this is also important, we have not been allowed to observe—translates, strictly speaking, into the allegation that somebody who is subject to extensive stereotyping meets those stereotypes too perfectly, the allegation made, in fact, by those who have produced and are continuously reproducing those stereotypes. Apparently, verisimilitude orders adhere to the convention that a narrative is not allowed to be too conventional. This is particularly strange, as the decision makers seem to take a quite positivistic stance by judging the plausibility of a narrative by means of its reference to stereotypes.

Throughout their conversation, the camera captures the two federal employees from an angle that signals distance. Calm, medium point-of-view shots contribute to a setting in which the spectator is made complicit with the camera rather than embarking on a search for the truth in the Somali's account of events. What also makes this scene so hard to grasp is how the decision maker in fact delegitimizes her doubt and her emotional involvement in such an interrogation—in order to restore the representational orders that provide her daily business with legitimacy. It seems to be the only option in order to be able to continue doing the job she is doing.

In yet another step, the image's resemblance and its conventionality turn against the Somali when the interrogator denies taking him at face value and rejects his asylum claim. She finds the story too good to be true, knowing very well that the repercussions of images of undocumented migration produced in the West are not limited to the West. She assumes—and in the logic of the European migration regime and *Borderland Schengen* this does definitely make sense—that the Somali, in other words, mingled other asylum seekers' stories into his own, putting together bits and pieces in order to *perform* an expedient migration story. Instead of scrutinizing the man's motivation, the interrogator puts his narration into question. In the hierarchically structured relationship between the man and the decision maker, it is the latter who generates the necessary images in order to assess the credibility of the asylum seeker—in the end, it is all about *her* imagination and knowledge, *her* in/ability to make sense of a narrative she was presented with. Rather than understanding the contrast between the Somali's narrative and the decision maker's reading of the narrative, the viewer can experience the contradictions and the man's hopelessness and incapacity to react on an affective level.

While, in other words, from a European perspective those images, representations, and stereotypes are legitimate elements of particular image politics, outside the European order one is apparently not allowed to strategically reorganize one's self-representation to accord with the expectations those images encompass. Furthermore, while the interrogators scrutinize the authenticity of the asylum seekers' stories, the authenticity of all those well-known icons of undocumented migration is not being called into question at all; and the seemingly unambiguous images of *illegal* migrants and *legitimate* refugees dominate the European migration regime. Even more, all the figures, places, practices, and narratives of migration seem to be conventionalized to an extent that it is irrelevant how far and in what way the subjects of migration actually correspond to the reproduction of their images.

Figures of the Crisis

The two film examples used in this chapter also emphasize the paramount necessity to approach the field of undocumented migration in general and *Borderland Schengen* in particular as fields in which the political and the visual cannot be understood independently from each other. In fact, the political and the visual merge in debates around immigration to Europe. Migration movements enter a complex interplay of political decision-making, social relations, legal status, and visual representations. The Swiss asylum officer, for instance, is not only justifying her decision-making by means of accounting for stereotypical figures and images, she is also interacting with those images much more profoundly than with the individual asylum seeker himself. While images play an increasingly important role in shaping political debates and laws, as well as our perceptions and understandings of them, policies at the same time do not exclusively aim at regulating immigration itself but just as much at governing and recoding its visibilities,[39] meanings, and interpretations.

Considering the *refugee crisis* in a more general sense, political measures in this regard seem to react much more to the visuality of the crisis than to what usually is considered to be at the core of political discourses and decision-making, its roots, implications, and consequences—which, in return, also points to the paramount significance of film and visuality concerning the institutionalization of the rejection of immigration.[40] The images do not bear witness only to self-evident events; at the same time, they already include the form of and justification for the legislative or executive responses to it.

What has happened since mid-2015, when the *refugee crisis* was proclaimed in an interplay between the political sphere and the media, cannot per se be considered an unsolvable crisis—but it has been turned into, and still is being perpetuated as, a crisis by means of a complex political–visual process. The media render particular elements and aspects visible and others invisible, dramatizing certain facts and events, and suggesting particular interpretations that, in many cases, are closely linked to national agenda-setting and national identities. Consequentially, the images are embedded in an accelerated nationalistic discourse that complements the mediated events with an even more insistent claim for integration as a disciplining dispositive.[41]

This is also connected to a clear allocation of roles in, for example, the Mediterranean area or the Aegean Sea—while Europe states its desire to protect those refugees in Europe, it denies responsibility for those who are caught in the border zones. Moreover, government rhetoric and political measures regarding the smugglers and so-called traffickers[42] operating in the European border zones are extremely harsh and its responses are highly militarized. While "the ruthless smuggler" and "the criminal trafficker" are important narrative figures when it comes to the justification of harsh and militarized political responses and measures, the central figure of undocumented migration discourses is, however, the "illegal immigrant." Visual processes contribute considerably to the construction of this figure and, in general, to the construction of groups as insiders or outsiders, and to the definitions of memberships. As the example from "La Forteresse" illustrates, they play, at the same time, an important part in the production of the very categories applied to describe such groups. Illegalization, in other words, is not merely a political or juridical process or discourse; it is, to a remarkable extent, a visual process: while "those immigrants are made *illegal* by political and juridical strategies,"[43] the production of the categories and the perception of a state of exception are entangled with the visual processes, with the images and the knowledge they imply and transport. As Mitchell puts it,

> law and migration engage the realm of images as the location of both the sensuous and the fantasmatic: concrete, realistic representation of actuality, on the one hand, and idealized, or demonized fantasies of migrants as heroic pioneers or invading hordes, on the other.[44]

Reichert[45] emphasizes the key role that media images play not only in reiteration of the figures but also in the very construction and dissemination of border spaces and facilities—like the border fences of the Spanish exclaves in Morocco, Ceuta and Melilla—as icons for *Fortress Europe*. In order to provide a certain border (and border policy) with legitimacy and authority, it has to be made plausible and politically justified in the context of its media representation. Visuality hence signifies "a change in consciousness, which accords visual practices a . . . substantial role in thought processes and in the acquisition of 'knowledge'."[46] "La Forteresse" highlights such a moment, when knowledge is acquired and applied to the disadvantage of the Somali refugee. As Bischoff et al. stress in their assessment of the production of the "illegal migrant" as a category of knowledge, the representations and visualizations of processes of illegalization and of illegality, as well as reversed processes of recognition, can "only be properly analyzed in relation to the actual concrete form . . ., the material forms—in which symbolic meaning is circulated"[47] and in which "the illegal" as a subject is at stake. This is actually what Scheffner and Melgar also aim at.

Images are, however, not immediately connected to the arrival or the emergence of the migrant; they precede him/her, even more so in the case of undocumented migration that, per se, lacks a certain visibility—"before the immigrant arrives, his or her image comes first, in the form of stereotypes [of, for example, ethnicity, gender, race], search templates, tables of classification, and patterns of recognition."[48] But not only are images quicker than the immigrants, they are, in most cases, much more successful in crossing geographical distances and borders, in contrast, for example, with the Somali refugee in "La Forteresse"; the adequacy of those images is, however, only rarely put under scrutiny.

CONCLUSIONS: *BORDERLAND SCHENGEN'S* COUNTER-TOPOGRAPHIES

On a more general level, both films implicitly or explicitly address spaces and iconologies of *illegal* migration and document frictions between European migration policies, iconologies of migration, and the dialectics of migrants' invisibility and visibility. They can be read as filmmakers' attempts at discursive participation as an aesthetic political practice, and as aiming to establish and recognize the (undocumented) migrants they portray as subjects in the first place. At the same time, the contradiction of the terms documented/undocumented is an implicit central element. The act of documenting human beings that, by definition, are invisible—and, in many cases, have to remain invisible for their own protection—poses challenges to filmmaking.

The directors pursue different strategies to trace undocumented migration and reflect on the spatial dimensions of the borderland, and to "stitch together the global archipelago of exclusion: dispersed sites of enforcement and detention where people are rendered stateless by geographical design."[49] Transgressing concepts of belonging and aiming to illustrate multilayered transnational social spaces of undocumented migration that go beyond the binary of inside and outside, the films are only occasionally set at the actual political borders. Instead, they detect the various invisible and yet tangible borders that structure movement through the border zones.

On a formal level, the films do not present their images as reproducing reality, nor do the images dissolve into being mere cultural codes—rather, they refer to, and at the same time render, the rhetoric, attitudes, epistemologies, and demands of the documental problematic in a sort of meta-documental discourse.[50] Reality, in this regard, is localized in two different sites—it is, on the one hand, created in its perception and display[51]; on the other hand, the images' relation to their protagonists' life realities is a subtext that contributes to the films' relevance as political statements. The films also apply a practice that, at the same time, imparts a reflection on the conditions for construction of the images; in this sense, they may be considered as applying a "specific mode to evoke reality."[52]

The two examples presented also illustrate the validity of Jacques Rancière's assumption that documentary film is capable of greater fictional invention than what is usually understood as fictional film—because the latter is necessarily devoted to producing the impression of the real and bound to particular stereotypes of action and characters.[53] This provides documentary film in general with a specific privilege because its complex entanglements with the true and the real release it from being "obliged to create the *feeling* of the real, and this allows it to treat the real as a problem and to experiment more freely with the variable games of action and life, significance and insignificance."[54] In return, this implies that documentary film carries the potential to thwart the hierarchies of the representational regime and make way for "aesthetic operations that calculate, withhold or construct meanings by playing with combinations of text and image, bodies and voices, fiction and fact, to offer reality and the very relation between cinema and reality, as an arena of contestation."[55]

Moreover, what "Havarie" and "La Forteresse" highlight is that documentary film extracts its fictional capacities not only from the fact that it is a cinematographic mode, but also from film being a historicizing mode, a means of memory. The term *memory* in this sense may, at first, appear to be an ambiguous one, particularly when it comes to a phenomenon, such as undocumented migration, that is hardly linked to collective memory, that hardly has memorizable subjects, and whose existential myth includes a fundamental invisibility. But as Rancière outlines, memory is not about preservation but about creation. Memory is the work of fiction in a sense that does not refer to the story or the lie, considered less as an act of feigning and more as an act of forging.[56]

In this sense, the films do "provide a splendid opportunity to incredulously reflect the conditions of . . . the status of the realistic image in general"[57]; different authors in this regard emphasize the paradoxical effect that the more the documental form critically and openly reflects its ambiguous relationship to reality, and the more it relativizes its significance as a carrier of truth, the more it is acknowledged as a tool extrapolating reality and truth.[58] In being factual and fictional at the same time, the films bear witness not so much to *reality* as to the context of the image, the factual and potential reverberations and after-images of events. Understanding "the skin of the film not as a screen, but as a membrane that brings its audience into contact with the material forms of memory,"[59] the form of the images' construction may be read, above all, as making the conditions of its production evident. Regardless of whether an image is congruent with reality or not, its form will always tell the truth about the context of the image itself[60]—that is, its production, its constructedness, the power relations it imparts and potentially reiterates.

The films discussed uncover the fundamental disparity that characterizes *Borderland Schengen*—the different processes are in a permanent state of tension; the invisible necessarily points to the visible, mobility to immobility, legality to illegality, and so on. They deploy a practice of documentary filmmaking investigating European borderlands as contact zones composed of sites where a complex web of articulations and demands is not only expressed but also negotiated and contested.[61] While the film images may be understood as counter-images—in the sense that they put the self-evident and the intolerable under scrutiny—opacity, resistance, and creativity are, in this regard, the cornerstones of *Borderland Schengen* as a counter-topographical space. It is a space in which the films must also be understood as mobilizing their images, as bringing back their differences, dynamisms, movements, and changes,[62] and at the same time linking the analysis of existing conditions to a critique of the *structure* of representation; what they observe, in this sense, are the ruins of representation and the disassembly of hierarchically ordered time and space, life and thought.[63]

The films also aim to establish a relationship with the undocumented migrants that allows for perceiving them as subjects, recognizing them as agents and appropriators of their own narrative, not least by putting the iconologies underlying current migration discourses under scrutiny. Instead of applying representative modes, the films' images and motives are characterized by visual performative approaches—focusing their own mediality, as well as deploying the fictional capacities of documentary film in a way that allows new perspectives on the phenomenon and its protagonists. In this regard, "Havarie" and "La Forteresse" are interested not so much in their protagonists' mere visibility as in their recognition and opacity. On a visual and a narrative level, they aim at irritating the self-evident in order to reveal the intolerable. Although most of the protagonists—the Algerian–French couple, thirteen 13 refugees on the rubber boat, and the Somali migrant—remain in a protracted state of transit, they none the less inhabit those border zones and constitute a social space including specific routes, places, artefacts, social practices, geographies, and symbols of migration. Philip Scheffner and Fernand Melgar investigate those border zones of migration also as spaces of autonomy and appropriation; they wander through both strictly regulated spaces under close surveillance and the clandestine spots that allow people to have a break—their temporary homes, so to speak—not least following a participative approach to filmmaking themselves.

Notes

1. Generally speaking, the definition of "undocumented" applied in this chapter aims, in the widest possible sense, to account for migrants who, according to European legislation, do not have legal status (who have, in other words, been illegalized), who are threatened with the loss of legal status, or who are in some sort of conflict with the European border regime, although they move only through its peripheries.

2. Ruben Andersson, *Illegality, Inc.: Clandestine Migration and the Business of Bordering Europe* (Oakland: University of California Press, 2014), 2–10.
3. Ruben Zaiotti, *Cultures of Border Control: Schengen and the Evolution of European Frontiers* (Chicago and London: University of Chicago Press, 2011).
4. Transit Migration Forschungsgruppe, *Turbulente Ränder: Neue Perspektiven auf Migration an den Grenzen Europas* (Bielefeld: transcript, 2007), 41–58.
5. Paul Mecheril, "Wirklichkeit schaffen: Integration als Dispositiv," *Aus Politik und Zeitgeschichte* 61, no. 43 (2011): 49–54.
6. Tom Holert, *Regieren im Bildraum*, PoLYpeN (Berlin: b_books, 2008), 13–22.
7. Jacques Rancière, *Film Fables*, reprint (London and New York: Berg, 2006), 157–70.
8. H. Adlai Murdoch, "Glissant's Opacité and the Re-Conceptualization of Identity," in *Theorizing Glissant: Sites and Citations*, ed. John E. Drabinski and Marisa Parham (London: Rowman & Littlefield International, 2015), 7–28.
9. Dimitris Papadopoulos and Vassilis Tsianos, "The Autonomy of Migration: The Animals of Undocumented Mobility," *Translate*, 2008, available at <http://translate.eipcp.net/strands/02/papadopoulostsianos-strands01en#redir> (last accessed December 17, 2016).
10. Ruben Andersson, "Europe's Failed 'Fight' against Irregular Migration: Ethnographic Notes on a Counterproductive Industry," *Journal of Ethnic and Migration Studies* 42, no. 7 (2016): 1055.
11. Holert, *Regieren im Bildraum*, 94.
12. Helena Smith, "Shocking Images of Drowned Syrian Boy Show Tragic Plight of Refugees," *The Guardian*, September 2, 2015, available at <http://www.theguardian.com/world/2015/sep/02/shocking-image-of-drowned-syrian-boy-shows-tragic-plight-of-refugees> (last accessed September 9, 2015).
13. C. Bischoff, F. Falk, and S. Kafehsy, eds, *Images of Illegalized Immigration: Towards a Critical Iconology of Politics* (Bielefeld: transcript, 2010), 7.
14. Christoph Rass and Melanie Ulz, "Migrationsforschung und Film: Interdisziplinäre Perspektiven," ed. Christoph Rass and Melanie Ulz, *IMIS-Beiträge* 46 (2015): 7–20.
15. Martina Benz and Helen Schwenken, "Jenseits von Autonomie und Kontrolle: Migration als eigensinnige Praxis," *Prokla* 35, no. 3 (2005), 363–77.
16. Upon premiering at the 2016 Berlinale's Forum section and receiving several euphoric reviews, the film found a distributor and had a regular film release in Spring 2017.
17. Terry Diamond, *Refugees*, Stream, 2012, available at <https://www.youtube.com/watch?v=CRAmCO2ilrg> (last accessed August 14, 2016).
18. The information that what we are seeing is a rubber boat has also been taken from the production company's website; it is nothing that can actually be identified in the film. Pong Film, "Havarie: Synopsis," *Pong*, 2016, available at <http://havarie.pong-berlin.de/en/9/synopsis> (last accessed August 14, 2016). Also, from the original film material it is impossible to tell the number of refugees on the boat; this information is provided halfway through Scheffner's film by means of a radio statement from the cruise ship captain.
19. Pong Film, "Havarie: Synopsis."
20. At the premiere at the 2016 Berlinale, Scheffner disclosed that he originally recorded the different sequences of the film planning to interweave the found footage and

additional material. Eventually, however, he decided to use the audio only. "Havarie" in this regard also documents the failed search for adequate depictions of the refugee crisis.

21. Esther Buss, "Postcards from the 66th Berlinale," *Frieze*, February 19, 2016, available at <https://www.frieze.com/article/postcard-66th-berlinale> (last accessed August 20, 2016).
22. Nicole Wolf, "Sea Sight," Pong, 2016, available at <http://havarie.pong-berlin.de/en/9/nicole-wolf> (last accessed August 19, 2016).
23. Indeed, the film itself also becomes very long and strenuous. In her review, Cosima Lutz documents this in two regards; on the one hand, she mentions that, during the Berlinale press screening, about a dozen of the film critics left the cinema during the first 40 minutes, unable to stand the waiting and the uneventfulness. On the other hand, her review carries the words "sinking raft" in its title, which clearly documents the viewer's longing for something to happen; but in fact, neither do the refugees sit on a raft, nor is their boat sinking. Cosima Lutz, "Das sinkende Floß trifft auf ein Kreuzfahrtschiff," *Die Welt*, February 12, 2016, available at <http://www.welt.de/kultur/kino/article152183604/Das-sinkende-Floss-trifft-auf-ein-Kreuzfahrtschiff.html> (last accessed August 15, 2016).
24. Wolf, *Sea Sight*.
25. Karl Ludwig Pfeiffer and Ralf Schnell, eds, *Schwellen der Medialisierung: Medienanthropologische Perspektiven—Deutschland und Japan*, Medienumbrüche 28 (Bielefeld: transcript, 2008), 7.
26. Sabine Hess and Vassilis Tsianos, "Europeanizing Transnationalism! Provincializing Europe! Konturen eines neuen Grenzregimes," in *Turbulente Ränder: Neue Perspektiven auf Migration an den Grenzen Europas*, ed. Transit Migration Forschungsgruppe (Bielefeld: transcript, 2007), 23–38.
27. Anna Triandafyllidou and Ruby Gropas, eds, *European Immigration: A Sourcebook*, 2nd edn, Research in Migration and Ethnic Relations series (Farnham: Ashgate, 2014), 1–18.
28. Hess and Tsianos, "Europeanizing Transnationalism," 36.
29. Joris Schapendonk, "Turbulent Trajectories: African Migrants on Their Way to the European Union," *Societies* 2 (2012): 27.
30. Marie Fröhlich, "Routes of Migration: Migrationsprojekte unter Bedingungen europäisierter Regulation," in *Movements of Migration: Neue Perspektiven im Feld von Stadt, Migration und Repräsentation*, ed. Sabine Hess and Torsten Näser (Berlin: Panama, 2015), 150–62.
31. Giorgio Agamben, *Homo Sacer: Sovereign Power and Bare Life* (Stanford: Stanford University Press, 1998).
32. Alison Mountz, "Where Asylum-Seekers Wait: Feminist Counter-topographies of Sites between States," *Gender, Place & Culture* 18, no. 3 (2011): 380–99.
33. Kirsten Maas-Albert, "Hightech gegen Asyl," in *Europa-Atlas*, ed. Heinrich-Böll-Stiftung (Berlin: Heinrich-Böll-Stiftung, 2014), 32–3.
34. Papadopoulos and Tsianos, "The Autonomy of Migration."
35. Papadopoulos and Tsianos, "The Autonomy of Migration."

36. Cindi Katz, "Accumulation, Excess, Childhood: Toward a Countertopography of Risk and Waste," *Documents d'Anàlisi Geogràfica* 57, no. 1 (2011): 47–60.
37. The presence of an interpreter certainly adds an additional layer to the whole scene. Not only does she translate the Somali's words into her own, but also there are statements that she apparently shortens or summarizes, or does not translate at all—thus also playing an important role in shaping the narrative. Moreover, the French parts of her and the pastor's speech are subtitled; the man's original statements are not.
38. Anna Gibbs, "After Affect: Sympathy, Synchrony, and Mimetic Communication," in *The Affect Theory Reader*, ed. Melissa Gregg and Gregory J. Seigworth (Durham, NC: Duke University Press, 2010), 200.
39. Sehrat Karakayalı and Vassilis Tsianos, "Movements that Matter: Eine Einleitung," in *Turbulente Ränder: Neue Perspektiven auf Migration an den Grenzen Europas*, ed. Transit Migration Forschungsgruppe (Bielefeld: transcript, 2007), 7–17.
40. Rass and Ulz, "Migrationsforschung und Film," 13.
41. Mecheril, "Wirklichkeit schaffen," 49.
42. The terms "smuggler" and "trafficker" are often—and incorrectly—used interchangeably in media and European Union statements; while smuggling usually takes place with the consent of the smuggled person and does not involve any kind of exploitation, victims of human trafficking are usually either moved from one place to another against their will or exploited during or after the journey. Smugglers, not traffickers, are consequently the primary targets of the European Union mission (Human Rights Watch, "Smuggling and Trafficking Human Beings," July 7, 2015, available at <https://www.hrw.org/news/2015/07/07/smuggling-and-trafficking-human-beings> (last accessed November 21, 2016).
43. Bischoff et al., *Images of Illegalized Immigration*, 7.
44. W. J. T. Mitchell, "Migration, Law, and the Image: Beyond the Veil of Ignorance," in *Images of Illegalized Immigration: Towards a Critical Iconology of Politics*, ed. C. Bischoff, F. Falk, and S. Kafehsy (Bielefeld: transcript, 2010), 13.
45. Ramón Reichert, "Das Geschlecht der Grenze: Genderrepräsentationen von der Berliner Mauer bis zur EU-Außengrenze," in *Identitäten in Bewegung: Migration im Film*, ed. Bettina Dennerlein and Elke Frietsch (Bielefeld: transcript, 2011), 35–56.
46. Bischoff et al., *Images of Illegalized Immigration*, 7.
47. Bischoff et al., *Images of Illegalized Immigration*, 7.
48. Mitchell, "Migration, Law, and the Image," 13.
49. Mountz, "Where Asylum-Seekers Wait," 385.
50. Holert, Regieren im Bildraum, 192.
51. Renate Wöhrer, *Dokumentation als emanzipatorische Praxis: Künstlerische Strategien zur Darstellung von Arbeit unter globalisierten Bedingungen* (Paderborn: Wilhelm Fink, 2015), 9–14.
52. Renate Wöhrer, ed., *Wie Bilder Dokumente wurden: Zur Genealogie dokumentarischer Darstellungspraktiken*, Kaleidogramme, vol. 119 (Berlin: Kulturverlag Kadmos, 2015), 7.
53. Jacques Rancière, *The Politics of Aesthetics: The Distribution of the Sensible* (New York and London: Continuum, 2004), 12–19.
54. Rancière, *Film Fables*, 17–18.

55. Nico Baumbach, "Jacques Rancière and the Fictional Capacity of Documentary," *New Review of Film and Television Studies* 8, no. 1 (2010), 60.
56. Rancière, *Film Fables*, 158.
57. Holert, *Regieren im Bildraum*, 191.
58. For example, Wöhrer, *Dokumentation als Emanzipatorische Praxis*; Holert, *Regieren im Bildraum*; Hito Steyerl, *Die Farbe der Wahrheit: Dokumentarismen im Kunstfeld*, Republicart 8 (Vienna: Turia + Kant, 2008).
59. Laura Marks, *The Skin of the Film: Intercultural Cinema, Embodiment, and the Senses* (Durham, NC: Duke University Press, 2000), 243.
60. Steyerl, *Die Farbe der Wahrheit*, 12.
61. Philipp Schorch, "Contact Zones, Third Spaces, and the Act of Interpretation," *Museum and Society* 11, no. 1 (2013): 68–81.
62. Amy Herzog, "Images of Thought and Acts of Creation: Deleuze, Bergson, and the Question of Cinema," *In [] Visible Culture* 3 (2000), available at <http://www.rochester.edu/in_visible_culture/issue3/IVC_iss3_Herzog.pdf> (last accessed July 7, 2016).
63. Dorothea Olkowski, *Gilles Deleuze and the Ruin of Representation* (Berkeley: University of California Press, 1999), 177–210.

Works Cited

Agamben, Giorgio. *Homo Sacer: Sovereign Power and Bare Life*. Stanford: Stanford University Press, 1998.

Andersson, Ruben. *Illegality, Inc.: Clandestine Migration and the Business of Bordering Europe*. Oakland: University of California Press, 2014.

Andersson, Ruben. "Europe's Failed 'Fight' against Irregular Migration: Ethnographic Notes on a Counterproductive Industry." *Journal of Ethnic and Migration Studies* 42, no. 7 (2016): 1055–75.

Baumbach, Nico. "Jacques Rancière and the Fictional Capacity of Documentary." *New Review of Film and Television Studies* 8, no. 1 (2010): 57–72.

Benz, Martina and Helen Schwenken. "Jenseits von Autonomie und Kontrolle: Migration als eigensinnige Praxis." *Prokla* 35, no. 3 (2005): 363–77.

Bischoff, C., F. Falk, and S. Kafehsy, eds. *Images of Illegalized Immigration: Towards a Critical Iconology of Politics*. Bielefeld: transcript, 2010.

Buss, Esther. "Postcards from the 66th Berlinale." *Frieze*, February 19, 2016, <https://www.frieze.com/article/postcard-66th-berlinale> (last accessed August 20, 2016).

Diamond, Terry. *Refugees*. Stream, 2012 <https://www.youtube.com/watch?v=CRAmCO2ilrg> (last accessed August 14, 2016).

Fröhlich, Marie. "Routes of Migration: Migrationsprojekte unter Bedingungen europäisierter Regulation." In *Movements of Migration: Neue Perspektiven im Feld von Stadt, Migration und Repräsentation*, ed. Sabine Hess and Torsten Näser, 150–62. Berlin: Panama, 2015.

Gibbs, Anna. "After Affect: Sympathy, Synchrony, and Mimetic Communication." In *The Affect Theory Reader*, ed. Melissa Gregg and Gregory J. Seigworth, 186–205. Durham, NC: Duke University Press, 2010.

Herzog, Amy. "Images of Thought and Acts of Creation: Deleuze, Bergson, and the Question of Cinema." In [] *Visible Culture*, no. 3 (2000), <http://www.rochester.edu/in_visible_culture/issue3/IVC_iss3_Herzog.pdf> (last accessed July 7, 2016).

Hess, Sabine and Vassilis Tsianos. "Europeanizing Transnationalism! Provincializing Europe! Konturen eines neuen Grenzregimes." In *Turbulente Ränder: Neue Perspektiven auf Migration an den Grenzen Europas*, ed. Transit Migration Forschungsgruppe, 23–38. Bielefeld: transcript, 2007.

Holert, Tom. *Regieren im Bildraum*. PoLYpeN. Berlin: b_books, 2008.

Human Rights Watch. "Smuggling and Trafficking Human Beings," July 7, 2015, <https://www.hrw.org/news/2015/07/07/smuggling-and-trafficking-human-beings> (last accessed November 21, 2016).

Karakayalı, Sehrat and Vassilis Tsianos. "Movements that Matter. Eine Einleitung." In *Turbulente Ränder: Neue Perspektiven auf Migration an den Grenzen Europas*, ed. Transit Migration Forschungsgruppe, 7–17. Bielefeld: transcript, 2007.

Katz, Cindi. "Accumulation, Excess, Childhood: Toward a Countertopography of Risk and Waste." *Documents d'Anàlisi Geogràfica* 57, no. 1 (2011): 47–60.

Lutz, Cosima. "Das sinkende Floß trifft auf ein Kreuzfahrtschiff." *Die Welt*, February 12, 2016, <http://www.welt.de/kultur/kino/article152183604/Das-sinkende-Floss-trifft-auf-ein-Kreuzfahrtschiff.html> (last accessed August 15, 2016).

Maas-Albert, Kirsten. "Hightech gegen Asyl." In *Europa-Atlas*, ed. Heinrich-Böll-Stiftung, 32–3. Berlin: Heinrich-Böll-Stiftung, 2014.

Marks, Laura. *The Skin of the Film: Intercultural Cinema, Embodiment, and the Senses*. Durham, NC: Duke University Press, 2000.

Mecheril, Paul. "Wirklichkeit schaffen: Integration als Dispositiv." *Aus Politik und Zeitgeschichte* 61, no. 43 (2011): 49–54.

Melgar, Fernand. "La Forteresse." DVD. Switzerland: Climage, 2008.

Mitchell, W. J. T. "Migration, Law, and the Image: Beyond the Veil of Ignorance." In *Images of Illegalized Immigration: Towards a Critical Iconology of Politics*, ed. C. Bischoff, F. Falk, and S. Kafehsy, 13–30. Bielefeld: transcript, 2010.

Mountz, Alison. "Where Asylum-Seekers Wait: Feminist Counter-topographies of Sites between States." *Gender, Place & Culture* 18, no. 3 (2011): 380–99.

Murdoch, H. Adlai. "Glissant's Opacité and the Re-Conceptualization of Identity." In *Theorizing Glissant: Sites and Citations*, ed. John E. Drabinski and Marisa Parham, 7–28. Creolizing the Canon. London: Rowman & Littlefield International, 2015.

Olkowski, Dorothea. *Gilles Deleuze and the Ruin of Representation*. Berkeley: University of California Press, 1999.

Papadopoulos, Dimitris and Vassilis Tsianos. "The Autonomy of Migration: The Animals of Undocumented Mobility." *Translate*, 2008, <https://translate.eipcp.net/strands/02/papadopoulostsianos-strands01en.htm> (last accessed December 8, 2020).

Pfeiffer, Karl Ludwig and Ralf Schnell, eds. *Schwellen der Medialisierung: Medienanthropologische Perspektiven—Deutschland und Japan*. Medienumbrüche 28. Bielefeld: transcript, 2008.

Pong Film. "Havarie: Synopsis." *Pong*, 2016, <http://havarie.pong-berlin.de/en/9/synopsis> (last accessed August 14, 2016).

Rancière, Jacques. *The Politics of Aesthetics: The Distribution of the Sensible.* New York and London: Continuum, 2004.
Rancière, Jacques. *Film Fables.* Reprint. London and New York: Berg, 2006.
Rass, Christoph and Melanie Ulz. "Migrationsforschung und Film: Interdisziplinäre Perspektiven," ed. Christoph Rass and Melanie Ulz. *IMIS-Beiträge* 46 (2015): 7–20.
Reichert, Ramón. "Das Geschlecht der Grenze: Genderrepräsentationen von der Berliner Mauer bis zur EU-Außengrenze." In *Identitäten in Bewegung: Migration im Film*, ed. Bettina Dennerlein and Elke Frietsch, 35–56. Bielefeld: transcript, 2011.
Schapendonk, Joris. "Turbulent Trajectories: African Migrants on Their Way to the European Union." *Societies* 2 (2012): 27–41.
Scheffner, Philip. "Havarie." Stream. Germany: Pong, 2016.
Schorch, Philipp. "Contact Zones, Third Spaces, and the Act of Interpretation." *Museum and Society* 11, no. 1 (2013): 68–81.
Smith, Helena. "Shocking Images of Drowned Syrian Boy Show Tragic Plight of Refugees." *The Guardian*, September 2, 2015, <http://www.theguardian.com/world/2015/sep/02/shocking-image-of-drowned-syrian-boy-shows-tragic-plight-of-refugees> (last accessed September 9, 2015).
Steyerl, Hito. *Die Farbe der Wahrheit: Dokumentarismen im Kunstfeld.* Republicart 8. Vienna: Turia + Kant, 2008.
Transit Migration Forschungsgruppe. *Turbulente Ränder: Neue Perspektiven auf Migration an den Grenzen Europas.* Bielefeld: transcript, 2007.
Triandafyllidou, Anna and Ruby Gropas, eds. *European Immigration: A Sourcebook*, 2nd edn. Research in Migration and Ethnic Relations series. Farnham: Ashgate, 2014.
Wöhrer, Renate. *Dokumentation als emanzipatorische Praxis: Künstlerische Strategien zur Darstellung von Arbeit unter globalisierten Bedingungen.* Berliner Schriften zur Kunst. Paderborn: Wilhelm Fink, 2015.
Wöhrer, Renate, ed. *Wie Bilder Dokumente wurden: Zur Genealogie dokumentarischer Darstellungspraktiken.* Kaleidogramme, vol. 119. Berlin: Kulturverlag Kadmos, 2015.
Wolf, Nicole. "Sea Sight." *Pong*, 2016, <http://havarie.pong-berlin.de/en/9/nicole-wolf> (last accessed August 19, 2016).
Zaiotti, Ruben. *Cultures of Border Control: Schengen and the Evolution of European Frontiers.* Chicago and London: University of Chicago Press, 2011.

11. CIRCULATING IMAGES OF DEATH: FESTIVAL FILMS AND THE SYRIAN REFUGEE CRISIS

Michelle Baroody

> on witnessing
>   a photograph, still
>   unmoving
>   and trauma
>   frozen
>   without time
>
>   through the safety of zeros and ones
>
>   Andrea Shaker, from the film *on silence*[1]

INTRODUCTION

In Andrea Shaker's short film *on silence*, the filmmaker interrogates the "luxury of a photograph."[2] Presented like a poem alongside moving images, the film begins with a shot of a closed window as rain beats against the glass. Shaker's experimental short juxtaposes similar shots with the image of Alan Kurdi, the young Syrian boy found dead on a beach in Bodrum, Turkey, whose photograph went viral in 2015, causing a momentary stir in the global news cycle. As it transitions to the photograph, *on silence* pauses on the image of Kurdi's body as it is carried from the shore by a Turkish soldier; the poetic voiceover and music cut, and the still shot shifts from color to black and white. In this moment, time becomes suspended and the audience is forced to look at the image without the chatter of the internet, Facebook, or the nightly news, seemingly without "the safety of zeros and ones." At the same time, the film mimics the conditions under which most spectators likely first experienced the photograph in the US and Western Europe, from a position of safety, "peace," and presumed "civilization." It reminds US and European viewers that they are both inundated with images of violence from war-torn regions like Syria and disconnected from the reality of that violence; however, it also signals their indirect participation in it by forcing the spectator to witness the child's death and the repetition of its representation.

Shaker's short film serves as an entry point to a larger discussion about the global reception of images from the fraught and overdetermined Middle East. *on silence* exposes the dominant viewing practices in the "West" that shape the reception of films and photographs from the "East." In its particularity, Shaker's film calls attention to the global system of circulating media through its intermediality: by blending poetry, moving and still images, performance, and newsreel footage, *on silence* breaks the wall between fact and fiction, and between reality and its representation. The film confronts the practice of looking by self-reflexively calling attention to itself as a work of art and displaying the apparatus of mediation inherent to viewing. Embedded within these practices of looking are colonialist relationships that theorists like Louise Spence and Robert Stam argue are part of the cinematic apparatus, such that all viewers are "unwittingly sutured into a colonialist perspective."[3] The space of viewing produces attendant fantasies of what life is like in the Middle East. Protected by their perceived distance to the violence on screen, the viewing public imagines a superficial kinship with those inside the theater. These forces combine to create the mask of innocent consumption in the West.

Shaker's *on silence* calls attention to the act of looking at the image of Kurdi's death as it is bound up in commodity culture, a "luxury" that is far removed from the beach and the struggle for life itself. The audience has the option to close their eyes, to look away, to like or dislike the experimental style of Shaker's work, and perhaps most importantly, to forget, as the images on screen shift to the next shot, to the next film that the spectator's purchased ticket promises. Moreover, the film's experimental form rejects realism and situates the spectator's gaze as one that can engage only at the level of artistry, engaging with images divorced from their historical and social context. This is the "luxury of a photograph."

In contemporary global media culture, Shaker's film, like the morbid image it repeats, is necessarily experienced as a remediation, several steps removed from the realities of migration that lead to Kurdi's death. It is a self-funded production. Shaker has Lebanese origins, but lives and works in Minneapolis, Minnesota, where her films screen at high-brow art institutions like the Walker Art Center and events like the Twin Cities Arab Film Festival and the Altered Aesthetics Film Festival, all located in and around Minneapolis. This means that even as a challenging and experimental film, *on silence* screens as art cinema and its circulation is confined to the discursive loop that recreates the sense of stability in American and European life, positioning the Arab or Muslim as always "other." Photographs of death, violence, suffering, and war in the Middle East might cause a momentary stir among the global community and Midwestern viewers, but, more immediately, they affirm the way of life and presumed community in zones of reception; they insist on and reproduce the conditions that allow spectators to position themselves outside of the violence, removed from the exploitative nature of capitalism and ongoing imperial efforts masked as globalization.[4] Shaker's film transforms our perception of Kurdi's image by exposing the mediating practices of viewing in the West. Still, imprisoned by its dominance, *on silence* recreates the very spectator position it critiques.

In this chapter, I will not focus on images of migration as such, but on the homology between viral photos like Kurdi's that represent the deaths of Syrian refugees and films that screen for limited and specialized audiences at international film festivals, like Shaker's *on silence*. I argue that these films and photographs are recognized or "liked" by the global community not because viewers connect to the images, but because they promote a counter-identification that highlights and maintains a difference between the viewing "West" and the dying Middle East. This discussion is supplemented with observations about the circulation of these films on the "festival circuit." I track the way images of violence, suffering, and death from places like Syria are carried across global markets to local theaters, traded and passed around festivals that serve as forums for the spectacle of humanitarian crisis.

To examine these ideas, I look specifically at two films that circulated widely in Europe and America, and which document Syria's war and those who flee its violence. My central analysis focuses on Ossama Mohammed and Wiam Simav Bedirxan's *Silvered Water, Syria Self-Portrait*, which edits together found and cell-phone footage collected from various civilians and soldiers living inside Syria's war.[5] I supplement my reading of *Silvered Water* by examining the filmmaking techniques, self-reflexivity, and revolutionary possibilities of Mohammad Ali Atassi and Ziad Homsi's *Our Terrible Country*, which follows well-known Syrian intellectual Yassin al-Haj Saleh and photographer Ziad Homsi as they travel from Damascus to Raqqa before fleeing to Istanbul.[6] Like Shaker's *on silence*, these films expose and refuse historical trends in the representation of Arabs and Muslims, and their approach operates as a critique of the dominant viewing practices of Western festival audiences. These films show violence and death, making them complicit in the visual narratives that already circulate in Western media. Yet, *Silvered Water* and *Our Terrible Country* highlight the meaning behind such limitations, revealing the discourse that interpolates viewing subjects as safely removed from Syria's violence.

It is worth noting that, in itself, this account is limited, as it reaches only a particular type of viewer: those who attend film festivals in Europe and the US, spectators who are educated and often upper-class. Ironically, though, these films can experience success only by screening in major international festivals, networks of circulation and distribution that determine where these films go and what their future viewership will be. Films from underdeveloped and "Third-world countries have to rely on [this] mediating agency—an advocate in the guise of a film critic, historian, scholar, or other certified 'expert' with media access."[7] The film festival becomes this mediation—through inclusion within its limited time and space, the festival situates itself and the films it screens in the process of determining what images are relevant and worth showing. Since films like *Silvered Water* are unlikely to have a wide commercial release in the US or Europe, these films' only chance of being seen is at a festival.

Furthermore, as Bill Nichols argues in his piece "Global Image Consumption in the Age of Late Capitalism," festival films "circulate, in large part, with a cachet of locally inscribed difference and globally ascribed commonality. They both attest to the uniqueness of different cultures and specific filmmakers and affirm the underlying qualities of an 'international cinema.'"[8] It has become an increasing trend of major international festivals to distinguish themselves by premiering political films, especially documentaries that highlight a contemporary world crisis. Yet such films also demonstrate "local difference" and ascribe a global commonality in image production and consumption. They affirm that the world can and must be represented and circulated on a global market and that media images provide the framework for understanding the world. However, they also maintain the necessary level of difference and "uniqueness" of the world's many cultures. As a result, these films work less to demonstrate the need for global exposure and a response from the global community to crises like the one in Syria, and instead function as an index for the unrelenting war zone of the Middle East, which has become a defining characteristic of the region. When screened at festivals like Cannes or Toronto, films about war and struggle reproduce the images that already circulate in the global imaginary and reinforce the fantasy of safety elsewhere. Shaker projects levels of meaning onto Kurdi's short life, for his death, captured by the viral photograph, creates a momentary local stir, but does little to transform the global response to Syria's refugees. In fact, the photo reinforces the status quo elsewhere, and as Shaker's film demonstrates, "the luxury of forgetting" mediatized images.

Syria's "Self-portrait" on International Screens

Violence against those who are already not quite living, that is, living in a state of suspension between life and death, leaves a mark that is no mark. There will be no public act of grieving.

Judith Butler, *Precarious Life*[9]

Silvered Water, Syria Self-Portrait opens with sound: a slow drip against a black screen, followed by an utterance from a soft voice speaking Arabic, "shāhadtuhu." Transcribed in the subtitles as "I saw it," the phrase more closely translates as "I watched it," or "I witnessed it," and its meaning refers to the film's images of life, torture, and death, various glimpses into Syria's conflict, which began in 2011. Presented as a series of impressions with intertitles that appear without any semblance of chronology, *Silvered Water* addresses the spectator's inability to see what the narrator sees, mobilizing "sight" as a privilege, a gesture that disrupts audience expectations of a documentary film about Syria's war and its refugees. Significantly, the film locates "seeing" as if it is always in the past tense – "I saw [or watched] it" – and possessed by a viewing subject within the film rather than one inside the theater. It produces a kind of witnessing that mitigates the spectator's view of the images, even when the screen is completely blank.

The film's present, subject to the authority of the camera or the temporality of the festival screen, merges with its spectacle, drawing attention to the voyeuristic gaze of the viewer and monitoring the film's content through a manipulation of its form. Among other techniques, in the opening sequence, this effect occurs through voiceover and discontinuity between sound and image, a practice that destabilizes the certainty of both looking and listening. The "self-portrait" emerges as a representation that is always mediated and predetermined by geopolitics and festival policies, and the film's events unfold as a looped image that continually circulates and resurrects Syria's self-determination in a space and time both in and outside the film.

As the narrator sees through the blackness of the film's opening, *Silvered Water* connects the act of looking to production and consumption. The familiar ding associated with receiving a Facebook message cues the first images of film, offering the disassociated dripping sound a visual source. A shaky camera reveals a leaky faucet amidst indistinct rubble, an inanimate object out of context and framed by chaos. The image appears as if it was brought to the screen by the social media platform and its instant ability to transmit and archive digital forms. The film presents "seeing," "viewing," and transmitting Syria's war as its main subject matter. The viewer's experience of Syria is situated as a type of looking that is always mediated by its form and its method of transmission, an encounter with the medium and the cinematic apparatus rather than war itself.

Mohammed and Bedirxan worked collaboratively between France and Syria to make the film. The two met on Facebook and used social media to share footage and ideas while Mohammed lived in exile in France and Bedirxan worked as a teacher, and a budding filmmaker, in Syria. *Silvered Water* is a collection of YouTube videos and online postings, recordings shot and shared by dozens of Syrians and edited together with Bedirxan's footage from the Syrian city of Homs. In France, Mohammed compiled this footage, juxtaposed images, and added chapter titles to shape the film. He determined the order and repetition of specific scenes and incorporated sound in silent moments and vice versa. Mohammed's narration, presented as an exchange with Bedirxan and the other Syrians left behind, and also as a discourse on the necessity and function of cinema, gives the audience a frame through which to consider the relationship between images and war, between moving pictures and life, and between transmission and death. Evidenced in its opening sequence, rather than directly documenting Syria's contemporary struggle, *Silvered Water* takes visibility as its primary subject, signaling a type of restricted filmmaking premised on the unrepresentability of reality. The blackness of its first moments acts as a buffer between the audience and the lives portrayed in the film. As for the spectators, denied access to Syrian lives or struggles, they must witness representation marked as such.

As a refugee himself, co-director Mohammed's exile represents the film's condition of possibility. For the filmmaker, Syria can be experienced only through picture and memory, and the frame he places around the images through a carefully constructed cinematic apparatus mimics for the audience his own distance from the war. Mohammed "left Syria on May 9, 2011, the anniversary of the day Nazi Germany surrendered to the Soviet Union. Destination: Cannes, not with a film, but as witness and repository of images."[10] He traveled to participate in a panel discussion, where he demanded the release of Syrian political prisoners. As a result, he received several death threats, making it impossible for him to return home. Since then, he has watched from Paris as his country is destroyed. A filmmaker by trade, he felt compelled to tell the story he witnessed through YouTube videos and other online platforms, which became possible when he heard from Kurdish–Syrian filmmaker Bedirxan. Living in the occupied city of Homs, she sparked the project by reaching out to Mohammed for filmmaking advice; what followed was an exchange across international lines and the conversation that transmits *Silvered Water*.

In 2014, the film brought Mohammed back to Cannes for its premiere. It was the only Arab film at the elite international festival that year, but the urgency of its message made the case for its inclusion.[11] After screening at Cannes, the film has been shown all over the world: Bergen, Turin, Yamagata, London, New York, Jihlava, Istanbul, Valdivia, Minneapolis, Basel, and dozens of other cities. *Silvered Water* was an official selection at the Toronto International Film Festival (2014), at the Arab Brazilian Film Festival (São Paolo, 2015), at the Viennale (2014), and at Locarno International Film Festival (2014), to name only a few. During its two-year run, *Silvered Water* has screened in a variety of international festivals, been promoted through special screenings, appeared in human rights and documentary festivals, and been showcased in festivals by filmmakers living in diaspora and/or exile. While the film, with its devastating footage of death and destruction, certainly establishes a need for foreign intervention in the

Syrian war and refugee situation, it was also made to move on festival circuits. Its poignant and topical content are the major thrust behind the film's success, and its attention to cinematic technique and emphasis on aesthetics draw attention to the market in which in circulates.

Silvered Water's critique of cinematic production develops in the sequence that follows the film's establishing shot of the grainy footage of a leaky faucet. The screen reverts to blackness before the sound of a woman humming enters the dark frame. As her voice slowly fades into silence, a single word is printed on the black screen: "*Sūrīyā.*" Whispering "Syria" in Arabic, her disembodied voice metonymically stands in for the country and for hope, and after a moment of silence, her loud exhalation calls forth new life: out of the black screen, the picture of a squirming newborn emerges. When the narrator's voice again cuts into the silence to tell the audience "I saw it," the voice and image combine to pronounce "Syria" through the darkness, in the rubble, and in everything that goes unseen. From the outset, the film establishes a pattern, one that oscillates between what can and cannot be seen by its viewer. This method separates sound from image to situate its major thesis, a comment offered by Bedirxan late in the film: "what you see isn't as it was." The spectator perceives this disconnect first with the rhythmic drip against blackness that reveals a surviving faucet, and then with the hum that reveals Syria. However, the source of the hum does not present a one-to-one relationship, as we never see the body which produces it. Instead, it enters the scene like an echo of the images that follow, a melodic and disembodied vibration that makes Syrian cinema manifest.

Silvered Water intercuts online postings shot and shared by dozens of Syrians with footage shot by co-director Bedirxan. While in France, co-director and editor Mohammed compiled this footage, juxtaposed images, and added chapter titles to shape the film. He determined the order and repetition of specific scenes and incorporated sound in silent moments, and vice versa. Mohammed's narration, presented as an exchange with Bedirxan and the other Syrians left behind, and also as a discourse on the necessity and function of cinema, gives the audience a frame through which to consider the relationship between images and war, between moving pictures and life, and between transmission and death. The film provides a familiar form, documentary, to critique spectator positions and filmmaking conventions as part of Syria's ongoing conflict.

Evident in the scenes that follow the film's opening, the narrator tells the audience that "cinema began" in Syria only after the violence. The spectator witnesses grainy footage of a baby squirming while its umbilical cord is cut, emerging out of the blackness of an empty screen. After an edit, the muted scene's silence forms a sound bridge with the image of an almost naked teenage boy, framed in the shape of a smartphone camera. He sits huddled in a ball in the corner of a small space, wearing only his underwear. There is no sound, but the story is clear. It shows the young man kissing the foot of a leg decked out in military fatigues that kicks him repeatedly against the wall. As this action continues, a man in a plaid shirt enters the frame and assaults the young man with a long white baton. The scene remains muted, but the text that follows informs the audience:

> After a school day, this boy wrote on a wall "the people want to topple the regime." He was detained. His nails were pulled out. This happened in Dar'a. His family ran to the officer demanding his release. "Forget him," the officer said. "Go make yourselves a new one! If you can't, send your women here—we shall help you."

Printed in white letters on a black screen in Arabic, French, and English, these statements appear against the backdrop of a droning white noise and contextualize the scene that will repeat in fragments throughout the film. The text lays the groundwork for the encounter between the boy and the regime, and draws a connection to the rhetorical tropes of the Arab Spring with a borrowed slogan from the Egyptian and Tunisian uprisings in 2010 and 2011: "the people want to topple the regime." Moreover, it recalls the story of the missing teens in Dar'a, whose writing on the wall was the impetus for Syria's uprising. However, this scene also situates the boy's torture as a repetition of the war's violence, and perhaps more candidly, it marks the possibility of a revolutionary cinema. It does not aim to represent the individual struggle, but only to critique the ways that audiences engage with images of violence and torture. The low-quality images of this boy's torture gesture toward the real, where violence and death stand in as the raw materials of life in Syria, but they also gesture toward cinema's revolutionary potential. The "reality" of this scene is not the boy's suffering, but the medium itself; film acts as a site for change.

In the early scene of torture, what Peter Bloom calls the "visual representation of an anarchic" need for colonial intervention manifests in the soldier's response to the boy's family, as it is made clear to the viewer that the boy will not return, that this was his final scene.[12] Perhaps more sinister, the soldier's threats extend beyond the image and include the boy's family with a veiled reference to rape, inserting violence into reproduction, the reproducibility of human life, and the reproducibility of images. In her discussion of the "poor image," Steyerl argues that "the poor image is an illicit fifth-generation bastard of an original image," which gives it a freedom to reach beyond representation to a kind of "visual becoming."[13] Steyerl puts faith in the poor image, especially one that generates from the copy rather than the original. Her piece explodes the need for an original, placing meaning into a spiral of "upload[s], download[s], share[s], reformat[s], and reedit[s]."[14] Similarly, in *Silvered Water*, a kind of re-edited upload, the copy does not represent Syrian struggling, but calls attention to the repetition of its images and forms. In the scene of torture, it is language that implies what image cannot, insisting that the boy's torture incites more shock than sympathy, read as reference to the continual violence in the Middle East. Yet, *Silvered Water* compels the audience to contend with death as an aesthetic practice, a repetition that displays the horrors of war, while also wresting the image from its representational duty. The film attempts to capture the violence inherent to the cinematic process itself by repeating this sequence throughout the film, like a refrain or a copy of a copy.

As the soldiers casually suggest the family forget their son and go make themselves a new one, human reproduction signifies a threat and an aesthetic. As a threat, the film locates what terrifies Western viewers the most, the reproducibility of Syrian lives and culture, as even in the face of torture and war, the newborn baby suggests that Syrian life might persevere. However, its placement in the film, alongside the scene of torture, suggests this child's fate is bound for a similar end. The boy's life is traded for a more universal image of violence, and *Silvered Water* invites the audience to imagine this boy's death: a demonstration of the endless war and failed revolution. The filmmakers try to highlight that the boy's life and its reproduction on screen stand in as a mere function of aesthetic practice, where European managers monitor the images of Syria's war.

In his foundational essay, "The Work of Art in the Age of its Technological Reproducibility," Walter Benjamin suggests that while art has always been "reproducible," technological reproducibility accelerates this process and transforms it. This mode "devalues the here and now" of the artwork, undoing "its unique existence in a particular place."[15] It does not evacuate the work of its history, but the reproduction no longer "bears the mark of the history to which the work has been subject."[16] This shift in production also marks a shift in perception of the artwork, and in many cases, art is made to be reproduced, like film. In this frame, art loses its ritualistic meaning and "changes the relation of the masses to art," and art becomes commodity. In regard to cinema in particular, Benjamin suggests that

> the critical and uncritical attitudes of the public coincide. The decisive reason for this is that nowhere more than in cinema are the reactions of individuals, which together make up the massive reaction of the audience, determined by the imminent concentrations of reactions into a mass.[17]

Thus, cinema, according to Benjamin, creates a situation where the masses can be manipulated into particular reactions by the exhibition process and the apparatus of filmmaking itself. In the case of films like *Silvered Water*, the response to Syria's "humanitarian crisis" is produced by the screening situation and the conditioned responses to images of violence and war that dominate modern depictions of the Middle East.

The image of the tortured boy positions two related embodiments of the Arab "other": the oppressor and the oppressed. Both subject positions reiterate the dialectic that maintains Western hegemony, supplying the images "necessary" for interventionist policies and force. However, by including and repeating the boy's image, the film simultaneously refuses and affirms the possibility that brown lives and deaths are frivolous, easily created and lost with little disturbance to the universe, similar to commodities bought, sold, and discarded. The soldier's assertion gives a nod to the value of human life under a dictatorial regime and under capital—and in death, the same message resounds. As General William Westmoreland states in *Hearts and Minds*, an American documentary about the Vietnam War that premiered at the Cannes Film Festival in 1974, "The Oriental doesn't put the same high price on life as does a Westerner. Life is plentiful. Life is cheap in the Orient."[18] While his comments refer to the Vietnamese and the United States' long war with their country, his sentiments apply here as well. The justification for international wars and intervention covers its tracks with a desire to save the other from themselves, to bring Western moral values and systems of value, capitalism, to non-Western spaces. However, Westmoreland's comments only imply the business of war itself: that is, the profit generated by military intervention, the monetary value of war weighed against the value of human life. In *Silvered Water*, the audience contends with the superficiality of the individual life, each viewer obliged to consider the value and meaning of their own lives in relation to the bodies on screen presented by the film's confrontational aesthetic.

Silvered Water addresses the ways that representations of life in Syria will be folded back into a dialectical relationship with the film's Western viewer, and the film oversteps the process of grieving for lives whose meaning and value are overdetermined by repeating images of war and death. Instead, the film posits a new beginning as the narrator attests that, in this scene, "cinema began," as if cinema's formal practices and circulation were always already tied to violent encounters. From birth, death, and violence, cinema emerges as if reborn and the boy's torture and subsequent death are liberated from signifying nothing more than the endemic violence that Western viewers conventionally attribute to the Middle East. In this moment, sound, separated from its image, returns to the theater: the audience hears the cries of the baby as his or her cord is cut, alongside the image of the teenager being tortured. The parallelism in this scene draws attention to the similarities between the beginning and end of life, as the cut cord references the film's cut to the next scene, a visual act of severing the first breath from the last. Here, cinema is determined by the convergence of life and death, where the original and its copy overwhelm the first minutes of the film—all that follows is repetition. The film removes the feeling of distance between the audience and the leg that indiscriminately kicks its target, because the very act of viewing forces spectators to consider how witnessing the violence on screen makes them complicit in the production of Syria's war, based on the simple fact that consuming the film at festivals creates the market in which such documentaries circulate.

In an interview, Mohammed describes seeing the YouTube video of the tortured teenager. This, he says,

> really set things off . . . This is my "primitive scene." In this instance, the image serves as an archetype of violence, but also helps to spread violence . . . that scene found its way into the film and was one of the triggers of the Syrian revolution.[19]

Mohammed's filmmaking process builds out from the scene of the teenager. This sequence is simultaneously the origin of filmmaking and of Syria's violence, but it is also repetition, mythologized and codified by its recording. Furthermore, Mohammed's formulation situates the scene of violence, bursting forth alongside new life, in a way that distorts the audience's relationship to the images of Syria's war, because the boy is not humanized in this scene, but instead transformed into a mode of cinematic violence. As "primitive scene," the sequence cannot be read as derivative and *Silvered Water*'s collection of images demands a different mode of viewing.[20]

In terms of production, Kamran Rastegar makes an argument in his work *Surviving Images* that resonates with all films relying on found video recordings of political upheaval. He states that, after the 2009 presidential elections in Iran,

> mobile-phone video recordings came to play a defining role in producing narratives of the events on the ground, especially in the absence of more traditional modes of news reporting. Discrete acts of defiance and repression were captured by cameras discreetly angled by street-level passersby, or held furtively out of apartment windows. These scenes, when uploaded for viewing across the globe, acted as powerful gestures of witnessing, despite appearing to be lacking in analysis or context.[21]

In *Silvered Water*, Syrians employ this practice of rogue journalism, witnessing violence and oppression in the country through the lens of discreetly placed camera phones or fearlessly posted videos. These images provide the frame through which to view them; in fact, since the outbreak of war, journalists' limited access to the situation in Syria has made it necessary for ordinary citizens to risk themselves for images and, like the uploaded web images from Iran, the assembled footage in *Silvered Water* doubles the process of witnessing. At once, the recordings transmit the internal struggle, which highlights the importance of seeing in the face of violence and oppression, and display a gap in "witnessing," demonstrating the "luxury" of distance for those only viewing the conflict on screen. *Silvered Water*'s style emphasizes the transgressive force of the image: cinema in practice offers freedom, as the untrained cinematographer takes control of the transmission. It is this articulation of "freedom" that allows Bedirxan to argue, "what you see isn't as it was." The spectator does not see the cameraman's intention, nor the reality of the situation on the ground.

About thirty minutes into the film, *Silvered Water* begins to feel like a direct dialogue between filmmaker Bedirxan and the viewer, her camera becoming a recurring protagonist. She states, "in Homs, clocks have no hands. I have a story." As she speaks, the camera shows images of carrier pigeons on a roof through a slightly cracked door. In the background, the viewer can hear the ding of a Facebook message being received, representing the mode of exchange, messages circulating on a global interface and mediating what the audience sees. The juxtaposition draws a link between technologies of communication—the camera, the internet, the pigeons—forging connections between spaces and temporalities often read as uneven. Moreover, the limited view of the rooftop pigeons, through a small crack in a heavy door, indexes all that is lost in translation, all that cannot be scrawled onto a note and sent in a bird's talons. What the audience sees is not what they had previously seen; instead, they see a set of images mediated by processes of looking and recording. Bedirxan's "story" does not depend on time, as she represents a kind of tradition—marked by the pigeons—and modern mode of communicating—marked by cinema— with a distant audience; in this mode, the film must break through linguistic and cinematic registers, and across transnational and transtemporal lines. Screening for Western viewers, Bedirxan's footage must confront the global imaginary and a particular type of cinephilia that exists at the international festival. As a result, the film must communicate on superficial and subversive levels. Thus, the tension between *Silvered Water*'s destination and origins operates openly in the film's message.

Their reflexive approach accounts for the reality of distributing a film like *Silvered Water*. For example, Dina Iordanova argues that

> besides the official film markets that accompany some of the big festivals and that remain the domain of film industry professionals and clear-cut distributors, there is the informal but increasingly networked and efficient system of international flow through festival links, where a small film from an obscure source is picked up by a succession of festivals and shown consecutively in various countries, thus getting truly global exposure, even if this exposure does not bring along measurable financial gains.[22]

In addition, globalization and a switch to digital formats have made foreign cinema more accessible and relevant across Europe and the US, and an increasing number of small festivals that highlight particular regions or themes have popped up almost everywhere. This means that films are relevant for longer, screening first at major festivals and then circulating between hundreds of smaller events across the globe beyond their first or second year. This has a dual effect on international films that depend on festivals for circulation, like those from Syria or other Arabic-speaking countries that have little chance of commercial distribution in countries like the US. On the one hand, it provides a market and screening audience for films outside the country of production or origin. Yet problematically, this practice leads to films that are produced specifically for these international festival audiences, made to circulate globally rather than being screened locally.

Kenneth Turan argues that festivals render film circulation possible, and that success in this market determines whether or not a film will be seen at all. He writes:

> Festivals have become, in effect, what Piers Handling, head of the powerful Toronto Film Festival, has called "an alternative distribution network. A lot of work only gets shown now at festivals. A lot of foreign-language film that would get distribution ten years ago doesn't get seen anymore." France has been especially assiduous in using festivals around the world to get its cinema seen, and it's impossible to imagine the current rage for Iranian films without the intense exposure these works have gotten at Cannes, New York, and elsewhere.[23]

Opening at a festival like Cannes determines the screening trajectory of a film like *Silvered Water*. Moreover, as a French production that is also distributed by the Paris-based company Doc and Film International, *Silvered Water* screens across the globe by representing France and Syria simultaneously. In Minnesota in 2016, for example, the Film Society of Minneapolis–St Paul ran the film as part of their Lumières Françaises series, which "showcase[d] a selection of today's best independent French films and filmmakers."[24] Screening in this series, alongside contemporary French cinema from native French filmmakers, speaks to *Silvered Water*'s awkward position in the world of Arab images.

Funding for *Silvered Water* came from two major sources: Les Films d'Ici, a thirty-year old French production company that finances documentary cinema, and Proaction Films, a Syrian production company founded in 2002 in Syria and recreated in 2013 in Egypt.[25] By naming *Silvered Water* among the "best independent French films," the Film Society in Minnesota renders the film French, even if its images depict Syria's ongoing war. Production, it seems, undermines content, and in this configuration, not only does the film screen for Western audiences, but it is also claimed by a Western nation. This type of screening positions *Silvered Water* as if it belongs to France and speaks for the diversity of the French nation, influence, and projects. The Lumières Françaises series enlists the film for France, and effaces an aspect of its particularity, presenting it as a document for Western consumption rather than an instance of Syrian action.

Moreover, European and US funding and screening are necessary elements of Arab cinema, a truth that has unexpected and incompatible results. Such financing continues a narrative of economic and cultural dependency, a form of imperialism couched in the rhetoric of humanitarian aid, which suggests that Middle Eastern films must reflect, speak to, or help define the West in some way in order to circulate globally. Dependent on Euro-American support and viewers, images of the Middle East begin and end in the West, like an echo or reflection in a two-way mirror—the spectator sees inside, but for those in country, there is only repetition and painted glass.

Initiatives like Cinephilia Bound perpetuate a similar level of surveillance and control over Arab cinema. The project, sponsored by French non-profit Maison des Scénaristes, accepts applications from emerging and prospective filmmakers from eighteen Arab countries (plus Turkey and Iran) to travel to Cannes for the international festival. While in attendance, those chosen meet with industry professionals, discuss their ideas with a script consultant, and learn filmmaking skills, as well as marketing techniques for their projects. Such outreach allows access to funding for filmmakers from countries in the Middle East and North Africa, which otherwise do not always have the infrastructure or financing for cinema. However, European distribution and production companies then decide what will be produced, and initiatives like Cinephilia Bound transform the festival from merely a site of reception and consumption to one of production as well.

Responding to the West's demand for cinema from the Arabic-speaking world, Mohammed and Bedirxan begin their film by claiming its images for Syria and Syrians. Situated as a collaborative effort between the two co-directors and the brave Syrians who posted their stories online, the film captures protests, destruction, torture, fear, and anger in Syria. *Silvered Water* deliberately removes the function of the film's director, who serves more as an editor-in-chief or an interpreter for the film's final result. In this move, the film erases the notion of a single story and aligns the process of production with the practice of viewing—like the prominent director, the spectator views the film as a piece of cinema, rather than as a series of facts about Syria's war and its refugees. The film casts off the myth of the brilliant artist at the helm, who presumably projects his or her intentional ideas and fantasies onto the image. Instead, *Silvered Water* offers a collective process of filmmaking that reclaims the act of recording and transmitting for Syrians on the ground.

In fact, Mohammed describes this in an interview from 2014: "For all the people, demonstrating against Assad was an explosion of cinema. People screaming 'Freedom! Freedom!' and filming for the first time . . . It was a revolution of cinema, of images, of expression.'"[26] In Mohammed's view, cinema and its expressive possibilities mimic the relationship between protest and "freedom," which finds shape in the technical practice of production, made manifest in the circulation of its final form. He reads the revolution as not only a moment of political upheaval, but one that unleashes expression and imagines a new role for cinema in the country. "For the first time," average protestors could hold up their video phones and record this shout for "freedom," and they could post it on social media for all the world to see. For Mohammed, the revolution redefines cinema as a collective act and not the vision of the auteur, similar to the proponents of Third cinema elsewhere. While he and Bedirxan might have the final word on the film's shape and content, the goal of cinema is linked to protest, and its expressive possibilities are a direct cry for "freedom."

Bedirxan's position in the film establishes two major points of critique that produce and challenge its revolutionary effects. First, her filming grounds the project, as Mohammed lives in exile and remains unable to film Syrian life himself. However, his role in editing, arranging, and narrating the final product decides how the audience will engage with Bedirxan's footage. Perhaps this justifies the film's self-reflexivity and its continual reference to the cinematic process and spectatorship over and above the situation in Syria. Put differently, maybe Mohammed's desire to emphasize the many levels of mediation at play in *Silvered Water* means to establish the feeling of distance between the audience and the war depicted on screen. This possibility also speaks to the choice of submitting this film to festivals like Cannes and Toronto, screening venues that reduce Syria's particularity to a cinematic object for consumption by Western viewers, where Syria's war becomes part of the larger global imaginary that stages the Middle East as a continual war zone and site of human rights violations.

The second critique challenges this cynical view, as Bedirxan's footage presents life amidst death and rubble. In his review of the *Silvered Water*, Jay Weissberg argues that "Bedirxan shoots a lot of scenes with children, always an incongruous notion in bombed-out cities where life, at least young life, isn't supposed to exist."[27] According to Weissberg, children feel like an anomaly in the war-torn Syrian landscape. He suggests that this scene feels out of place in Syria, as this is a place where life, particularly "young life, isn't supposed to exist." However, Weissberg's review makes a telling point, as one of the film's most jarring sequences occurs when Bedirxan follows a child walking through "bombed-out" streets alone, a scene that presents hope and life alongside heart-wrenching hopelessness. As the boy skips along a broken road, he carries a flower and passes demolished buildings and fences, as if he cannot see the destruction around him. In this scene death reigns supreme, but the child strolls casually through the streets to the sound of gunfire and bombs in the distance. His closeness to death is apparent through the surrounding scene, and yet his life archives the possibility of something else.

Nevertheless, death shadows life in the film. Introducing a screening in Japan, journalist Kaori Shoji exclaimed, "no matter how hard you brace yourself, the film will shred your nerves, wring your heart dry and leave you enveloped by a sadness so pervasive you'll be left speechless."[28] In fact, several points in the film pronounce the death toll in Syria's streets. The narrator speaks English as if he directs the action on screen—"take one," "take two," "take three," and so on—while the camera cuts between images of dead young Syrians, their bodies, their faces, and a man clutching the corpse of his dead child. In the background, the spectator can hear a cell phone vibrate, as if to drive home the point that these are the images transmitted from Syria, this is what the camera captures: death. Photographs and videos of death sent like an everyday text message, shot by another cell phone. *Silvered Water*'s effect visualizes beyond its cell-phone images and found footage as it advocates for a type of cinematic experience that uses images of war and destruction to present a political and aesthetic fact—the circulation of images of death creates the very possibility of cinema in Syria. Discussing the work of Bedirxan, Mohammed states that "the whole cinematic language, with its close-ups, wide-angle shots and tracking shots, was being reinvented. It was a moment of truth, a moment close to death, a moment of urgency that desperately needed to be expressed."[29]

To return to the epigraph, Judith Butler's makes a claim there that violence against those "who are not quite living . . . leaves a mark that is no mark." For these lives, "there will be no public act of grieving." Most viewers of *Silvered Water* read Syrians against a backdrop of violence, suffering, religious fanaticism, or rebellion, and the country is judged as oppressed or oppressing by a century of discourse and decades of degrading images; consequently, an increasing global Islamophobia and anti-Arab and anti-Muslim ideology dehumanize the entire Syrian population. Mohammed and Bedirxan's frame anticipates this interpretation in order to insist on a new vision. By revealing the democratization of the filmmaking process, its reproducibility and ability to determine responses from the masses, as Benjamin suggests, *Silvered Water* removes the generous buffer between the spectator and the spectacle, and calls attention to the human element of the cinematic process, making commodified Arab lives visible. In this frame, Syrians participate in the production of images rather than being enemies of visual production. The narrator speaks to the audience, providing a kind of authenticity, but more importantly, acknowledging the 1,001 cinematographers who risked their lives to share what they witnessed: videos of violence and war that position them as both viewers and directors of the world they inhabit, rather than victims of it. "A dead body itself doesn't say anything," Mohammed argues, "so you have to reconnect it to the movement of time and life."[30]

Silvered Water does not discuss migration, but still the film evokes the motivations of millions of Syrians to leave their homes and seek life elsewhere. The film insists that while the streets of Syria remain war-torn, such death drives cinematic production. The film transforms death into a revised vision of the world. Emphasized in the image of a dark street, where streetlights provide the scene's natural lighting, a cameraman shouts into the night, "the world is not yours alone! There's a place for all of us! You don't have the right to own it all!" Behind his shaking camera, which films the empty street and the sound of occasional gunfire, the unseen filmmaker calls out to the regime and to the viewer to recognize his right to life, to his street, and to his world.

Migrating Images

In her book, *States of Emergency: Documentaries, Wars, Democracies*, Patricia Zimmermann argues that filming on the ground in a war zone changes "the relationship between filmmaking and subjects . . . from a strategy of representation to a strategy of transaction, a moving across different spaces, domains, discourses, actions, politics, and subject positions."[31] The "state of emergency" demands this tactical shift; it reorganizes the power of the image to move across discursive, geographical, and geopolitical boundaries, making exchange across borders possible. Moreover, Zimmermann suggests that "rather than exclusively representing those . . . marginalized by dominant culture in the modality of the visual, these on-the-ground works function within a different political agenda: they operate more as transcriptions across and through technologies of representation to inscribe political action and active spectator positions within the work itself."[32] The viewer is, as Zimmerman suggests, drawn "into direct encounter with the filmmaker," and in this schema, the viewer becomes an active witness-turned-participant through technologies of representation and the cinematic process rather than merely a voyeur watching from afar.[33]

Zimmermann's claims about the transactional nature of cinema made in crisis are compelling, as she suggests a kind of relationship between documentary filmmaking and reality that moves outside the framework of representation to one of exchange, a method that promotes a certain level of agency for the subjects and a type of participation for the audience. Yet, images taken in a war zone act as "transcriptions across and through technologies of representation to inscribe political action," a visual index for the possibility of global involvement. While this paradigm feels productive, as it creates subjects and spectators that are actively engaged with the events on the ground, the images of nations in "states of emergency" instead expose Bloom's "colonial media apparatus," which embeds a colonial engagement with documentary footage and promotes a kind of viewing that "mak[es] the colonies visible . . . [by] diagnosing invisible agents that can be detected only by technologies of vision and know-how."[34]

According to Bloom, these "techniques of magnification . . . rend[er] the invisible visible as part of a . . . social and moral imperative to transform the colonial landscape."[35] Not only do the images of suffering produce a justification for colonial intervention, but they virtually transform the landscape of the colonies, archiving the social and moral imperative of the West with regard to the "Third World." Likewise, Stam and Spence argue that "just as the camera might . . . be said to inscribe certain features of bourgeois humanism, so the cinematic and televisual apparatuses, taken in their most inclusive sense, might be said to inscribe certain features of European colonialism."[36] It is not merely the images that are called into question, but the gaze of cinema itself.

Mohammad Ali Atassi and Ziad Homsi's film, *Our Terrible Country*, immediately blurs the line between filmmaker, subject, and spectator. The film opens with a group of young men under siege, each of them armed with a rifle and dressed in street clothes as they duck behind the remains of a bombed-out building in the city of Douma. The makeshift battalion attempts to take down a sniper in a tower across the way and the camera focuses on one of the film's protagonists and filmmakers, Homsi, who is among the besieged men. When the situation resolves, Homsi photographs the ragtag bunch of fighters, the average-looking, untrained, young and middle-aged civilians forced to take up arms and defend their streets. In the next sequence, Homsi sits in front of the camera, his face cut off by the top of the frame, holding a rifle in one hand and wearing a shabby kufiyah around his neck. The filmmaker discusses the battle, which lasted four days and nights. In the background, there is only rubble and the ruins of the city. Homsi explains that when you are holding a gun and a camera, you often have to put down your camera; sometimes you have to fight. *Our Terrible Country* draws the spectator into this immediate action, as the situation on the ground in Syria introduces the viewer to the filmmakers, and positions the spectator to identify with the filmmaker who has traded his camera for a loaded weapon.

In the film's press kit, the synopsis posits the question that looms above the film's action: "how [does one] make a film on violence without directly showing or reproducing it . . . [without] inflicting the violence a second time?"[37] Taken from the film's promotional materials, this demonstrates the way that this film understands its own task, as if it might present a solution to this tangled question. *Our Terrible Country* approaches the task by tracking filmmaker Homsi, twenty-four, and Syrian intellectual and dissident Yassin al-Haj Saleh, fifty-two, as they travel across the country to ISIS-occupied Raqqa. Throughout the film, the two bond as they travel with a group of young men on a treacherous journey. On the road, they spend much of the film discussing Saleh's activism and membership of the Syrian Communist Party in the 1980s. His activism led to a sixteen-year imprisonment and encouraged many young Syrians in the film to draw from his experience and insight. His writing, which is inserted during poetic interludes in *Our Terrible Country*'s narrative, serves to frame the revolution for the viewer. As a result, the film presents the violence in Syria less as a brutal power grab and more as an uprising motivated by political ideas. This distinction shapes the film's aesthetic form, presented as a narrative of travel and eventual exile; the spectator follows Homsi and Saleh's developing relationship and the narrative thus follows their escape to Istanbul in real time, avoiding the violence of Syria's war.

Perhaps it is for this reason that *Our Terrible Country* received less attention than *Silvered Water*. *Our Terrible Country* also circulated on festival networks and carried its story across many international lines, but was featured at about half as many festivals. In fact, *Our Terrible Country* did not premiere at a major festival like Cannes or Toronto. While it did screen in France, Germany, Portugal, Brazil, and the US, and won the grand prize in the international competition at FID Marseille,[38] *Our Terrible Country* also screened in Jordan, Turkey, and Morocco, unlike *Silvered Water*. This difference delineates these two films' production histories: *Our Terrible Country* was produced by Syrian non-profit Bidayyat Audiovisuals, an organization created in 2013 to fund documentary projects by Syrians and Syrian Palestinians, while, as I discussed above, *Silvered Water*'s funding came from both French and Syrian companies.

Another reason for this discrepancy in screening spaces might also have something to do with the fact that, besides the film's opening sequence, *Our Terrible Country* shows little death and destruction that are not filtered through the perception of Homsi, the filmmaker, and Saleh, an intellectual. Nevertheless, close-up shots and monologues from the film's protagonists describe the post-trauma of Syria's violence and the interpretive possibilities of such scenes. As Benjamin argues, "with the close-up, space expands."[39] The close-up does not reveal something about Homsi or Saleh, but instead, "expands" the possibility of their being. We find this approach in many of the film's contemplative scenes. For example, before the journey to Raqqa, the camera follows Saleh through the streets of Douma and captures civilians maintaining the roads and cleaning the rubble from the streets. Saleh and his wife participate in this action, drawing the spectator into the process of rebuilding and carrying on in the face of war, rather than witnessing the violence of the brutal regime first hand. Instead, the bombed-out city stands as the backdrop for what seems like normal life, while Saleh tells the viewer "you won't find a place where life and death are in closer proximity."[40] The juxtaposition of men playing soccer in a square, next to what Saleh explains is a tent where corpses are washed before burial, disrupts the expectation for war on screen. Instead, death and war feel like only an aspect of life, represented through the calm smile of Saleh, who seems to recognize the irony of the scene.

The shots of Saleh as he wanders the streets of Douma map easily onto the sequences on the road, as Saleh walks through the empty desert on the road to

Raqqa with a similarly composed gait. The political dissident strolls alone across the rocky terrain of the back roads as he remembers his adolescence in Syria in a voiceover, the sound design also revealing Assad's air force flying overhead. His voiceover monologue ends with the harsh reality that their destination, Raqqa, is now controlled by ISIS. The empty landscape and Saleh's monologue foreshadow Homsi's capture by ISIS fighters. The filmmaker is held captive as Atassi and Saleh escape to Istanbul. The narratives of violence, terrorist cells, oppressive regimes are mediated by Saleh's poetic voiceovers and through the stories of the film's protagonists. The viewer does not see Homsi's capture, but only hears of it when he eventually makes his way to Istanbul. The film withholds the spectacle and the spectator is thus forced to imagine the experience of captivity from the safety of Istanbul's cafés. In this way, the film reproduces the situation of the spectator through an identification with Homsi and Saleh. It draws the spectator into the action by positioning them within the developing relationship between the film's protagonists, rather than merely as a witness to Syria's war.

When the two find each other again, both Saleh and Homsi are overcome with emotion. As they cry together in a crowded restaurant in Istanbul, a medium shot captures the two at the table. Homsi chain-smokes and says,

> I'm going to get my mother out. I'm going to get my brother out. I'm going to get my father out. Because they can't live inside. People who want to live should get out. They shouldn't stay inside . . . because inside there's death . . . We used to have one enemy: the regime. Now we have a thousand enemies. Add to that the enemy inside us, which we don't know, which we need someone to tell us to fear.

For the filmmaker, there is no option: he must fight, either with images or a gun, even in the face of death and "a thousand enemies." In the tight close shot, the two men huddled together in a booth crying, smoking, lamenting the family they have left behind, the camera stands in for the spectator to sit across from Homsi and Saleh on the other side of the booth. This is not a display of death and destruction, but instead an index of the life that remains in Syria and the necessity of migration. The sequence thus begs the viewing public to see the reasons for fleeing Syria's war without partaking in the reproduction or consumption of images of violence.

In fact, *Our Terrible Country* archives an overwhelming desire for return. The film ends with Saleh walking through a wooded area on a hiking trail in Istanbul. In the voiceover that accompanies this image, Saleh states, as if to himself,

> I don't know exactly what I will do in exile. I have long felt uneasy about this word. It seemed like mockery coming from those who remained in the country. Today, its meaning might change to include our overwhelming

experience, the experience of uprooting, escape and dispersal, and the hope of return. I don't know what I'll do, but I am part of this great Syrian exodus, and of this Syrian hope of return. Even though it resembles a slaughterhouse today, this is our country, we have no other. And I know that no country will be kinder to us than this terrible country.

The shots that accompany this monologue parallel earlier images of Saleh walking on the rocks and sand of the desert. Here, surrounded by life as he walks among blooming plants and flowering trees, the writer speaks of return to the "terrible country" called home. His words seem to contradict the mise en scène as he speaks of being "uprooted" while surrounded by the branches of enormous trees, whose roots in Turkey's soil no doubt run deep. Having witnessed the violence through the eyes of the filmmaker, Homsi, and the film's subject, Saleh, the spectator identifies with the characters and relationships that have developed on screen, not with the violence of Syria's war. Violence is never directly shown on screen, only alluded to by the stories Saleh and Homsi share with the audience. These stories are told through close-up shots, a device that draws the spectator to connect to the human element of the refugee crisis, figures that are struggling to survive and eventually return home. The kinship amongst viewers that might be developed in the local theater through the act of viewing Middle Eastern violence on screen is rejected and replaced by simulating a connection between the spectator and the subjects whose participation in the narrative and filmmaking process creates the viewer's only access to the world presented inside the film.

Conclusion

While these films offer some productive forms of identification between the viewer and the subjects on screen, the fact remains that the spectator does not connect to or identify with Syria, its people, or its culture, but instead with the images themselves. Through film and viral images, the bodies of refugees speak to Western audiences as their exile is put on display for international spectators. Western viewers consume these images and this process reinforces their own safety and difference from the violence and death on screen, as they engage with films like *Our Terrible Country* and *Silvered Water* in the same way that they engage with Kurdi's image. Moreover, in response to festival film specifically, spectators are drawn into an institutional framework of looking, where viewers are "transform[ed] . . . into armchair conquistadores, affirming [the viewer's] sense of power while making the inhabitants of the Third World objects of spectacle for the First World's voyeuristic gaze."[41] In some ways, it is as if the "Western" viewer might escape death by watching "others" die, as if seeing the brutality of death and war might preserve the distance between "us and them."

In *Regarding the Pain of Others*, Susan Sontag argues that "catch[ing]" death as it is "actually happening and embalm[ing] it for all time is something only cameras can do, and pictures taken by photographers out in the field of the moment of (or just before) death are among the most celebrated and reproduced of war photographs."[42] There is an "authenticity" to images of death and war, but more relevant here is the authentic experience of looking: watching the death and pain of others confirms one's experience and reproduces a sense of life and purpose in one's everyday reality, no matter how mundane or constructed that reality might be. For the spectator who is "forever looking at death," watching Syrians, Arabs, and Muslims "forever about to be murdered, forever wronged," their life feels safe and the ability to skirt death and avoid suffering feels almost possible.[43] I do not mean to suggest that there is a kind of comfort in seeing the objects of one's fear murdered and "forever wronged" on screen, but that when seen from afar, images of death sustain the practices of everyday life in countries with the "luxury" of viewing war through images alone. And watching this continual violence reiterates the notion that these lives matter less, that these deaths are "but an irrelevant fleck along the international news cycle, something that happens in those parts of the world," and something that does not happen at home.[44]

In Shaker's film, the photograph of Alyan Kurdi, "still / unmoving," demonstrates the reality of Syria's war to the audience, but this feeling passes quickly, and the reality of Kurdi's death gets lost in representation, an image of war that has become commonplace. Kurdi and his family, like millions of Syrian migrants since 2011, were fleeing their war-torn home, risking their lives for the possibility of life in another country. The image of young Kurdi might have shocked and horrified the world, briefly changing the global conversation about Syrian refugees from fear to sympathy, but most countries maintained their strict immigration policies, as anti-Muslim sentiments continued to proliferate in Europe and America. After the image went viral, many argued that Kurdi, a child, dead and helpless on the beach, elicited empathy from spectators, even those inundated with images of Syrian death and destruction, because many could imagine him as a "son." For a moment, this connection even humanizes the body of the refugee more generally, but in reality, Kurdi is not a European or American child; he is fleeing war in Syria for the very possibility of life in a place that does not want him or his family. In fact, it is only in death that his story is told and that his image circulates. Kurdi's figure gains popular attention not because he could be "our" child, but because he will never grow up to be a Syrian adult.

Notes

1. *on silence*, film, directed by Andrea Shaker (2016; Minneapolis: Altered Aesthetics Film Festival).

2. *on silence*.
3. Robert Stam and Louise Spence, "Colonialism, Racism, and Representation: An Introduction," *Screen* 24, no. 2 (1983): 12.
4. This type of analysis is reflected in works like Susan Sontag's *Regarding the Pain of Others* (New York: Picador, 2003). Here Sontag discusses Virginia Woolf's *Three Guineas*, and the author's "revulsion" at war-time photographs. Woolf's text reproaches those who proclaim that their work will bring war to an end while continually producing more violence: "The photographs are not an argument," Woolf claims, "but those certainly are dead children" (Virginia Woolf, *Three Guineas* (Orlando: Harcourt, 1966), 10–11. According to Woolf, photographs of war used as propaganda by the Spanish government do not make rhetorical arguments, but instead represent facts of war and circulate gruesome images of death and destruction. However, Sontag argues that Woolf's gripe is not "any less conventional in its rhetoric, in its summations, rich in repeated phrases" than those of the warmongers she condemns. Rather, in its reliance on the image as factual record, Woolf's discussion of "photographs of the victims of war are themselves a species of rhetoric. They reiterate. They simplify. They agitate. They create the illusion of consensus" (pp. 10–11) What Sontag isolates calls attention to the discourse that extends from images of violence. Using Woolf's essay to ground this claim, Sontag demonstrates the ways that we engage with the pain and death of others in photographs, and shows how these images become tied to the very rhetoric that creates and reproduces violence: they "reiterate" and "simplify."
5. *Silvered Water, Syria Self-Portrait*, film, directed by Ossama Mohammed and Wiam Simav Bedirxan (2014; Cannes: Doc and Film International).
6. Our Terrible Country, film, directed by Mohammad Ali Atassi and Ziad Homsi (2014; Marseille: Biddayat Audiovisuals).
7. Julianne Burton-Carvajal, "Marginal Cinemas and Mainstream Critical Theory," *Screening World Cinema*, ed. Catherine Grant and Annette Kuhn (London: Routledge, 2006), 19.
8. Bill Nichols, "Global Image Consumption in the Age of Late Capitalism," *East-West Film Journal* 8, no. 1 (1994): 69.
9. Judith Butler, *Precarious Life: The Powers of Mourning and Violence* (London: Verso, 2004), 36.
10. Jay Weissberg, "Cannes Film Review: 'Silvered Water, Syria Self-Portrait,'" *Variety*, May 16, 2014, <http://variety.com/2014/film/festivals/cannes-film-review-silvered-water-syria-self-portrait-1201183212/> (last accessed December 1, 2020).
11. Nick Vivarelli, "Cannes: Syrian Director Talks 'Silvered Water,' Filming Revolution on Cell Phones," *Variety*, May 17, 2014, <http://variety.com/2014/film/festivals/cannes-syrian-director-talks-silvered-water-filming-revolution-on-cell-phones-1201184769/> (last accessed December 1, 2020).
12. Peter J. Bloom, *French Colonial Documentary: Mythologies of Humanitarianism* (Minneapolis: University of Minnesota Press, 2008), vii–viii.
13. Hito Steyerl, "In Defense of the Poor Image," *e-flux* 10 (November 2009), available at <http://www.e-flux.com/journal/10/61362/in-defense-of-the-poor-image/> (last accessed December 1, 2020).

14. Steyerl, "In Defense of the Poor Image."
15. Walter Benjamin, "The Work of Art in the Age of its Technological Reproducibility," *Walter Benjamin: Selected Writings, Volume 4*: 1938–1940, ed. Michael W. Jennings (Cambridge, MA: Harvard University Press, 2006), 253.
16. Benjamin, "The Work of Art," 253.
17. Benjamin, "The Work of Art," 264.
18. *Hearts and Minds*, film, directed by Peter Davis (1974; France: BBS Productions).
19. Ossama Mohammed, "An Interview with Ossama Mohammed" (*Silvered Water, Syria Self-Portrait* press materials, Doc and Film International, France, 2014).
20. Furthermore, the "primitive scene" recalls Freud's discussion of the "primal scene" and Deleuze's rereading of it in relation to cinema. For Freud, this scene emerges from a childhood trauma as the child witnesses the parents engaged in sexual activity. In dealing with the subsequent trauma of this moment, one creates fantasy images by combining experience and history. Freud's primal scene relies on the past to create an image of the present, culling both individual experience and the experience of ancestors into the production of fantasy. Yet, Deleuze adds to this configuration. He rereads the "primitive scene" through the cinematic apparatus, which layers the past and future into the present moment: "to film what is *before* and what is *after* . . . Perhaps it is necessary to make what is before and after the film pass inside it in order to get out of the chain of presents" (Gilles Deleuze, *Cinema 2: The Time Image*, trans. Hugh Tomlinson and Robert Galeta (Minneapolis: University of Minnesota Press, 1989), 37–8). Rather than indexing past, present, and future diachronically, as a series of present moments that will become past and lead to the future, Deleuze argues that the temporality of the image can be mapped synchronically. Defined as "time-image," this translates into the cinematic as an experience where past, present, and future overlap as a collection of presents. In Mohammed's film, this process is visually represented by the image fragment of the teenage boy, a refrain that continually repositions individual scenes in the film as always in relation to cinema's beginning and becoming.
21. Kamran Rastegar, *Surviving Images: Cinema, War, and Cultural Memory in the Middle East* (Oxford: Oxford University Press, 2015), 206.
22. Dina Iordanova, "Rise of the Fringe: Global Cinema's Long Tail," *Cinema at the Periphery*, ed. Dina Iordanova, David Martin-Jones, and Belén Vidal (Detroit: Wayne State University Press, 2010), 31.
23. Kenneth Turan, *Sundance to Sarajevo: Film Festivals and the World They Made* (Berkeley: University of California Press, 2002), 8.
24. "Lumière Françaises Film Series," Film Society of Minneapolis St Paul, <http://mspfilm.org/lumieres-francaises/> (last accessed December 1, 2020).
25. Proaction Films has moved to Berlin, Germany, and is now known as No Name Film.
26. Vivarelli, "Cannes."
27. Weissberg, "Cannes Film Review."
28. Kaori Shoji, "The 'Silvered Water' of 'Syria Mon Amour,'" *The Japan Times*, June 15, 2016, <http://www.japantimes.co.jp/culture/2016/06/15/films/silvered-water-syria-mon-amour/#.WKFRarTFuCQ> (last accessed December 1, 2020).

29. *Silvered Water* press materials.
30. *Silvered Water* press materials.
31. Patricia R. Zimmermann, *States of Emergency: Documentaries, Wars, and Democracies* (Minneapolis: University of Minnesota Press, 2000), 91.
32. Zimmermann, *States of Emergency*, 91–2.
33. Zimmermann, *States of Emergency*, 92.
34. Bloom, *French Colonial Documentary*, viii, x.
35. Bloom, *French Colonial Documentary*, viii, x.
36. Stam and Spence, "Colonialism, Racism, and Representation," 4.
37. *Our Terrible Country* press materials, Biddayat Audiovisuals.
38. Festival International de Cinéma de Marseille.
39. Walter Benjamin, "The Work of Art," 265.
40. *Our Terrible Country*, film, directed by Mohammad Ali Atassi and Ziad Homsi (2014; Marseille: Biddayat Audiovisuals).
41. Stam and Spence, "Colonialism, Racism, and Representation," 12.
42. Sontag, *Regarding the Pain of Others*, 59.
43. Sontag, *Regarding the Pain of Others*, 61.
44. Anne Barnard, "Beirut, Also the Site of Deadly Attacks, Feels Forgotten," *The New York Times*, November 15, 2015, <https://www.nytimes.com/2015/11/16/world/middleeast/beirut-lebanon-attacks-paris.html?_r=1> (last accessed December 1, 2020).

Works Cited

Barnard, Anne. "Beirut, Also the Site of Deadly Attacks, Feels Forgotten." *The New York Times*, November 15, 2015, <https://www.nytimes.com/2015/11/16/world/middleeast/beirut-lebanon-attacks-paris.html?_r=1> (last accessed December 1, 2020).

Benjamin, Walter. "The Work of Art in the Age of its Technological Reproducibility." *Walter Benjamin: Selected Writings, Volume 4: 1938–1940*, ed. Michael W. Jennings, 251–83. Cambridge, MA: Harvard University Press, 2006.

Bloom, Peter J. *French Colonial Documentary: Mythologies of Humanitarianism*. Minneapolis: University of Minnesota Press, 2008.

Burton-Carvajal, Julianne. "Marginal Cinemas and Mainstream Critical Theory." *Screening World Cinema*, ed. Catherine Grant and Annette Kuhn, 17–35. London: Routledge, 2006.

Butler, Judith. *Precarious Life: The Powers of Mourning and Violence*. London: Verso, 2004.

Deleuze, Gilles. *Cinema 2: The Time Image*, trans. Hugh Tomlinson and Robert Galeta. Minneapolis: University of Minnesota Press, 1989.

Iordanova, Dina. "Rise of the Fringe: Global Cinema's Long Tail." *Cinema at the Periphery*, ed. Dina Iordanova, David Martin-Jones, and Belén Vidal, 23–45. Detroit: Wayne State University Press, 2010.

"Lumière Françaises Film Series." Film Society of Minneapolis St Paul, <http://mspfilm.org/lumieres-francaises/> (last accessed December 1, 2020).

Mohammed, Ossama. "An Interview with Ossama Mohammed." *Silvered Water, Syria Self-Portrait* press materials, Doc and Film International, France, 2014.

Nichols, Bill. "Global Image Consumption in the Age of Late Capitalism." *East-West Film Journal* 8, no. 1 (1994): 68–85.

on silence. Film. Directed by Andrea Shaker. 2016. Minneapolis: Altered Aesthetics Film Festival.

Our Terrible Country. Film. Directed by Mohammad Ali Atassi and Ziad Homsi. 2014. Marseille: Biddayat Audiovisuals.

Rastegar, Kamran. *Surviving Images: Cinema, War, and Cultural Memory in the Middle East*. Oxford: Oxford University Press, 2015.

Shoji, Kaori. "The 'Silvered Water' of 'Syria Mon Amour.'" *The Japan Times*, June 15, 2016, <http://www.japantimes.co.jp/culture/2016/06/15/films/silvered-water-syria-mon-amour/#.WKFRarTFuCQ> (last accessed December 1, 2020).

Sontag, Susan. *Regarding the Pain of Others*. New York: Picador, 2003.

Stam, Robert and Louise Spence. "Colonialism, Racism, and Representation: An Introduction." *Screen* 24, no. 2 (1983): 2–20.

Steyerl, Hito. "In Defense of the Poor Image." *e-flux* 10, November 2009, <http://www.e-flux.com/journal/10/61362/in-defense-of-the-poor-image/> (last accessed December 1, 2020).

Turan, Kenneth. *Sundance to Sarajevo: Film Festivals and the World They Made*. Berkeley: University of California Press, 2002.

Vivarelli, Nick. "Cannes: Syrian Director Talks 'Silvered Water.' Filming Revolution on Cell Phones." *Variety*, May 17, 2014, <http://variety.com/2014/film/festivals/cannes-syrian-director-talks-silvered-water-filming-revolution-on-cell-phones-1201184769/> (last accessed December 1, 2020).

Weissberg, Jay. "Cannes Film Review: 'Silvered Water, Syria Self-Portrait.'" *Variety*, May 16, 2014, <http://variety.com/2014/film/festivals/cannes-film-review-silvered-water-syria-self-portrait-1201183212/> (last accessed December 1, 2020).

Woolf, Virginia. *Three Guineas*. Orlando: Harcourt, 1966).

Zimmermann, Patricia R. *States of Emergency: Documentaries, Wars, Democracies*. Minneapolis: University of Minnesota Press, 2000.

THE CONTRIBUTORS

Michelle Baroody holds a PhD in Comparative Literature from the University of Minnesota. Her research interests include archival studies, film history and exhibition, Arab cinema, and Arab American studies. She has served as curator of multiple film projects, including Mizna's Arab Film Festival and the Arab Film Fest Collab.

Valerie Behiery is a Canadian art historian, writer, and academic whose work focuses on historical and contemporary visual culture from or relating to the Middle East and North Africa region, with a special emphasis on gender, cross-culturality, and the politics of representation. She is currently Assistant Professor at Al Faisal University in Riyadh.

William Brown is an independent scholar, as well as an Honorary Fellow for the School of Arts at the University of Roehampton, London. He is the author of *The Squid Cinema from Hell: Kinoteuthis Infernalis and the Emergence of Chthulumedia* (with David H. Fleming, 2020) and *Non-Cinema: Global Digital Filmmaking and the Multitude* (2018).

Mohannad Ghawanmeh earned his PhD from University of California, Los Angeles (UCLA) in Cinema and Media Studies. He is co-founder of the Twin Cities Arab Film Festival, and curated the first editions of the Arab American National Museum's film festival and the Minneapolis/St Paul Italian Film Festival, as well as the Melnitz Movies series at UCLA. His research examines such intersecting fields as governmentality, migration, nativity, religion, theater, music, literature, industrialization, and modernity.

Colleen Hays is an independent scholar. Her research interests include original texts from the French colonial period, methods of teaching the Algerian War of Independence in France, French films concerning cultural diversity and conflict, and the role of immigration in relationship to French citizenship.

Frank Jacob is Professor of Global History at Nord Universitet, Norway.

Jan Kühnemund completed his PhD at Berlin University of the Arts (UdK). He also holds an MA degree in Political Science, Visual Media, and English. Currently, he is a research assistant at Europa-Universität Flensburg, Germany. From 2010 to 2017, he was involved in the academic coordination of the African–European Erasmus Mundus Master Course "European Migration and Intercultural Relations" (EMMIR) at Carl von Ossietzky University Oldenburg. His publications include "Topographies of 'Borderland Schengen': Documental Images of Undocumented Migration in European Borderlands" (2018) and "Exploring Intervention: Displacement, Cultural Practices and Social Knowledge in Uganda" (with L. Tommila, 2019).

Drew Paul is Associate Professor of Arabic at the University of Tennessee, Knoxville. His research focuses on modern Arabic literature and film, with particular interests in space, mobility, and sexuality.

Marta F. Suarez is Lecturer in Latin American Studies at Manchester Metropolitan University. At the time of going to press, she was due to defend her PhD thesis on Screen Studies at Liverpool John Moores University. She has lectured on film theory, screenwriting, race/gender on screen, and expressions of the nation through genre. Her thesis explores the portrayal of Latin American and African immigration in contemporary Spanish film, and discusses issues of globalization, (post)colonialism, and national identity. Her research interests approach themes of intersectionality and identity in a variety of screen media, from Latin American and Spanish film to popular TV narratives and alternative worlds. She is editor for *Open Screens*.

Nicole B. Wallenbrock is Assistant Professor of French and Francophone Studies at Hostos Community College of the City University of New York and previously taught at Syracuse University.

INDEX

A escondidas, 163
action, 23, 78, 100, 110, 157n10, 192, 195, 222, 237, 243, 245, 247–9
  political, 57, 59, 64, 246
aesthetic, 7, 19–22, 26, 30, 50, 81n7, 211, 221–2, 238–9, 245, 248
Africa, 28, 36, 91, 132, 157n8, 162–6, 168, 170–2, 176–7, 196–8, 201
  North, 31, 69, 84n50, 186, 188, 191, 243
African, 118, 130, 143, 161–8, 170–1, 173, 175–7
  immigrants, 162–3, 148, 166
  immigration, 162–3, 166–8, 196–7
  migration, 164, 187–8, 198
  women, 6, 187, 189, 192, 198–200
Agamben, G., 98, 191–2
Algiers, 29–31
Amorim, V., 5, 110, 128–9, 132
Amur Society, 123
Anglo-Egyptian Treaty, 70
Arab, 51, 62, 70–7, 79–81n7, 82n24, 232, 235, 239, 242–3, 245
  countries, 50, 71, 75, 243
  League, 71, 76

nationalism, 68, 71, 75–6
Spring, 4, 77, 84n49, 237
Unity, 69–76
world 4, 50, 70, 72, 81n7
Arabic, 31, 36, 52, 68, 70, 72, 77, 80, 193, 234, 236–7
Archipelago, 29
Asia, 29, 124; *see also* Asian
Asian, 108, 112, 117, 121, 124, 127–8
asylum, 23, 36, 216–19

Bedirxan, W. S., 7, 234–6, 241, 243–5
birth, 8, 62, 119, 157n10, 239
border, 5, 7, 48, 53, 56–7, 61, 74, 81, 88–91, 100, 157n7, 161–2, 164, 166–7, 171–2, 177, 181n48, 182n61, 205, 207, 213–15, 220–1, 223n1
Border zones, 7, 213–14, 220–1, 223
Borderland Schengen, 205–6, 212–15, 218–19, 222–3
Brazil, 108–30, 132–3, 248
Brazilian, 5, 108–33, 235
British Embassy, 124–6
Burkina Faso, 5, 144, 146
Bwana, 164–6

INDEX

camera, 2, 6, 20, 26–7, 29, 32, 50, 53–4, 56, 58–9, 61–2, 64, 78–9, 95, 97, 100–1, 105n22, 148–9, 153, 157n7, 170, 174, 177, 187, 192–3, 195–6, 198–200, 208–10, 215–16, 218, 234, 236, 240–1, 245–9
camp, 3, 46–8, 58–63, 76, 171, 182n61
Cannes, 109, 143, 233, 235, 239, 242–4, 248
century, 2, 6, 18, 30, 68–70, 74, 76–7, 79–80, 90, 108, 110–11, 113–15, 120, 128, 132–3, 162, 177, 187, 192, 245
cinema, 1, 3, 5–6, 18–19, 28, 40n17, 91, 96–7, 101–3, 153, 156, 191–2, 196, 198, 222, 225n23, 231, 233, 235–9, 241–7, 253n20
   Arab countries, 70, 72–3, 75, 80–1
   Brazilian, 109–10, 114–15, 133
   Palestinian, 49–51
   Spanish immigration, 161, 164–5, 167, 170–2, 176–7, 181n48
cinematic, 2, 4, 18, 29, 49–51, 91, 96–7, 103, 105n22, 187, 196, 206, 208, 210, 231, 234–6, 238, 240–1, 244–7, 253n20
citizenship, 17, 19, 21, 41n24, 77, 108–9, 114, 144–5, 147, 153, 191, 199
city, 4, 23, 26, 31, 72, 91, 100–1, 116, 119–20, 125, 234–5, 247–8
civil war, 3, 59, 76
community, 2–4, 37, 56, 80–1, 97, 108–16, 118–29, 132–3, 155, 175, 182n71, 193, 232–3
Coraçōes Sujos
criminal, 101, 145, 153, 155, 157n10, 176–7, 220, *see also* illegal
crisis, 15–17, 39, 69, 112, 128, 133, 161, 164–6, 172–3, 176–7, 178n3, 205–8, 212, 219, 230, 232–3, 238, 246, 250
culture, 2, 17–19, 26, 41n20, 49, 54, 56, 76, 78–80, 93–4, 122–3, 144, 162, 205, 213, 231, 238, 246, 250

Dabashi, H., 50–1
Dardenne Brothers, 5–6, 143–5, 147, 153
Dark Ocean Society, 123
death, 7, 20, 36, 62, 68, 74, 77–8, 97–9, 103, 105n22, 125–7, 130–1, 143, 145, 151, 153, 164–5, 199, 200, 231–9, 244–6, 248–51, 252n4
Diamantes negros, 6, 161, 169, 173–4, 176
diaspora, 5, 108–9, 111, 235
director, 3, 48, 51, 72, 77, 80, 84n46, 91, 104n7, 110, 114–16, 119, 125, 189, 193–4, 196–8, 200–1, 235–6, 243
discourse, 5–6, 29, 32–3, 35, 39, 47, 53, 69, 110, 114, 128, 168, 219–21, 232, 235–6, 245, 252n4
discrimination, 2, 20, 116, 122, 124, 187, 192, 200
displacement, 19, 32, 38, 40n17, 52, 57, 63–4, 69, 116, 164–5, 169, 176, 217
documentary, 6, 23, 31, 38, 51, 79, 81, 91, 102, 114, 143, 167–8, 177, 195, 198, 205–6, 208, 215, 222–3, 234–6, 239, 242, 246, 248
Dussel, E., 88, 92–4, 98, 101–2

East Asian, 112, 121, 127–8
Eastern European, 144–5
economy, 35, 76, 92, 102, 162, 170, 176, 187, 192, 195, 197, 202n17, 112
Egypt, 70–2, 75–7, 80–1, 82n24, 242
Egyptian, 48, 51, 69–73, 75–6, 79–81, 237
ethnographic, 187, 195–6
El traje, 166
English, 20, 26, 31, 40n17, 41n28, 82n21, 89, 98, 237, 245
Euro-American, 16, 19, 38, 39n2, 243
Europe, 4, 6–7, 15–17, 19, 26, 31, 36, 50–1, 68–9, 77, 92, 113, 132, 145–6, 161–3, 168–71, 173, 175–7, 186–8, 190, 199–201, 202n7, 210, 213, 217, 219–20, 231–3

259

INDEX

European, 4–7, 23, 31, 38, 57, 93, 114, 120, 144–7, 150, 162–3, 165, 173–6, 187–8, 192–3, 196, 201n7, 205–7, 212–13, 215, 217, 220, 223n1, 231–2, 238, 243, 247, 251
   migration, 7, 205, 212, 215, 218–19, 221
   refugee crisis, 205–6, 212
   Union, 7, 207, 215, 218–19, 221
   Western, 147, 150, 155
   see also migration industry
European Union, 146, 161, 213–14, 226n
exchange, 122, 127, 145, 171, 173, 175, 195, 197–9,214, 235–6, 241, 246
exile, 4, 19, 46–53, 56, 58, 234–5, 244, 248–50

father, 6, 53, 62, 88, 95, 129–30, 132, 144, 147–9, 155, 174, 199, 249
family, 46, 61, 71, 91, 95–6, 98, 113, 115–16, 132, 136n77, 147–8, 150, 164–6, 174–5, 189, 199, 237–8, 249, 251
female, 31, 41n20, 110, 114–16, 118–19, 129, 144–9, 157n8, 187, 189, 192, 195, 197–200
Fedayeen, 48, 53, 56, 62
Festival, 1, 4, 7, 23, 28, 80, 103, 109, 114, 165–6, 168, 173, 191, 201, 231–6, 239, 241–3, 248, 250
festivals, 7, 65n11, 80, 83n26, 103, 143, 232–3, 235, 240–2, 244, 248
France, 4, 21–1, 28, 35–6, 41n24, 144, 173, 188, 194–5, 210–11, 234, 236, 243
French, 6, 20–1, 27–8, 30–1, 36, 41n24, 41n28, 83n28, 109, 145–6, 155, 187, 191, 193–8, 214, 223, 226n37, 237, 242–3, 248
Fukunaga, 5, 88, 103

Gaijin, 5, 109–10, 114–15, 119–20, 129, 132, 134n12
Galeano, E., 4, 88, 90, 92, 96, 103

gang members, 95, 101–2, 89
Gate of the Sun, 4, 46–8, 51–3, 57–61, 63–4
gender, 3, 6, 21, 25, 114–15, 186–93, 195–6, 198–200, 221
generation, 47, 60, 63, 128, 133, 167, 191, 237
Ghazel, 4, 17, 19–24, 26–8, 38, 41n20, 41n24, 41n28, 42n33
global, 7, 16, 19, 21, 26, 31, 34, 47, 50, 81n7, 92, 108–9, 112, 121, 157n10, 161, 163, 170, 173, 175–7, 194, 196–8, 221, 230, 241, 244–6, 251; see also globally
globally, 15, 18, 39, 47, 233, 242–3
government, 5, 20, 65n7, 71–5, 79, 90, 104n1, 113, 120–2, 124, 126, 129, 136n77, 148, 154, 158n20, 181n48, 182n70, 191, 220, 252n4
group, 6, 47, 61, 79, 101, 114, 119, 126, 145, 154–5, 162, 164, 166, 171, 182n61, 194, 196, 247
Guatemala, 88–9, 93, 96–7, 100

Havarie, 206, 208–10, 212, 214–15, 222–3
heritage, 4, 108, 124, 128–9
historical, 3, 5, 18, 30–1, 50, 68–9, 72, 91–2, 102, 109–10, 115, 129–30, 132, 156, 158n21, 163–5, 172, 176–7, 179n22, 197, 231–2
history, 5–6, 8, 16, 22, 29–32, 35, 41n26, 48–50, 70, 73–4, 76, 88, 90, 92, 96, 99, 109–11, 114–15, 119–20, 127–9, 132–3, 156, 158n21, 163, 170, 177, 181n49, 189, 205, 238, 253n20
homeland, 46–9, 52–3, 64, 74–5, 92, 108–9, 167
Homsi, Z., 232, 247
Hope, 6, 186–8, 190–2, 195–6, 198–9, 201
Hope (movie character), 187–9, 191–7, 199–200

hope, 58, 62, 64, 90, 93, 153, 161, 168, 171–2, 176, 189, 194, 236
human, 20, 32, 37, 88, 90–2, 94, 96–7, 101, 145, 152, 155, 166, 168, 173, 175, 177, 186, 189, 221, 221n42
humanitarian, 6, 145, 154–6, 164, 207, 232, 238, 243
husband, 20–1, 116–17, 119, 129–32, 144, 146, 148–50, 193, 196, 210
Hussein, S., 26, 75–6

icons, 207–9, 219–20
identity, 3–4, 16–17, 19, 25–6, 31, 46, 64, 99–102, 108–11, 113–15, 117, 119, 123, 127, 130, 132–3, 163, 173, 175, 191, 194
Igor, 144–50, 152–3, 155–6, 157n7
Ilegal, 164, 167
illegal, 2–3, 5, 17, 20–1, 23, 25–6, 32, 36, 68, 91–2, 96, 101, 145–8, 150, 161–2, 166–7, 173, 176, 187–8, 207, 219–21
image, 4, 17, 20–2, 25–6, 29, 32–4, 37–9, 53, 61, 73, 95–7, 116–19, 164–5, 188–9, 205–14, 218, 221–2, 230–4, 236–41, 243, 246, 249–51, 252n4, 253n20
In the last days of the City, 68–71, 75–81
in-transit, *see* transit
Iran, 19–21, 23, 35, 240, 243
Iraq, 73, 75–6, 80
Iraqi, 20, 32, 51, 71, 74–8, 80, 144
Israel, 49–51, 53, 59, 63, 73–4, 76
Italy, 21, 28, 35–6, 113, 188

Jacir, A., 47, 51
Japanese, 5, 108–32
journey, 3, 6, 31, 34, 36, 48, 89–90, 98, 100, 116, 148, 161, 164, 166–75, 186–92, 196, 198–200; *see also* The Mapping Journey Project

Kanafani, G., 71–2, 74
Khalil, 46–8, 52, 59, 61, 63

Khalili, B., 4, 17, 19, 28–38
Kokunjükay, 123–4
Kosovo, 23, 40n9, 146
Kravagna, C., 25
Kuwait, 73, 76, 80

La Fille inconnue, 143
La Forteresse, 7, 206, 215–16, 220–3
La jaula de oro, 88–9, 93–4, 98, 103
La venta del paraíso, 173
labor, 5, 90, 92, 113, 118–19, 121, 147, 167, 169, 191
Latin America, 29, 89–90, 93–4, 96, 98, 101–3, 121, 162–3
Le Jeune Ahmed, 143
Le Silence de Lorna, 6, 144–6, 152, 154–6
Lebanon, 46–8, 57, 75–6
Lesser, J., 110, 112, 127
liberation, 29, 31, 64, 71, 73–4, 92–3, 98, 100, 169
Liberation of Palestine (DFLP), 30, 49
Liberation Organization (PLO), 49
Lorna, 144–7, 150–3, 155–6
luxury, 90, 98, 230–1, 233, 240, 251

makegumi, 123, 125, 127–8, 130
male, 25, 31, 91–2, 100, 116, 144–5, 147, 149–50, 156, 165, 187–90, 192–4, 197–200
map, 29, 33, 37
March, L. S., 109–10, 116–17
Marco, 23, 25–8
marginalized, 16–17, 19, 21–2, 26, 29, 32, 38, 39n5, 75, 157n10, 164, 196, 246
marriage, 6, 20–1, 61–2, 116–17, 144, 150, 169–70, 187, 189, 191, 193, 198
massacre, 51, 57–8
media, 4, 15–16, 18–19, 23, 79, 81, 84n49, 93–4, 111, 162–6, 172, 177, 182n61, 186, 188–90, 206–7, 219–20, 231–4, 244, 246

INDEX

memory, 4, 25, 46, 50, 56, 61, 109, 163, 165, 167, 176–7, 179n22, 222, 235
Middle East, 4, 29, 69, 71, 76, 231–3, 238–9, 243–4
Middle Eastern, 4, 21, 69–70, 74, 77, 79, 82n21, 243, 250
Mignolo, W., 88, 92
migrants, 2–8, 15–19, 21, 23, 25–6, 28–9, 32, 34–8, 39n2, 68–9, 89–90, 97–100, 102–3, 118, 132–3, 165–6, 171, 186–9, 205–6, 208, 212, 214, 219–21, 221n1, 251
migration industry, 89–91, 96; *see also* European migration
mobility, 6, 18, 36, 161, 167, 186–9, 195, 198–201, 205, 213–14, 222
Mohammed, O., 232, 234–6, 240, 243–5
Morocco, 6, 28, 146, 162, 173, 177, 179n15, 182n61, 186, 188, 196, 220, 248
mother, 5, 47, 53–4, 57, 73, 78, 99, 101, 149, 153, 175, 249
movement, 3–5, 7–8, 18, 22, 36, 53, 68, 71, 76, 88, 96–8, 103, 105n22, 115, 126, 146, 152, 186, 193–5, 198, 205, 207, 209, 221, 245
movie, 20–1, 78, 99, 118–19, 147
moving image, 4, 15, 18–19, 34, 38–9
Moyano, E., 167

Nasrallah, Y., 46, 48, 51, 61, 64
nationalism, 29, 49, 52, 68, 70–1, 75–6, 108, 122, 124, 128–30, 132
neoliberal, 100–2, 161, 164, 175
Nikkei, 109–12, 114, 121, 127–9, 133
North America, 16, 19, 92, 96; *see also* United States, USA

on silence, 230–2
orientalism, 6, 163
Ouedraogo, A., 5, 144, 146–50, 152–3, 155–6

Pacific war, 5, 112, 122, 123–4, 126, 129, 132
Palestine, 30, 46–54, 56–7, 59–64, 71, 74; *see also* Palestinian
Palestinian, 4, 34, 46–53, 55–65n11, 70–4
pan-Arabism, 4, 68–71, 76–7, 80
Papadopoulos, D., 2–3
Paris, 21, 36
people, 3, 5, 7, 8, 22, 26, 30, 32, 39, 47, 52–4, 61, 69, 71, 73–6, 78–9, 81, 89–92, 97, 99–101, 112, 116–17, 126–7, 148, 154–5, 166, 170, 182n61, 196, 207, 211–12, 221, 223, 237, 243, 249–50
Pérez, J., 164, 171–2
perspective, 2–5, 7, 8, 18, 38, 41n22, 42n37, 64, 91–3, 98, 110, 112, 114, 116, 122, 129, 132, 144, 155, 187, 187, 192–4, 197, 200, 212, 218, 231
photograph, 20, 95–6, 98–9, 103, 230, 233, 251
photography, 5, 15, 79, 84n49, 88–9, 94–100
pictures, 5, 100, 188, 235–6, 251
plantation, 116–19
    owners, 113, 117–18
    system, 109, 113
    workers, 109, 118, 120–1
plot, 2, 73, 115, 146, 150, 153, 174, 190, 192, 200
policy, 16, 73, 76, 121, 157n10, 181n48, 194, 205, 207, 213, 215, 220
Poniente, 164, 166
Port Santos, 111. 121
postcolonial, 29, 31, 39n5, 41n22, 163, 165, 170
power, 8, 16, 19, 25, 29, 33, 35–7, 41n22, 71, 92, 154, 156, 158n21, 166, 172, 175, 191, 193, 198, 222, 246, 248, 250
Princesas, 167

Querida Bamako, 164, 167–8
Quijano, A., 88, 92

racism, 29, 36, 165, 167, 178
rape, 193–5, 237
refugees, 1, 3–5, 15, 17–18, 25, 35–8, 46–7, 49, 53, 58–9, 63, 68–71, 206, 208, 211–12, 215–16, 219–20, 223, 225n23, 232–4, 243, 250–1
relationship, 1, 16, 18, 20, 26–7, 31, 41n21, 48, 51–2, 61, 95, 102, 121, 146–8, 150–1, 153–6, 165, 192, 200, 205, 210, 213, 218, 222–3, 235–6, 239–40, 244, 246, 248–9
religion, 70, 76, 146
Retorno a Hansala, 162, 164, 167
Roger, 144–5, 147–9, 155, 157n7
Rouch, J., 195

Sahara, 6, 168, 177, 186, 188, 190, 192
Saleh, T., 4, 51, 72–5, 80, 83n28
Saleh, Y. al-Haj, 232, 247–50
Saloul, I. 52–3
Salvajes, 166
Salvatrucha, M., 89, 94–5, 99–102
Santos, C., 118–9
Santos, M. I., 164
Santos, N. P. dos, 115
São Paulo, 108, 111–12, 114, 116–17, 119–20, 122, 125–7
Sasaki, 129–31
Sayra, 88, 95, 99–100
separated, 53, 127, 132, 199, 210, 214, 239
separation, 51–2, 64, 112, 214
sex, 6, 257n8, 191–3, 195, 197
sex work *see* sex
Silvered water, 7, 232–46, 248, 250
Sin nombre, 5, 88–91, 93–103
Smiley, 99, 101, 89, 97
smugglers, 90. 166, 171–2, 220, 226n42
social, 2, 8, 17–18, 23, 25, 30, 32, 36, 72–3, 75, 94, 116, 129, 143, 156, 164, 167, 172, 179n22, 205, 210, 213–15, 219, 221, 223, 231, 247
  media, 84n49, 234, 244
  problems, 23, 72, 74

society, 2, 5–6, 23, 37, 49, 61, 71, 75, 78, 98, 101, 103, 111, 116, 123–5, 127, 150, 166, 169–71, 174
  Belgian, 143–5, 147–8
  Brazilian, 115, 122, 133
  civil, 154–6, 158n20, 21
socio-economic, 79, 191
South American country, 108–10, 112–13, 116, 120–1, 125, 128, 133
Spain, 6, 93, 113, 161–8, 171–7, 188, 200–1, 210
Spanish, 6, 90, 93–4, 98, 118, 120, 161–174, 176–7, 179n13, 182n61, 182n70, 208, 220, 252n4
spectator, 6–7, 17–18, 20, 23, 25–7, 33, 41n21, 144, 153, 187, 212, 218, 231, 232, 236, 241, 243, 245–51
sub-Saharan, 6, 164–6, 170, 172–3, 177, 181n48, 186, 188, 191–2, 196, 198
survival, 3, 5, 25, 146, 187, 189, 191–2, 198
Syria, 7, 50, 64, 71–3, 75, 80, 231–7, 239–40, 242–51
Syrian, 3, 7, 64, 70, 72–3, 165, 230, 232, 234–8, 240, 242–5, 247–8, 250–1

Tapachula, 89, 95, 100–1
Tarek, 47–8, 53–4, 56–7, 75, 77–8
Taxi, 164, 166
technology, 4, 20–1, 84n50, 96, 154, 208
television, 18, 20, 27, 93–4, 168
The Dupes, 4, 50, 68–70, 72–5, 80–1
The Mapping Journey Project, 15–18, 22, 29, 33–9
Tonho, 117–19
torture, 20, 41n22, 234, 237–9, 243
Trade, 88, 91–2, 98, 100
trade, 94, 120–2, 144–5, 188, 235
trafficking, 91–2, 101, 147, 173, 220, 226n42
transformation, 31, 49, 61–3, 113, 132, 156, 162, 191
transit, 186–92, 194, 197–200, 213, 223

transnational, 17, 19, 48, 50–1, 58, 88–9, 91, 101–3, 121, 173, 206, 210, 213–14, 221, 241
transnationalism, 70
Tsianos, V. S., 2–3
Turkey, 15, 21, 146, 202n7, 230, 243, 248

Ultranationalist, 109, 123–4, 129
United Arab States, 71–4
United States, 3, 5, 21, 29, 51, 76, 89–90, 93, 111–13, 121, 239; *see also* North America, USA
Un novia para Yasmina, 162, 167
USA, 88–103; *see also* North America, United States

Vargas, G., 5, 121–2, 124
violence, 3, 7, 36, 48, 75–6, 92, 102, 118, 123, 151, 163–4, 166, 172, 187, 198, 217, 231–3, 236–40, 245, 247–51, 252n4

war, 3–5, 20, 28, 47, 49, 59, 61, 64, 65n7, 68, 70–1, 74–6, 78, 111–12, 122–7, 129–32; *see also* civil war

watan, 47–9, 51–4, 56–8, 60–1, 63–4
water, 28, 32, 73–4, 100, 151, 175, 188–9, 201, 207, 210
Western, 6–7, 16–17, 41n22, 79, 95–6, 98, 108, 117, 144–7, 150, 155–6, 169, 188, 196, 231–2, 238–9, 241–2, 244, 250
women, 6, 41n20, 54, 79, 99, 110, 112, 115–18, 132, 144, 156, 169, 187–90, 192–3, 195, 198–200, 237; *see also* African women
work, 15, 19–21, 28–32, 37–8, 41n22, 42n33, 53, 72–4, 77–9, 82n21, 88, 90, 92, 98, 100, 103, 111–12, 115–20, 128, 133, 144–5, 147, 155
World War I, 70, 108, 121
World War II, 64, 92, 109, 114, 121, 128

Yamada, 117–19
Yamasaki, T., 109–10, 114–15, 119

Zimmermann, P., 246